Theory and Application of Multi-Formalism Modeling

Marco Gribaudo
Politecnico di Milano, Italy

Mauro Iacono
Seconda Università degli Studi di Napoli, Italy

A volume in the Advances in Systems
Analysis, Software Engineering, and High
Performance Computing (ASASEHPC)
Book Series

Information Science
REFERENCE
An Imprint of IGI Global

Managing Director:	Lindsay Johnston
Production Manager:	Jennifer Yoder
Publishing Systems Analyst:	Adrienne Freeland
Development Editor:	Christine Smith
Acquisitions Editor:	Kayla Wolfe
Typesetter:	Christina Barkanic
Cover Design:	Jason Mull

Published in the United States of America by
Information Science Reference (an imprint of IGI Global)
701 E. Chocolate Avenue
Hershey PA 17033
Tel: 717-533-8845
Fax: 717-533-8661
E-mail: cust@igi-global.com
Web site: http://www.igi-global.com

Library of Congress Cataloging-in-Publication Data

Theory and application of multi-formalism modeling / Marco Gribaudo and Mauro Iacono, editors.
    pages cm
  Includes bibliographical references and index.
    ISBN 978-1-4666-4659-9 (hardcover) -- ISBN 978-1-4666-4660-5 (ebook) -- ISBN 978-1-4666-4661-2 (print & perpetual access) 1. Mathematical models. I. Gribaudo, Marco, 1972- II. Iacono, Mauro, 1975-
  TA342.T478 2014
  003--dc23
                                        2013026788

This book is published in the IGI Global book series Advances in Systems Analysis, Software Engineering, and High Performance Computing (ASASEHPC) (ISSN: 2327-3453; eISSN: 2327-3461)

British Cataloguing in Publication Data
A Cataloguing in Publication record for this book is available from the British Library.

All work contributed to this book is new, previously-unpublished material. The views expressed in this book are those of the authors, but not necessarily of the publisher.

For electronic access to this publication, please contact: eresources@igi-global.com.

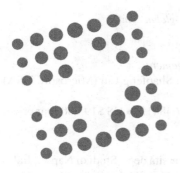

Advances in Systems Analysis, Software Engineering, and High Performance Computing (ASASEHPC) Book Series

ISSN: 2327-3453
EISSN: 2327-3461

MISSION

The theory and practice of computing applications and distributed systems has emerged as one of the key areas of research driving innovations in business, engineering, and science. The fields of software engineering, systems analysis, and high performance computing offer a wide range of applications and solutions in solving computational problems for any modern organization.

The **Advances in Systems Analysis, Software Engineering, and High Performance Computing (ASASEHPC) Book Series** brings together research in the areas of distributed computing, systems and software engineering, high performance computing, and service science. This collection of publications is useful for academics, researchers, and practitioners seeking the latest practices and knowledge in this field.

COVERAGE

- Computer Graphics
- Computer Networking
- Computer System Analysis
- Distributed Cloud Computing
- Enterprise Information Systems
- Metadata and Semantic Web
- Parallel Architectures
- Performance Modeling
- Software Engineering
- Virtual Data Systems

IGI Global is currently accepting manuscripts for publication within this series. To submit a proposal for a volume in this series, please contact our Acquisition Editors at Acquisitions@igi-global.com or visit: http://www.igi-global.com/publish/.

Titles in this Series

Enabling the New Era of Cloud Computing Data Security, Transfer, and Management
Yushi Shen (Microsoft, USA) Yale Li (Microsoft, USA) Ling Wu (EMC, USA) Shaofeng Liu (Microsoft, USA) and Qian Wen (Endronic Corp, USA)
Information Science Reference • copyright 2014 • 336pp • H/C (ISBN: 9781466648012) • US $195.00 (our price)

Theory and Application of Multi-Formalism Modeling
Marco Gribaudo (Politecnico di Milano, Italy) and Mauro Iacono (Seconda Università degli Studi di Napoli, Italy)
Information Science Reference • copyright 2014 • 319pp • H/C (ISBN: 9781466646599) • US $195.00 (our price)

Communication Infrastructures for Cloud Computing
Hussein T. Mouftah (University of Ottawa, Canada) and Burak Kantarci (University of Ottawa, Canada)
Information Science Reference • copyright 2014 • 583pp • H/C (ISBN: 9781466645226) • US $195.00 (our price)

Organizational, Legal, and Technological Dimensions of Information System Administration
Irene Marie Portela (Polytechnic Institute of Cávado and Ave, Portugal) and Fernando Almeida (Polytechnic Institute of Gaya, Portugal)
Information Science Reference • copyright 2014 • 321pp • H/C (ISBN: 9781466645264) • US $195.00 (our price)

Advances and Applications in Model-Driven Engineering
Vicente García Díaz (University of Oviedo, Spain) Juan Manuel Cueva Lovelle (University of Oviedo, Spain) B. Cristina Pelayo García-Bustelo (University of Oviedo, Spain) and Oscar Sanjuán Martinez (University of Carlos III, Spain)
Information Science Reference • copyright 2014 • 424pp • H/C (ISBN: 9781466644946) • US $195.00 (our price)

Service-Driven Approaches to Architecture and Enterprise Integration
Raja Ramanathan (Independent Researcher, USA) and Kirtana Raja (Independent Researcher, USA)
Information Science Reference • copyright 2013 • 411pp • H/C (ISBN: 9781466641938) • US $195.00 (our price)

Progressions and Innovations in Model-Driven Software Engineering
Vicente García Díaz (University of Oviedo, Spain) Juan Manuel Cueva Lovelle (University of Oviedo, Spain) B. Cristina Pelayo García-Bustelo (University of Oviedo, Spain) and Oscar Sanjuán Martínez (University of Oviedo, Spain)
Engineering Science Reference • copyright 2013 • 388pp • H/C (ISBN: 9781466642171) • US $195.00 (our price)

www.igi-global.com

701 E. Chocolate Ave., Hershey, PA 17033
Order online at www.igi-global.com or call 717-533-8845 x100
To place a standing order for titles released in this series, contact: cust@igi-global.com
Mon-Fri 8:00 am - 5:00 pm (est) or fax 24 hours a day 717-533-8661

Editorial Advisory Board

Table of Contents

Detailed Table of Contents

Section 1
Methodology and Problems

This section presents contributions about the main themes around multiformalism modeling.

The chapter introduces the main themes concerning multiformalism modeling: advantages and disadvantages, research experiences and directions, existing solutions, and open questions. After an introduction to the basic ideas behind multiformalism modeling, the authors propose some informal definitions and classifications, useful to build a common discussion background and to support the analysis and the comparison of the main existing solutions. A brief review of literature about the most widespread frameworks is given to support the reader interested in further readings.

The chapter deals with the application of model transformation-based approaches to multiformalism modeling. The authors examine the advantages of model transformation primitives and principles to design consistent modeling frameworks capable of conjugating the benefits model composition, multiformalism, and high-level abstract representations. Effectiveness of the proposal is demonstrated by a case study.

The chapter deals with the problem of enabling multisolution of high-level representation-based models. The authors, exploiting the conceptual tools typical for the Model-Driven Engineering field, propose a transformation-based approach founded on the automatic generation of models, written in different performance-oriented formalisms, starting from a Performance Model Interchange Format description of a system. The approach is demonstrated by showing how it is possible to generate some example transformations that are applied in a case study.

The chapter presents multimodeling techniques and an application of workflow languages to the solution of multiformalism models. The authors propose a modeling methodology built on a semantic background, aiming to the evaluation of metrics over scenarios developed in a given domain. The proposed methodology guides the modeler from an ontological description of a given domain to a dedicated workflow language that implements the analysis. The approach is demonstrated by a drug interdiction and intelligence case study.

The chapter deals with the problem of compositionality in multiformalism models. The author analyzes the main results of research activities in this field, comparing the most known frameworks and tools with special reference to the solutions implemented in the SIMTHESys framework, which is used as an example. For each of the examined approaches, the mechanisms to obtain the interactions between heterogeneous submodels are reported.

The chapter deals with the problem of result representation and manipulation in multiformalism frameworks. The authors show how a proper application of metamodeling techniques enables the creation of a common method to report and reuse the (intermediate) results in a solution process that involves different cooperating solvers. The approach is demonstrated by applying it to Petri net-based models.

Section 2
Exploiting Multiformalism: Tool Design Experiences

This section presents design experiences of multiformalism tools.

The chapter presents a tool that exploits Petri nets to analyze models based on the Generalized Continuous Time Bayesian Network Formalism. The authors describe the architecture of the tool, together with the considerations that guided its design and the transformation rules applied to obtain the formalism translation as a guideline that can be generalized to deal with multiple formalisms. The tool is applied to a case study to show the solution process.

The chapter proposes a multiformalism-based tool capable of facing models with large-scale population. The tool applies a multisolution approach that includes a mean field analysis solution engine. The approach is validated by studying a chemical case study. The architecture of the tool is discussed to show how different solvers are integrated.

Chapter 9

The chapter deals with the problem of representing a high number of states in state-space-based solvers. The authors show how it is possible to apply an efficient state representation technique to support solution processes for models of large systems, proposing this method for the implementation of multiformalism-oriented solvers. The method is used to produce a Markov reward models-based solver capable of supporting composed models in which submodels interact by shared state variables or synchronization.

Chapter 10

In this chapter, the potential of the SIMTHESys approach to formalism design is demonstrated by presenting the general formalism description framework, a complete example, and a number of specifically targeted formalism examples, already applied to case studies to face different problems. The reader is guided through the design choices taken in the examples to suggest how to develop solutions.

Section 3
Applying Multiformalism: Case Studies

This section presents modeling experiences coming from industrial applications.

Andrea Bobbio, University of Piemonte Orientale, Italy
Daniele Codetta-Raiteri, University of Piemonte Orientale, Italy
Luigi Portinale, University of Piemonte Orientale, Italy
Andrea Guiotto, Thales Alenia Space, Italy
Yuri Yushtein, ESA-ESTEC, TheNetherlands

The chapter presents a dependability application in the aerospace sector that exploits multiformalism to provide probabilistic diagnosis and prognosis of the state of an autonomous spacecraft capable of self-repair. The integration of the chosen formalisms, oriented to assess different characteristics of the system, allows one to obtain a unified modeling framework for all the relevant aspects.

Roberto Nardone, Università di Napoli "Federico II", Italy
Stefano Marrone, Seconda Università di Napoli, Italy

The chapter presents an application of multiformalism modeling exploiting Model-Driven Engineering to the assessment of metropolitan train systems. The authors propose a framework to support performability evaluation during design and in-service phases by automatic generation of the required models.

Preface

The term "multiformalism models" describes a complex research area that has become a reality through the years. "Models" refers to one of the most important tools used by scientists in many fields, such as physics, system theory, economics, and computer science. As defined by E.D. Lazoswka (1984) in his *Quantitative System Performance* book, "A model is an abstraction of a system: an attempt to distill, from the mass of details that is the system itself, exactly those aspects that are essential to the system's behavior." "Formalism" includes the word "formal"; it describes the importance of having a set of rules, precisely specified and unambiguous, which must be followed to fulfill a task. Although this might seem to be somehow limiting, this "formality" is what allows automatic techniques to be employed. Since the features that can be used are limited and fixed, algorithms can interpret them with the need of any type of intelligence. In our context, formalism refers to the rules that can be used to describe a model.

"Multi" is a Latin word including the concept of multiplicity. This somehow opens new horizons previously shrunk by the formalism; we must adhere to a set of fixed and unambiguous rules, but we can use several different sets of them. Depending on the particular modeling task we are facing, this gives us the opportunity to choose the most suitable tool to obtain the expected result either more precisely or more efficiently.

The focus of this book concerns *multiformalism modeling*, that is tools, techniques, and practical examples of models exploiting several different formalisms to achieve a specific goal, which would not be possible, or simply not convenient, if pursued with a single modeling paradigm.

Before providing a better specification of multiformalism, it is helpful to present the evolution that led to the definition of this paradigm. As soon as new formalisms were studied, new techniques to automatically perform some kind of analysis on the models described according to the proposed formalism were introduced. The next step was to develop a tool to support the use of both the formalism and the proposed analysis techniques.

Tool development is always a long, demanding, and not a rewarding task. A tool, to be successful, requires a good user interface and must support the user in the task of writing a model. It must perform the required analysis with the least hassle, and it must present the results in the form in which they are easiest to read and to interpret. This, however, requires very long programs to be written: they must predict all the possible actions taken by the users and must guide the actions to be coherent with the selected formalism. Worst of all, a tool developer is hardly rewarded for his job; modeling tools are rarely sold (since in most of the cases they are just used by a research center for experimentations and not for production), and even when they are commercially successful, the budget that can be planned for further development and support is usually very limited. From a scientific point of view, the quantity of time spent on tool development can be an order of magnitude greater than the one required to formulate a hypothesis, verify it, and describe it in a paper for a top-class journal. Usually a tool can lead to a minor contribution, such as a poster or a two page description in a track of a specialized conference.

However, tools are important for modeling: they are what can lead the scientific community to choose one particular formalism over another. For example, in the mid 1980s, several different formalisms were being studied to add timing to Petri Nets models. In particular, there were two main lines being followed: adding time to places, or to transitions. For the latter, a tool with one of the first Graphical User Interfaces (GUI), based on X-Windows and Motif, was developed. It was called the *GreatSPN* tool, and it was developed by G. Chiola and others. The tool allowed drawing Generalized Stochastic Petri Nets models (GSPNs) by graphically inserting primitives in a window. The tool had enormous success and gave a big contribution to the adoption of the GSPN formalism where time was associated with Petri Nets Transitions.

Let us return to multiformalism models. Why did tools play an important role in the development of multiformalism? Well, whoever has worked on a tool, despite all the problems previously pointed out, has usually enjoyed the experience, and most likely repeated with another one! Of course, this has deeper reasons than the willingness to pursue difficult results and to sacrifice themselves for the community. In most of the cases, the developers working on tools also work on formalism specification. As the formalism under study evolves, the tools follow accordingly. Sometimes formalisms evolve in something completely different; this leads to the requirement of completely new tools.

When developing a second, third, or n-th tool, one usually finds a very large similarity with the one previously created. Such similarity can reside in the user interface, in the solution algorithms, in the support library created to analyze the models, or in the modules exporting the results. When there is a need to write a tool from scratch, it is easy to realize that creating it to support a larger number of formalisms is usually only a fraction of work harder than developing it formalism-locked on a single specific modeling paradigm.

The earliest examples of multiformalism tools were thus multiformalism in the sense that they could analyze models described in different languages but just one at a time. Although being a good starting point, since the users would have had to learn just one common interface to be able to experiment with different modeling formalisms, their features were still very limited. Once the modeling language was chosen, the user was stuck with it. If a model could be split in several different parts, where each of them could be better expressed using a different language, the modeler would have to choose one and try to use it to model the components of the system where that particular formalism was sub-optimal.

In parallel to tool development, theoretical researchers were trying to understand the expressive power of the various formalisms that were introduced. This was achieved by formal proofs, where models defined in a specific formalism were transformed in equivalent models of another formalism whose properties and expressiveness were already known. Formalism transformations led to a first type of multiformalism modeling: one could create a model using a paradigm, transform it in an equivalent model for a different formalism, and then use it in the target language.

Both the tools and the language transformations approaches led to the idea that allowing a modeler to use more formalisms at the same time can provide large benefits. In particular, it allows one to use the language that is most suited for each particular component of the system, leading to models that are clearer to read, easier to understand, and more efficient to analyze.

Of course, this is not always possible. Sometimes formalisms are so different they simply cannot be integrated in any meaningful way. In other cases, what can be described with a simple connection of elements coming from multiple specification languages hides a large set of details that should be specified to make the model "formal" enough to be analyzed by a tool. These difficulties led the research in multiformalism modeling recently.

Several different approaches for the multiformalism have been introduced; each one has its own target, its own goal, and its specific set of applications where it can work at its best. Some of them are well defined and well known to the whole modeling community. Among them, we must emphasize the *Möbius* tool, by W. H. Sanders, which currently is the state-of-the-art of multiformalism tools. In particular, it allows one to define (sub)-models in different formalisms and to compose them in a larger multiformalism model. Some other approaches are lesser known but interesting for the way in which the problem is approached, solved, and presented.

A concept tightly coupled with the multiformalism model and how multiformalism models can be analyzed is *multisolution*. The term multisolution refers to the ability of integrating different tools to perform different analyses on the considered multiformalism models. It has two main advantages: it allows using the most mature and well performing tools already developed for a particular formalism, and it reduces the time required to develop multiformalism analysis algorithms, since the task usually reduces to the orchestration of existing software components. However, multisolution has several drawbacks. The main one is that it can be applied only to a few very specific (but important) interpretations of multiformalism modeling. The second practical concern is the standardization of results and interchange formats, which must be present to allow the interaction of different tools.

In this book, we provide a picture of the current state of multiformalism modeling and multisolution, continuing a work that was started with the organization of the WRUMMM ("Workshop on Research and Use of Multiformalism Modeling Methods") workshop during the QEST 2012 conference in London, UK. The workshop was held in London on September the 17th 2012, with the aim of gathering researchers, practitioners, and users of whatever is related to multiformalism modeling methods and techniques. It was guided by the idea that multiformalism modeling methods may constitute a powerful tool to improve modeling and model evaluation experiences in every application field. Within the goals of WRUMMM there was the creation and coordination of a community of modelers and theoreticians to develop and spread multiformalism approaches and to allow an easy information and collaboration exchange inside academia and with industrial partners. The original aim of the workshop was to collect original papers related to theoretical and methodological issues as well as case studies and automated tool support in the research areas related to multiformalism modeling, which were identified in:

- Multiformalism theoretical foundations.
- Methodological approaches.
- Modeling techniques.
- Modeling experiences.
- Multisolution approaches.
- Heterogeneous models composition.
- Case studies from different disciplines.
- Tools integration.
- Results presentation and analysis.
- Standard interchange modeling language definitions.

Many of the contributions of this book come from the participants of that conference but many others are from other researchers who decided to describe their vision of the subject specifically for this work. Contributions has been chosen to focus on what we believe to be the emerging directions of multiformalism modeling, leaving the more consolidated approaches to the references that will presented at the end of each chapter.

The book is organized as follows. It is divided in three sections: the first focuses on the theoretical aspects, the second the practical concerns, while the last one presents successful applications of the considered techniques.

The first section, called "Methodology and Problems," presents contributions about the main themes around multiformalism modeling. Its purpose is to introduce the theoretical aspects of the topic and to make a deep review of the related literature. It is composed of six chapters, written by some of the most active researchers in the field.

The 1st chapter is an introduction to multiformalism modeling. The chapter introduces the main themes concerning multiformalism modeling, presenting their advantages and disadvantages, research experiences and directions, existing solutions, and open questions. After an introduction to the basic ideas behind multiformalism modeling, the chapter proposes some informal definitions and classifications. This allows building a common discussion background as well as supporting the analysis and the comparison of the main existing solutions. The chapter also gives a brief review of literature about the most widely spread frameworks, supporting the interested reader in further readings.

The 2nd chapter studies techniques to combine heterogeneity, compositionality, and automatic generation in formal modeling. It mainly deals with the application of model transformation-based approaches to multiformalism modeling. The chapter examines the advantages and the principles of this technique to design consistent modeling frameworks capable of conjugating the benefit model composition, multiformalism, and high-level abstract representations. Effectiveness of the proposal is demonstrated by a case study.

The 3rd chapter traces the directions towards a multiformalism multisolution framework for model-driven performance engineering. It deals with the problem of enabling multisolution of high-level representation-based models. The chapter, exploiting the conceptual tools typical of the Model-Driven Engineering field, proposes a transformation-based approach founded on the automatic generation of models, written in different performance-oriented formalisms, starting from a Performance Model Interchange Format description of a system. The approach is demonstrated by showing how it is possible to generate some example transformations, which are applied in a case study.

Multi-modeling, meta-modeling, and workflow languages are considered in chapter 4. Multi-modeling techniques and an application of workflow languages to the solution of multiformalism models are presented. The chapter proposes a modeling methodology, built on a semantic background, aiming to evaluate metrics over scenarios developed in a given domain. The proposed methodology guides the modeler from an ontological description of a given domain to a dedicated workflow language that implements the analysis. The approach is demonstrated by a case study that considers an application to drug interdiction and intelligence.

The SIMTHESys framework, working on multiformalism modeling and compositionality, is described in chapter 5. The problem of compositionality in multiformalism models is considered in depth by first analyzing the main results of research activities in this field and then by comparing the most well-known frameworks and tools, with special reference to the solutions implemented by the SIMTHESys framework, which is used as an example. For each of the examined approaches, the mechanisms to obtain the interactions between heterogeneous sub-models are reported.

The issues of result representations are considered in the 6th chapter, which focuses on a meta-model based approach to the definition of the analysis results of Petri net models. The chapter shows how a proper application of meta-modeling techniques can enable the creation of a common method to report and reuse the (intermediate) results in a solution process that involves different cooperating solvers. The approach is applied to Petri Net-based models.

The second section, called "Exploiting Multiformalism: Tool Design Experiences," presents design experiences of multiformalism tools. Its aim is to give an idea of the challenges that must be faced when creating a multiformalism tool. This is accomplished by presenting three examples in three different chapters.

Chapter 7 describes a Petri Net-based tool for the analysis of Generalized Continuous Time Bayesian Networks. In particular, it presents a tool that exploits Petri nets to analyze models based on the Generalized Continuous Time Bayesian Network Formalism. The chapter describes the architecture of the tool, together with the considerations that guided its design and the transformation rules applied to obtain the formalism translation. This chapter can serve as a guideline that can be generalized to deal with multiple formalisms. The tool is applied to a case study to show the solution process.

Chapter 8 proposes a multiformalism, multisolution approach to efficient analysis of large-scale population models. This is accomplished by a multiformalism-based tool capable of facing models with large-scale populations. The architecture of the tool is discussed showing how different solvers are integrated. The tool applies a multisolution approach that includes a mean field analysis solution engine. The approach is validated by a case study of a chemical process.

Chapter 9 studies a symbolic approach to the analysis of multiformalism Markov reward models. The chapter deals with the problem of representing a high number of states in state-space-based solvers. The authors show how it is possible to apply an efficient state representation technique to support the solution processes for models of large systems. The proposed method can be used for the implementation of multiformalism-oriented solvers. The technique can produce a solver based on Markov reward models that is capable of supporting composed models in which sub-models interact by shared state variables or synchronization.

Chapter 10 proposes the experiences developed within the SIMTHESys project with several user-defined formalisms, chosen to demonstrate how complex features can be embedded in various design languages to face specific problems. The chapter briefly introduces the framework to offer a complete modeling example and a number of formalisms through which the reader is guided to inspire and stimulate new custom solutions.

The final section of the book presents two interesting case studies. In particular, it focuses on modeling experiences coming from industrial applications.

Chapter 11 considers a unified modeling and operational framework for fault detection, identification, and recovery in autonomous spacecraft. The chapter presents a dependability application in the aerospace sector that exploits multiformalism to provide probabilistic diagnosis and prognosis of the state of an autonomous spacecraft, capable of self-repair. The integration of the chosen formalisms, oriented to assess different characteristics of the system, allows obtaining a unified modeling framework for all the relevant aspects.

Finally, chapter 12 presents a Model-Driven Methodology to Evaluate Performability of Metro Systems. It considers an application of multiformalism modeling in Model-Driven Engineering to the assessment of metropolitan train systems. The chapter proposes a framework to support performability evaluation during design and in-service phases, which exploits automatic generation of the required models.

We hope that this book will help interested readers in having a broader picture of multiformalism modeling. Our goal is to build a community to continue to study this fascinating and open problem and to apply this technique to more and more case studies. We think that the advantages that can be obtained in many fields by using such techniques can reward the difficulties that this topic poses, especially at the beginning of its study.

Marco Gribaudo
Politecnico di Milano, Italy

Mauro Iacono
Seconda Università degli Studi di Napoli, Italy

REFERENCES

Lazowska, E. D., Zahorjan, J., Graham, G., & Sevcik, K. (1984). *Quantative system performance: Computer system analysis using queueing network models*. Upper Saddle River, NJ: Prentice Hall..

Section 1
Methodology and Problems

This section presents contributions about the main themes around multiformalism modeling.

Chapter 1
An Introduction to Multiformalism Modeling

Marco Gribaudo
Politecnico di Milano, Italy

Mauro Iacono
Seconda Università degli Studi di Napoli, Italy

ABSTRACT

The fundamental need for models in every field of design stems from the absolute and essential necessity for complexity domination. The prediction and verification competence is a must-have ability to allow an efficient and effective design cycle, as much as the complexity of the requirements, in specification, extension or criticalness of the design object, grows. Researchers and practitioners have developed different modeling languages to suit the needs of special classes of problems, such as general formalism like Fault Trees for dependability and availability models, several Petri Nets variants for performance and correctness evaluation, or dedicated modeling languages that map model elements onto domain entities. Richness and variety of formalisms, each of which tailored on a specific problem, empowers the modeling process, but also results in the explosion of many different submodels when coping with a complex and articulated system. These models are logically correlated and are used to take local decisions about single aspects of the overall problem. In practice they might not be aligned to each other and the mutual influences connecting them could be lost, compromising the general results. Multiformalism is an approach to modeling that aims to enable modelers to exploit together different formalisms for different aspects of the same system, while keeping the coherence and the mutual influences of the different parts of the overall model. Different concepts and interpretation of multiformalism modeling (and related problems, such multiparadigm and multisolution) have been experimented and are documented in literature. In this chapter, the main ideas and results in the field are introduced, together with an analysis and comparison.

DOI: 10.4018/978-1-4666-4659-9.ch001

INTRODUCTION

As rich hardware becomes more and more a commodity and the availability of reliable high speed network technologies increases, the expectations in terms of complexity of functions and integration of components about systems and applications grow, posing significant design challenges. Systems and applications consequently grow in scale, number of components and articulation of internal relationships. More constraints on performance, reliability, safety, security are expected to be satisfied during the design process. The result is that the process of specification of artifacts becomes a design into the design. Keeping the coherence between specifications expressed at different degrees of abstractions, related to different problems (but mutually influential on each other), requires a significant effort and consequent resources.

Moreover, the number of different logical and physical layers of artifacts possibly requires the collaboration of experts, with specialized backgrounds and skills, each used to a proper modeling logic, tools and methodology, and generally focused on different areas of the project.

Each of the problems faced during the design process led, with time, to the definition of a different approach to modeling, capturing and abstracting all the elements and the relations that influence or describe the system under that specific perspective. Such an abstraction process led to the birth and the definition (and generally the formalization) of proper modeling languages, which are a mean to produce abstraction artifacts (in graphical or textual form) by which problems can be described, communicated, documented, eventually analyzed and evaluated. The possibility of obtaining a manual or, even better, an automatic evaluation process producing qualitative or quantitative results in the field of interest is a useful feature. In general it is considered as the main goal in the definition of a modeling language supporting and speeding up the design cycle, in the early decision phases or as a verification tool to be applied to design choices, as an alternative or an integration to more classical test- or prototype-based approaches. In the rest of this chapter, the focus will be on the subset of all possible modeling languages aiming to offer a tool producing and/or transforming automatically evaluable models (let this informally defined subset be dubbed for convenience in the rest of this chapter *solvable modeling languages* or, alternatively, in coherence with the terminology that will be introduced in the following, *solvable formalisms*).

Solvable modeling languages imply the existence of proper *solving processes*, i.e. sequences of operations or transformations or other manipulations producing the final goal of the evaluation. They are implemented by *solvers*, software tools that perform such processes by steps or integrally. Solving processes for different solvable modeling languages (e. g. performance and availability oriented languages) are generally different, and based on different principles; as a consequence, it is unlikely that a single approach to solution could encompass all possible needs. One of the main challenge with multiformalism modeling is the invention of a possible solving approach to handle this problem. For example, when the dynamic aspects of a system are involved in the evaluation and probabilistic description of its elementary behaviors are available, a possibility is given by general-purpose event-based simulators. However, this approach presents some drawbacks: i) it does not preserve the richness of description proper of specific modeling languages, and could produce approximate results, ii) it requires long setups of the simulation scenario due to the complexity of the modeling power that multiformalism modeling offers, iii) it requires long simulations for systems with many interactions and many different aspects of it modeled together. iv) it requires the modelers to focus on the design and implementation of the simulation process rather than on the modeling process itself, and v) it can force modelers to acquire a different background with respect to their own specialization. Resorting to such a non-specialized solution could become itself a critical factor, artificially inserted into the design process and maybe too resource consuming to get to a profitable application of the tool for complex systems.

The multiformalism modeling approach rather aims to the definition of techniques and methods that allow i) to coordinate modeling of different aspects or different components of a system by means of heterogeneous contributions, or ii) to compose a single, unique macro-model by a set of proper submodels, for each of which it should be possible to use the most suited modeling language without losing the unitarity and the coherence of the overall model (Sanders, 1999). Coordination and unitarity are extremely important goals, as mutual influences between different aspects of a model (or of the submodels of different components of a same model) can significantly change the final result. Consider for example a system in which one of its subsystems, *A*, must process some information and transmit it to another subsystem, *B*, before a certain deadline. Imagine that *B* is designed to produce a failure signal and start a safety procedure if some other subsystem is faulty. If maximum performances of *A* are not sufficient to process information before the deadline in some case, *B* could consider *A* as faulty and react. As *A* is actually not damaged nor behaving abnormally a pure dependability model of the system would not be able to catch the problem,, while a performance model of *A* would be suited to correctly evaluate that limit, but incapable of direct influences on the dependability model.

Multiformalism is thus an approach to modeling that aims to enable modelers to exploit together different modeling languages for different aspects of the same system, while keeping the coherence, the coordination and the mutual influences of the different parts of the overall model. Different concepts and interpretation of multiformalism modeling (and related problems, such multiparadigm and multisolution) have been experimented and are documented in literature.

Obviously, multiformalism modeling is not a silver bullet, as, in most of the cases, a careful, informed, experienced, flexible use of traditional modeling techniques can obtain the same final result in the hands of a skilled modeler. In some cases, results obtained with a single formalism approach by an elite modeler can even be more accurate and efficiently obtained than using multiformalism models: but, multiformalism modeling can support with profit the design of complex systems by allowing field experts to use familiar tools, with a minimal semantic gap and learning effort, giving them back familiar results, and composing and coordinating their efforts.

The chapter is organized as follows: the next section is devoted to give some reference definitions; subsequently, model description, solution description and result description will be examined in the respective sections.

DEFINITIONS

Let *formalism* define a formal or formalized syntactical definition for a modeling language, be it textual, graphical or in other form, aiming to the description of abstractions of a system, by proper distinguishable syntactical *elements* to represent atomic or non atomic components of the system with their *properties*, and syntactical *constructs* that describe the rules by which elements can be used to form a well formed representation. A formalism is thus a description tool to capture and abstract some specific aspects of a system and provide a coherent and formal representation of it.

Literature offers plenty of examples of formalisms, such as Fault Trees, Petri Nets, Process Algebra, Unified Modeling Language and many others.

Let *model* define a description of a system obtained by the correct use of a formalism, and *submodel* define a subset of a model, that represents a description of a subsystem obtained by the correct use of a formalism and syntactically structured to interact with other submodels according to a desired and proper interaction syntax. Submodels usually correspond to given components of a system: e. g., in the model of a server, its disks can be defined by submodels, as well as its network connection, and the description of the workload that it has to serve. Let the expression *heterogeneous submodels* define two (or more) submodels using a different formalism each. Let *evaluable formalism* be a formalism that is designed to produce models that can be in some way processed to obtain additional or new information that is not immediately represented by the properties of model or of some part of it, and consequently let *evaluable model* be a model expressed in an evaluable formalism.

Let *solvable formalism* be an evaluable formalism for which models can be automatically processed for their evaluation, and consequently let *solvable model* be a model expressed in a solvable formalism.

Let *representation formalism* be a formalism that is not an evaluable formalism, and let *representation model* be a model expressed in a representation formalism.

Between the given examples, Fault Trees, Petri Nets, Process Algebra are solvable formalisms, while Unified Modeling Language is a representation formalism.

Let *results* be the output of the evaluation of a solvable model. In order to automatically obtain results from a solvable model, proper tools and algorithms are needed, that must be used according to a certain *solution process*, depending on the nature and the complexity of the model. Let *solver* be a software tool capable of implementing a solution process, and *solution engine* be a software tool capable of implementing a self-contained step of a solution process.

Whenever not specified, the rest of this chapter deals with solvable formalisms and solvable models, respectively shortly referred as formalisms and models, abusing the introduced notation.

MAIN ISSUES

According to the informal definitions of the previous section, the traditional modeling techniques can be seen in the multiformalism perspective as a simple case of multiformalism based on a single formalism, for which the solution process is based on a solver composed by a single solution engine. However, in the case of multiple formalisms involved, a more complex scenario should be considered to describe the possibilities and the needs.

In order to present the main issues related to multiformalism, it is useful to separate the topics into three main interrelated levels: i) the level of model representation, ii) the level of model solution and iii) the level of results.

The main problems on the level of model representation are related to information consistency, representability and sharing. Whenever different formalisms are used together, their different natures should coexist and be represented in a way that allows keeping their original semantics (representability) while letting information being fit for manipulations that involve elements from different formalisms (sharing). Moreover, the representation should offer a common general approach in order to let the user perceiving all the information in a homogeneous way (consistency). One of the possibilities to face these issues is resorting to a modular and hierarchical organization of the model by composition of heterogeneous submodels or more elaborate solutions, with syntactical interaction mechanisms, which can be dependent (or not) on a given combination of formalisms.

The main problems on the level of solution process representation are related to process representation and process enactment. Depending on the complexity and the flexibility offered by the modeling process in terms of extension, variety, heterogeneity and extensibility of the set of the admissible formalisms, the solver most be able to support diverse solution processes. If the set of formalism is fixed, the solution process could be predetermined: consequently the solution process can be considered as implicitly described by the internal algorithms of the solver; if the set of formalisms can vary, its solution process will vary as well, and should be also described in order to be implemented in a proper solver, which will use the needed solving engines or aggregate them. For example, many formalisms such as Generalized Stochastic Petri Nets, Queuing Networks with Finite Capacity, Repairable Fault Trees, can be transformed into an equivalent Continuous Time Markov Chain, by generating their state space, and accounting for the speed at which the model jumps from one state to another to define the transition rates of the underlying stochastic process. All this formalism can then be analyzed using similar solution processes. Other formalisms, such as Product Form Queuing Networks, can instead be analyzed using different tools, such as the Mean Value Analysis. If we want to combine this type of models with the ones in the formalisms previously introduced, some aggregation and integration technique must be applied. The enactment of the described process by the solver is not obvious as well, as the solver acts as a bridge between the three levels, and it should consequently implement proper solutions for all the problems presented. Moreover, the solution process can adopt advanced techniques, such as multisolution and model transformations, which are described in the next sections.

The main problems on the level of result representation are related to local and global results representation (and generation), results traceability, handling and reuse of intermediate results. Depending of the formalism, the effects of the solution process may generate results that are local (related to some elements of the model) or global (related to the model as a whole): it is the case of a Stochastic Petri net, for which the probability of a marking constitutes a local result for each place, while soundness and the existence of deadlocks constitute a global result. A correct representation of results requires a formal specifi-

cation, related to the nature of the formalism and of the solution process. Moreover, a solution process may in some cases transform the structure of a model or its elements, thus producing results that cannot be bound anymore to an element nor to the whole model. A proper representation of results is crucial to support their correct management: in facts, results may be i) intermediate products of the solution process, ii) byproducts of the solution process with no direct connection to the model, iii) inputs needed to complete the solution process, or iv) significant products obtained by solving a part/submodel and needed necessary to process another part/submodel to get to the final result.

THE MODELING LEVEL

A Proposal of Classification Criteria

At the modeling level, a first classification criterion to attempt a systematization is the possibility of structuring models. Let *flat multiformalism* define the case in which a multiformalism model is not partitionable into submodels, and *modular multiformalism* define the case in which it is possible to obtain a model as composition of (heterogeneous) submodels, or to decompose a model into (heterogeneous) submodels. Since a single model can contain elements belonging to different formalisms mixed together, a flat multiformalism can be viewed as a single formalism that supports all formalism elements from all formalisms; the case of modular multiformalism is more appealing, since it allows isolation of different aspects of the model in different submodels, it potentially supports reuse of submodels and it can be more fit to support complex specification, design and verification methodologies.

A second classification criterion can result from the extent of syntactic interaction mechanisms. Let *isolated multiformalism* be the case in which syntactic interactions are not allowed between generic formalism elements from different formalisms; let *mixed multiformalism* be the case in which syntactic interactions are potentially allowed between any meaningful combination of generic elements from different formalisms. To enable inter-formalism interactions in isolated multiformalism, proper inter-formalism interface elements should be provided: i) either by adding specific connection primitives inside a formalism: this approach implies in some way a support for a sort of communication protocol between formalisms; ii) or by introducing proper syntactic mechanisms to allow the explicit definition of some elements of a model as inter-formalism interfaces: this approach implies the possibility of information hiding with regard to the other model elements, that are not reachable from outside the model iii) or defining inter-formalism interactions at the level of submodels: this approach implies a hierarchical organization in blackbox-like submodels that behave analogously to software components.

A third classification criterion is founded on the nature of the set of formalisms that should be supported. Neglecting the case of single formalism, let *closed multiformalism* be the case in which models can only exploit a fixed, predetermined set of formalisms; let *open multiformalism* be the case in which models can exploit a non-predetermined, theoretically infinite set of formalisms. The problem of representation is different in the two cases. In case of closed multiformalism, all syntactic aspects of all combination of elements can be aprioristically studied, once the exact set of formalisms is known: this fact reduces the complexity of designing formalisms and interactions, at least for what concerns the coherence of representation (and also simplifies the design of solvers, which do not need to handle model elements and elements interactions that are not known yet at the moment of solver implementation). In case of open multiformalism, new formalisms are supposed to be designed by users. Consequently, a framework supporting open multiformalism should i) provide functionalities allowing the specification of new syntactical constructs, and

ii) define a general interaction syntax, that can be used by heterogeneous submodels. The more general is the interaction syntax, the more coherent with the field of application of a given formalism will be the actual interaction syntax. However, the possibility of having too general interactions makes formalism and model specification more similar to using a standard simulation package (like Arena), and thus a little bit far away from the main motivations of using multiformalism models. Open multiformalism also complicates the design of solvers, that should support solution for models using formalisms not yet known in the implementation phase.

A fourth possible classification criterion is the relation between different formalisms. Let *horizontal multiformalism* define the case in which two (or more) heterogeneous submodels can directly interact with each other, provided proper interaction mechanisms. Let *vertical multiformalism* define the case in which two heterogeneous submodels cannot interact with each other, but in which one of them (*high level submodel*) can be used to obtain the other (low level submodel), e. g. by generation or transformation. Horizontal multiformalism is suited to support compositional modeling techniques; vertical multiformalism can be used to support solution processes based on transformation of heterogeneous submodels towards submodels written in formalisms for which a solving engine is available: e. g. to define user-specified domain oriented formalisms without the need for a solving engine.

A further, peculiar case of classification is defined in (Vittorini et al., 2004): the case in which, in a framework that allows the use of components that can be defined as blackboxes (i.e. where the internal specification cannot be directly seen by a modeler that uses the component), multiformalism is visible to the user is called *explicit multiformalism*, while the case in which multiformalism is exploited internally, during the solution process, is called *implicit multiformalism*.

Tackling the Representation Problem

Many different solutions have been used in literature to tackle the model representation problem. The various solutions are influenced by the main goals of the tools and the frameworks that have been designed, and closely depend from the kind of multiformalism that authors want to support. With no claim for completeness, some relevant cases can be identified.

The most simple case from the conceptual point of view concerns cases of closed multiformalism. By exploiting the complete knowledge of formalisms, it is possible to completely analyze the representation needs, and it is not necessarily needed to explicitly represent formalisms, as they can be internally represented by solver/editor data structures and directly handled as a part of the software architecture of the tools. It is the case of SHARPE (Trivedi, 2002), one of the earliest multiformalism tools, SMART (Ciardo & Miner, 2004; Ciardo et al., 2009) and, to some extent, of Möbius (Sanders et al., 2007), probably the most advanced multiformalism modeling and analysis tool[1]. An example of such a solution is given in Chapter 8.

A second case, based on the explicit production of proper representations for formalisms, is the adoption of *metamodeling techniques* (Vittorini et al., 2004; Iacono et al., 2012). Metamodeling techniques allow a multi-level description of a domain, in which, if a model can be described by using the elements and the syntactic rules defined in a formalism, in turn a formalism can be described using the elements and the syntactic rules defined in a *metaformalism*. This approach is specially profitable for frameworks aiming to support open, horizontal multiformalism, as in the case of OsMoSys (Vittorini et al., 2004) and SIMTHESys (Iacono et al., 2012, Gribaudo et al., 2005). An example of such a solution is given in Chapter 11. More details on metamodeling are given in Chapter 4 and in the references given in this paragraph.

A third case, again based on the explicit production of proper representations for formalisms, exploits model transformation techniques. Model transformations, typical of the field of Model Driven Engineering, use *transformation description languages,* and some related standard tools, to implement and perform mappings between different formalisms (including semi-formal model description languages) and convert models. Transformations, consequently, take a model using a certain formalism as input and produce a model using another formalism as output. Transformation descriptions operate on formalisms by specifying the rules by which elements or groups of elements from a formalism must be rendered by elements or group of elements in another formalism. This approach is very fit to support open, vertical multiformalism, as in the case of AToM[3] (de Lara & Vangheluwe, 2002). Examples of such a solution are given in Chapter 11. A deeper analysis of model transformations techniques is given in Chapter 2 while relations with Model Driven Engineering are presented in Chapter 3.

It is worth of noting another case, in which a submodel is implicitly specified as a *parametric submodel* using a given formalism. Let a parametric submodel be a submodel that is incompletely described, or described as a black box with respect to the rest of the model, keeping part of its structure or part of its elements unspecified until the overall model is solved. The solution process will consequently include a sort of pre-solving step (analogously to the pre-processing step in the executable generation process of programming languages like C, or to sophisticated binding mechanisms in object oriented programming languages), during which all parametric submodels will be transformed in conventional submodels according to information about the rest of the model, e. g. by means of automatic submodel generation or model transformation techniques. Automatic submodel generation and (eventually naive) model transformations can be performed by dedicated tools, that can be considered a special category of solving engines. This kind of approach is reported in (Raiteri et al., 2004), a case of implicit multiformalism, and is also used in OsMoSys (Vittorini et al., 2004; Franceschinis et al., 2009) to support object oriented and object based features in formalism and model descriptions.

THE SOLUTION LEVEL

The nature of a solution process depends on the nature of the results that constitute its goal. A solution process could produce quantitative or qualitative information, as well as less conventional forms of results, including the case in which the result of a solution process applied to a model is another model: consequently, there could be cases in which a solution process consists in a pure transformation. Multiformalism allows the use of transformation or generation of models to tackle situations in which a solving engine for the original formalism is not available. A related concept is multisolution, that is the possibility of applying, selectively or in parallel, different solving engines to the same model, e.g. to optimize a solution process accordingly to some characteristics of the specific model. With relation to multisolution, there could be a correspondence between a given formalism and a set of applicable solving engines, or there could be complete independence. The case of multisolution requires a framework to have a proper solving engine management mechanism.

Tackling the Solution Problem

Literature reports several different categories of *solution strategies*, some of which are borrowed from other fields.

Analogously to what seen for the model description problem, a first case is given by *monolithic solvers*, that directly implement one (or more, selectable) solution process(es). In this case, the solver is a single tool, eventually encompassing model editing facilities as well. The advantage of such an approach is generally that it is possible to design very optimized solvers, since they are unique, coherent pieces of software, with complete visibility of all data structures and model information and complete knowledge about all the possible situations. The main drawback is generally that the more the available formalisms and the available solving engines are, the more complex is the design of the tool and the more difficult is to optimize it and to extend it with other formalisms or other solvers. Thus, for frameworks that support open multiformalism, other solutions are preferable. Examples of monolithic solvers are given by SHARPE and SMART.

A second solution relies on *automated solver generation*. In this case, solvers are obtained by a proper tool that analyzes the model and synthesizes a self-contained piece of software, capable of independently solving the model. The advantages of automated solver generation are given by the fact that it is possible to support open multiformalism and to extend the set of available solving engines, adding flexibility to the framework, and enabling the automatic support of new formalism combination also for non-expert modelers. The disadvantages of this approach are: i) the need for a solver generation tool, capable of analyzing formalism and model descriptions to derive information about the actual scenario to manage with; ii) the fact that the generation of the solver requires an explicit or implicit description of the semantic interactions between heterogeneous models over formalism elements, thus potentially complicating the specification and design of models and formalisms and requiring a mean to describe interactions; iii) the fact that the solver is potentially assembled by integrating solving engines without the experience and the contribution of a human designer, that could affect optimality. The synthesized solver can be *model specific* or *formalism set specific*. Model specific solvers include a suitable description of the model together with the needed solving engines in a single tool, e. g. a simulator or an analytical solver for that specific model. Formalism set specific solvers are basically monolithic solvers suitable for the solution of all models based on that specific formalism set, thus partially conjugating the advantages of open multiformalism and monolithic solvers. An example of model specific automated solver generation is given by Möbius, while an example of formalism set specific automated solver generation is given by SIMTHESys.

A third solution, that constitutes an extension of monolithic solvers towards open multiformalism/multisolution, consists in designing the monolithic solver with a plugin architecture, that allows to increase the number of solving engines and/or supported formalisms. Such an approach can be seen as a compromise between the first two solutions: the advantage is a lower design complexity with respect to the second and a higher flexibility with respect to the first; the disadvantage is that the effectiveness of this approach heavily depends on the design choices taken about the plugin mechanism. An example is given by (Bohnenkamp et al., 2003).

A fourth solution, already mentioned for what concerns model descriptions, is the approach based on transformations. In this case, the simplest solver architecture can be thought as made up of a transformation engine, capable of executing the transformations required by the solution process, and a solution engine (eventually based on transformations as well, if sufficient to obtain the desired results) capable of solving models in a base formalism. This solution is particularly fit for vertical multiformalism support. Examples of transformation based approaches are given by AToM[3] and DEDS (Bause et al., 1998). More details can be found in Chapter 2.

A fifth solution is based on *solving engine orchestration*. In this case, solving engines are designed to be used as independent services and orchestrated as specified by the solution process, that can be viewed as a business process or a workflow (van der Aalst & ter Hofstede, 2012). Rather than on a solver, this approach is based on a workflow engine, that executes the solution process. The advantages of this approach derive from the fact that solution engines are not part of the workflow engine, and can consequently be designed and implemented independently, by experts of the specific techniques used in each solving engine, at the point that they can be standalone tools, made compatible with the framework by means of proper wrapper. The main disadvantages of the approach are i) the fact that it only allows a loose interaction between submodels, since different parts of the model or submodels are solved in isolation by the required solving engine, and ii) the fact that the nature of the interactions between different submodels heavily depends on the sophistication degree of the workflow engine and the description language for the solution process. This is potentially a limiting factor with respect to approaches that enable a closer integration between different solving engines, or that allow to manage the model as a whole. This solution is particularly fit for modular, horizontal multiformalism support. An example of this solution is given by OsMoSys (Moscato et al., 2007).

Tackling Model Composition

Model composition (or decomposition) potentially offers some advantages in managing the complexity of a model. While, with respect to the model description problem, modularity helps usability, breaking big models in submodels and isolating into them different problems or different parts of a system, and reusability, allowing libraries of submodels, applying modularity to solution offers the chance to lower the computational or spatial complexity needs of the solver (e. g., by allowing a separate processing of subsets of the overall state space of the model). Let *composed model* be a model obtained by composition of submodels. Model composition can be exploited in many ways, as in the case of Möbius (Deavours et al., 2002).

Let *composition semantics* define a mechanism by which, during a solution process for a composed model, submodels can interact. A given composition semantic can be applied in any step of any of the solution strategies presented.

The case in which two or more submodels are directly translated into a single flat model by transformations will be here neglected, as it is based on a syntactical approach, rather than on a semantical approach, and has been thus already covered.

The simplest type of composition semantics consists in *parameter value exchange* between submodels. In this case submodels can be basically solved in isolation, and the solution process is properly structured to get partial results from and provide them to submodels according to the needs. This is a case of a loose interaction, as it does not require any knowledge about the internal structure of submodels, with the exception of the interface elements. It can separately exploit different solving engines for different submodels, without the need for specific information about them, the algorithms used or their internal details, with the exception of what is needed for their proper execution. This kind of composition semantics is fit for supporting solving engine orchestration solution strategy based frameworks and tools. The advantage of this semantics is that it is relatively easy to implement and exploit. The disadvantage is that this semantics, given its loose nature, does not easily allow optimizations, as it does not get into the nature of interfaced formalisms nor allows sharing parts of the submodels internal solution structures: e. g., if two homogeneous submodels are composed by parameter value exchange composition semantics, they will be solved in isolation even if more sophisticated composition semantics would improve the efficiency of the solution. Parameter value exchange is supported in OsMoSys.

A more sophisticated composition semantics is given by *state superposition* (or *parameter superposition*, or *variable superposition*). State superposition consists in the sharing of parts of submodels, able to store information, that can be accessed and eventually modified by all the submodels involved. Such parts (being them or not identifiable as shared submodel elements or dedicated data structures of the specific implementation framework) are used during the solution process to synchronize submodels and generate or handle actual interactions between them. This is a case of tight interaction, as it does require more knowledge about the internal structure of submodels and their nature and representation, even if also in this case it is possible to resort to interface elements. Solution processes that implement this strategy generally process the model as a whole, and exploit modularity for other means than independent partial resolution. This kind of composition semantics is more fit for supporting frameworks and tools that adopt solver generation or monolithic solver solution strategies. The advantage of this semantics is that it is relatively easy to obtain optimization and synchronize submodels; the disadvantage is that this semantics, given its tight nature, could lose the peculiarities of the original formalisms of the submodels, or could in general make difficult to keep the optimizations that characterize of specific formalism-oriented solving engines, e. g. optimizations that exploit a different internal representation of the model. Usually, it also produces models that are larger to analyze, and consequently for which results can be compute less efficiently (or could not be computed at all). Parameter value exchange is supported in Möbius, which offers a very sophisticated bouquet of solution optimization methods by exploiting adaptive multisolution.

A third approach, that could be considered as complementary to the second one, is *synchronization* (or *message exchange*) based composition. This technique is an application of classical message passing concurrent programming paradigm, and is not typical nor specific of multiformalism modeling frameworks (although the actual enactment of some solution processes could rely on it at the execution level).

Synchronization consists in implementing a communication protocol between submodels, to exchange events that can carry event ordering or quantitative information. This semantics is more commonly applied to solving engines, rather than directly to submodels, and can support concurrent execution of solving engines as well as the implementation of other semantics (e. g. parameter value exchange); in this case, there is no need to explicitly represent in models or formalisms the interaction semantics. This kind of composition is specially fit for frameworks in which some of the solving engines are e. g. existing event simulators or in-the-loop simulators. The advantage of this semantics is that it supports concurrent solvers; the disadvantage is that it discourages further optimizations based on tight submodel integrations. A variant of this semantics, namely *arc superposition*, is adopted in SIMTHESys: SIMTHESys formalisms also explicitly specify the behaviors (sort of execution semantics) of formalism elements, and this feature can be used to specify custom interaction semantics, that exploit and couple peculiarities of different formalisms. The advantage of this approach is that the description of the interactions is available for processing by the solver generator, and can be implemented in the generated solver in different ways, adding flexibility and independence from the need for actual protocol implementation between submodels or solving engines; the disadvantage of this approach is that the generation of concurrent solvers is more complicated with respect to the concurrent execution of natively concurrent solving engines by the coordination by means of the solution process.

A more deep description of how modularity is adopted and applied in literature is given in Chapter 5, in which all the main multiformalism frameworks and tools are analyzed and compared.

THE RESULTS LEVEL

As seen, the nature of results substantially impacts the general organization of a multiformalism framework. A solution process can produce very complex and structured outputs, as final result or as intermediate results (and, conceptually, one could consider as final result of a framework a tool, as in Möbius, or a solver, as in SIMTHESys). The optimal representation for results in a framework heavily depends from its design choices. The main problems are traceability (that is, the possibility of mapping back to a given formalism element of a formalism the related data obtained by the solution process) and management of results that are not related to any given element in the model. While the case of closed multiformalism is relatively easy to manage, the case of open multiformalism requires that results are described similarly to models. Multisolution or non-invertible model transformations complicate the problem. Metamodeling offers good advantages also for result representation, and is exploited by OsMoSys (Gribaudo et al., 2003); internal representations are used by Möbius and SIMTHESys.

The problem of results representation is examined in Chapter 6.

A REVIEW OF LITERATURE

Multiformalism modeling for performance evaluation of systems is widely present in scientific literature as a solution to cope with heterogeneity and complexity of systems. Different approaches to multiformalism modeling can be found in literature. A first, loose classification suggests either extensible or non extensible frameworks. With no claim for completeness, in the first category, SHARPE, SMART and DEDS are the key references, while AToM[3], Möbius, OsMoSys and SIMTHESys to different extents fall in the second category.

Early experiences with multiformalism modeling are given by SHARPE (Trivedi, 2002), in which models are composed by submodels in a fixed set of different formalisms, that are solved by different solvers. SHARPE is a modeling framework capable of studying Markov models, queuing networks expressed in product form and Generalized Stochastic Petri Nets. In SHARPE submodels interact by exchanging probability distributions to obtain the global result and the solution process is determined by the user. SMART (Ciardo & Miner, 2004; Ciardo et al., 2009) is a software package for designing complex discrete-state systems; it provides both numerical solution algorithms and discrete-event simulation techniques. DEDS (Bause et al., 1998) is able to integrate models defined according to different formalism by creating a translation to a common abstract notation while AToM[3] (de Lara & Vangheluwe, 2002) exploits metamodeling to implement model transformations, used to solve models by its solver.

The main references for this chapter are Möbius (Sanders, 1999; Clark et al., 2001; Courtney et al., 2009; Deavours et al., 2002; Derisavi et al., 2002; Sanders et al., 2007), OsMoSys Franceschinis et al., 2002a; Franceschinis et al., 2002b; Franceschinis et al., 2004; Franceschinis et al., 2009; Gribaudo et al., 2003; Vittorini et al., 2004) and SIMTHESys (Barbierato et al., 2011a; Barbierato et al., 2011b; Barbierato et al., 2011c; Barbierato et al., 2012a; Barbierato et al., 2012b; Barbierato et al., 2012c; Barbierato et al., 2013; Castiglione, 2013; Iacono & Gribaudo, 2010; Iacono et al., 2012). All of them aim to provide a methodology and a tool for extensible multiformalism models design and evaluation and consider model composition and multiple solution methods as the foundation of their model solution process. From the point of view of multiformalism modeling, the three approaches use submodel composition to support formalism interaction, but with different premises.

Möbius supports Stochastic Activity Networks (SANs), Petri nets, Markov chains and Performance Evaluation Process Algebra (PEPA), and offers a very articulated complex model composition technique, that allows the generation of optimized solutions. OsMoSys can create multi-formalism models and uses workflow management to achieve multi-solutions, relying on meta-modeling and object-orientation in models and formalisms. SIMTHESys is a multiformalism framework for the definition of new formalisms and the generation of related solvers, based on the description of elements behavior and behavioral interfaces to integrate elementary solvers. In Möbius submodels interact by sharing state variables and by superposing events between submodels; in OsMoSys interactions are defined by using operators, which formally describe the semantics of information exchange between submodels; in SIMTHESys interactions are defined by arc superposition.

Extensibility is another common goal of the three research initiatives: Möbius is designed to be extended by third-party formalism that can be integrated in the framework through proper APIs, while OsMoSys exploits a sophisticated object-oriented metamodeling approach to allow users to include new formalisms by specifying their description in terms of elements and constraints; SIMTHESys is based on the explicit definition of both syntax and semantics of all atomic components of a formalism and on a set of non-specialized solving engines, that are used to automatically and transparently generate (multi)formalism-specific reusable solvers. From the point of view of solution processes, Möbius offers a very flexible and complete execution policy for model elements, that is implemented by a framework of specialized solution algorithms, and allows the automated generation of a custom software that solves the specific model; OsMoSys exploits external existing solvers by encapsulating them in proper software components (namely adapters) and using them to build solution processes in the form of workflows, which structure is generated by examining the model and its operators; SIMTHESys allows rapid prototyping of new formalisms and solution techniques, with native multiformalism support, and the deployment of new solvers (and new interfaces that can be used to characterize different classes of formalisms) without modifying the existing ones.

In the majority of these approaches, modularity or compositionality are supported, and in some cases exploited to enhance the solution process. In SHARPE modularity is managed at model level by its source code; in Möbius complex model composition policies allow optimized solution; in OsMoSys composed models are solved by the orchestration of different solvers for different submodels in a workflow (Franceschinis et al., 2009). In other cases, multiformalism and/or modularity are not explicitly used by the modeler but used for optimized analysis (e.g. (Raiteri et al., 2004)): in general, modularity suggests the possibility of a solution in parts, which is possible if certain hypotheses are verified.

The solution process can be based on the translation to single solution formalism, as in AToM[3] and, to some extent, Möbius, or by using native solvers and composition formalism, as for OsMoSys, or by a combination of the two techniques, as in SIMTHESys. SIMTHESys provides a more general modeling environment with respect of Möbius at a price of reduced solution efficiency. The Abstract Functional Interface (AFI) (Derisavi et al., 2002) that defines all the possible evolution is not required in SIMTHESys. In a certain sense, Möbius AFI can be considered as a specific set of Solver Interfaces and Solver Helper Interfaces in the SIMTHESys methodology. Concerning SHARPE and SMART, SIMTHESys does not currently provide optimized solution engines as they do. However, its set of existing solution engines is planned to be expanded in order to provide solutions that exploit some of the basic principles on which such tools are based. Regarding OsMoSys and SPE-ED (Smith & Williams,

2002), SIMTHESys focuses on a primitive level interaction among the elements of the formalisms, and not only on the multisolution obtained by mixing existing solvers throughout the definition of a workflow. Such techniques can also be included into SIMTHESys by the creation of a suitable set of behaviors. Similarly to AToM[3], SIMTHESys formalisms and models are described as graphs based on a metaformalism, and the integration with DrawNET (Gribaudo et al., 2005) similarly allows to visually manipulating models described in specified formalisms. Both approaches greatly consider the relevance of the operational semantics of formalisms, AToM[3] for simulators generation and SIMTHESys for multiformalism solvers generation. However, AToM[3] privileges model transformations, while SIMTHESys relies on extensibility through the behaviors.

REFERENCES

Barbierato, E., Bobbio, A., Gribaudo, M., & Iacono, M. (2012). Multiformalism to support software rejuvenation modeling. In *Proceedings of ISSRE Workshops* (pp. 271-276). IEEE.

Barbierato, E., Dei Rossi, G., Gribaudo, M., Iacono, M., Marin, A. (2012). Exploiting product form solution techniques in multiformalism modeling. *Electr. Notes Theor. Comput. Sci.*

Barbierato, E., Gribaudo, M., & Iacono, M. (2011a). Defining formalisms for performance evaluation with SIMTHESys. *Electronic Notes in Theoretical Computer Science*, 275, 37–51. doi:10.1016/j.entcs.2011.09.004.

Barbierato, E., Gribaudo, M., & Iacono, M. (2011b). Exploiting multiformalism models for testing and performance evaluation in SIMTH-ESys. In *Proceedings of the 5th International ICST Conference on Performance Evaluation Methodologies and Tools*. Paris, France: ICST (Institute for Computer Sciences, Social-Informatics and Telecommunications Engineering).

Barbierato, E., Gribaudo, M., & Iacono, M. (2013). A performance modeling language for big data architectures. In *Proceedings of HiPMoS 2013 – ECMS 2013*. ECMS.

Barbierato, E., Gribaudo, M., Iacono, M., & Marrone, S. (2011). Performability modeling of exceptions-aware systems in multiformalism tools. In K. Al-Begain, S. Balsamo, D. Fiems, & A. Marin (Eds.), *ASMTA* (pp. 257–272). Berlin: Springer. doi:10.1007/978-3-642-21713-5_19.

Barbierato, E., Iacono, M., & Marrone, S. (2012). PerfBPEL: A graph-based approach for the performance analysis of BPEL SOA applications. In *Proceedings of VALUETOOLS* (pp. 64-73). IEEE.

Bause, F., Buchholz, P., & Kemper, P. (1998). A toolbox for functional and quantitative analysis of DEDS. In R. Puigjaner, N. N. Savino, & B. Serra (Eds.), *Computer Performance Evaluation (Tools)* (pp. 356–359). Berlin: Springer. doi:10.1007/3-540-68061-6_32.

Bohnenkamp, H. C., Hermanns, H., Katoen, J.-P., & Klaren, R. (2003). The modest modeling tool and its implementation. In P. Kemper, & W. H. Sanders (Eds.), *Computer Performance Evaluation / TOOLS* (pp. 116–133). Berlin: Springer. doi:10.1007/978-3-540-45232-4_8.

Castiglione, A., Gribaudo, M., Iacono, M., & Palmieri, F. (2013). Exploiting mean field analysis to model performances of big data architectures. *Future Generation Computer Systems*. doi:10.1016/j.future.2013.07.016.

Ciardo, G., Jones, R. L., Miner, A. S., & Siminiceanu, R. I. (2006). Logic and stochastic modeling with SMART. *Performance Evaluation*, *63*(6), 578–608. doi:10.1016/j.peva.2005.06.001.

Ciardo, G., & Miner, A. S. (2004). SMART: The stochastic model checking analyzer for reliability and timing. In *Proceedings of QEST* (pp. 338-339). IEEE Computer Society.

Ciardo, G., Miner, A. S., & Wan, M. (2009). Advanced features in SMART: The stochastic model checking analyzer for reliability and timing. *SIGMETRICS Performance Evaluation Review*, *36*, 58–63. doi:10.1145/1530873.1530885.

Clark, G., Courtney, T., Daly, D., Deavours, D., Derisavi, S., Doyle, M., et al. (2001). The Möbius modeling tool. In *Proceedings of the 9th international Workshop on Petri Nets and Performance Models* (PNPM'01). IEEE Computer Society.

Courtney, T., Gaonkar, S., Keefe, K., Rozier, E., & Sanders, W. H. (2009). Möbius 2.3: An extensible tool for dependability, security, and performance evaluation of large and complex system models. In *Proceedings of DSN* (pp. 353-358). IEEE.

de Lara, J., & Vangheluwe, H. (2002). AToM[3]: A tool for multi-formalism and meta-modelling. In R.-D. Kutsche, & H. Weber (Eds.), *FASE* (pp. 174–188). Berlin: Springer.

Deavours, D. D., Clark, G., Courtney, T., Daly, D., Derisavi, S., & Doyle, J. M. et al. (2002). The Möbius framework and its implementation. *IEEE Transactions on Software Engineering*, *28*, 956–969. doi:10.1109/TSE.2002.1041052.

Derisavi, S., Kemper, P., Sanders, W. H., & Courtney, T. (2002). The Möbius state-level abstract functional interface. In T. Field, P. G. Harrison, J. T. Bradley, & U. Harder (Eds.), *Computer Performance Evaluation / TOOLS* (pp. 31–50). Berlin: Springer. doi:10.1007/3-540-46029-2_2.

Franceschinis, G., Gribaudo, M., Iacono, M., Marrone, S., Mazzocca, N., & Vittorini, V. (2004). Compositional modeling of complex systems: Contact center scenarios in OsMoSys. In J. Cortadella, & W. Reisig (Eds.), *ICATPN* (pp. 177–196). Berlin: Springer. doi:10.1007/978-3-540-27793-4_11.

Franceschinis, G., Gribaudo, M., Iacono, M., Marrone, S., Moscato, F., & Vittorini, V. (2009). Interfaces and binding in component based development of formal models. In G. Stea, J. Mairesse, & J. Mendes (Eds.), *VALUETOOLS* (p. 44). ACM. doi:10.4108/ICST.VALUETOOLS2009.7677.

Franceschinis, G., Gribaudo, M., Iacono, M., & Vittorini, V. (2002). Towards an object based multi-formalism multi-solution modeling approach. In *Proceedings of Second International Workshop on Modelling of Objects, Components, and Agents* (MOCA'02). Aarhus, Denmark: MOCA.

Franceschinis, G., Gribaudo, M., Iacono, M., Vittorini, V., & Bertoncello, C. (2002). DrawNet++: A flexible framework for building dependability models. In *Proceedings of DSN* (p. 540). IEEE Computer Society.

Gribaudo, M., Codetta-Raiteri, D., & Franceschinis, G. (2005). DrawNET, a customizable multi-formalism, multi-solution tool for the quantitative evaluation of systems. In *Proceedings of QEST 2005*. QEST.

Gribaudo, M., Iacono, M., Mazzocca, N., & Vittorini, V. (2003). The OsMoSys/DrawNET XE! Languages system: A novel infrastructure for multi-formalism object-oriented modelling. In *Proceedings of ESS 2003: 15th European Simulation Symposium And Exhibition*. ESS.

Iacono, M., Barbierato, E., & Gribaudo, M. (2012). The SIMTHESys multiformalism modeling framework. *Computers & Mathematics with Applications (Oxford, England)*, *64*, 3828–3839. doi:10.1016/j.camwa.2012.03.009.

Iacono, M., & Gribaudo, M. (2010). Element based semantics in multi formalism performance models. In *Proceedings of MASCOTS* (pp. 413-416). IEEE.

Moscato, F., Flammini, F., Di Lorenzo, G., Vittorini, V., Marrone, S., & Iacono, M. (2007). The software architecture of the OsMoSys multisolution framework. In P. W. Glynn (Ed.), *VALUETOOLS* (p. 51). ACM. doi:10.4108/valuetools.2007.1913.

Raiteri, D. C., Iacono, M., Franceschinis, G., & Vittorini, V. (2004). Repairable fault tree for the automatic evaluation of repair policies. In *Proceedings of DSN* (pp. 659-668). IEEE Computer Society.

Sanders, W. H. (1999). Integrated frameworks for multi-level and multiformalism modeling. In *Proceedings of the 8th International Workshop on Petri Nets and Performance Models*. Washington, DC: IEEE.

Sanders, W. H., Courtney, T., Deavours, D., Daly, D., Derisavi, S., & Lam, V. (2007). Multiformalism and multi-solution-method modeling frameworks: The Möbius approach. In *Proceedings of Symp. on Performance Evaluation–Stories and Perspectives*, (pp. 241–256). IEEE.

Smith, C. U., & Williams, L. G. (2002). *Performance solutions: A practical guide to creating responsive, scalable software*. Boston, MA: Addison-Wesley.

Trivedi, K. S. (2002). SHARPE 2002: Symbolic hierarchical automated reliability and performance evaluator. In *Proceedings of DSN* (p. 544). IEEE Computer Society.

van der Aalst, W., & ter Hofstede, A. (2012). Workflow patterns put into context. *Software & Systems Modeling*, *11*, 319–323. doi:10.1007/s10270-012-0233-4.

Vittorini, V., Iacono, M., Mazzocca, N., & Franceschinis, G. (2004). The OsMoSys approach to multi-formalism modeling of systems. *Software & Systems Modeling*, *3*, 68–81. doi:10.1007/s10270-003-0039-5.

ENDNOTES

[1] The set of formalisms of Mobius can be extended by properly extending the software tool with data structures and solving engines.

Chapter 2
Combining Heterogeneity, Compositionality, and Automatic Generation in Formal Modelling

Stefano Marrone
Seconda Università di Napoli, Italy

Nicola Mazzocca
Università di Napoli "Federico II", Italy

Roberto Nardone
Università di Napoli "Federico II", Italy

Valeria Vittorini
Università di Napoli "Federico II", Italy

ABSTRACT

Critical computer-based systems have an increasing complexity due to the number of components, to their heterogeneity, and to the relationships among them. Such systems must meet strict non-functional requirements and should be able to cope with competitive market needs. The adoption of formal methods is often advocated in order to provide formal proof, but their application does not scale with the growing size of systems. The aim of this chapter is to introduce a modelling and analysis methodology that allows the combination of three proven research trends in formal modelling of large systems: formal model generation (by means of model-driven techniques), multiformalism, and compositional approaches. In this chapter there is also a discussion about enabling techniques. The proposed approach has been applied to the performability modelling and evaluation of flexible manufacturing systems.

DOI: 10.4018/978-1-4666-4659-9.ch002

FORMAL MODELLING OF CRITICAL SYSTEMS

Computer-based systems are now present in our daily life and affect many aspects providing essential support to several human activities, from transportation to industrial automation systems. They generally have large distributed architectures where the complexity is due to heterogeneity of system elements which are not only hardware and software components, but also procedures and people. Their criticality implies the necessity to meet several requirements, often dictated by international standards, whose fulfillment must be demonstrated in order to achieve necessary certifications. The application of formal methods in industry (highly recommended if not mandatory) is slowed down by the complexity of the model and heterogeneity (which reflects the system complexity), and by the need to have highly skilled personnel involved in model development. In other words, there is a request for modelling methodologies and supporting tools which can hide the complexity of the modelling process, without losing expressive power and solving efficiency.

The scientific literature addresses three main research directions in order to overcome the described problems:

- **Divide-and-Conquer:** Focusing on methods and techniques for developing models through submodel composition.
- **Multi-Formalism and Multi-Paradigm:** Exploring the possibility of combining different formalisms and modelling paradigms in defining the overall model.
- **Automatic Generation:** Generating formal models suitable for the analysis from high-level specifications.

In the first approach a model consists of several submodels tied together by appropriate rules and composition operators: in order to provide appropriate methods for solving submodels and aggregating results, composition techniques and operators definition are necessary. In (Nicol, 2004) a comprehensive review of the state of the art in such techniques is presented. These methods include techniques to limit the size of the state space (*largeness avoidance*) and techniques to manage the size of the models (*largeness tolerance*).

The second approach deals with the integration between submodels expressed by different formalisms and also based on different modelling paradigms. The first steps in this direction have been made by SMART (Ciardo, 2001) and SHARPE (Trivedi, 2002): the first integrates Stochastic Petri Nets, Markov chains in continuous and discrete time, while the latter integrates Fault Trees (FT), Generalized Stochastic Petri Nets (GSPN), some types of queuing networks and Markov Processes. Then, some approaches and tools based on explicit methodologies for the development of multiformal models have been proposed: two different frameworks described in literature are Möbius (Deavours, 2002) and OsMoSys (Vittorini, 2004). An interesting example of multi-paradigm modelling is realized by AToM[3] (de Lara, 2002), which implements an approach based on meta-modelling and graph transformation techniques. Other recent frameworks focuses the attention on the practical use of these techniques (Iacono, 2012).

The third approach deals with the generation of formal models from high-level specifications. As surveyed in (Bernardi, 2011b), the scientific community has also explored such way and several approaches presented in the literature are: in (Pai, 2002) and in (D'Ambrogio, 2002) the generation of Fault Tree and Dynamic Fault Tree (DFT) models from a set of UML diagrams is described; in (Bondavalli, 2011), UML diagrams are used to generate Timed Petri Nets-based models; generation of Stochastic Reward Nets from Statechart and Activity Diagrams are presented respectively in (Huszerl, 2002) and (Tadano, 2011). These approaches often rely on high-level languages oriented to Non-Functional Properties (NFPs) modelling; some of these approaches are based on the usage of MARTE and AADL languages. In a recent work (Bernardi, 2011b) the "Dependability Analysis and Modelling" (DAM) profile has been proposed as a MARTE specialization. A MARTE-DAM annotation stereotypes a UML design model element, thereby extending its semantics with dependability concepts (e.g., annotating a generic transition of UML State Machines as a failure step). Hence, DAM is useful to annotate dependability requirements and properties in UML specifications, in particular, reliability, availability, maintainability and safety attributes.

A criticism often advanced, as stated in (Montecchi, 2011), shows how these approaches are seldom integrated into a broader development process: the development of business transformations is not engineered enough and it is often related to very specific application domains, resulting in flexibility and low reusability. There is not a general framework in which Model-Driven approaches are integrated with the ones described above. This need has been collected from several European projects as SATURN (SysML bAsed modelling, architecTUre exploRation, simulation and syNthesis for complex embedded systems) (SATURN 2009) and the ARTEMIS JU-CHESS (Composition with guarantees for High-integrity Embedded Software component aSsembly) (CHESS 2009) whose goal is to create a framework for critical system analysis using model-driven approaches that support the entire development cycle of systems.

This paper has the objective to describe the steps necessary to move towards a formal modelling approach which can integrate the three discussed approaches and can exploit the benefits brought by each of them. The proposed approach is developed according to Model-Driven methods and techniques. According to such paradigm, software and systems design can be achieved by using high level specifications expressed in proper modelling languages (usually called Domain Specific Modelling Languages - DSMLs) and by

defining automatic transformation chains, able to incrementally generate new design artifacts. The methodology should be implementable into cost-effective processes in order to reduce time-to-market specifically in verification stages of critical system development lifecycles. Such objective will be achieved by both improving usability and reusability of typical Model-Driven artifacts. Thus, the definition of languages and model transformations cannot be a handcrafted discipline but must be ruled by mechanisms and techniques with the aim of improving reuse. The proposed approach is built on top of OsMoSys methodology and framework but is quite generic to be adapted to other multiformal approaches.

The original contribution of this paper is in combining the three main research approaches in a comprehensive methodology based on Model-Driven principles and that are able to generate multiformalism and component based formal models by means of transformational techniques. A strong emphasis is placed on the study of enabling techniques by which the proposed methodology can be put in practice inside cost-effective system development processes. This work constitutes an extension of two previous papers (Bernardi, 2011a; Marrone, 2010); in these works the enabling techniques that are described in this paper have been introduced and discussed. A work that is very close to the one here presented is in (Harrison, 2009): one of the main difference between these two works (the cited and this chapter) is on the focus: while focuses more on performance modeling, this chapter wants to give a wider overview of this kind of approaches.

The paper is structured as follows: section 1 gives motivations for the research and related works. Section 2 describes some techniques that enable effective and efficient implementation of the proposed methodology. Section 3 introduces the methodology. Section 4 provides a deep description of MARTE and MARTE-DAM UML profiles while section 5 focuses on Repairable Fault Trees. Section 6 summarizes the proposed approach by applying it on Flexible Manufacturing System example. Section 7 ends the paper giving some concluding remarks and addressing future works.

ENABLING TECHNIQUES

In order to be feasible and cost-effective, the methodology we are going to propose must be supported by proper techniques which make possible a high level of automation. In this section some of these techniques are addressed.

Domain Specific Modelling Language definition

The first enabling technique we focus on is related to Domain Specific Modelling Language construction. The effective usage of Model-Driven Development solutions in industrial settings asks for the availability of specialized modelling languages well focused on domain scope, able to simplify the design process. Domain specific concepts are grouped into a domain meta-model, which defines the relationships among them and precisely specifies semantics and constraints associated with the domain concepts. The definition of a DSML is an activity performed by "language engineers" and it is still an emerging discipline with few established guidelines and patterns. Three main approaches to the definition of a DSML are reported in the literature (Selic, 2007):

1. Definition of a new modelling language from scratch.
2. Extension of an existing modelling language by supplementing it with fresh domain specific constructs.
3. The refinement of an existing more general modelling language, as UML, by specializing some of its general constructs to represent domain specific concepts.

Clearly the first one allows a precise characterization of domain specific concepts, but it requires the implementation of the model editors that involves an extra effort when put into practice. The second one suffers from the same problems, but it can rely on the experience. The third one is more practical and reduces development and maintenance costs: it is based on the UML profiling technique when UML is the chosen general modelling language.

Independently from the chosen technique, language construction should promote reuse by means of language inheritance and formalism hierarchies. In (Taivalsaari, 1996) a very deep analysis of inheritance mechanisms has been done with particular reference to programming languages while in (Barbero, 2007) the focus shifts to models and metamodels.

Let us consider the taxonomy of the DSMLs in vertical and horizontal (Kleppe, 2008). Vertical DSMLs focus on concepts that are common to several application domains: data modelling, testing, performance, etc.; they are characterized by high usability and low re-usability as opposed to technical DSMLs that focus on specific business contexts (telecommunication, railway, automotive, etc.). It is reasonable that the new language would gain the advantages of both the two kinds of languages by means of language composition techniques. In (Ldeczi, 2001) authors define several composition operators for metamodels and in (Sanchez, 2010) a focus on embedded systems is done: here a series of techniques in DSMLs family creation have been addressed such as importation or extension.

UML Profiling

The Unified Modeling Language (UML) is a well known general purpose standardized modelling language for software system specification (OMG 2011). The system structure is typically specified by a Component Diagram and/or a Class Diagram.

The behavioural view of the system is instead specified using Use Cases, Activity Diagrams, Sequence Diagrams and State Machines, or a combination of them.

UML is a semi-formal specification language: the semantics of UML diagrams are expressed in natural language while the abstract syntax is provided in terms of UML meta-models. A UML meta-model is actually a Class Diagram that represents the UML concepts and their relationships as meta-classes and meta-associations, respectively. Constraints on the meta-classes and meta-associations are expressed with OCL (OMG 2012).

UML is also equipped with a profiling mechanism that allows customizing UML for a particular domain or platform. The UML profiling is actually a lightweight meta-modelling technique to extend UML, since the standard semantics of UML model elements can be refined in a strictly additive manner. Stereotypes, tags and OCL constraints are the extension mechanisms used to define a UML profile. In particular, a stereotype extends one or more UML meta-classes and can be applied to those UML model elements that are instantiations of the extended meta-classes. The profiling mechanism has been addressed in literature as an alternative approach for creating DSML (Selic 2007).

For example, in Figure 1, the *Resource* stereotype extends the *Class* meta-class, then the former can be applied to a class in a Class Diagram. Just like classes, a stereotype can have properties which are referred to as tag definitions: in the previous example *resMult* and *isProtected* are tags. When a stereotype is applied to a model element, the value assigned to a stereotype property is called *tagged-value*.

Creating a UML profile is not a mechanical task since, according to (Selic, 2007) and (Lagadre, 2007), it starts from a conceptual modelling that may be a metamodel or a more "UML-friendly" domain model expressed in UML itself.

Figure 1. Example of stereotype definition and application

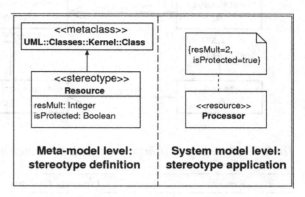

Then concepts of the domain model have to be mapped into a concrete profile. Each class, as well as its attributes, associations and constraints, is considered and the most suitable UML concepts are identified, according to the cited guidelines. The outcome of this iterative process is a UML profile which provides the UML extensions as well as a datatype model library.

Inheriting Transformations

It is necessary at this point to understand how the extension of metamodels can be exploited in order to achieve a greater level of reuse of model transformations. In this paper we refer to a technique that tries to exploit the relationship between a base language and a derived language in order to define the relationship between rules in base and derived transformations. This would allow a mechanism of transformation inheritance. Such methodology is fully explained in (Marrone, 2010) where four cases of *language elements inheritance / transformation rules inheritance* are described (see Figure 2 and Table 1).

The description refers to the following case: if *A* language extends *A* and we have *A-to-B* transformation, we want to understand the inheritance relationships between *A-to-B* and *A -to-B*.

Figure 2. Transformation inheritance schema

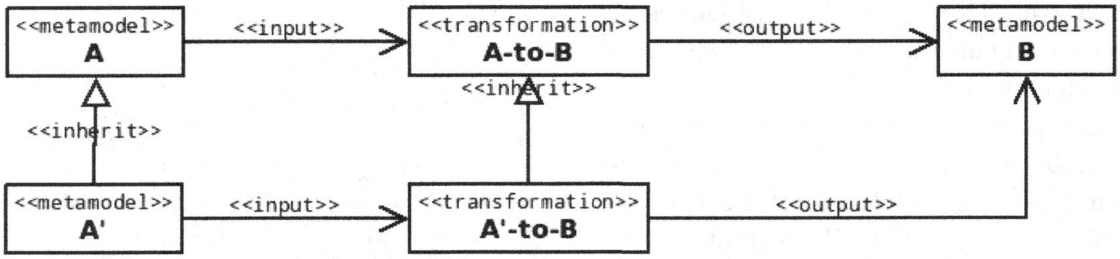

Table 1. Summary of transformation inheritance methodology

Name	Language Elements	Transformation Rules
Addition	A extends A by adding a new element	a new rule must be defined that maps the new source element onto the target one
re-definition (new context)	an element in A is inherited without changes but it may be used within a new context in A	the rules in A-to-B related to the translation of inherited elements are extended and/or partially redefined in A-to-B
re-definition (old context)	an element defined by A assumes a new meaning within A, but the context in which it is used does not change	the rules in A-to-B related to the translation of inherited elements must be redefined
full reuse	an element defined in A is inherited by A without modifications	the rules in A-to-B that are related to the translation of inherited elements are fully reused by A-to-B

Two main mechanisms have been defined in the literature for transformation composition that we exploit for implementing transformation inheritance: *superimposition,* that allows for overlaying several transformation definitions and executing them as they were a single transformation, and *rule overriding*, that substitutes an existing rule by a new one with the same name (Wagelaar, 2009).

Model Composition

The increasing complexity of systems is more and more reflected by the incapability to create a single model of a system: system models are often composed of several submodels. One of the most important activities in a model-based automated approach is model composition. Scientific literature has strongly invested in research on this topic traditionally focusing on the composition problem inside a single formalism.

As an example Petri Net and its derived formalism compositions have been extensively studied under both theoretical and technical aspects and well supported by proper tools. It is possible with such approaches to model in a compositional way very complex IMS networks[1] such as in (Marrone, 2012). A comprehensive discussion of such methods and the proposal for a unifying framework is in (Reisig, 2009).

Another compositional technique relies on the definition of compositional operators: this is an approach typical of multiformalism frameworks (Vittorini, 2004) (Deavours, 2002). We refer to OsMoSYS where, in brief, there are four compositional operators that link together two models, say M_A and M_B:

- **Copy Properties Operator (CPP):** The operator copies the property value of a M_A's element into the value of the property of M_B's element.

- **Copy Elaborated Properties Operator (CEP):** The operator copies a transformation of the property value of a M_A's element into the value of the property of M_B's element.
- **Copy Results Operator (CPR):** The operator copies the value of one of the outputs of M_A's solution into the value of the property of M_B's element.
- **Copy Elaborated Results Operator (CER):** The operator copies a transformation of the value of one of the outputs of M_A's solution into the value of the property of M_B's element.

A further discussion of these operators is out of the scope of this chapter, see (Vittorini, 2004) for further details.

These last years have seen an increasing research interest around model composition: the affirming trend is to consider compositionality in high level modelling language (such as UML) in order to define model composition approaches in the model driven perspective. Several approaches are present in literature (Del Fabro, 2007) (Fleuery, 2007) some of them describing the model composition as model transformation. In fact the problem of compose two models can be easily solved by defining an endogenous model transformation[2] that compose two source models into a target one (Baudry, 2005).

TOWARDS A COMPREHENSIVE MODELLING METHODOLOGY

In this Section we propose a three stage approach (Figure 3) in order to combine heterogeneity, compositionality and automatic generation in formal modelling: the stages are described in a top-down manner.

The first stage covers all phases of high-level modelling and meta-modelling of the system and its requirements. In order to establish an auto-

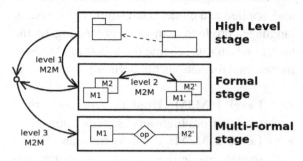

Figure 3. Conceptual schema of the methodology

mated method, it is necessary that all models comply with languages whose syntax has been formally defined. At this stage, the creation of high level models requires the use of a DSML that can be eventually defined from existing ones.

At the second stage several formal models are generated on the basis of high-level one: each of the generated models can be expressed in a different formal language. In this context "formal" means that these languages are based on strong mathematical bases. Languages at this stage include, but are not limited to: Petri Net, Fault Tree, Queuing Network, Process Algebra and their extensions. The choice of the language depends on the specific characteristics of the high level model and on the type of the requirement whose fulfillment has to be verified.

At the third stage single-formalism models are tied together in order to create a multiformal model of the entire system. The relationships among high level model sub-parts are translated into compositionality operators, which define the rules of passing parameters and/or results between models. The importance of having a multiformalism approach is twofold: on the one hand we can express each aspect of the system by choosing the best fitting formalism; on the other, we can exploit this decomposition in order to solve efficiently the model by solving each submodel with the most appropriate solver.

Passing from a stage to another is possible by means of model-to-model transformations (M2M). These transformations are defined between two formalized languages (a source and a target one) and, applied to a model conforming to the source language, produce a model conforming to the target one. In this scheme the following kinds of model transformations are defined:

- **Level 1 M2M:** Used to generate formal models from high-level specifications.
- **Level 2 M2M:** Used to translate formal models inside the second stage. Such passage is often desirable in order to simplify the final multiformal model and therefore the solution process (e.g. Fault Trees can be expressed through a Generalized Stochastic Petri Nets). It is important to clarify that this transformation passage is optional when possible.
- **Level 3 M2M:** It generates a multiformalism model by adding compositional operators among the models at the second stage. In order to accomplish this purpose, this kind of transformations has as inputs both models at the first stage and models on the second stage.

THE MARTE AND MARTE-DAM PROFILES

The *UML Profile for Modelling and Analysis of Real-Time and Embedded systems (MARTE)* (OMG 2002) adds capabilities to UML for modelling Real Time and Embedded Systems. MARTE is an OMG standard profile enabling the description of non-functional properties (NFP) of a system under analysis, such as timing or performance-related properties; it is useful in all the development cycle, from specification to verification and validation phase. The main advantage brought by MARTE is related to capacity of this language to capture essential features of real-time and embedded systems and to annotate application models in order to support analysis of system properties. Specifically for the analysis aim, MARTE contains a general package called

General Quantitative Analysis Model (GQAM): the object of this package is to represent some general analysis concepts and describe how the system behaviour uses resources, although different domains have different terminology, concepts, and semantics.

A key feature of MARTE is the NFP subpackage. It provides a general framework to annotate UML models with NFPs, defining new NFP datatypes necessary for the definition of a specific analysis domain. In particular, a NFP datatype is characterized by several properties, such as the origin (that allows the modeller to specify whether an NFP is a requirement or a metric to be estimated), the type of statistical measure associated to a NFP (e.g. mean), the type of the quality order relation in the value domain of an NFP for comparative analysis purposes. A Value Specification Language (VSL) has been defined in MARTE in order to specify expressions for constraints, properties, and stereotype attributes. In fact, this expression language enables the value specification, at model level, in tagged values, body of constraints, and in any UML element.

The *Dependability Analysis and Modelling (DAM)* (Bernardi, 2011b) specializes general concepts of MARTE-GQAM for dependability analysis. The DAM domain model is a set of UML Class dDiagrams, structured into packages that represent the main dependability concepts (Figure 4). The main package is the *System*, decomposed in turn in two subpackages: the *Core* and the *Redundancy* packages. The former contains concepts to model a system as a set of components, according to a component-based view of the system to be analysed, bound together by connectors, in order to interact. They deliver a set of high-level services that can be detailed as a sequence of steps. The latter package represents possible component redundancies, contained in redundant structures.

The *Threats* model adds threats to the system: impairments of the system can run against the services and are represented as the fault-error-impairment chain. At last, the *Maintenance* pack-

Figure 4. DAM domain model packages

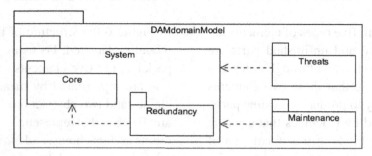

age includes maintenance concepts: it is possible to model both service recoveries and system component repairs. The involvement of external agents (e.g. maintenance staff and test equipment) has been contemplated.

The DAM profile has been defined by mapping, systematically, the concepts of the DAM domain model onto UML extensions and onto MARTE concepts. Each domain class was examined, together with its attributes, associations and constraints, to identify the most suitable UML base concepts for it. Finally, only a subset of the domain classes was mapped to stereotypes and the remaining classes were mapped to datatypes (e.g. fault, error and failure classes).

THE REPAIRABLE FAULT TREE FORMALISM

The Repariable Fault Tree (RFT) formalism was introduced to ease the modeler's approach to complex repair policy modeling and evaluation (Codetta-Raiteri, 2004) as a result of the application of the OsMoSys multi-formalism multi-solution methodology (Vittorini, 2004). RFTs preserve the modeling simplicity of FTs and allow to exploit the expressive power of Petri Nets by implementing where possible an efficient divide-et-impera solving process (Codetta-Raiteri, 2004). At the state, RFTs allow to model a series of complex maintenance policies and extend the well known FT formalism by adding a new ele-

ment, called Repair Box (RB), that is able to take into account:

- Which fault condition will start a repair action (trigger event.)
- A repair policy, including the repair algorithm, the repair timing and priority, and the number of repair facilities.
- The set of components in the system that are actually repairable by the RB.

Graphically, a RFT model is a simple FT with the addition of the RBs. The FT is obtained exactly as for usual FT models, then RBs are added to implement repair actions. A RB is connected to the tree by arcs linking the trigger event to the RB and the RB to all the Basic Events in the FT (that are the elementary events, at the bottom of the tree) on which the repair operates. The RFT model of a system can be obtained in two steps. First, the FT of the system is built by inspection of its structure; then the chosen repair policies are applied to the model by evaluating which conditions will trigger the repair and on which sub-tree the repair will be applied.

AN EXAMPLE FROM AUTOMATION DOMAIN

To better explain the meaning of each phase of the methodology we introduce an example taken from Flexible Manufacturing Systems (FMS) domain. In Figure 5 a simple FMS production cell is depicted.

In this kind of cell, five types of elements are present: raw material and unfinished parts are loaded/unloaded into the cell through entry and exit areas; we suppose that these two elements have infinite capacity to produce/consume parts. Materials are worked by machines that are able to accomplish some kinds of transformation of initial material. Materials can be moved only by armed robots that transfer parts from/to machines and other places inside the cell. Finally semi-finished parts that need to be further worked by machines can be temporarily stored in buffers (with a finite capacity). In particular we suppose that R1 is fault-prone and can be repaired. We are interested in generating a model that can give us information on the performance of the production cell in the presence of failure of the robot R1 (i.e. a performability model). For this purpose we aim at the creation of a multiformalism model composed of a performance GSPN submodel of the entire cell and an availability Repairable Fault Tree model of robot.

The first stage of the methodology describes (1) the definition/choice of a proper DSML and (2) implementation of the DSML and (3) the creation of a high-level model of the cell to be studied. Then the model is transformed by (4) the Level 1 M2M in order to generate (5) formal models at the second stage. Finally the generated formal models are transformed into a multiformalism model by the (6) Level 3 M2M.

Definition of a DSML

In Figure 6 the structure of the defined domain model is depicted. Focusing on *production cell* package, the five elements of the FMS description are represented by means of five concrete classes and two abstract ones. These last classes are: *Worker*, that represents performing objects as robots and machines, and *Stage*, that is a concept related to material transformation and storing entities. *Stage*s are connected between them in order to define a workflow of the material: the workflow is modelled by the *flow* auto-association with the *Stage* class. The serves association between Robot and flow represents the movement of the material: in fact since Stage elements are unable to move material by themselves, Robots are needed in order to "serve" material flows. Two properties are present in the domain model: the *rate* of *Worker* that defines the production rate of *Machine*s and *Robot*s, and the *capacity* that represents the maximum amount of material units that can be stored in *Buffer*s.

Workers are fault-prone, thus it is natural to exploit existing metamodels that have already captured dependability aspects, so we use MARTE-DAM. In this way, *Worker* can be inherited from MARTE-DAM's *DaComponent* i.e. the class of MARTE-DAM domain model which represents objects characterized by Mean-Time-To-Failure (MTTF) and Mean-Time-To-Repair (MTTR).

In this example, we extend elements of a DSML by the elements of another language applying

Figure 5. Simple flexible production cell

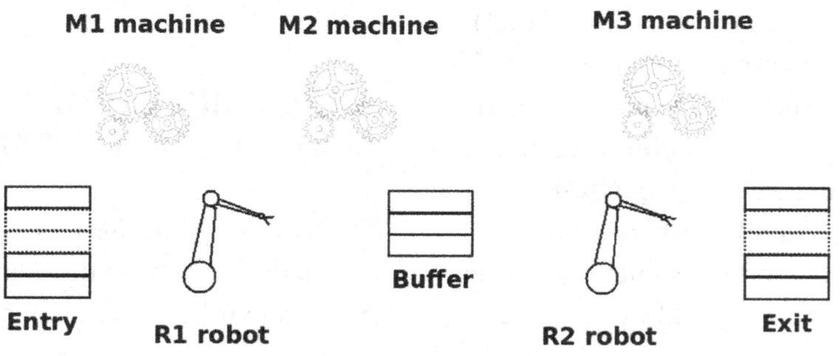

Figure 6. FMS domain model

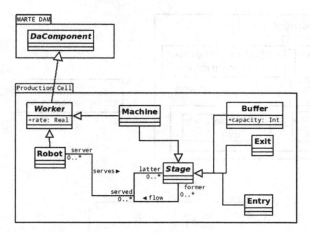

the technique described above. In particular we define the (vertical) FMS language on the base of MARTE-DAM (horizontal) language by deriving the *Working* concept from the *DaComponent* concept.

Implementation of the DSML

According to the domain model, a UML profile can be developed. More in detail, the FMS profile imports MARTE-DAM UML profile and contains a UML package of stereotype and tagged values related to the production cell package.

Creation of the High Level Model

We choose of course to model the cell by a UML model on which the defined FMS profile is applied. The model consists of two UML structural diagrams: a Class Diagram (Figure 7) and a Composite Structure Diagram (Figure 8). The first describes the layout of the production cell and highlights their elements by means of UML stereotypes and tagged values belonging to the production cell package; the second diagram gives insight into the structure of the robot R1 (the one that is fault-prone).

The second diagram also allows showing how single components can be described under fault and repairing aspects: it depicts R1 robot whose structure consists of three main components: a mechanical arm, a microcontroller and a power group. These elements are specified by means of MARTE-DAM stereotypes: in particular we use: the *DaComponent* stereotype to specify elements that are characterized by a MTTR and/or a MTTF, the *DaRedundantStructure* stereotype in order to

Figure 7. Model of the production cell

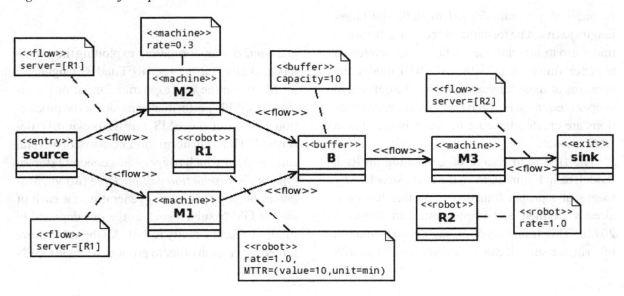

Figure 8. Model of the faulty-repairable robot

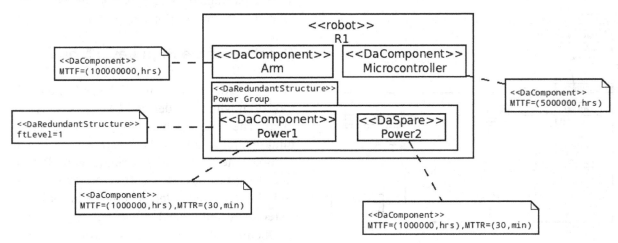

model redundant fault-tolerant structures and the *DaSpare* stereotype to model spare components. In particular, the *Arm* and *Microcontroller* cannot be repaired while the specification of a not null MTTR for the *Power1* and *Power2* model elements, gives us the opportunity to specify that a fault of a single *Power* unit can be repaired while the *R1* is on-line. More details on the specification of such models are in (Bernardi, 2011a) (Bernardi, 2013).

Level 1 M2M

In order to generate formal models, the target languages must be formalized according to model transformation techniques. Since we are interested in generating both a GSPN and a RFT model, the syntaxes of these languages have to be defined in proper metamodels. Then two model transformations are created in order to properly translate a UML model.

The first is in charge of generating an RFT model, as in Figure 9, from the robot structure by means of a proper transformation that has been already defined and implemented in Bernardi 2011a. This transformation uses transformation inheritance since it can be decomposed in *dam2ft*

Figure 9. Repairable fault tree model of robot structure

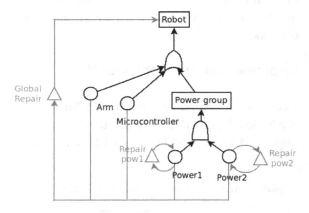

and *dam2rft* transformations exploiting the inheritance relationship between RFT and FT languages.

Moreover the *fms2gspn* transformation generates the GSPN performance model of the production cell from the FMS profile previously described. This transformation consists of several rules each of which triggers on a concrete stereotype of *the production cell package* (*Robot, Machine, Buffer, flow*, etc...) generating for each of them a GSPN subnet such as the one depicted in Figure 10 for the faulty Robot. All the subnets are linked together in order to produce a single GSPN

Figure 10. GSPN subnet of the faulty robot

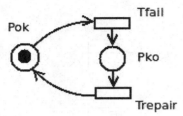

performance model. The result of this transformation is depicted in Figure 11.

Let us note that the *dam2rft* is built exploiting transformation inheritance as previously described. This is possible since RFT formalism is defined upon FT formalism. Figure 12 depicts the organization of such model transformation.

Formal Model Stage

In the proposed example a Level 2 M2M transformation has been used. The RB node of the RFT encapsulates a GSPN model of the repair action. Under proper hypotheses, a RFT model is solved by translating the parts affected by a repair into equivalent GSPN sub-models, in order to (efficiently) evaluate the steady-state probability of

the related subsystems failures. To this aim, in (Marrone, 2010) the *rft2gspn* model-to-model transformation is described: in this paper there is also the evidence that *rft2gspn* has been build by using the transformation inheritance technique, too.

Level 3 M2M

The RFT and GSPN model are now ready to be transformed into a multiformalism one. In order to make this passage two sources of information are necessary. From the high level model we understand which of the formal models are tied together: in the example, the R1 robot represents a single model element that is characterized by both performance and reliability aspects. Moreover the nature of the formal models (i.e. the formalisms in which they are expressed) determines how these models are tied together: in the example, the value of the probability of occurrence of the top event of the fault tree into the rate of the transition of the subnet related to R1 robot. The formalization of this connection is made by means of a compositional operator. In particular, according to the OsMoSYS methodology, we encapsulate the

Figure 11. GSPN of the overall FSM plant

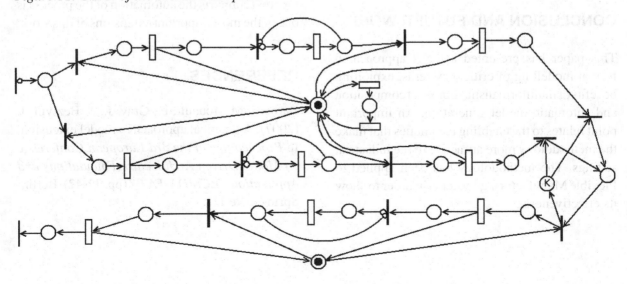

Figure 12. The dam2rft transformation structure

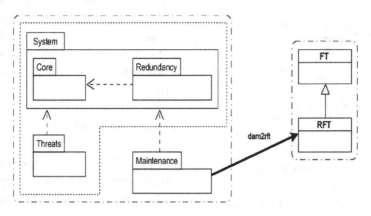

Figure 13. Multiformalism model of the FSM plant

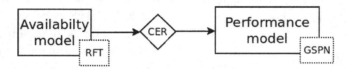

models described before by means of the Copy-Elaborated-Result (CER) operator. According to the semantics of this operator, the result of the analysis of a RFT model is copied as a parameter of GSPN one. The resulting model (depicted in Figure 13) can be further analysed by means of a proper automated solution process.

CONCLUSION AND FUTURE WORK

This paper has presented a novel approach in formal modelling of critical systems, exploiting benefits of multiformalism, submodel composition and automatic model generation. An important point relates to the enabling techniques that make the methodology more attractive to the industrial settings. The methodology has been applied to Flexible Manufacturing Systems in order to show its effectiveness.

Future research efforts will investigate on the application of the same methodology to more complex case studies, also in other application domains, focusing on other non-functional properties (security, safety, etc...) in order to adjust the methodology itself and to discover new techniques to be applied for a better industrial penetration. Moreover the description of a reference architecture that supports the automation of the process is one of the most important extensions of this work.

REFERENCES

Barbero, M., Jouault, F., Gray, J., & Bezivin, J. (2007). A practical approach to model extension. In *Proceedings of the 3rd European Conference on Model Driven Architecture-Foundations and Applications, ECMDA-FA'07* (pp. 32-42). Berlin: Springer-Verlag.

Barbierato, E., Dei Rossi, G., Gribaudo, M., Iacono, M., & Marin, M. (2013). Exploiting product forms solution techniques in multiformalism modeling. *Electronic Notes in Theoretical Computer Science, 296*(16), 61–77. doi:10.1016/j.entcs.2013.07.005.

Barbierato, E., Gribaudo, M., & Iacono, M. (2011). Defining formalisms for performance evaluation with SIMTHESys. *Electronic Notes in Theoretical Computer Science, 275*, 37–51. doi:10.1016/j.entcs.2011.09.004.

Baudry, B., Fleurey, F., France, R., & Reddy, R. (2005). *Exploring the relationship between model composition and model transformation.* Paper presented at the 7th International Workshop on Aspect-Oriented Modeling. Montego, Jamaica.

Bernardi, S., Flammini, F., Marrone, S., Mazzocca, M., Nardone, R., Merseguer, J., & Vittorini, V. (2013). Enabling the usage of UML in the verification of railway systems: The DAM-rail approach. *Reliability Engineering & System Safety.* doi:10.1016/j.ress.2013.06.032.

Bernardi, S., Flammini, F., Marrone, S., Merseguer, J., Papa, C., & Vittorini, V. (2011a). Model-driven availability evaluation of railway control systems. *Lecture Notes in Computer Science, 6894*, 15–28. doi:10.1007/978-3-642-24270-0_2.

Bernardi, S., Merseguer, J., & Petriu, D. C. (2011b). A dependability profile within MARTE. *Software & Systems Modeling, 10*(3), 313–336. doi:10.1007/s10270-009-0128-1.

Bondavalli, A., Dal Cin, M., Latella, D., Majzik, I., Pataricza, A., & Savoia, G. (2001). Dependability analysis in the early phases of UML-based system design. *Comput. Syst. Sci. Eng., 16*(5), 265–275.

CHESS. (n.d.). *Composition with guarantees for high-integrity embedded software components assembly.* Retrieved from http://www.chess-project.org

Ciardo, G., Jones, R. L., Miner, A. S., & Siminiceanu, R. (2001). SMART - Stochastic model analyzer for reliability and timing. In *Proceedings of Tools of Aachen 2001 Int. Multiconference on Measurement, Modelling and Evaluation of Computer Communication Systems* (pp. 29-34). Tools of Aachen.

Codetta Raiteri, D., Franceschinis, G., Iacono, M., & Vittorini, V. (2004). Repairable fault tree for automatic evaluation of repair policies. In *Proceedings of the Performance and Dependability Symposium.* Washington, DC: IEEE Computer Society.

Cuadrado, J. S., & Molina, J. C. (2010). A model-based approach to families of embedded domain specific languages. *IEEE Transactions on Software Engineering, 35*(6).

D'Ambrogio, A., Iazeolla, G., & Mirandola, R. (2002). A method for the prediction of software reliability. In *Proceedings of the 6th IASTED Software Engineering and Applications Conference (SEA2002).* IASTED.

de Lara, J., & Vangheluwe, H. (2002). ATOM3: A tool for multi-formalism and meta-modelling. [LNCS]. *Proceedings of Fundamental Approaches to Software Engineering, 2306*, 174–188. doi:10.1007/3-540-45923-5_12.

Deavours, D. D., Clark, G., Courtney, T., Daly, D., Derisavi, S., & Doyle, J. M. et al. (2002). The Möbius framework and its implementation. *IEEE Transactions on Software Engineering, 28*, 956–969. doi:10.1109/TSE.2002.1041052.

Didonet Del Fabro, M., & Valduriez, P. (2007). Semi-automatic model integration using matching transformations and weaving models. In *Proceedings of 22nd ACM Symposium on Applied Computing - Model Transformation Track (SAC 2007)* (pp. 963-970). ACM.

Fleurey, F., Baudry, B., France, R., & Ghosh, S. (2007). A generic approach for automatic model composition. In *Proceedings of AOM at MoDELS*. MoDELS.

Harrison, P. G., Lladó, C. M., & Puigjaner, R. (2009). A unified approach to modelling the performance of concurrent systems. *Simulation Modelling Practice and Theory*, *17*(9), 1445–1456. doi:10.1016/j.simpat.2009.06.003.

Huszerl, G., Majzik, I., Pataricza, A., Kosmidis, K., & Dal Cin, M. (2002). Quantitative analysis of UML statechart models of dependable systems. *The Computer Journal*, *45*(3), 260–277. doi:10.1093/comjnl/45.3.260.

Iacono, M., Barbierato, E., & Gribaudo, M. (2012). The SIMTHESys multiformalism multisolution framework. *Computers & Mathematics with Applications (Oxford, England)*, *64*(12), 3828–3839. doi:10.1016/j.camwa.2012.03.009.

Kleppe, A. (2008). *Software language engineering: Creating domain-specific languages using metamodels*. Reading, MA: Addison-Wesley Professional.

Lagarde, F., Espinoza, H., Terrier, F., & Gérard, S. (2007). Improving UML profile design practices by leveraging conceptual domain models. In *Proceedings of 22nd Int.l Conf. on Automated Software Engineering* (pp. 445-448). ACM.

Ledeczi, A., Nordstrom, G., Karsai, G., Volgyesi, P., & Maroti, M. (2001). On metamodel composition. In *Proceedings of the 2001 IEEE International Conference on Control Applications*. IEEE.

Marrone, S., Mazzocca, N., Nardone, R., Presta, R., Romano, S. P., & Vittorini, V. (2012). A SAN-based modeling approach to performance evaluation of an IMS-compliant conferencing framework. *T. Petri Nets and Other Models of Concurrency*, *6*, 308–333. doi:10.1007/978-3-642-35179-2_13.

Marrone, S., Papa, C., & Vittorini, V. (2010). Multiformalism and transformation inheritance for dependability analysis of critical systems. In *Proceedings of 8th Integrated Formal Methods, IFM'10* (pp. 215–228). Berlin: Springer-Verlag. doi:10.1007/978-3-642-16265-7_16.

Montecchi, L., Lollini, P., & Bondavalli, A. (2011). Towards a MDE transformation workflow for dependability analysis. In *Proceedings of ICECCS* (pp. 157-166). ICECCS.

Nicol, D. M., Sanders, W. H., & Trivedi, K. S. (2004). Model-based evaluation: From dependability to security. [IEEE.]. *IEEE Transactions on Dependable and Secure Computing*, *1*, 48–65. doi:10.1109/TDSC.2004.11.

OMG. (2002). *UML profile for MARTE: Modeling and analysis of real-time embedded systems, version 1.1, formal/11-06-02*. OMG.

OMG. (2011). *Unified modeling language: Infrastructure and superstructure, version 2.4, formal/11-08-05, May 2011*. OMG.

OMG. (2012). *Object constraint language, version 2.3, formal/12-01-01, January 2012*. OMG.

Pai, G. J., & Dugan, J. B. (2002). Automatic synthesis of dynamic fault trees from UML system models. In *Proceedings of the 13th International Symposium on Software Reliability Engineering* (pp. 243-254). Washington, DC: IEEE.

Reisig, W. (2009). Simple composition of nets. [LNCS]. *Proceedings of Applications and Theory of Petri Nets*, *5606*, 23–42. doi:10.1007/978-3-642-02424-5_4.

SATURN. (n.d.). SysML based modeling, architecture exploration, simulation and synthesis for complex embedded systems. Retrieved from http://www.saturn-fp7.eu/

Selic, B. (2007). A systematic approach to domain-specific language design using UML. In *Proceedings of 10th IEEE Int.l Symposium on Object and Component-Oriented Real-Time Distributed Computing (ISORC'07)*. IEEE.

Tadano, K., Xiang, J., Kawato, M., & Maeno, Y. (2011). Automatic synthesis of SRN models from system operation templates for availability analysis. In *Proceedings of the 30th International Conference on Computer Safety, Reliability, and Security, SAFECOMP'11* (pp. 296-309). Berlin: Springer-Verlag.

Taivalsaari, A. (1996). On the notion of inheritance. *ACM Computing Surveys*, *28*, 438–479. doi:10.1145/243439.243441.

Trivedi, K. S. (2002). SHARPE 2002: Symbolic hierarchical automated reliability and performance evaluator. In *Proceedings of the 2002 International Conference on Dependable Systems and Networks, DSN '02*. Washington, DC: IEEE Computer Society.

Vittorini, V., Iacono, M., Mazzocca, N., & Franceschinis, G. (2004). The OsMoSYS approach to multi-formalism modeling of systems. *Software & Systems Modeling*, *3*, 68–81. doi:10.1007/s10270-003-0039-5.

Wagelaar, D., Van Der Straeten, R., & Deridder, D. (2009). Module superimposition: A composition technique for rule-based model transformation languages. In *Software and Systems Modeling*. Berlin: Springer. doi:10.1007/s10270-009-0134-3.

ENDNOTES

[1] IMS stands for IP Multimedia Systems that are IP based networks at the base of multimedia applications such as VoIP

[2] An endogenous transformation is a transformation that has the same language as source and target languages.

Chapter 3
Towards a Multi–Formalism Multi–Solution Framework for Model–Driven Performance Engineering

Catalina M. Lladó
Universitat de les Illes Balears, Spain

Pere Bonet
Universitat de les Illes Balears, Spain

Connie U. Smith
Performance Engineering Services, USA

ABSTRACT

Model-Driven Performance Engineering (MDPE) uses performance model interchange formats among multiple formalisms and tools to automate performance analysis. Model-to-Model (M2M) transformations convert system specifications into performance specifications and performance specifications to multiple performance model formalisms. Since a single tool is not good for everything, tools for different formalisms provide multiple solutions for evaluation and comparison. This chapter demonstrates transformations from the Performance Model Interchange Format (PMIF) into multiple formalisms: Queueing Network models solved with Java Modeling Tools (JMT), QNAP, and SPE ED, and Petri Nets solved with PIPE2.

INTRODUCTION

Our approach to Model-Driven Performance Engineering (MDPE) is based on model interchange formats for creating and evaluating performance models. The goal is to transfer design specifications into a performance model that may be automatically solved by a variety of modeling tools. The overall approach begins with a formal specification of a system and/or software design and transforms it into a *Model (MIF)* as shown in the upper left of Figure 1. The *Model* may be created by translating design models into performance models (Balsamo & Marzolla, 2005) (Smith, Cortellessa, Di Marco, Lladó, & Williams, 2005), or created with one performance modeling tool

DOI: 10.4018/978-1-4666-4659-9.ch003

then converted into the MIF format. MIF formats have been defined for queueing network models (PMIF), software performance models (S-PMIF), layered queueing networks (LQN), UML, PNs and other types of models.

The upper right section of Figure 1 shows the Experiment Schema Extension (*Ex-SE*) that defines a set of model runs that vary parameters and the *output metrics* desired (Smith, Lladó & Puigjaner, 2011). It may be used to study how performance metrics change for different workload mixes, increasing service demands, etc. The *Model* and *Ex-SE* files together are used as input for one or more performance modeling tools; Qnap (Potier, D., & Veran, M., 1985), SPE-ED (www.spe-ed.com), JMT (Java Modeling Tools, jmt.sourceforge.net.), and PIPE2 (Bonet, P., Lladó, C.M., Puigjaner, R. & Knottenbelt, W.J., 2007) are illustrated but many such tools can be used.

Each tool generates the performance metric output as specified for each experiment and an Output Schema Extension (Output-SE) specifies

Figure 1. Model interoperatibility framework

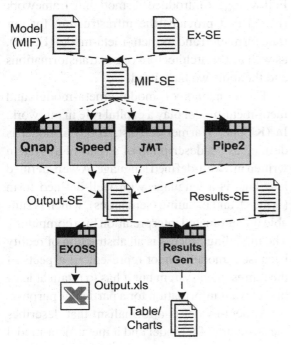

the XML format for these *output metrics*. The tool EXperiment Output to SpreadSheet (EXOSS) has been also developed *EXOSS* (Llodrà, J., Lladó, C.M., Puigjaner,R. & Smith.C.U., 2011), which takes the XML output from one or more experiments and produces a spreadsheet (xls) file for easily viewing the performance output. The last step transforms the output into desired results as specified by the Results-SE (Smith, Lladó & Puigjaner, 2011).

Note that Figure 1 illustrates abstract classes for the interchange formats that are instantiated into concrete realization(s). For example, the *Model* abstract class (or MIF) may be realized with the Performance Model Interchange Format (PMIF) (Smith & Williams, 1999) (Smith & Lladó, 2004). The performance model interchange format (PMIF) is a common representation for system performance model data that can be used to move models among modeling tools that use a Queueing Network Model (QNM) paradigm. A user of several tools that support the format can create a model in one tool, and later move the model to other tools for further work without the need to laboriously translate from one tool's model representation to the other. Without a MIF two tools would need to develop a custom import and export mechanism. A third tool would require a custom interface between each of those tools resulting in an order N^2 requirement for customized interfaces. With PMIF, tools export and import with the same format so the requirement for customized interfaces is reduced to $2 \cdot N$. The remainder of this paper assumes a familiarity with the MIF approach; see (Smith, Lladó & Puigjaner, 2010) for background information

The MIF could also be realized with the Software Performance Model Interchange Format (S-PMIF) (Smith, Cortellessa, Di Marco, Lladó, & Williams, 2005) for exchanging software performance model information. Similarly, the *Ex-SE* may have an instance for PMIF called PMIF-Ex (in other words, QN oriented), or for Petri Nets (PN) called PN-Ex (Smith, Lladó & Puigjaner, 2011).

This paper introduces the use of the model interoperability framework to support performance evaluation of systems using multiple formalisms and multiple solutions of the resulting models for comparison and evaluation. The framework can also be used for reliability, dependability, and other assessments; we focus on performance engineering for illustration. Model interchange fits well within the context of Model Driven Engineering (MDE), an approach to software development based on models and transformations between them (and Model Driven Performance Engineering - the extension for performance (Fritzsche & Johannes, 2008).The approach in Figure 1 relies on model transformations. Our earlier work (Smith & Lladó, 2004) (Smith, Lladó & Puigjaner, 2010) used custom translators to import/export models in the MIF formats into the input format of different tools. This paper uses Model-to-model (M2M) transformations to simplify the development and maintenance of tools that support the framework. As the individual meta-models evolve, it is only necessary to update the transformation specifications. M2M transformations are not aimed at refining an existing model. Instead, the transformations we focus on take place between a source and a target model that are at the same level of abstraction, but are represented in different notations, hence they comply with different meta-models.

Our M2M transformations have been implemented in Eclipse. Eclipse's IDE provides its own MDE platform: Eclipse Modeling Project (www.eclipse.org/modeling). One of its subprojects is the Eclipse Modeling Framework (EMF) (Steinberg, Budinsky, Paternostro & Merks, 2009). It is a modeling framework and code generation facility for building tools and other applications based on a structured data model. EMF features Ecore, a meta-meta-model based on the Essential MOF (Meta Object Facility) specification (Object Management Group, 2011), for describing meta-models. We use the Atlas Transformation Language (ATL, www.eclipse.org/atl/) for the M2M transformations.

We illustrate the multi-formalism and multi-solution approach with examples of QNM and Petri Nets. We use The Java Modeling Tools (JMT, jmt.sourceforge.net.) for modeling and analysis of queueing networks. It is a free, open source set of tools that provide different techniques for solving the models and for simulating the system behaviour (Bertoli, Casale & Serazzi, 2006). We use PIPE2 (Platform Independent Petri net Editor, pipe2.sourceforge.net) for analysis of Petri Net models. PIPE2 is an open source, platform-independent tool for creating and analyzing Generalized Stochastic Petri Nets (GSPNs) (Ajmone, M., Balbo, G., Conte, G., Donatelli, S., & Franceschinis, G., 1995).

This paper is organised as follows: we first describe background and related work. Following, the framework is described and presented in detail, and we finish with conclusions and future work.

BACKGROUND

Following, we introduce the modeling framework (EMF) that provides the infrastructure for our transformation and its meta-meta-model (Ecore), as well as the architecture of our transformations and the tools we have used.

The concepts of model, meta-model and meta-meta-model play a capital role in our work. In (Kleppe, Warmer & Bast, 2003) a model is defined as: "a description of a (part of a) system written in a well-defined language. A well-defined language is a language with well-defined form (syntax), and meaning (semantics), which is suitable for automated interpretation by a computer". The modeling process is an abstraction of reality because a model cannot represent all aspects of the represented system but it has to retain at least the relevant information for a particular purpose.

A meta-model is a formalism that describes the structure of a model and a meta-meta-model is a formalism that describes the structure of a meta-model. It also describes itself so it spares the need of a next level (meta-meta-meta-model).

Eclipse Modeling Framework

EMF (Eclipse Modeling Framework) is part of the Eclipse tools project. It is a modeling and meta-modeling framework and also a code generation framework. Other projects are built on EMF: Model to Model Transformation (M2M), Model to Text Transformation (M2T), etc. and a very diverse set of tools (as for example ATL and Acceleo (www.eclipse.org/acceleo/) have been developed around it. The common ground is provided by Ecore, the EMF's meta-meta-model. Ecore is a meta-language for defining models, which is based on and aligned with EMOF, the core of the MOF specification. Ecore is used to define models that are not specific to a technological platform (Platform Independent Models).

In Ecore, the model classes are represented by EClasses, the classes' properties are represented by EAttributes and the relations among classes, by EReferences. EAttributes have a name and a type, represented by an EDataType element.

Transformation Architecture

The general architecture of our transformations is shown in Figure 2. Both transformations are performed in two steps:

- A model to model transformation (M2M).
- A model to text transformation (M2T).

Given a source model (Ms) and a target model (Mt), we use the source model's meta-model (MMs) and the target model's meta-model (MMt) to build the M2M transformation. These meta-models must conform to a common meta-meta-model in order to be able to perform the transformation operations. In our case, this meta-meta-model is Ecore.

The source and the target models are stored in XMI (XML Metadata Interchange) files therefore our current target tools cannot work directly with the M2M transformation output. The second step, the M2T transformation, takes the M2M output and produces a text file that our tools can use.

The M2M transformation is performed using ATL, a transformation language that is described in the next subsection, whereas the M2T transformation is performed using Acceleo, which is a code generator based on templates that imple-

Figure 2. Transformation architecture

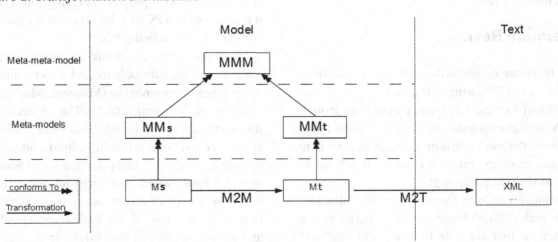

ment the OMG's Model-to-Text specification. Both ATL and Acceleo are fully integrated in the EMF framework

M2M Transformation Language: ATL

ATL (ATLAS Transformation Language) (ATL, www.eclipse.org/atl/) is a Domain Specific Language for specifying M2M transformations. It was developed as a response to the OMG's request for proposal for QVT, a specification for performing model transformations. ATL allows for the use of a mixture of declarative and imperative constructs though the declarative style is preferred.

An ATL transformation specification is composed of helpers and rules. Rules describe what target patterns are generated for each source pattern. Filters can be used to restrict the application of a rule to source elements that meet the requirements. Helpers define global variables and encapsulate functions. They can be called from rules and from other helpers.

ATL transformations are unidirectional. The source model is read-only (it can be navigated but it cannot be modified) whereas the target model is write-only (it cannot be navigated). ATL also provides a special operation called *resolveTemp* that can be used in an ATL rule. This operation points to any of the target model elements that will be generated from a given source model element by a matched rule.

Literature Review

The literature review is divided into two sections based on the following categories:

Model-to-model transformation: Even though M2M transformations are used in a wide range of areas, the most relevant to us are those where the source or the target formalism is related to performance engineering;

Multi-formalisms for performance evaluation: tools and methodologies used in performance evaluation that are able to work with multiple formalisms.

Model-to-Model Transformations

M2M transformations are a key component of Model Driven Engineering. The advantages of using a transformation language instead of Java-based transformations are discussed in (Cortellessa, Di Gregorio, Di Marc, 2008), where ATL is used in a transformation from UML models to Queueing Networks and it is also compared to the same transformation implemented in Java. Although it can initially be hard to use, a transformation language makes the transformation maintenance easier and provides traceability. Moreover, since the transformation language is formally defined, it is feasible to build formal proofs of correctness.

One of the first works that use M2M for performance evaluation is presented in (Petriu & Shen, 2002), that describes a model transformation from UML (Unified Modeling Language) augmented with the Schedulability, Performance, and Time (SPT) profile to Layered Queueing Networks. It performs the manipulation and transformation of the UML model at the meta-model level but it uses a different transformation language than ATL. Similarly, (Meier, Kounev & Koziolek, 2011) presents several transformations from software performance models (specified using the Palladio Component Model – (PCM)) to multiple formalisms. This transformation is implemented using ATL and a general purpose language (Java) and it is also part of a PCM solution method based on simulation of Queueing Petri Nets.

A methodology for combining formal model generation, multiformalism and compositional approaches is presented in (Marrone, Mazzocca, Nardone & Vittorini, 2012). The objective of this methodology is to integrate three different approaches (sub-models composition, combining formalisms and modeling paradigms, and generation of formal models from high-level specifications) by means of a three stage approach. The first stage consists of the high-level modeling and meta-modeling of the system; in the second stage, formal models are generated from the high-level one, and in the third stage single-formalism models are tied together creating a multiformal model of the system. M2M transformations are used to generate formal models from high-level specifications (1st stage), to translate between formal models (2nd stage) and to generate multifomal models (3rd stage).

A transformation from Æmilia architectural models to queueing network models is introduced in (Bernardo, Cortellessa & Flamminj, 2011). This transformation is part of a methodology that allows the analysis and comparison of software architectures based on their performance characteristics. It is a Java implemented tool integrated in Eclipse (www.eclipse.org), though the authors express their intention of rewriting the transformation using a model transformation language in the future.

Beyond single M2M transformations, Model-Driven Performance Engineering is defined as a process that combines MDE and performance engineering (Fritzsche & Johannes, 2008). MDPE can be applied if behaviour models of the system are available on abstraction levels where performance data can be defined based on experiences or measurements on existing systems. A case study that follows this approach can be found in (Fritzsche, Picht, Gilani, Spence, Brown & Kilpatrick, 2009). It features a chain of five M2M transformations implemented using ATL.

Multi-Formalisms for Performance Evaluation

A multi-formalism framework or methodology supports modeling and analysis of systems using different formal languages (or formalisms) simultaneously. The term multi-solution refers to the use of different tools to solve and analyze a model. Both concepts are related and usually happen together, though one of them does not imply the other. Recently, a lot of work has been done on multi-formalism performance modeling. There are several tools/frameworks that offer pow-

erful capabilities: Sharpe, Möbius, SIMTHESys (Structured Infrastructure for Multiformalism modeling and Testing of Heterogeneous formalisms and Extensions for SYStems), OsMoSys (Object-based multi-formaliSm MOdeling of SYStems) and Sirio, among others. All of them aim to provide a methodology and tool support for multi-formalism models, and consider model composition and multiple solution methods.

Next, a brief description of these tools/frameworks broadly illustrates their capabilities:

- SHARPE (Trivedi & Sahner, 2009), is one of the first tools that implemented the concept of multi-formalism. It supports a set of formalisms (e.g. Markov models, queuing models, stochastic Petri Nets, etc.) to describe models. Several models can compose a higher level model by exchanging its probability distributions.

- Möbius (Sanders, Courtney, Deavours, Daly, Derisavi & Lam, 2003) is a tool used mainly for performance and dependability modeling. It supports several formalisms: Stochastic Activity Networks, Performance Evaluation Process Algebra, Stochastic Petri Nets, and Queueing Petri Nets. Atomic models can be composed with other models (atomic or composed) by means of the Replicate/Join composition formalism. Once the complete model is built, the measures of interest can be specified using a reward formalism. Then the model can be solved with one of the solvers included in Möbius (as for example Direct steady-state solver, Iterative steady-state solver, Takahashi steady-state solver).

- SIMTHESys (Barbierato, Gribaudo & Iacono, 2011), is a framework for the definition of multiformalism composed models and the automatic generation of the corresponding solvers. SIMTHESys can integrate different models, formalisms and solvers within a framework through the use of Behavioural Facilities (BFs). These can be seen as a translation layer between formalisms and solvers. New solvers can be introduced adding a new implementation of those BFs.

- OsMoSys (Vittorini, Iacono, Mazzocca, & Franceschinis, 2004) supports the analysis of multi-formalism models through the composition of results obtained by different solvers. OsMosys is based on a three-layer structure: a language, called Meta-formalism that describes any graph-based formalism, Model MetaClasses, that are the formal languages specified by the meta-formalism, and Model Classes specifying the models that share a common structure. It allows building a model by composing several sub-models.

- Sirio (Carnevali, Ridi & Vicario, 2011) implements solution techniques for various extensions of Petri Nets: Time Petri Nets (TPNs), pre-emptive Time Petri Nets (pTPNs), stochastic Time Petri Nets (sTPNs) and stochastic pre-emptive Time Petri Nets (spTPNs). Its flexibility allows creating hybrid models by combining different types of Petri Nets. Sirio's solvers support evaluation of transient and steady state reward measures both via simulation and via analytical methods.

All these tools/frameworks follow approaches that exploit model composition. Differently, our approach uses M2M transformations following the model interoperability concept, which is based on using existing tools and not building new ones. M2M transformations are used to go from the PMIF to specific tool formats (for example, to JMT) and hence a model can be solved in the most convenient tool. Additionally, M2M transformations are used to go from one formalism to another (for example Queueing Networks to Petri Nets), so a model can also be solved using a different formalism when necessary.

M2M FRAMEWORK FOR MDPE

To start with the details of the M2M framework described in this paper, the PMIF and PMIF-Ex meta-models are described and presented as an Eclipse implementation. Following, the multi-solution related transformation is presented as well as the transformation from PMIF to Petri Nets to allow for multi-formalism, to end with the case studies showing viability of the approach.

PMIF and PMIF-EX Meta-Models

In this section, we introduce the PMIF and PMIF-Ex meta-models, the source models used for the transformations in this paper. The original PMIF and PMIF-Ex meta-models were implemented as an XML Schema in (Smith, Lladó & Puigjaner, 2010) and (Smith, Lladó, Puigjaner, 2011) respectively. However, as shown in the previous section, to implement the automated M2M transformations using the ATL transformation language, they need to be specified using Eclipse's EMF.

The PMIF meta-model specified in Eclipse is shown in Figure 3, which is based on the meta-model defined in (Smith, Lladó & Puigjaner, 2010) --a model of the information for constructing a Queueing Network Model (QNM). As shown in Figure 3, a *Queueing Network Model* is composed of one or more *Nodes*, zero or more *Arcs*, and one or more *Workloads*. An *Arc* connects one *Node* to another *Node*. Several types of *Nodes* may be used in constructing a *QueueingNetworkModel*:

Server: Represents a component of the execution environment that provides some processing service. A *Server* may be a *WorkUnitServer* that executes a fixed amount of work (processing service) for each *Workload* that makes a request for service.

Non-ServerNode represents nodes that show topology of the model, but do not provide service. There are two types of *Non-ServerNodes*: *SourceNode*: represents the origin of an *Open-*

Figure 3. PMIF meta-model

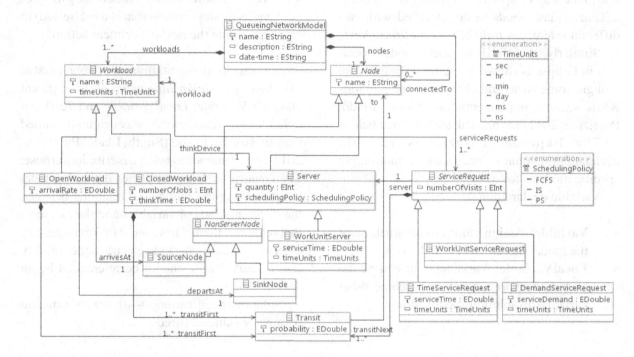

Workload and *SinkNode* represents the exit point of an *OpenWorkload*.

A *Server* provides service for one or more *Workloads*. A *Workload* represents a collection of transactions or jobs that make similar *ServiceRequests* from *Servers*. There are two types of *Workloads*:

OpenWorkload: Represents a workload with a potentially infinite population where transactions or jobs arrive from the outside world, receive service, and exit. The population of the *OpenWorkload* at any one time is variable.

ClosedWorkload: Represents a workload with a fixed population that circulates among the *Servers*. A closed workload has a *ThinkDevice* or independent delay node (for example, to model finite collections of users) characterized by its *ThinkTime* (average interval of time that elapses between the completion of a transaction or job and the submission of the next transaction or job).

Upon arrival, a *Workload Transits* to other *Nodes* with a specified probability. A service request associates the *Workloads* with *Servers*. A *ServiceRequest* specifies the average *ServiceTime*, *ServiceDemand* or *WorkUnitService* provided for each *Workload* that visits the *Server*. A *TimeServiceRequest* specifies the average service time and number of visits provided for each *Workload* that visits the *Server*. A *DemandServiceRequest* specifies the average service demand (service time multiplied by number of visits) provided for each *Workload* that visits the *Server*. A *WorkUnitServiceRequest* specifies the average number of visits requested by each *Workload* that visits a *WorkUnitServer*. Upon completion of the *ServiceRequest*, the *Workload Transits* to other *Nodes* with a specified probability.

The only differences in this Ecore meta-model and the earlier version (Smith, Lladó & Puigjaner, 2010) are implementation related. For example, due to the way Eclipses *Ereferences* are handled, a Transit class needs to be specified with two different references *transitFirst* and *transitNext*.

Similarly, the PMIF-Ex meta-model specified in Eclipse is shown in Figure 4. In this case though, some structural changes to the previous XML schema implementation (Smith, Lladó, Puigjaner, 2011) are needed, as described below.

The Experiment specifies variable declaration(s), solution specification(s) and output specifications as follows.

Variable declaration(s):

- **Variable:** Assign values to an attribute of the model, iterate over it and so on.
- **LocalVariable:** Variables that can be assigned to expressions that combine other variables in solution specifications.

- **TestVariable:** Metric produced by the previous model solution that is used (tested) to determine the next experiment action.

For this implementation, we have created the class *GenericVariable* as an abstract parent class for *Variable*, *LocalVariable* and *TestVariable* classes. *TestVariable* was originally called *OutputVariable* in and (Smith, Lladó, Puigjaner, 2011), now renamed to better describe its purpose. The *GenericVariable* simplifies the meta-model by decreasing the number of relations between the different kinds of variables and the elements that reference them. However, it makes necessary external semantic checks to ensure model validity (i.e. a *TestVariable* cannot be referenced by an *Assign* element).

Solution specification(s)—the model runs and parameter values desired:

Figure 4. PMIF-Ex meta-model

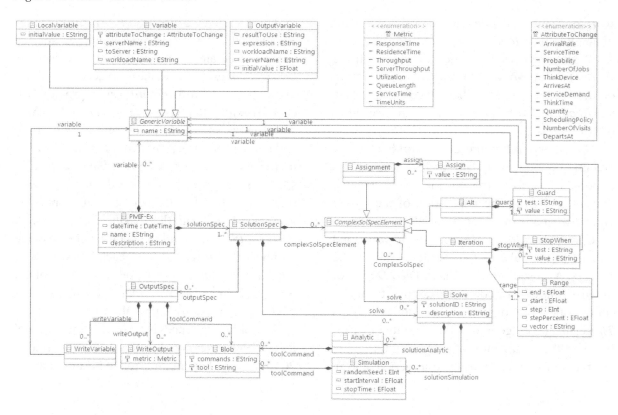

- **Assignment:** Assigns values to model attributes.
- **Iteration:** One or more range of values to be assigned, StopWhen conditions for termination and Solve specifications.
- **Alternation:** A test and action(s) to be taken when true.
- **Solve:** The type of solution desired and the point(s) in the experiment where it should be executed.

In order to maintain the flexibility of the PMIF-Ex schema, we have also introduced the *ComplexSolSpecElement* class. It is an abstract parent class of Alt, Iteration and Assignment that allows the nesting of these elements.

The order of the siblings in Ecore models cannot be easily specified. This was a problem because the xml schema specification of the experiments allowed an ordering of elements. For example, there can be several *Assigns* and a *Solve* followed by more *Assigns* and another *Solve*; a different order could completely change the results. To fix this problem we created the Assignment class which contains the group of *Assigns* for a *ComplexSolSpecElement* that must be done before the solution of the model.

Output specification(s)—the variables to be written, the metrics (e.g. throughput or utilization), and possibly tools specific output.

The experiment schema definition is included in the host schema, e.g. PMIF. The Ex-SE allows specification of:

- Changes in parameter values from one execution of a model to the next.
- Specification of control in performing model studies, including iteration and alternation.
- Variables that are local to the experiment to be used in computations and output.
- Model-results dependent execution.
- Use of previous output as input to subsequent runs.

- Specification of the output metrics to be returned.
- Solution-type specifications.

The expressive power of the PMIF-Ex metamodel is in general much larger than most available QNM tool experimenters provide. Our framework assumes that specific tools use only the specifications that they support. For example, a tool that does not have experimentation, or does not support the experiment specified, will just run the model once. In those cases, some sort of warning from the tool to the user is recommended.

Multi-Solution Transformation: PMIF-Ex to JMT

Our performance engineering framework allows for multi-solution and multi-formalism. This section describes one transformation example that allows for multi-solution. A model can be specified in PMIF and then solved by different QN based performance modeling tools. In our previous work we used an import and export mechanism among the different tool formats to and from the PMIF (Smith, Lladó & Puigjaner, 2010). This work migrates to M2M transformations to go from PMIF specifications to any specific QN tool's format. The main advantage is that the transformation is external to the tools, and is simpler than creating custom code that must be maintained.

The multi-solution transformation is demonstrated with JMT (Bertoli, Casale & Serazzi, 2006). JMT provides a command line wrapper so the model can be analyzed from outside the JMT GUI. We have developed an M2M transformation that uses a combination of two source models PMIF and PMIF-EX and has one target model, which is the one used by JMT's discrete-event simulation engine. We have also built a demonstration application (PMIF-Ex2JMT) that after generating the JMT model, evaluates it by invoking the JMT discrete-event simulation engine through the command line (a similar application could be done to invoke JMVA, the JMT Mean Value Analysis Solver).

Next, we describe JMT and its simulation meta-model to provide the reader with a better understanding of the M2M transformation section that follows.

JMT-Java Modeling Tools

The Java Modeling Tools (JMT) is an open source suite composed of a set of tools for performance evaluation, capacity planning, workload characterization, and modeling of computer and communication systems. Queueing Networks can be modelled through wizard dialogs or with a graphical modeler and can be solved analytically or by simulation. The simulations are performed by its JSIM simulation engine. It computes typical performance indexes: number of customers, queue time, residence time, response time, utilization and throughput among others.

JSIMgraph provides a graphical interface for the JSIM simulator and it is our transformation's tool target. JSIMgraph offers a simple experimenter called *what-if analysis* that performs a sequence of simulations for different values of some control parameters (number of customers, service times and arrival rates): given a *starting value* and an *ending value* for a certain control parameter, it runs as many simulations as specified by the *steps* parameter. These experiments are very limited compared to the ones that can be specified with PMIF-Ex, so only a small subset of PMIF-Ex experiments can be transformed for automated JMT *what-if analysis*. JSIMgraph meta-model

Using the Eclipse Modeling framework, we have automatically generated the JMT meta-model from the JMT simulator's (JMTSim) schema definition (provided by the authors). The JMTSim schema structures the model information in four parts: *Sim*, *Jmodel*, *Results* and *Solutions*. Only *Sim* and *Jmodel* are necessary to be filled in the transformation since *Results* and *Solutions* are the container elements for the results of the selected performance indices and are always filled when the model has been simulated or solved. A simplified version of this meta-model, which only includes the classes used in the transformation, is shown in Figure 5.

The *Sim* element contains five different types of children:

- **UserClass:** Defines an open or a closed customer class. It contains a *referenceSource* attribute that specifies which station is used to compute the system's throughput and response time of the class.
- **Node:** *Queueing* stations, *Delays*, *Sinks* and *Sources* are represented using the *Node* element. *Queueing* stations contain three elements: the queue, to specify the queueing capacity (finite or infinite) and its policy (FCFS, LCFS, FCFS with priority, LCFS with priority and Processor Sharing), the service (the service time distribution and the number of servers) and the routing (the path that customers follow after having received service). For *Delays*, there is no queueing element whereas the *Sources* only have the routing and *Sinks* are empty.
- **Measure:** Each *Measure* indicates a performance metric that will be computed in the simulation.
- **Connection:** Each *Connection* represents a directed arc from a source node to a target node.
- **Preload:** If there is a closed class, preload elements contain the information relative to the station's populations (how the total number of customers is distributed among the net nodes).

The *Jmodel* element specifies the model's graphical representation (currently not represented in PMIF) and the *what-if analysis* information with the elements:

Figure 5. JMTSim meta-model

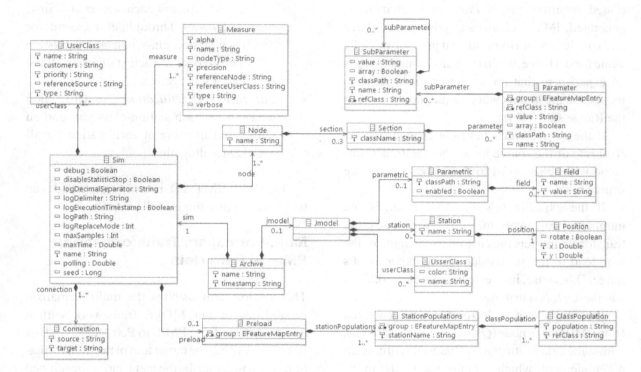

- **UserClass:** Assigns a color to a customer class;
- **Station:** Assigns a position to a net node;
- **Parametric:** Contains the information relative to an experiment if there is one.

M2M Transformation

The M2M transformation of the model itself is relatively straightforward, given that both source and target models represent Queueing Networks:

- For elements that are the same in both meta-models (*Source, Sink*) it just creates the JMT's counterpart.
- For each *Server* and *WorkUnitServer*, a JMT's *Delay* or *Queueing* station is created depending on the scheduling policy. If it is Infinite Servers (IS) is a *Delay* and a *Queue*ing station otherwise.

- For workloads (*OpenWorkload* or *ClosedWorkload*), a JMT workload is created (with type attribute open or closed correspondingly). Additionally, for each *ClosedWorkload*, a *StationPopulation* element that specifies the initial number of customers is also created.

On the other hand, due to the limitations of the JMT *what-if analysis,* the following requirements must be met in order for a PMIF-Ex experiment to be transformed into JMT's format:

- There can be one and only one *SolutionSpec*.
- There can be only one *Iteration* containing only a *Range* and a *Solve*.
- There cannot be any *Alt* or *Iteration* inside the *Iteration*.

Therefore, if the PMIF-EX fits the aforementioned requirements, a *Parametric* element is generated. JMT's *what-if* analysis does not have an explicit *start* attribute since it uses the model's value for it. Hence, when the transformation finds an experiment that meets the previous requirements, the attribute's value of the model is set to the Range start value.

If the experiment's *Iteration* changes the arrival rate of the source node, the iteration's start value will be assigned to the arrival rate of the source node.

If the experiment's *Iteration* changes the number of customers for closed workloads, the transformation sets the customers attribute of the workload to the start value of the experiment's range. Otherwise, it is set to the closed workloads *NumberOfJobs* attribute.

JMTSim's root node (*archive*) is generated from PMIF's root node (*QueueingNetworkModel*), with some default attributes. This node will contain a *Sim* element, which contains the model information, and a *jmodel* element with the graphical representation (automatically generated).

Finally, depending on the PMIF-Ex's *Write-Output* (WO) specifications, JMT *Measure* elements will be generated, as follows:

- For each WO ResponseTime:
  - A Response Time measure for each station-class and Sink-class pair and a Response Time measure for all classes altogether at each station and Sink.
  - System Response Time measure for each class and for all the classes altogether.
- For each WO *ResidenceTime* and each *Throughput*: a *Residence Time* and *Throughput* measure respectively for each class and for all the classes altogether.
- For each WO *Server Throughput*:
  - A Throughput measure for each station-class and Sink-class pair and a Throughput measure for all the classes altogether at each station and Sink.
  - A System Throughput measure for each station-class pair and a System Throughput at each station for all the classes altogether.
- For each WO *Utilization*: An Utilization measure for each station-class pair and an Utilization measure at each station for all the classes altogether.

The PMIF2JMT ATL transformation code can be viewed at dmi.uib.es/~cllado/mifs/.

Multi-Formalism Transformation: PMIF to Petri Nets

This section demonstrates the multi-formalism capabilities of our MDPE framework with a transformation from PMIF to Petri Nets. We first introduce PIPE2, the target tool of the transformation. Then we describe the meta-model developed for representing Petri Nets and the transformation itself.

PIPE2 (Platform Independent Petri Net Editor)

PIPE2 (Platform Independent Petri Net Editor 2, pipe2.sourceforge.net) is an open source, platform-independent tool for creating and analyzing Generalized Stochastic Petri Nets (GSPNs) - one type of Petri Net that allows for temporal specification using immediate and exponential delays. PIPE2 is implemented entirely in Java to secure platform independence and provides an elegant, easy-to-use graphical user interface that allows for the creation, saving, loading and analysis of GSPNs.

We implemented new PMIF import and transformation operations in PIPE2. Therefore, we can now open a PMIF model, as shown in Figure 8 and the tool automatically opens and shows the transformed PN model.

Petri Net Meta-Model

The target meta-model for the M2M transformation is a Petri Net meta-model (PetriNetMM) as shown in Figure 6, It represents the essential features of GSPNs without unnecessary details. The PetriNetMM is composed of the following entities:

- **Places:** With an initial marking and a capacity restriction.
- **ImmediateTransitions:** With a weight and a priority.
- **TimedTransitions:** With a firing rate.
- **Arcs:** With a weight. They may be *InhibitorArcs*.

In this meta-model there is no rule that prevents connecting two Places or two Transitions. This is not necessary in our case, since the models will be generated automatically by the transformation.

M2M Transformation

Given that the source and target models represent different formalisms, the transformation is non trivial. The key is that for each PMIF *Server* or *WorkUnitServer* a PN structure is created. This structure called *PNServer* is composed of an input place, a timed transition and an output place, as shown in Figure 7 - a . The input place acts as a queue whereas the output place stores the clients that have been served. The firing rate of the transition is the inverse of the service time of the *Server* or *WorkUnitServer*.

PMIF supports three queueing disciplines Processor Sharing (PS), First Come First Served (FCFC) and Infinite Server (IS). However, its implementation in a Petri net is not straightforward (Balsamo & Marin, 2008), hence the current transformation only considers a Service in Random Order (SIRO) policy. PS, FCFS and IS are considered for future work.

The rest of the transformation is:

- For each *SourceNode* a structure composed of a timed transition and an output place (PNSource shown in Figure 7 - b) is generated. The transition rate is the arrival rate of the customer class that arrives at the network through the source node.
- For each *SinkNode*, a structure composed of an input place and an immediate transition (PNSink show in Figure 7 - c) is

Figure 6. Petri Net meta-model

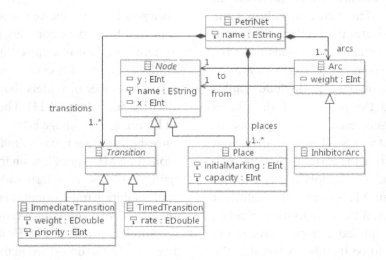

Figure 7. PNServer, PNSource and PNSink

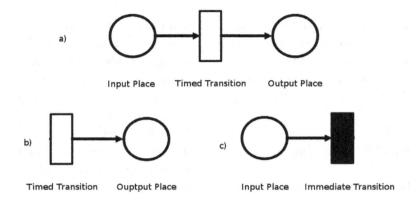

generated. This structure consumes the tokens that represent customers leaving the network.

- For each *Transit*, an immediate transition is generated. This transition will connect output places and input places of the structures generated in the target model. Its weight is equal to the Transit's probability attribute.

As for the *ClosedWorkloads*, its *ThinkDevice* will also be modelled by a *PNSever*, whose transition firing rate is the inverse of the *ClosedWorkload thinkTime*. The *PNServer* input place contains as many tokens as specified by the *ClosedWorkload numberOfJobs* attribute.

Since GSPN tokens are indistinguishable, in order to model the different customer classes, the transformation replicates the *PNServer* structure as many times as different workloads can visit this original PMIF *Server* or *WorkUnitServer*.

PMIF specification does not include graphical information so the position of the places and transitions is generated by adding constant offsets for the x and y axis. Therefore, the layout of the resulting Petri net is certainly not optimal. It would be convenient to apply a graph layout algorithm, but given ATL's declarative nature, it is hard to include it in the transformation rules. It would be better applied as a post processing algorithm, that could be then be included in the tools transformation.

Once the ATL transformation is done and we have a PN model, a model to text transformation is applied using Acceleo (www.eclipse.org/acceleo/) to convert it into PIPE2's input format, which is a pseudo PNML (Petri Net Markup Language, www.pnml.org). This way, we allow for different PN evaluation tools to use the first ATL transformation to a PN model. Only the model to text transformation would need to be written specifically for each tool that does not provide an xmi import feature.

The PMIF2PNML ATL transformation code can be viewed at dmi.uib.es/~cllado/mifs/.

Case Studies

As a proof of concept we use a simple case study followed by a more complex study of an actual system. The first is a closed manufacturing network composed of six single-server stations with a fixed number of pallets that circulate through the network (Blanc, 2011). The network is shown in Figure 8. This image is the one shown by JMT once the model has been automatically transformed from the PMIF specification to the JMT's format using the M2M transformation described in the multi-solution transformation section (this is also the reason that some lines cross each other).

Similarly, the same PMIF model is transformed to a Petri Net as described in the multi-formalism transformation section. Figure 9 shows the result-

Figure 8. Closed manufacturing network

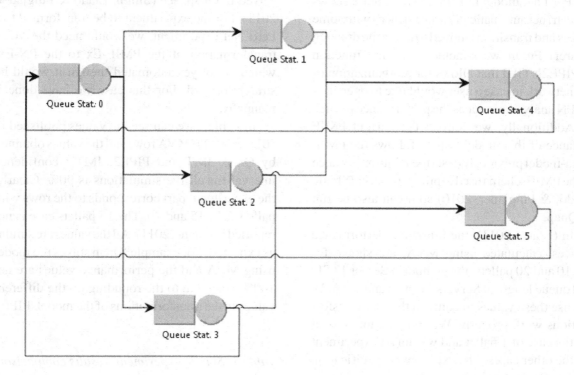

Figure 9. Closed manufacturing network as a Petri Net

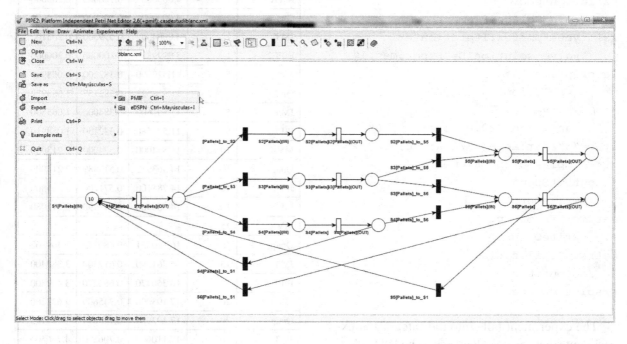

ing Petri net model in PIPE2. This Figure shows the Petri net automatically transformed (with some places and transitions moved to make the drawing clearer). Future work includes adding a function to PIPE2's GUI that allows for reorganization of the network in case a user would like to open it. A GSPN analysis produces the performance results.

Additionally, we convert the current PMIF instance of this model (which follows the PMIF meta-model previously described) into an instance of the PMIF schema used in previous works (Smith, Lladó, & Puigjaner, 2010) so it can also be run in Qnap.

In (Blanc, 2011), the following performance indices, calculated using MVA, are shown for 1,5,10 and 20 pallets: throughput at Server 1 (T1) and queue length at Servers 1 (QL1) and 2 (QL2). We use these values to confirm that our transformations work properly. We run a simple model for the case of 1 pallet and we run an experiment for the other cases. The experiment specification (PMIF-EX instance) is as follows:

```
<solutionSpec>
  <complexSolSpecElement
xsi:type="pmifex:Iteration">
    <solve solutionID="Experiment1"
description="">
      <solutionAnalytic/>
    </solve>
    <range end="20.0" start="5.0"
step="5" variable="//@variable.0"/>
  </complexSolSpecElement>
  <outputSpec>
    <writeOutput
metric="Throughput"/>
    <writeOutput
metric="Utilization"/>
  </outputSpec>
</solutionSpec>
```

The experiment falls into the category of experiments that can be solved using the JMT *what-if* analysis and it can also be transformed to and

solved in Qnap, see (Smith, Lladó & Puigjaner, 2011). For the experiment to be transformed to a Petri Net experiment, we would need the M2M transformation of the PMIF-Ex to the PN-Ex, which is not yet automated though it would be straightforward. For this case we have done it manually.

In Table 1 we can see the values published in (Blanc, 2011) (MVA row) and the values obtained by Qnap, JMT and PIPE2. JMT's confidence interval for all the simulations is 90%. Clearly, the experiment part corresponds to the rows with pallets 5,10,15 and 20. The 15 pallets case is not reported in (Blanc, 2011). All the values are similar as expected. For example, Qnap solves the model using MVA and the performance values are not 100% exact due to the rounding on the different values in the transformations of the model. PIPE2

Table 1. Simple experiment, results comparison

	Pallets	T1	QL1	QL2
MVA	1	4.000000	0.100000	0.200000
Qnap	1	4.000000	0.100000	0.200000
JMT	1	4.000400	0.099800	0.203100
PIPE2	1	3.999980	0.100000	0.200000
MVA	5	11.529000	0.382200	1.058900
Qnap	5	11.528627	0.382157	1.058922
JMT	5	11.501600	0.384000	1.065500
PIPE2	5	11.528580	0.382150	1.058910
MVA	10	14.864000	0.574000	2.213000
Qnap	10	14.863972	0.573989	2.213005
JMT	10	14.788100	0.571200	2.205800
PIPE2	10	14.863900	0.573990	2.212980
MVA	15	-	-	-
Qnap	15	16.360551	0.680275	3.409862
JMT	15	16.261300	0.677300	3.382400
PIPE2	15	16.360470	0.680270	3.409800
MVA	20	17.193000	0.745600	4.627200
Qnap	20	17.192983	0.745614	4.627193
JMT	20	17.110600	0.706500	4.766500
PIPE2	20	17.192900	0.745610	4.627090

gives similar values as well since the models are equivalent (except for the queueing discipline which is irrelevant in this case), with a maximum relative error of 0.013%. JMT values are a little bit different since the model is simulated instead of solved analytically. Even so, the maximum relative error is a 5.244% (QL1 for 20 clients).

To further illustrate the power of the framework we present a second case study, called RealStudy, that was presented in (Smith, Lladó, Puigjaner & Williams, 2007), where the xml import/export mechanism was used. This case uses an actual complex, large-scale model and compares the results of the original study, performed using SPE·ED (L&S Computer Technology Inc. Performance Engineering Services Division, www. spe-ed.com.) with those of a Qnap execution of a PMIF-Ex specification of the same study. For this paper we have done the transformation to JMT and added the performance metrics obtained when JMT is used as the tool solver.

The study has 4 workloads: Forms, Apply, Store, and Convert. Forms and Apply are user interaction scenarios for submitting some complex information to a Web Server. Upon submission, Store processes the data and archives it in a database. Convert transforms some of the data for storage in an image database. This is a challenging model for solvers because it includes coordination among workloads, large think times (e.g., up to 1 hour), small service demands (e.g., 0.000134 sec.), and long and different execution times (e.g., 20 sec. to 7 min.).

The results shown here are a portion of the model runs to determine the scalability of the application. These runs show the baseline platform with 1 CPU and 1 Disk. In the original study these experiments were repeated to study vertical scalability by increasing the number of CPUs and Disks of the Web Server platform. They were then repeated to increase the number of Web Servers to quantify horizontal scalability. This case study reports a small subset of those extensive experiments.

Table 2 shows the results originally produced with SPE·ED, and those produced by the PMIF-Ex translation using Qnap to solve the models as well as those produced by JMT. JMT cannot solve this case as an experiment since it cannot be written as a what-if analysis (this is due to the limitations of the tool itself and not of our approach), so the different instances of the model have to be run separately. Qnap and JMVA (JMT solver that uses MVA) performance results are exactly the same so they are shown in one column in Table 2 (named Q-JMT). The SPE·ED model is an advanced system execution model that explicitly represents coordination among the workloads. It uses a simulation solution. SPE·ED is oriented to design-time analysis before precise performance specifications are available. Therefore, the simulation stopping conditions default to a 90 percent probability that the simulation response result is within 30 percent of the mean. Because the model parameters are imprecise, we opt for shorter solutions that yield approximate results since they are usually sufficient to identify architecture and design performance problems. As shown in the table, the results are not exact but reasonably close. The Qnap and JMT models use an approximate think time for coordination, and solves the model analytically. We have also simulated the models with Qnap and JMT though, confidence intervals obtained are never good enough due to the nature of the study.

Most results are comparable; however, the Store workload shows some significant differences in CPU utilization and response time that would require further investigation. The difference is not due to the model transformation; the model parameters are equivalent (other than the think time). Unfortunately, it is not possible to compare to the original measured results because limited data was available. The case study models were created at design time by measuring, modeling, and validating against a prototype.

Table 2. Validation results for RealStudy

Experiment	Users	Response Time		Throughput		CPU Utilization	
		SPE·ED	Q-JMT	SPE·ED	Q-JMT	SPE·ED	Q-JMT
Run1-1							
Forms	18	451	446	0.005	0.005	0.39	0.44
Apply	32	194	177	0.014	0.016	0.15	0.16
Store	50	66	21	0.019	0.017	0.04	0.04
Convert	30	20	21	0.012	0.010	0.06	0.06
Total						0.64	0.70
Run1-2							
Forms	27	1125	1034	0.006	0.006	0.48	0.58
Apply	48	226	243	0.021	0.023	0.21	0.23
Store	75	236	40	0.027	0.026	0.05	0.06
Convert	45	69	61	0.017	0.015	0.09	0.09
Total						0.83	0.96
Run1-3							
Forms	36	2995	3003	0.005	0.006	0.42	0.53
Apply	64	300	457	0.025	0.028	0.24	0.28
Store	100	584	92	0.031	0.034	0.05	0.08
Convert	60	213	184	0.020	0.020	0.11	0.11
Total						0.82	1.00

CONCLUSION AND FUTURE WORK

This paper introduces the use of the model interoperability framework to support performance evaluation of systems using multiple formalisms and multiple solutions of the resulting models for comparison and evaluation. Model interchange fits well within the context of Model Driven Engineering and its extension for performance, MDPE. We have illustrated the multi-solution approach with examples of QNM interchange, with an M2M transformation from PMIF to JMT. We have also illustrated the multi-formalism approach with an example of a transformation that goes from QNM to Petri Nets and uses PIPE2 for analysis of Petri Net models. Our transformation converts both the model and the experiment that defines a set of model runs that vary parameters and the output metrics desired. Future work includes specific issues mentioned in this paper such as adding different queueing disciplines to the M2M transformation from QN to Petri Nets. We are also working on adding more tools and formalisms to the framework as well as the specification of higher level models that can combine different formalisms as different submodels.

ACKNOWLEDGMENT

This work is partially funded by the TIN2010-16345 EIGER project of the Ministerio de Educacion y Ciencia, Spain. Smith's participation was sponsored by US Air Force Contract FA8750-11-C-0059. Approved for public release 88ABW-2012-4628.

REFERENCES

Ajmone, M., Balbo, G., Conte, G., Donatelli, S., & Franceschinis, G. (1995). *Modeling with generalized stochastic petri nets*. Hoboken, NJ: Wiley.

Balsamo, S., & Marin, A. (2008). From BCMP queueing networks to generalized stochastic petri nets: An algorithm and an equivalence definition. In *Proceedings of the European Simulation and Modeling Conference*, (pp. 447–455). Academic Press.

Balsamo, S., & Marzolla, M. (2005). Performance evaluation of UML software architectures with multiclass queueing network models. In *Proceedings of the Fifth International Workshop of Software and Performance*, (pp. 37-42). Academic Press.

Barbierato, E., Gribaudo, M., & Iacono, M. (2011). Exploiting multiformalism models for testing and performance evaluation in SIMTHESys. In *Proceedings of the Fifth International Conference on Performance Evaluation Methodologies and Tools* (Valuetools), (pp. 121-130). Valuetools.

Bernardo, M., Cortellessa, V., & Flamminj, M. (2011). TwoEagles: A model transformation tool from architectural descriptions to queueing networks. In *Proceedings of Computer Performance Engineering, European Performance Engineering Workshop* (EPEW), (pp. 265-279). EPEW.

Bertoli, M., Casale, G., & Serazzi, G. (2006). Java modeling tools: An open source suite for queueing network modeling and workload analysis. In *Proceedings of Quantitative Evaluation of Systems*. QEST.

Blanc, J. P. C. (2011). *Queueing models - Analytical and numerical methods*. Retrieved from http://lyrawww.uvt.nl/~blanc/qm-blanc.pdf

Bonet, P., Lladó, C. M., Puigjaner, R., & Knottenbelt, W. J. (2007). PIPE v2.5: A petri net tool for performance modelling. In *Proceedings of 23rd Latin American Conference on Informatics* (CLEI 2007). CLEI.

Carnevali, L., Ridi, L., & Vicario, E. (2011). Sirio: A framework for simulation and symbolic state space analysis of non-markovian models. In *Proceedings of the 30th International Conference on Computer Safety, Reliability, and Security*, (pp. 409-422). Springer-Verlag.

Cortellessa, V., Di Gregorio, S., & Di Marc, A. (2008). Using ATL for transformations in software performance engineering: A step ahead of java-based transformations? In *Proceedings. of the 7th Int. Workshop on Software and Performance*, (pp. 127–132). ACM.

Fritzsche, M., & Johannes, J. (2008). Putting performance engineering into model-driven engineering: Model-driven performance engineering. In H. Giese (Ed.), *Reports and Revised Selected Papers* (pp. 164–175). New York: Springer. doi:10.1007/978-3-540-69073-3_18.

Fritzsche, M., Picht, M., Gilani, W., Spence, I., Brown, J., & Kilpatrick, P. (2009). Extending BPM environments of your choice with performance related decision support. In *Proceedings of the 7th Int. Conference on Business Process Management* (BPM '09), (pp. 97-112). Berlin: Springer-Verlag.

Kleppe, A., Warmer, S., & Bast, W. (2003). *MDA explained: The model driven architecture: Practice and promise*. Boston, MA: Addison-Wesley Longman Publishing Co.

Llodrà, J., Lladó, C. M., Puigjaner, R., & Smith, C. U. (2011). FORGE: Friendly output to results generator engine. In *Proceedings of the Second Joint WOSP/SIPEW International Conference on Performance Engineering* (ICPE '11). ACM.

Marrone, S., Mazzocca, N., Nardone, R., & Vittorini, V. (2012). *Combining heterogeneity, compositionality and automatic generation in formal modeling*. Paper presented at the International Workshop on Research and Use of Multiformalism Modeling Methods. London, UK.

Meier, S., Kounev, P., & Koziolek, H. (2011). Automated transformation of component-based software architecture models to queueing petri nets. In *Proceedings of 19th IEEE/ACM International Symposium on Modeling, Analysis and Simulation of Computer and Telecommunication Systems* (MASCOTS). IEEE/ACM.

Object Management Group. (2011). *MOF core specification*. Retrieved from http://www.omg.org/technology/documents/modeling_spec_catalog.htm#MOF

Petriu, D., & Shen, H. (2002). Applying the UML performance profile: Graph grammar-based derivation of LQN models from UML specifications. In *Proceedings of the 12th International Conference on Computer Performance Evaluation, Modeling Techniques and Tools,* (pp. 183-204). Academic Press.

Potier, D., & Veran, M. (1985). QNAP2: A portable environment for queueing systems modelling. In *Proceedings of the First International Conference on Modeling Techniques and Tools for Performance Analysis*, (pp. 25-63). IEEE.

Sanders, W. H., Courtney, T., Deavours, D., Daly, D., Derisavi, S., & Lam, V. (2003). Multiformalism and multisolution-method modeling frameworks: The Möbius approach. In *Proceedings of the Symposium on Performance Evaluation - Stories and Perspectives*, (pp. 241--256). IEEE.

Smith, C. U., Cortellessa, V., Di Marco, A., Lladó, C. M., & Williams, L. G. (2005). From UML models to software performance results: An SPE process based on XML interchange formats. In *Proceedings of the Fifth International Workshop of Software and Performance* (pp. 87–98). Palma de Mallorca, Spain: ACM.

Smith, C. U., & Lladó, C. M. (2004). Performance model interchange format (PMIF 2.0), XML definition and implementation. In *Proceedings of the First International Conference on the Quantitative Evaluation of Systems* (pp. 38-47). IEEE Computer Society Press.

Smith, C. U., Lladó, C. M., & Puigjaner, R. (2010). Performance model interchange format (PMIF 2): A comprehensive approach to queueing network model interoperability. *Performance Evaluation*, *67*(7), 548–568. doi:10.1016/j.peva.2010.01.006.

Smith, C. U., Lladó, C. M., & Puigjaner, R. (2011). Model interchange format specifications for experiments, output, and results. *The Computer Journal*, *54*(5), 674–690. doi:10.1093/comjnl/bxq065.

Smith, C. U., Lladó, C. M., Puigjaner, R., & Williams, L. G. (2007). Interchange formats for performance models: Experimentation and output. In *Proceedings of the Fourth International Conference on the Quantitative Evaluation of Systems* (pp. 91-100). IEEE Computer Society Press.

Smith, C. U., & Williams, L. G. (1999). A performance model interchange format. *Journal of Systems and Software*, *49*(1), 63–80. doi:10.1016/S0164-1212(99)00067-9.

Steinberg, D., Budinsky, F., Paternostro, M., & Merks, E. (2009). *EMF: Eclipse modeling framework 2.0* (2nd ed.). Reading, MA: Addison-Wesley Professional.

Trivedi, K. S., & Sahner, R. (2009). SHARPE at the age of twenty two. *ACM SIGMETRICS Performance Evaluation Review*, *36*(4), 52–57. doi:10.1145/1530873.1530884.

Vittorini, V., Iacono, M., Mazzocca, N., & Franceschinis, G. (2004). The OsMoSys approach to multi-formalism modeling of systems. *Software & Systems Modeling*, *3*, 68–81. doi:10.1007/s10270-003-0039-5.

ADDITIONAL READING

Brambilla, M., Cabot, J., & Wimmer, M. (2012). *Model-Driven Software Engineering in Practice*. Morgan & Claypool.

Frankel, D. S. (2003). *Model Driven Architecture: Applying MDA to Enterprise Computing*. John Wiley & Sons.

Jouault, F., & Kurtev, I. (2006). On the Architectural Alignment of ATL and QVT. In *Proceedings of ACM Symposium on Applied Computing (SAC 06), Model Transformation Track*. Dijon (Bourgogne, FRA).

Lazowska, V., Zahorjan, J. J., Graham, G., & Sevcik, K. (1984). *Quantitative System Performance: Computer System Analysis Using Queuing Network Models*. Prentice-Hall.

Melià, M., Lladó, C., Smith, C., & Puigjaner, R. (2008). An experimental framework for PIPEv2.5. In *5th International Conference on Quantitative Evaluation of Systems*. IEEE Computer Society Press.

Melià, M., Lladó, C., Smith, C., & Puigjaner, R. (2008). Experimentation and output interchange for Petri net models. In *Proceedings of the Seventh International Workshop on Software and Performance (WOSP)*, 133–138. ACM

Menascé, D. A., Almeida, V. A. F., & Dowdy, L. W. (2004). *Performance by Design: Computer Capacity Planning by Example*. Prentice Hall.

Peterson, J. L. (1981). *Petri Net Theory and the Modeling of Systems*. Prentice Hall.

Schmidt, D. (2006). Guest editor's introduction: Model-driven engineering. *IEEE Computer, 39*(2), 25–31. doi:10.1109/MC.2006.58.

Smith, C. U., & Williams, L. G. (2002). *Performance Solutions: A Practical Guide to Creating Responsive, Scalable Software*. Addison-Wesley.

KEY TERMS AND DEFINITIONS

Model Driven Engineering (MDE): A software development methodology that focuses on creating and exploiting domain models (abstract representations of the knowledge and activities in a particular application domain), rather than on the computing (or algorithmic) concepts.

Model Driven Performance Engineering (MDPE): Methodology that extends the Model Driven Engineering with Performance Engineering. It helps to analyze performance models, to detect performance issues and to get performance feedback into the model driven process.

Meta-Modeling: Construction of a collection of "concepts" (things, terms, etc.) within a certain domain. A model is an abstraction of phenomena in the real world; a meta-model is yet another abstraction, highlighting properties of the model itself.

Multi-Formalism: Tools and methodologies used in performance evaluation that are able to work with multiple formalisms.

Multi-Solution: Integration of several analysis tools to obtain relevant performance indexes for a model.

Petri Nets: A Petri Net is a mathematical modeling language for the description of distributed systems. It is a directed bipartite graph composed by transitions (events) and places (conditions); directed arcs (arrows) describe the pre-conditions and post-conditions for the occurring of the transitions.

Performance Engineering: Systematic, quantitative approach to the cost-effective development of systems to meet performance requirements.

Performance Modeling: A structured and repeatable approach to modeling the performance of a system.

Queueing Networks: Formalism used in performance modeling. A Queueing Network is a network composed of nodes that are servers with queues. It is represented as a directed graph where the clients/jobs receive service at a node and then transit to another node.

Chapter 4
Multi–Modeling, Meta– Modeling, and Workflow Languages

Alexander H. Levis
George Mason University, USA

Ahmed Abu Jbara
George Mason University, USA

ABSTRACT

Models, created using different modeling formalisms or techniques, usually serve different purposes and provide unique insights. While each modeling technique might be capable of answering specific questions, complex problems require multiple models interoperating to complement/supplement each other. This Multi-Modeling approach for solving complex problems is full of syntactic and semantic challenges. In this chapter, a systematic methodology for addressing Multi-Modeling problems is presented. The approach is domain specific: domain identification and domain analysis are the first steps in which the multi-modeling concepts and modeling techniques associated with a domain of interest are identified and analyzed. Then a new Domain Specific Multi-Modeling Workflow Language supported with a domain ontology is used to construct the workflow that defines the interoperation of the selected models. The domain ontology provides semantic guidance to affect valid model interoperation. This general approach is illustrated using a case study from the Drug Interdiction and Intelligence application domain. Analysis of diverse intelligence and sensor data using various modeling techniques is essential in identifying the best courses of action. For this example, the created workflow focuses on the interoperation of Social Networks, Timed Influence Nets, and Geospatial Models.

INTRODUCTION

The modeling of systems that include humans for the analysis of their behavior in response to external stimuli is an example of a complex problem that requires development and interoperation of a set of several models. Each model, developed using a different modeling language or formalism, but having access to a common shared data repository, offers unique insights and makes specific assumptions about the system being modeled. Interoperation of such models can produce a

DOI: 10.4018/978-1-4666-4659-9.ch004

more robust modeling and simulation capability to support behavior and performance analysis and evaluation.

In order to address the modeling and simulation issues that arise when multiple models are to interoperate, four layers need to be addressed (Figure 1). The Physical one, in which Hardware and Software reside, is a platform that enables the concurrent execution of multiple models expressed in different modeling languages or formalisms and provides the ability to exchange data and also to schedule the events across the different models. The Syntactic layer ascertains that the right data are exchanged among the models. The Physical and Syntactic layers have been addressed by the development of several testbeds that enable model interoperation. Two such examples are the SORASCS test bed (Garlan et al., 2009) and the C2 Wind Tunnel platform (Hemingway et al., 2011). Once this is achieved, a third problem needs to be addressed at the Semantic layer, where the interoperation of different modeling formalisms is examined to ensure that conflicting assumption in different modeling languages are recognized and form constraints to the inter-operation and the exchange of data. Finally, in the Workflow layer, valid combinations of interoperating models are linked to address specific issues. The focus of this chapter is the description of a systematic methodology for creating and implementing Multi-Modeling Workflows that are both syntactically and semantically correct, i.e., the focus is on the Semantic and Workflow layers.

The methodology is illustrated in an application from the Drug Interdiction and Intelligence application domain. The Joint Interagency Task Force - South (JIATF-South), an agency well known for interagency cooperation and intelligence fusion (Munsign and Lamb, 2011), receives large amounts of data from diverse sources regarding drug smuggling efforts. Analysis of such data using various modeling techniques is essential in identifying best Courses of Action. The methodology is applied to the solution of a class of problems in this domain by creating workflows of model interoperations involving Social Networks, Timed Influence Nets, and Geospatial models.

In the background section, a discussion of the basic concepts and approaches is presented. In the following section the key steps in the methodology are described. The domain specific illustrative application is described in the fourth section. Conclusions and discussion of future work are in the final section.

BACKGROUND

The idea of using a variety of modeling formalisms to solve a complex modeling and analysis problem is not a new one: an earlier survey and a collection of papers on the use of multiple *strategies* for machine learning problems can be found in (Michalski and Tecuci, 1994). Some examples of more recent work employing multi-modeling are: the integration of First-order Logic with Bayesian probability theory in the form of an approach called MEBN (Carvalho et al., 2008), Interoperable Technosocial Modeling (ITM) which focuses on the integration and evaluation of human and physical models across diverging modeling platforms, e.g., Bayesian Nets and System Dynamics (Whitney and Walsh, 2010), and

Figure 1. The four layers of multi-modeling

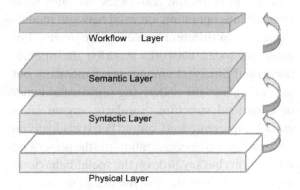

the interoperation between organizational decision models and socio-cultural trait models in Kansal et al. (2007). Other examples of multi-modeling include AToM³, a tool for multi-modeling that allows both meta-modeling and model-transformation (de Lara and Vangheluwe, 2002). In AToM³, formalisms are described as graphs. From a meta-specification of a formalism, AToM³ generates a tool to visually manipulate models described in the specified formalism. Model transformations are performed by graph rewriting. The transformations themselves can thus be declaratively expressed as graph-grammar models. The Object-based multi-formaliSm MOdeling of SYStems (OsMoSys) is a framework that provides capabilities of multi-formalism modeling of systems. Its approach is based on meta-modeling, allowing to easily define and integrate different formalisms, and on some concepts from object orientation (Vittorini et al., 2004). Its main objectives are the interoperability of different formalisms and the definition of mechanisms to guarantee the flexibility and the scalability of the modeling framework. Structured Infrastructure for Multiformalism modeling and Testing of Heterogeneous formalisms and Extensions for SYStems or SIMTHESys (Iacono et al., 2012) is an approach to multi-formalism compositional modeling, that is based on the possibility of freely specifying the dynamics of the elements of a formal modeling language in an open framework. Möbius is a software tool for modeling the behavior of complex systems and supports multiple modeling languages based on either textual or graphical representations. (Clark et al., 2002)

Model interactions can take a wide variety of forms (Levis et al., 2012). In research performed so far we have identified five types of meta-modeling operations for performing multi-modeling. All these model interactions require semantic interoperability:

- **Concatenation:** Models share representations and can get instances from each other.

- **Amplification:** Model adds or augments class representation from another.
- **Parameter Discovery:** One model provides parameters to another model's method.
- **Model Construction:** One model is used to construct models of another type.
- **Model Merging:** Meta-model for a new model type created by merging structure from one model with methods from another.

To understand modeling language semantics so that multiple models can be used together, i.e., can interoperate, Concept Maps (Novak and Cañas, 2006) are used to describe the characteristics of the set of modeling languages and data that are available to support analysis. It is assumed that two models can interoperate (partially) if some concepts appear in both modeling languages. By refining this approach to partition the concepts into modeling language input and output concepts and also defining the concepts that are relevant to the questions being asked, it becomes possible to determine which sets of models can interoperate to address some or all of the concepts of interest, and which sets of models use different input and output concepts that are relevant to those questions. This meta-modeling approach extends earlier work by (Kappel et al., 2006) and (Saeki and Kaiya, 2006) for a class of modeling languages primarily used for behavioral modeling problems.

Therefore, meta-modeling analysis based on concept maps and ontologies indicates what types of interoperation are valid between models expressed in different modeling languages. For example, social networks describe the interactions (and linkages) among group members but say little about the underlying organization and/or command structure. Similarly, organization models represented as Colored Petri nets focus on the structure of the organization and the prescribed interactions but say little on the social/behavioral aspects of the members of the organization.

MODELING, MULTI-MODELING, AND META-MODELING

Modeling is the process of producing a model; a model is a representation of the construction and working of some situation of interest (Maria, 1997). Figure 2 represents the modeling hierarchy where a Model is obtained using a Modeling Tool that applies a Modeling Language to represent a specific situation. The model itself should always conform to the Modeling Language used to create it. We call this combination of model, a modeling language and a modeling tool a Modeling Technique.

Multiple models are used because each modeling technique provides certain capabilities and makes specific assumptions about the domain being modeled. In this context, a Multi-Modeling process addresses a complex problem through the use of a number of interconnected domain-specific models where each model contributes insights to the overall problem. The interoperation between the interconnected models could serve different purposes and can happen in various forms.

In achieving Multi-Modeling, and to provide powerful supporting platforms, many challenges have to be faced. Beside the technical issues that usually arise in allowing interoperations between models through their modeling tools, there is also a

Figure 2. Modeling hierarchy

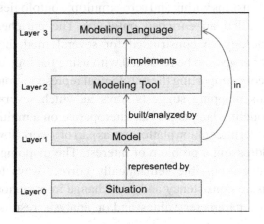

major challenge of improving the human interface to the Multi-Modeling process itself (Fishwick, 2004). This includes addressing both syntactic and semantic aspects of interoperation. Consequently, the development and employment of a systematic methodology for addressing multi-modeling problems is needed. The approach taken in this chapter is domain specific but applies to any domain. It requires the identification of the domain and the specification of the relevant supporting modeling techniques. The rationale behind this is twofold. First, problems to be solved by employing Multi-Modeling techniques are usually domain specific themselves. Second, by narrowing the scope of meaningful interoperations among several modeling techniques, where each technique offers unique insights and makes specific assumptions about the domain being modeled, it is possible to get concrete results and implement the methodology.

The general methodology begins with identification and characterization of an application domain of interest and the supporting modeling techniques. A Domain Analysis (DA) follows aiming to provide formal representations of syntactic and semantic aspects of the domain. A new Domain Specific Multi-Modeling Workflow Language is then developed to construct workflows that capture multi-modeling activities in the selected domain. A domain ontology resulting from the domain analysis step is utilized to provide semantic guidance that effects valid model interoperation.

A Meta-Model is an abstraction layer above the actual model and describes the modeling language used to create the model; a model has to conform to its Meta-Model. A Meta-Model conforms itself to a higher Meta-Model (Meta²-Model) which describes the Meta-Modeling Language as shown in Figure 3. The typical role of a Meta-Model is to define how model elements are instantiated. Meta-Modeling is defined to be the process of constructing a Meta-Model in order to model a specific problem within a certain domain. In the context of this Multi-Modeling research effort, the Meta-Modeling concept is extended to include the

Figure 3. Meta-model hierarchy

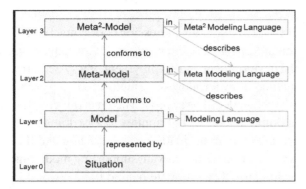

analysis of the conceptual foundations of a model ensemble. These models interoperate as part of a workflow developed to address a specific problem. Meta-Modeling then becomes a process of constructing a Meta-Model of a Multi-Modeling Workflow Language that captures interoperations between models.

Ontology-Based Meta-Modeling

Ontology is the term used to refer to the shared understanding of a domain of interest. It entails some sort of a global view of a specific domain. This view is conceived as a set of concepts, their definitions and their inter-relationships; this view is referred to as conceptualization. In computer systems, ontologies can be thought of as a means to structure a knowledge base (Uschold and Gruninger, 1996). The use of ontologies as a means for representing the semantic aspects of model interoperability has been explored in (Levis et al.,2012) and (Höfferer, 2007). The first approach is based on comparing ontologies (for each Modeling Technique) to help identify the similarities, overlaps, and/or mappings across the models under consideration and then constructing a higher level "meta" ontology that determines which sets of models can interoperate. The second maintains a clear distinction between meta-models and ontologies; they are different but complementary

concepts, and both are needed to allow for model interoperation.

The first approach starts by specifying a modeling language by constructing a generalized concept map (Novak and Cañas, 2008) that captures the assumptions, definitions, and elements and their properties and relationships relevant to the paradigm. This is termed as the "Conceptual Modeling Level" in Figure 4. This concept map model is a structured representation albeit not a formal one and, therefore, not amenable to machine reasoning. The concept map representation is then formalized using a syntactic model. The aim of constructing the syntactic model is to reveal the structural aspects of the modeling technique and to lay down the foundation for its ontology. This step is identified as the "Syntactic Modeling Level" in Figure 4. Then a basic ontology, referred to as a pseudo ontology, is constructed which mirrors the meta-model and serves as the foundation ontology; it does not contain any semantic concepts (related to the modeling technique and to the modeled domain) but acts as the skeleton for the ontology. In the next step, semantic concepts and relationships are added to this basic ontology to obtain the refactored ontology. This is done for each modeling language to be included in the multi-modeling construct.

Once the individual ontologies are completed for each modeling technique, mapping of concepts across the ontologies is started. The resulting ontology, which contains these concepts and relationships within and across multiple ontologies, is called an enriched ontology. The enriched ontology so constructed for several modeling languages can be reasoned with using the logical theory supporting the ontological representation. This mapping suggests ways in which several modeling languages can interoperate on a multi-model integration platform or as part of a workflow addressing a problem of interest. The mappings suggest possible semantically correct ways to ensure consistency and to exchange information (i.e., parameter values and/or analysis results)

Figure 4. Overview of the meta-modeling approach

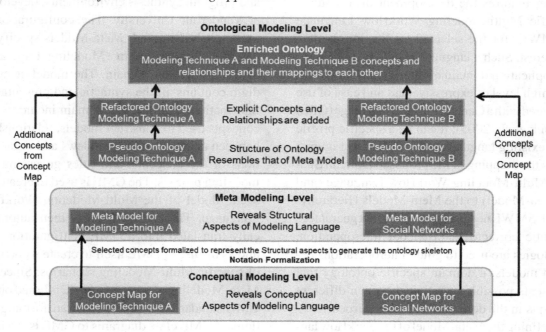

between different types of models when they are used in a workflow. The steps of constructing the pseudo, refactored and enriched ontologies are carried out as part of "Ontological Modeling Level" in the proposed approach (Figure 4).

The fusion of concepts from both types of refactored ontologies inside the enriched ontology is achieved by defining additional object properties in related classes and asserting them in the new ontology.

The process described in this section is repeatable for any set of modeling techniques. For instance, to extract semantic knowledge about a Modeling Technique C, similar concept maps (for the defined focus questions) can be developed, followed by the syntactic model, and then the pseudo and refactored ontologies. By the time the refactored ontology is completed, enough insight into the modeling technique should have been achieved that the ontology designer would easily be able to map the modeling technique C concepts to the related modeling techniques A and B concepts (if any). These newly mapped concepts can then

be incorporated into this enriched ontology and an updated enriched ontology can be obtained which would serve as the knowledge container for all three modeling techniques.

MULTI-MODELING WORKFLOWS

The Workflow layer in Figure 1 is where workflows of interoperating models are captured. A multi-modeling workflow is itself a model of an analysis process. A formal approach to capture a workflow for a multi-modeling activity requires a workflow modeling language with its own rules. Developing workflows using a domain specific language allows for translating visual views of model interoperation into an executable implementation. There already exist techniques for designing and implementing workflows such as Business Process Model and Notation (BPMN) (OMG, 2011) and Business Process Execution Language (BPEL) (OASIS, 2007). The domain specific nature of the approach described in this chapter requires the development of a Domain Specific Multi-Modeling Workflow Language (DSMWL) for the selected application domain of interest. Such a language should be tailored to the application domain of interest and should offer a high level of expressiveness and ease of use compared with a General Purpose Language (GPL) (Mernik et al., 2005); it can be a specific profile of an existing language such as BPMN. Figure 5 shows the mapping of the proposed Domain Specific Multi-Modeling Workflow Language (and its Meta-Model) to the Meta-Models Hierarchy.

A DSMWL needs a mechanism that guarantees semantic correctness of model interoperation. Ontologies are used to guide interoperations between models: a domain specific ontology that represents possible mappings between different concepts in the domain serves this purpose.

Defining the Meta-Model of the workflow language in Layer 2 in Figure 5 is a Meta-Modeling process itself. To capture those constructs of the Meta-Model that define the new language, a Meta-Modeling Language that conforms to a higher Meta-Model, Meta^2-Model, is also required. The research community in this area has addressed such hierarchy from different perspectives and many approaches were developed. One of these approaches is the Generic Modeling Environment (GME) (Davis, 2003), a configurable toolkit for creating domain-specific modeling languages

and program synthesis environments, developed at Vanderbilt University. The configuration is accomplished through Meta-Models specifying the modeling paradigm (Modeling Language) of the application domain. The modeling paradigm contains all the syntactic and presentation information regarding the domain including the concepts used to construct models, relationships between concepts, different views and organizations of the concepts, and rules governing the modeling process. The GME is used to create the Meta-Model of the Multi-Modeling Workflow Language. This Meta-Model is then automatically translated into a GME configuration that allows the use of GME itself to create workflows of specific Multi-Modeling scenarios. Since the Meta-Modeling paradigm in GME is based on the UML standard, the process of transforming the domain UML class diagrams to GME is straightforward. In general, a profile of BPMN (OMG, 2011) is used as the basis of a Domain Specific Multi-Modeling Workflow Language.

The methodology presented in this chapter can be viewed as a two phase approach (Figure 6). Phase 1 is where the first three steps, Domain Identification, Domain Analysis, and Workflow Language Definition take place; they are described in detail in this section. For a specific domain, this phase goes into multiple iterations until the Domain Specific Multi-Modeling Workflow Language

Figure 5. Mapping the domain specific multi-modeling workflow language to the meta-models hierarchy

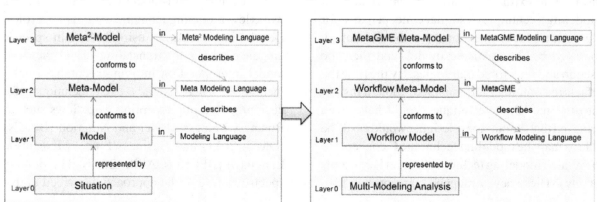

Figure 6. Methodology overview

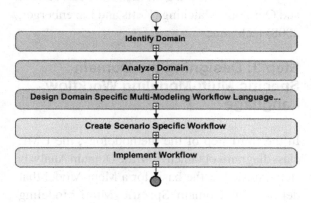

that addresses a domain of interest and is capable of capturing model interoperations is obtained. Phase 2 takes place when the DSMWL is used to create specific workflows for specific scenarios. These are described in the fourth section. It is always possible to go back to Phase 1 to refine and enhance the Domain Specific Multi-Modeling Workflow Language; this might be the case when a new modeling technique (or model formalism) is introduced in the domain of interest.

Step 1: Domain Identification

Since the proposed multi-modeling approach for solving complex problems is domain specific, domain characterization becomes an essential task to be conducted prior to any other activity. The output of the domain characterization should provide enough information to perform domain analysis, construct the domain ontology, and develop a meta-model of a Domain Specific Multi-Modeling Workflow.

In the context of software and systems engineering, a domain is most often understood as an application area, a field for which systems are developed (Prieto-Diaz, 1990). It is also defined to be a class of problems, where the types of problems to be solved and the context in which the system elements can be used are clearly identified (Ferré and Vegas, 1999). In this chapter, a domain

is considered to be a specific class of problems to be solved using a set of modeling techniques and the appropriate required data.

The domain identification process itself has been approached in many research efforts, especially the research on software reusability in the late 80's and early 90's. Ferré and Vegas (1999) provide a comparison of Domain Analysis approaches for software reuse purposes. Domain identification was characterized as a first and essential step prior to any domain analysis activities. Domain identification methods in those approaches include informal description in the form of statements, use of object oriented techniques, employing classification schemes, determining domain boundaries and collecting examples of similar problems.

As shown in Figure 7, the process begins with an informal description of the domain in the form of statements that try to identify the problems to be solved, modeling techniques usually used in solving these problems, data sources and types, and main actors involved including domain experts, modelers and analysts. Then the domain boundary is determined in order to scope the domain and to exclude any unrelated elements. Finally, a classification of concepts applicable to the domain

Figure 7. Domain identification process

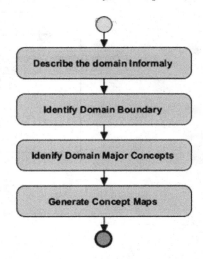

takes place. These concepts serve as a repository for constructing the Concept Maps. Generating Concept Maps is an iterative process until a satisfactory domain representation is reached.

Step 2: Domain Analysis

Once satisfactory Concept Maps that represent the domain of interest and its supporting modeling techniques are ready, the Domain Analysis (DA) process starts. The process, as shown in Figure 8, goes into two parallel, but complementary, paths. On the outer path, UML class diagrams derived from the concept maps are produced to capture the structural aspects of the domain and its supporting modeling techniques. A mapping between these class diagrams follows to produce consolidated diagrams that include interoperations between the modeling techniques. On the inner path, the ontologies based on the concept maps of the domain and the modeling techniques are constructed to capture the semantic aspects. These ontologies are represented using the formal Web Ontology Language (OWL) standard (W3C, 2004). Mapping of these ontologies follows by em-

ploying Upper Ontology (Niles and Pease, 2001) and Ontology Matching (Kotis and Lazenberger, 2008) techniques.

Step 3: Designing the Domain Specific Multi-Modeling Workflow Language

In the third step of the methodology, the UML class diagrams obtained from the Domain Analysis step are used as the basis for a Meta-Model that defines the Domain Specific Multi-Modeling Workflow Language (Figure 9)

Domain Specific Modeling Languages (DSMLs), i.e., languages tailored to a specific domain, offer a high level of expressiveness and ease of use compared with a General Purpose Language (GPL). Development of a new DSML requires both domain knowledge and language development expertise. DSMLs were developed simply because they can offer domain-specificity in better ways. According to Mernik et al. (2005), the development of any new DSML should proceed as follows:

Figure 8. Domain analysis

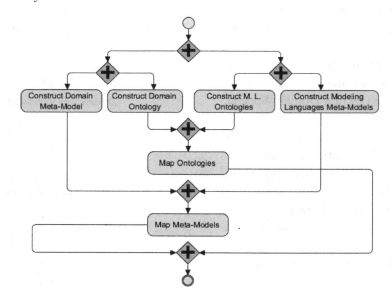

Figure 9. Multi-modeling workflow language definition

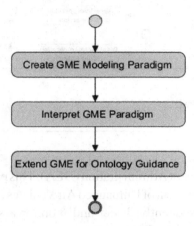

- **Decision:** The decision phase should balance the tradeoffs between the benefits of using an existing general purpose language or developing a new specific language.
- **Analysis:** The problem domain should be identified and domain knowledge should be gathered.
- **Design:** Basically there are two main approaches for designing new DSMLS: (a) base a new DSML on an existing Language, and (b)invent a new language.
- **Implementation:** Implementing a DSML involves the selection of a suitable implementation pattern. This depends on the purpose of the language and other factors such as the need for this language to be visual or executable.

This same approach is now used to design the Domain Specific Multi-Modeling Workflow language. The semantic concepts identified in the domain identification process and then captured using ontologies in the Domain Analysis step are utilized in obtaining a Domain Ontology that guarantees constructing semantically correct multi-modeling workflows. Since the workflows are meant to capture interoperations between models, the semantic concepts captured in these ontologies should be mapped and matched so that they can be used effectively. A systematic way of transforming initial pseudo ontologies of a specific domain into an Enriched Ontology (Levis et al., 2012) that incorporates the techniques described in (Niles and Pease, 2001) and (Kotis and Lanzenberger, 2008) is now employed to obtain an Upper Enriched Ontology for the domain of interest.

OWL is used as the standard language to represent the ontologies. Since the approach uses GME to create multi-modeling workflows, and since the final Domain Ontology is captured in OWL, there should be a way to allow communication between GME and the Domain Ontology while creating workflows for specific problems. This communication is required to ensure that interoperations captured in any workflow are semantically correct. Checking the domain Ontology for the correctness of workflow interoperations requires the capability of querying the Ontology for such information. The SPARQL (W3C, 2008) Ontology Query Language is used for this purpose.

GME allows for different types of extensions to the environment (Ledeczi, et al. 2001). Utilizing these GME extensibility features and in order to address the semantic guidance issue, a GME Add-on extension was implemented. This extension reacts to GME events, and in the case of creating a connection that represents interoperation between models, the OWL ontology is queried on the semantic validly of this connection. SPARQL queries are passed to a Fuseki (Fuseki, 2011) SPARQL server that utilizes the Jena (Jena, 2001) SPARQL query engine to query the ontology. Based on the query result, the GME extension could allow or disallow any interoperation connection. Figure 10 shows an overview of this process.

The meta-model of the new language has to be created and it should include the set of fundamental language constructs that represent the essential concepts of the domain, the set of valid relationships that exists between the domain concepts, and a set of constraints that govern how the language constructs can be combined to pro-

Figure 10. Overview of the semantic guidance process

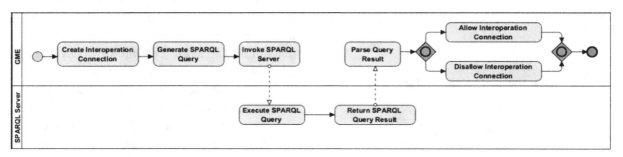

duce valid models. The final step is to implement our workflows in an appropriate platform. In order to achieve this, an interpretation of the workflow to an executable form is required. For this purpose, a GME interpreter can be coded. One example platform that can be used to execute our workflows is the SORASCS test bed that utilizes BPEL to execute workflows of analysis activities. Since the Domain Specific Multi-Modeling Workflow Language is based on BPMN, which can be mapped to BPEL, workflows created using the just created Multi-Modeling Workflow Language can be converted to executable workflows that SORASCS can execute.

APPLICATION TO A DOMAIN: DRUG INTERDICTION

Before applying Steps 4 and 5 of the methodology described in Figure 6 a domain must be specified. The selected application domain is a decision making problem in drug interdiction. The Joint Interagency Task Force - South (JIATF-South) is a drug Interdiction agency well known for interagency cooperation and intelligence fusion (Munsing and Lamb, 2011). The agency usually receives diverse types of data regarding drug trafficking and drug cartels from a wide variety of sources. Quick and accurate analysis of data is essential in addressing drug trafficking threats effectively. A typical case begins with JIATF-South receiving information from the U.S. Drug

Enforcement Administration (DEA). This prompts the deployment of Unmanned Air Vehicles (UAVs) that subsequently detect and monitor a suspect vessel until JIATF-South can sortie a US Coast Guard cutter to intercept. If drugs are found, jurisdiction over the vessel and disposition of the drugs and crew are coordinated with other agencies and countries. Courses of Actions (COAs) identified by the agency are dependent on timely and accurate analysis of received data.

The two modeling languages selected for this study are Influence Nets (Wagenhals and Levis, 2007) and Social Networks (Carley, 1999). Influence Net models, a variant of Bayesian Networks, describe cause-and-effect relationships among groups at a high level (Haider and Levis, 2007). Social Networks describe the interactions (and linkages) among group members (Carley, 1999). A considerable number of models for real world applications have been developed and analyzed using both techniques. A brief description of each technique follows.

Influence Nets: Based on two well established techniques, i.e., Bayesian inference net analysis and Influence diagramming, Influence nets are primarily used to perform probabilistic modeling of cause and effect relationships. In an Influence Net model, the nodes represent random variables (propositions) such as beliefs, actions, events, etc., whereas an edge represents a causal relationship (influence) between two nodes (propositions). The parent and child nodes are often called cause and effect, respectively. The causal relationship between a cause and an effect can either be promoting or inhibiting as identified by the edge attributes as shown in Figure 11a: Event A has an inhibiting influence on Event B (round arrowhead) and a promoting influence on Event C (pointed arrowhead), similarly Event B has a promoting influence on Event C. A tool called Pythia (Pachowicz et al., 2007) supports modeling of the timed version of Influence Nets called Timed Influence Nets (TINs) (Haider and Levis, 2005).

Social Networks: The Social Network definition used here is that of Carley (1999), where a Social Network is a structure composed of real world entities and associations among them. In this definition, a node, or an entity, can be an agent, organization, action, knowledge, and/or resource. In the sample Social Network shown in Figure 11b, the nodes represent entities such as human beings and the edges connecting these entities represent associations (e.g., relationship) between them. The graphical form of the social network can also have a matrix representation in which the entities are represented in the matrix rows and columns and the matrix entries indicate their interaction. ORA, a Social Network analysis tool (Carley and Columbus, 2012), supports constructing these matrices and the models. These matrices can either be single-mode or multi-modal. Single-mode matrices represent networks containing only one type of entities (e.g., people

or agents only) while multi-modal matrices consider networks with multiple types of entities (e.g., agents, action, organizations, knowledge etc.). These matrices collectively make up a meta-matrix, a framework that integrates multiple and related network matrices into a single interrelated unit.

A step-by-step application of the approach described in Figure 4 applied to the two modeling techniques follows.

Conceptual Modeling Level: The first step is the construction of Concept maps for each modeling language under consideration. In a Concept map, a concept is represented using some type of geometrical shape (rectangle, circle, ellipse, etc.) and is connected with other concepts using a directed link. This link can be tagged with a description of the relationship between the two concepts. Concepts connected together with a relationship referring to a meaningful entity define a proposition, for example, *Influence Net is composed of Nodes and Links.* Concept *Influence Net* is connected with concepts *Node* and *Link* with a relationship *is composed of.* The aim of constructing a Concept maps is to gain a syntactic and semantic, albeit informal, insight into the modeling techniques to reveal aspects which will ultimately facilitate the ontology construction process later on. The construction of a Concept map is an iterative process that requires brainstorming and frequent

Figure 11. (a) Example influence net; (b) Example social network

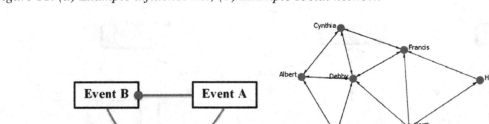

(a)   (b)

revisions until a final, concrete Concept map is developed. The steps of constructing a Concept map include (a) identification of focus questions, (b) construction of parking lot (pool of concepts) and (c) establishing cross links between these concepts. Figure 12 shows a fragment of a Concept map constructed for Influence Nets in an attempt to address the following focus question: *What are the constructs of an Influence Net?*

Syntactic Modeling Level: After the conceptual modeling level, only selected concepts from it are formalized to represent the structural aspects of the modeling techniques in the form of a syntactic model. A syntactic model is an abstraction layer above the actual models and can be considered a meta-model describing the syntactical rules and requirements for the construction of an instance model. The objective at this level is to retrieve a basic ontology skeleton. Syntactic

models do not contain any detailed concepts and relationships of the domains they model, but their structure can be used as the basis for the first ontology to be constructed in the next level. Figure 13 shows the syntactic model for the Influence Net modeling language expressed in the form of a UML class diagram.

Ontological Modeling Level: There are three sub-levels in this step that eventually yield an ontology enriched with concepts and relationships from both modeling languages. (Kappel et al., 2006) refer to the process of formalism shifting as reducing the gap between the implementation oriented focus of syntactic models and the knowledge representation oriented focus of ontologies. This formalism shift is led by the syntactic model developed in the previous level. Kappel's technique has been enhanced with the addition of the Conceptual Modeling Level as the first attempt

Figure 12. A sample concept map for constructs of influence nets

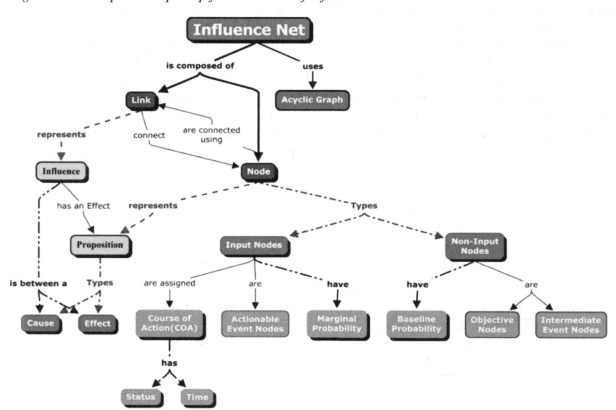

Figure 13. Influence net syntactic model

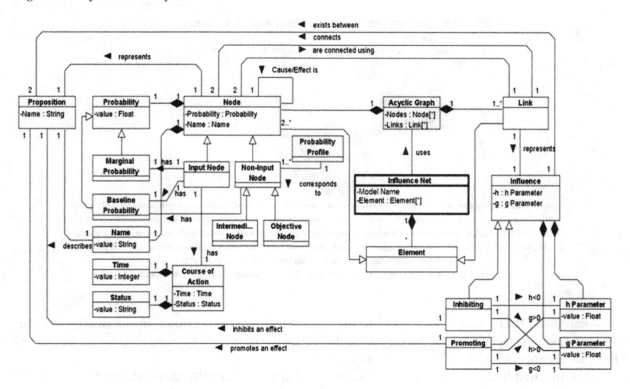

in understanding the underlying syntactic and semantic constructs of a modeling language and the generic domain concepts that are used in the models. At this point, some semantic equivalences between refactored ontologies are asserted manually.

The first ontology that is constructed is called *pseudo ontology* and resembles its syntactic model equivalent. Explicit domain concepts and relationships used by the modeling technique are added into the pseudo ontology to construct a *refactored ontology*. Mapping of concepts between the refactored ontologies of both techniques is partly done manually and partly by invoking an ontology "reasoner" to construct an *enriched ontology*. This enriched ontology contains the individual and mapped concepts and relationships of both modeling techniques. It can be considered as a template ontology which contains the intra and inter-modeling technique concepts

and relationships. An ABox of this ontology can be instantiated for a specific domain which will serve as the knowledge container for that domain. For instance, *Agent* and *Organization* classes from a Social Network refactored ontology can be mapped to the *Subject* and *Object* classes of an Influence Net refactored ontology by adding *hasSubjectValue* and *hasObjectValue* object properties to the existing object property of the Agent and Organization classes (Figure 14).

Step 4: Create Scenario Specific Workflow

A fictitious scenario of a possible drug trafficking activity has been created. The scenario is presented briefly in Figure 15, while Figure 16 shows a hypothetical geographic description of the situation.

Figure 14. Enriched ontology classes

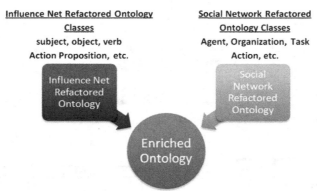

Influence Net Refactored Ontology Classes
subject, object, verb
Action Proposition, etc.
Social Network Refactored Ontology Classes
Agent, Organization, Task
Action, etc.
Influence Net Refactored Ontology
Social Network Refactored Ontology
Enriched Ontology
subject (hasSubjectValue some subject or hasAgentValue some Agent or hasOrganizationValue some Organization)
object (hasObjectValue some object or hasAgentValue some Agent or hasOrganizationValue some Organization)
Agent (hasAgentValue some Agent or hasSubjectValue some subject or hasOrganizationValue some Organization)
Organization (hasAgentValue some Agent or hasSubjectValue some subject or hasObjectValue some object)
verb (hasVerbValue some verb or hasTaskValue some Task) etc.
Action (hasElements some subject, verb and object or hasActionValue some Action)

Analysts at JIATF-South are trained to use various modeling techniques to analyze data and then to identify possible Courses of Action (COAs). In a traditional manner, analysts would be using each modeling technique individually. Applying this multi-modeling methodology, would make such analysis process more accurate and faster. The rationale is that while each modeling technique might be capable of capturing certain aspects of the available data, interoperation between models will definitely improve the results of the overall process. Also, the ability for analysts to create visual workflows of the Multi-Modeling activity provides a mean of reusability of the constructed workflows in addressing similar scenarios.

Step 1: Domain Identification

First, an informal description of the domain is developed. Looking back at the JIATF-South operations description and the brief scenario, the following partial list of statements shown in Figure 17 describes the main concepts of the domain.

These informal statements are then revised to scope the domain and exclude any concepts that are outside its boundary. In this example, the Asset Allocation and Scheduling problem is not

Figure 15. Scenario brief

- Drug Interdiction involves information sharing, fusion of intelligence data and monitoring of drug trafficking activities.
- Given (incomplete and uncertain) information, decisions to be made on best COAs.
- Drug Interdiction involves dealing with Drug Cartels and Smugglers (RED groups) and Law Enforcement and Intelligence (Blue groups).
- Drug Smuggling takes different routes and originates from different sources.
- Analysts use Social Networks, GIS, Influence Nets, Asset Allocation and Scheduling and Organization Models techniques.

Figure 16. Scenario visualization

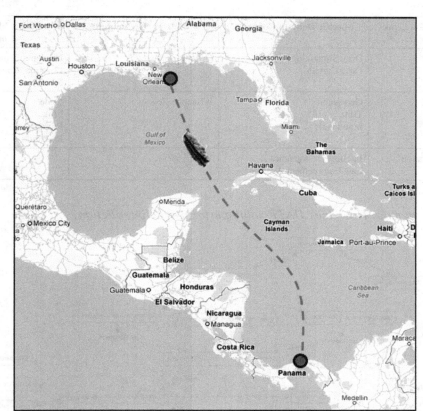

Figure 17. Informal description of domain

- Drug Interdiction involves information sharing, fusion of intelligence data and monitoring of drug trafficking activities.
- Given (incomplete and uncertain) information, decisions to be made on best COAs.
- Drug Interdiction involves dealing with Drug Cartels and Smugglers (RED groups) and Law Enforcement and Intelligence (Blue groups).
- Drug Smuggling takes different routes and originates from different sources.
- Analysts use Social Networks, GIS, Influence Nets, Asset Allocation and Scheduling and Organization Models techniques.

addressed. A repository of related concepts is then identified. Table 1 shows examples of some related concepts. The concepts are classified into two major categories, Domain Concepts, and Modeling Techniques Concepts.

After identifying related concepts, concept maps are constructed to capture the relations between these concepts. Figure 18 shows a concept map that addresses the question: How does JIATF-South perform Drug Interdiction? Other relevant questions are posed and the answers to them lead to the development of corresponding concept maps.

Table 1. Domain and modeling techniques concepts

General Domain Concepts	Specific Domain Concepts	Modeling Techniques Concepts	Specific M. Techniques Concepts
Drug Interdiction	Drug Smuggling Drug Cartels	Geospatial Analyses	Incidents, Time Location, Route WebTas
Data	Geospatial Time Individuals	Influence Nets	Node Link Proposition Probability
Interagency Collaboration	Intelligence Agencies Law Enforcement Agencies		

Figure 18. Concept map: How does JIATF-south perform drug interdiction?

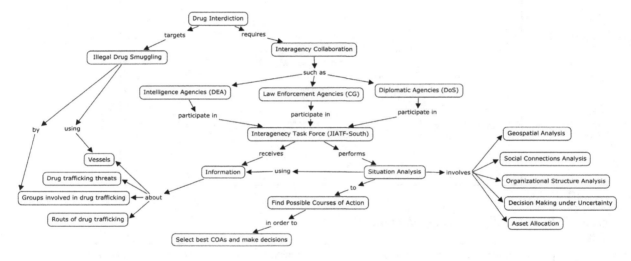

Step 2: Domain Analysis

In this step, the generated concept map of Figure 18 is used to perform domain analysis. The UML class diagram is derived from the concept map to represent the constructs of the domain and the Modeling Techniques. Parallel to that, semantic concepts and relations are identified and captured in the OWL ontology. Figure19 shows a partial UML class diagram that represents the constructs of the drug interdiction domain. Figure 20 (a) and (b) show the multi-modeling domain ontologies: (a) focuses on the modeling techniques and data while (b) focuses on the models that are used.

Step 3: Domain Specific Multi-Modeling Workflow Language

Using GME, a meta-model for the domain's workflow multi-modeling language is defined based on the UML class diagrams resulted from the domain analysis. This meta-model defines the constructs of this new language. Figure 21 shows part of GME meta-model of the proposed domain specific multi-modeling workflow language. In addition to basic constructs borrowed from BPMN, some new constructs have been introduced and some constraints imposed. The workflow in this domain has two types of activities, operations and interoperations. Operations are those activities

Figure 19. UML class diagram representing main constructs of the drug interdiction domain

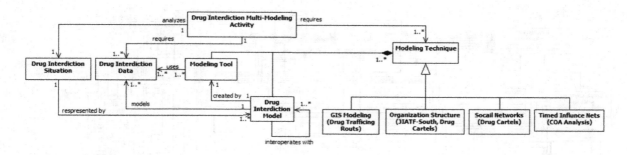

Figure 20. The multi-modeling onntologies: (a) modeling techniques and data; (b) models

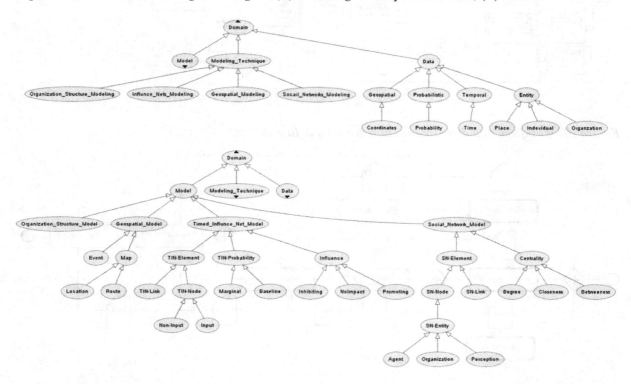

performed on a specific model using the modeling tool that supports its modeling language. Interoperations are those activities that involve operations across models through their modeling tools. Operations in this workflow language can be either Thick or Thin operations. Thin Operations represent the case when service based integration takes place, given that the modeling tool of interest exposes its functionalities as services.

Thick Operations represent the case in which the whole modeling tool is integrated as a package in the multi-modeling platform. Multi-modeling platforms can support the integration of modeling tools in these two forms.

Figure 21. GME meta-model of the domain specific multi-modeling workflow language

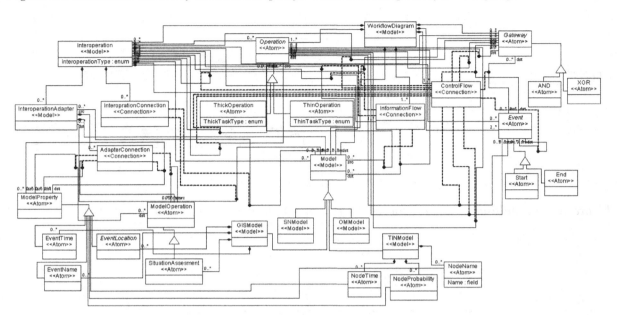

Figure 22. Workflow of a drug interdiction multi-modeling activity

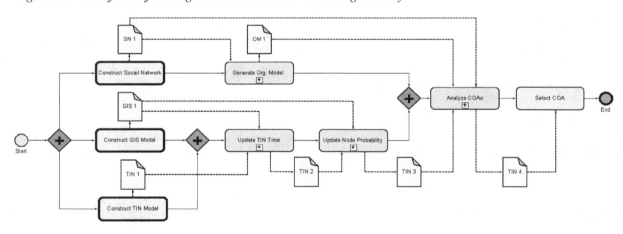

Step 4: Scenario Specific Workflow Creation

Once the GME meta-model of the Domain Specific Multi-Modeling Workflow Language is interpreted and registered as a new Modeling Paradigm in GME, the GME environment is used to create workflows that capture specific domain scenarios. Figure 22 shows a workflow that includes the use of GIS, Timed Influence Nets, Social Networks and derived Organization Models to analyze data and then generate and select best courses of action.

Figure 23 shows an example of an interoperation between a GIS model and a Timed Influence net model captured using the Domain Specific Workflow Language. Interoperations between models can be of different types. This example represents an interoperation where the time of an

Figure 23. Model interoperation between models

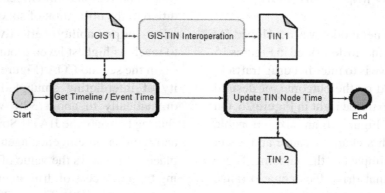

Figure 24. Interoperation adapter

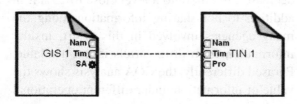

event in the GIS model is used to update the time of a node in a Timed Influence Net. Adapters in this DSMWL, such as the "GIS-TIN Interoperation" rounded box in Figure 23, capture the low level details of the interoperation as shown in Figure 24. The notation used in Figs. 23 and 24 is defined in Figure 25.

The enforcement of semantic rules captured in the domain Ontology takes place on the Interoperation Adapter level. Whenever the modeler tries to establish connection between two models on this level, the GME extension that has been included in the Domain Specific Workflow language is triggered to check the semantic correctness of the connection. The extension formulates a SPARQL query based on the models being connected, sends the query to the SPARQL server and then parses the returned result to determine the validity of the connection. Based on the query result, the connection might be allowed or disallowed.

Figure 25. The domain specific workflow language notation

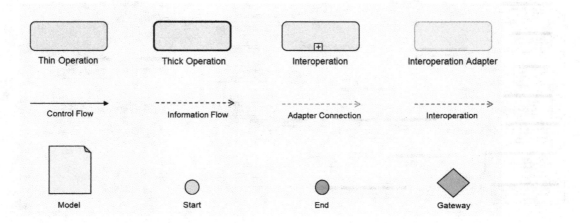

Step 5: Workflow Implementation

A Timed Influence net model was developed for the JIATF-South scenario described in Figures 15 and 16. The objective is to interdict drug trafficking; this is reflected by the outcome, or desired effect, node at the extreme right in Figure 26. On the extreme left of Figure 26 are six actionable events that, through a chain of cause and effect influences, have an impact on the outcome. These actionable events that drive the scenario range from "Share information with other agencies" to "Send UAVs for surveillance over international waters" to "Get information from insider informant in drug cartel in Country R."

The TIN model developed for the scenario was analyzed using the Pythia tool (Wagenhals and Levis, 2007) to select the best course of action for the agency to take. Pythia provides means for COA analysis where different combinations of action events are examined to determine the COA/s that give highest probability for achieving a specific node goal such as successful drug interdiction in this scenario. The results of three COAs are presented to show the effect of different combinations of action events.

The first COA (Figure 27) shows that sharing information between the JIATF-South and other (local and regional) intelligence agencies in addition to the utilization of surveillance resources allows the probability of effective drug interdiction to reach its highest level, around 68%.

In the second COA (Figure 28), the probability of interdicting smuggled drugs decreases dramatically to about 32% when information sharing between the JIATF-South and other local and regional intelligence agencies does not take place. This shows the value of information sharing to the success of drug interdiction efforts.

The third COA (Figure 29) shows how the probability of effective drug interdiction can decrease even more to a level close to 25% if in addition to not sharing information among the many agencies involved in this effort, insider information from drug cartels is not available. Phrased differently, the COA analysis shows the value of information under different operational conditions.

The comparison between the three COAs tells clearly that in order for an agency like the JIATF-South to be effective and successful in its drug interdiction efforts, all available resources should be utilized. It is also evident that information sharing and exchanging real time data about any specific drug smuggling scenario increases the probability of success significantly.

Figure 26. The timed influence net model for drug interdiction

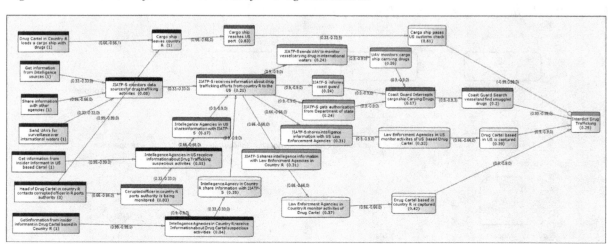

Figure 27. The probability of achieving drug interdiction with COA 1 as a function of time

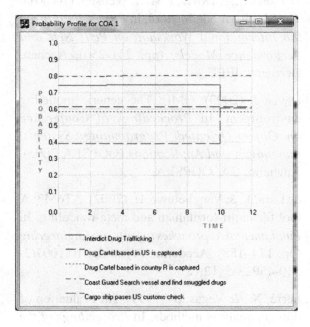

Figure 28. The probability of achieving drug interdiction with COA 2 as a function of time

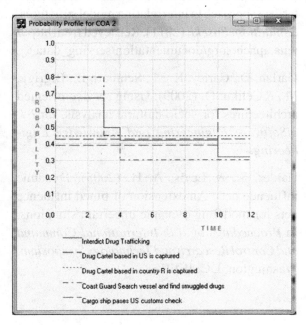

Figure 29. The probability of achieving drug interdiction with COA 3 as a function of time

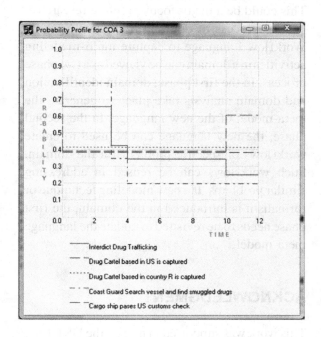

CONCLUSION

A systematic methodology for addressing multi-modeling problems by employing a Domain Specific Multi-Modeling Workflow Language and a supportingdomain ontology has been described. The approach is domain specific and allows for visual representation of Multi-Modeling activities.However, it requires the characterization of a specific domain, modeling techniques used in solving problems in that domain, and data sources available for creating models of specific scenarios in that domain. Domain characterization is a complex problem by itself. It has been addressed in this methodology by exploiting previous research in this area.

The utilization of a domain ontology to guarantee the creation of semantically correct Multi-Modeling workflows is an area of research that requires further attention. Creating a domain specific ontology is an iterative process that requires domain experts' knowledge and advanced techniques to match and combine low-level ontologies into a higher-level "Upper" domain ontology. This could be a major focus in future research.

The process of defining a Domain Specific Workflow Language to capture multi-modeling activities in a domain can be viewed as a two phase process. In the first phase, domain identification and domain analysis take place to generate the meta-model of the new language. In the second phase, the new language can be used to create workflows of specific problems in the domain. Such workflows can be reused in addressing similar problems. If a new modeling technique or formalism is introduced in the domain, the first phase needs to be revisited to update the language meta-model.

ACKNOWLEDGMENT

This work was supported in part by the US Office of Naval Research under contract no. N00014-11-1-0129.

REFERENCES

Carley, K. M. (1999). On the evolution of social and organizational networks. *Research in the Sociology of Organizations*, *16*, 3–30.

Carley, K. M., & Columbus, D. (2012). *Basic lessons in ORA and AutoMap 2012*. Pittsburgh, PA: Carnegie Mellon University, School of Computer Science, Institute for Software Research.

Carvalho, R., Santos, L., Matsumoto, S., Ladeira, M., & Costa, P. (2008). UnBBayes - MEBN: Comments on implementing a probabilistic ontology tool. In *Proceedings of IADIS, Applied Computing 2008 Conference*. Algarve, Portugal: IADIS.

Clark, G., Courtney, T., Daly, D., Deavours, D., Derisavi, S., & Doyle, J. M. … Webster, P. (2001). The Mobius modeling tool. In *Proceedings of the 9th International Workshop on Petri Nets and Performance Models,* (pp. 241-250). Aachen, Germany: IEEE.

Davis, J. (2003). GME: The generic modeling environment. In *Proceedings of Conference on Object-Oriented Programming, Systems, Languages, and Applications* (OOPSLA 2003). Anaheim, CA: OOPSLA.

de Lara, J., & Vangheluwe, H. (2002). AToM3: A tool for multi-formalism and meta-modeling. In *Fundamental Approaches to Software Engineering* (pp. 174–188). Academic Press. doi:10.1007/3-540-45923-5_12.

Ferré, X., & Vegas, S. (1999). An evaluation of domain analysis methods. In *Proceedings of the 4th CASE/IFIP8 International Workshop in Evaluation of Modeling Methods in Systems Analysis and Design*. CASE/IFIP.

Fishwick, P. A. (2004). Toward an Integrative multimodeling interface: A human-computer interface approach to interrelating model structures. *Simulation. Fuseki*. (2011). Retrieved from http://jena.apache.org/documentation/serving_data

Garlan, D., Carley, K. M., Schmerl, B., Bigrigg, M., &Celiku, O. (2009). Using service-oriented architectures for socio-cultural analysis. *Int'l J. ofSoftware Engineering and Knowledge Engineering*.

Haider, S., & Levis, A. H. (2005). Dynamic influence nets: An extension of timed influence nets for modeling dynamic uncertain situations. In *Proceedings of 10th International Command and Control Research and Technology Symposium*. Washington, DC: IEEE.

Haider, S., & Levis, A. H. (2007). Effective course-of-action determination to achieve desired effects. *IEEE Trans. on Systems, Man, and Cybernetics, Part A: Systems and Humans, 37*(6), 1140–1150. doi:10.1109/TSMCA.2007.904771.

Hemingway, G., Neema, H., Nine, H., Sztipanovits, J., & Karsai, G. (2011). Rapid synthesis of high-level architecture-based heterogeneous simulation: A model-based integration approach. *Simulation*. PMID:22919114.

Höfferer, P. (2007). Achieving business process model interoperability using metamodels and ontologies. In *Proceedings of 15th European Conference on Information Systems*. IEEE.

Iacono, M., Barbierato, E., & Gribaudo, M. (2012). The SIMTHESys multiformalism modeling framework. *Computers & Mathematics with Applications (Oxford, England), 64*, 3828–3839. doi:10.1016/j.camwa.2012.03.009.

Jena. (2011). Retrieved from http://jena.apache.org/about_jena/about.html

Kansal, S., Abusharekh, A., & Levis, A. H. (2007). Computationally derived models of adversary organizations. In *Proceedings of the IEEE Symp. On Computational Intelligence for Security and Defense Applications*. Honolulu, HI: IEEE.

Kappel, G., Kapsammer, E., Kargl, H., Kramler, G., Reiter, T., & Retschitzegger, W. …Wimmer, M. (2006). Lifting metamodels to ontologies: A step to the semantic integration of modeling languages. In Model Driven Engineering Languages and Systems (pp. 528-542). Berlin: Springer.

Kotis, K., & Lanzenberger, M. (2008). Ontology matching: Current status, dilemmas and future challenges. In *Proceedings of International Conference on Complex, Intelligent and Software Intensive Systems*. IEEE.

Ledeczi, A., Maroti, M., Bakay, A., Karsai, G., Garrett, J., & Thomasson, C. … Volgyesi, P. (2001). *The generic modeling environment*. Paper presented at the Workshop on Intelligent Signal Processing. Budapest, Hungary.

Levis, A. H., Zaidi, A. K., & Rafi, M. F. (2012). *Multi-modeling and meta-modeling of human organizations*. Paper presented at the 4th International Conference on Applied Human Factors and Ergonomics. San Francisco, CA.

Maria, A. (1997). Introduction to modeling and simulation. In *Proceedings of the 29th Winter Simulation Conference*. IEEE.

Mernik, M., Heering, J., & Sloane, A. M. (2005). When and how to develop domain-specific languages. *ACM Computing Surveys, 37*, 316–344. doi:10.1145/1118890.1118892.

Michalski, R., & Tecuci, G. (Eds.). (1994). *Machine learning: A multistrategy approach*. San Mateo, CA: Morgan Kaufmann.

Munsing, E., & Lamb, C. (2011). *Joint interagency task force - South: The best known, least understood interagency success*. Washington, DC: National Defense University Press.

Niles, I., & Pease, A. (2001). Towards a standard upper ontology. In *Proceedings of International Conference on Formal Ontology in Information Systems*. IEEE.

Novak, J. D., & Cañas, A. J. (2006). *The theory underlying concept maps and how to construct and use them*. Pensacola, FL: IHMC.

OASIS. (2007). *Business process execution language*. Retrieved from https://www.oasis-open.org/committees/wsbpel/

OMG. (2011). *Business process model and notation (BPMN)*. Retrieved from http://www.omg.org/spec/BPMN/

Pachowicz, P., Wagenhals, L. W., Pham, J., & Levis, A. H. (2007). Building and analyzing timed influence net models with internet-enabled pythia. In *Proceedings of SPIE, Defense and Security Symposium*. Orlando, FL: SPIE.

Prieto-Diaz, R. (1990). Domain analysis: An introduction. *Software Engineering Notes, 15*(2), 47. doi:10.1145/382296.382703.

Saeki, M., & Kaiya, H. (2006). On relationships among models, meta models and ontologies. In *Proceedings of the 6th OOPSLA Workshop on Domain-Specific Modeling*. Jyväskylä, Finland: University of Jyväskylä.

Uschold, M., & Gruninger, M. (1996). Ontologies: Principles, methods and applications. *The Knowledge Engineering Review, 11*, 93–136. doi:10.1017/S0269888900007797.

Vittorini, V., Iacono, M., Mazzocca, N., & Franceschinis, G. (2004). The OsMoSys approach to multi-formalism modeling of systems. *Software & Systems Modeling, 3*, 68–81. doi:10.1007/s10270-003-0039-5.

W3C. (2008). *SPARQL query language for RDF*. Retrieved from http://www.w3.org/TR/rdf-sparql-query/

Wagenhals, L. W., & Levis, A. H. (2007). Course of action analysis in a cultural landscape using influence nets. In *Proceedings of the IEEE Symp. On Computational Intelligence for Security and Defense Applications*. Honolulu, HI: IEEE.

Whitney, P. D., & Walsh, S. J. (2010). Calibrating Bayesian network representations of social-behavioral models. [LNCS]. *Proceedings of Advances in Social Computing, 6007*, 338–345. doi:10.1007/978-3-642-12079-4_42.

KEY TERMS AND DEFINITIONS

Meta-Model: A description of the modeling language used to create the model, the model has to conform to its Meta-Model. It is a level of abstraction above a model.

Modeling Language: A modeling formalism.

Multi-Modeling: The use of multiple interoperating models expressed using different modeling formalisms.

Multi-Modeling Workflow Language: A language that enables the design and specification of the interoperation of multiple models expressed using different formalisms.

Social Network: A structure composed of real world entities and associations among them.

Timed Influence Net: A special form of Bayesian networks that describes cause and effect relationships with associated delays as an acyclical graph.

Chapter 5
Multiformalism Modeling Compositionality in SIMTHESys

Enrico Barbierato
Università di Torino, Italy

ABSTRACT

Multiformalism has emerged as a sound technique to define a complex system as the composition of a set of sub-components, each one modeled according to the best-suited formalism. Existing literature offers a wide choice of frameworks and tools that exploit model composition following different approaches. This chapter provides an insight into the composition approach used by SIMTHESys (a framework for the development of modeling languages and the solution of multiformalism models) in order to compose easily and consistently primitives belonging to different (custom) modeling languages. A case study is presented to illustrate the effectiveness of the proposed composition formalism.

INTRODUCTION

The modeling of real world systems is intrinsically complex.

The issue arises from the fact that several factors must be taken in account: for example, a system can be distributed over different components or can be characterized by an intricate dynamics. As some of the aspects of the system can be ignored, the researcher can invest more time and efforts to study the most relevant aspects. This classification suggests the possibility of building an abstraction of the system or a model that is defined according to a formalism. The advantages provided by these approach are several, being the most notable the capability of measuring the system dependability (the ability of a system to provide a specific ser-

vice) and its performability (how well a system performs, including the occurrence of faults).

One of the most powerful ways to understand how the parts of a system interact is modeling. Modeling power and Decision power of a formalism play an important role in this field. The former corresponds to the capability of describing efficiently a real system. The latter is inversely proportional to the complexity of computation and the set of computing resources requested to define properties and to execute the model (i.e. to implement a control function defined in terms of the formalism). Sub-formalisms originated by structural restrictions reduce modeling power and tend to increase the model size. On the other hand, they increase the decision power.

DOI: 10.4018/978-1-4666-4659-9.ch005

A further level of analysis considers qualitative and quantitative modeling. In the first case, the models are characterized by a variable with finite value domains and rely on an abstract logic description of the system behavior. In the second case, real valued variables are used to describe physical entities of a system through differential and algebraic equations.

The scale of the systems currently in charge to support human activities and the concurrency of different non-functional specifications require that modeling techniques would offer abstraction mechanisms that allow modelers to face such complexity while exploiting mathematically founded methods. Such abstraction mechanisms can be constituted of formal modeling languages and their solution algorithms, that can be based either on simulation or analytical methods. A broad and well spread example set is given by stochastic modeling techniques such as Petri nets, fault trees, stochastic automata, process algebras, queuing networks and many others that have been given a stochastic variant or interpretation.

During the last decades the intricacy of modern systems has grown significantly, including operating systems, networks, hardware and applications. Not only the choice of a specific formalism to build a model is difficult, but experience has shown that there is no a unique formalism able to model a system the best. Even in a specific domain the specifications used to build a system may vary. In a similar way, there is no a unique solution method.

The need to investigate disciplines such as engineering and biology characterized by complexity and heterogeneity has seen the rapid development of different formalisms and solution techniques supporting research in these fields. Informally, these approaches can be classified within three categories: i) sub-models composition, ii) multiformalism integration and iii) formal models generation from high-level specifications. Multiple tools integration in a common environment plays an important role. A common approach in the Software Performance Engineering area consists of implementing model-to-model transformations from UML description to formal models oriented to performance and dependability. However, integrating different tools raises different issues.

Firstly, it is necessary to understand how to report the results from a tool in a common way and secondly how to build the interoperability between the tools, considering the output values provided by one tool as the input for another tool.

Model composition has emerged as a sound technique showing how a complex model can be described as the composition of a set of sub-models. Initially, modelers consider several abstractions of the system under study, then they decompose it into two or more sub-components in order to analyze and understand more easily the single parts. Finally, the sub-components are put together following a bottom-up fashion in order to generate the initial system.

Literature offers different approaches to model composition describing different techniques and operators required. The most notable proposals include i) combinatorial methods, ii) qualitative model checking and iii) state-based stochastic methods.

The advantage of multiformalism results from the capability to assign the modeling of each sub-component to an expert in the specific subject, who is free to model that part using the most suitable formalism. Multiformalism has proven to be successful in different areas such as biology, fault-tolerant computing and disaster recovery being the most notable. As a result, this interdisciplinary aspect has created interesting links between different communities of modelers.

A variety of different software tools have been implemented to date. Early attempts included SHARPE (Trivedi 2002), a modeling framework capable of studying Markov models, queueing networks expressed in product form and generalized stochastic Petri Nets (GSPN). SMART (Ciardo G., Jones R. L. et al. 2006) is a software package used to design complex discrete-state systems; it provides both numerical solution algorithms and discrete-event simulation techniques. More recent approaches include Möbius (Clark G., Courtney T. et al. 2001), OsMoSys (Franceschinis G., Gribaudo M. et al. 2002), PRISM (Kwiatkowska M., Gethin N. et al. 2011), GRIF (TOTAL 2007), ModHel'X (Boulanger F. and C. 2008), Oris ((Bucci G., Sassoli L. et al. 2004) and BIO-PEPA (Ciocchetta F. and Hillston J. 2009).

Users who need to design new heterogeneous formalisms on Möbius are requested to refer to a meta-model interface called Abstract Functional Interface (AFI).

Möbius supports stochastic activity networks (SANs), Petri nets, Markov chains and performance evaluation process algebra (PEPA). OsMoSys can create multi-formalism models and workflow management to achieve multi-solution. The key idea of OsMoSys relies on meta-modeling and the concept of object-oriented paradigms. Though PRISM and BIO-PEPA are not oriented to multiformalism, they introduce some interesting perspectives in modeling composition.

PRISM provides capabilities oriented to formal modeling and analysis for systems exhibiting probabilistic, nondeterministic and real-time characteristics, in addition to discrete and continuous-time Markov chains and Markov decision processes. It also provides a modeling language.

BIO-PEPA is based on PEPA, a process algebra historically designed to study the performance analysis of computer systems. BIO-PEPA extends PEPA to describe biochemical networks and some kinds of kinetic laws. Analysis based on ordinary differential equations, model checking and stochastic simulation are available too.

The foundation of this approach - inspired to the Model Driven Engineering principle that uses models in the software construction - consists of a process algebra connecting different levels of abstraction through message channels in order to assemble a set of submodels into a model. It is particularly well suited to the modeling of cell behavior and its interactions. Considering the vari-

ety of scientific disciplines where multiformalism is used and the vast number of multi-modeling tools, the problem arises of understanding which kind of formalism can be used according to the model class.

SIMTHESys (Barbierato E., Iacono M. et al. 2012) is a framework for the definition of new multiformalism composed models and the automatic generation of the corresponding solvers. The contribution of this chapter relates to the SIMTHESys Composition Formalisms (CF, a set of formalisms capable of composing models based on different languages) with respect to other approaches.

The remainder of this chapter is organized as follows: the Background Section introduces the aspects of the theory of models composition and reviews some of the most important approaches to Compositionality. A state of the art follows. The SIMTHESys Section explains the key principles of this framework with respect to the Composition Formalisms; the Case study Section shows how the SIMTHESys Composition Formalism can be deployed to model a system; finally, the last Sections include conclusions and future work.

BACKGROUND

Composability is defined in as the capacity to assemble different subcomponents in one system. Informally, composability can be considered from a syntactic or a semantic point of view. In the former, the single components are implemented compatibly with the resulting configurations (i.e. they fit together), while in the latter the single components are assembled in a meaningful way (i.e., the resulting computation is still valid semantically). Note that the former doesn't necessarily imply the latter. A formal theory of composability includes the concept of Model (a representation of the system under study) that can be seen as a computable function. This definition not only allows the use of function compositionality concepts but also suits users interested in simulating the model (more formally, to execute it over time).

Thus Composability is defined as a technique used to compose models in a valid way. The notion of validity is more complex. Besides being a comparison between a simulated model and the perfect model, it is necessary to consider also which model inputs or applications need to be considered for a model to be valid. Syntactic composability is discussed in (Szabo C. and M. 2007) where the authors raise a number of issues that can be described as i) determining a common model by which all the components are requested to comply, ii) tackling the heterogeneity of both simulation components and their respective application domains and iii) extending the coverage to many and specific domains.

CODES (COmposable Discrete-Event scalable Simulation) is a framework accounting for these problems and consists of component discovery, model validation, model execution and model deployment, defining in this way an architecture based on component based simulations. Regular grammars allow the framework to perform model composition and reuse rules; on the one hand, this choice allows the composed model to be represented as production strings, on the other it formalizes syntactic composability.

Multi-layer modeling relies on the observation that very often a real system can be abstracted in two components called plant and controller and regarded as computations able to exchange information about states and commands. This subdivision concerns also the task carried out by this pair, i.e. the plant works on operations at low-level while the controller carries out high-level operations. A controller can be regarded as a plant whose operations are determined by another controller; as a result, it is possible to define multi-layer plant/controller specifications and, at higher level, separating conceptually knowledge. Both plant and controller can be described by a single or multiple formalism (the latter solution is preferable if the components of the system fol-low different embedded dynamics). The authors define a modeling formalism consisting of the specification of a model and the algorithm that defines its execution. Simple scenarios where a single formalism is sufficient to model a system exploit mono and super modeling formalisms.

The former refers to cases where a single modeling formalism captures one aspect of a real world system.

Most complex cases where different formalisms are required to model different system components use meta and poly modeling formalism. In the former, the model specifications are abstracted to another modeling formalism; this approach must be capable of coping with the differences between the different model specifications that need to be composed.

The latter (also called multi-formalism modeling) can compose different models exploiting a formalism (Knowledge Interchange Broker) handling the differences between disparate modeling formalisms. In the latter, a modeling formalism is encapsulated into a super formalism. An important condition is that the encapsulated modeling formalisms have a well-defined relationship with respect to each another. These kind of formalisms adopt composition of state-based models instead of composing a state-based model and an input/output model. Solution integration plays an important role in composability theory as it defines how the different submodels pass the results.

The approach can be static or dynamic depending on whether results are shared during or after the solution process takes place. Service-oriented techniques are an interesting approach enabling components to exchange messages.

In the case of mono composability, as all the models are specified using the same formalism, it is necessary to define an execution protocol. Using a super compositionality approach, it is necessary to implement an inter-operation policy between the encapsulated models and the enclosing ones. In the poly composability approach, inter-operability occurs at both model level (i.e.

the model specifications of two models α and β are composed using a model specification γ) and execution level (the execution algorithm of γ takes in account the execution algorithms α and β). Finally, in a meta composability approach, the execution algorithms are encapsulated in a set of constructs oriented to inter-operability. The High-Level Architecture HLA ((SISC) 2000) essentially focuses on inter-operability across simulation systems while other technologies like Web service, Java-RMI and CORBA concern the exchange of messages between loosely-coupled software applications.

HLA architecture allows the definition of distributed simulations (federation) and includes the following components: i) a set of rules, ii) a template to unify coherently the description information provided to the distributed simulators and iii) an interface specification denoting the functional interfaces between the simulators and the Run-Time Infrastructure (RTI), which determine the way in which a simulator will be executed. The elements in the federations can communicate either by modifying the properties of an object and then notifying the change to other elements that need to access the object or just by using specific interactions to communicate that a certain event has occurred. The approach used complies to two different requirements, i.e. the support to data transformations between the models and the preservation of the semantic integrity when composition occurs. The former requirement is satisfied by a component acting as broker (Knowledge Interchange Broker or KIB) while the latter is taken in account by implementing a common model that provides a common vocabulary denoting constraints on the decision and physical models. Some behavioral aspects have to be considered though. Firstly, the KIB must implement the causality when the messages are sent between the decision and the process models; as causality is already included in DEVS but not in LP (as models don't depend on time), it is necessary to modify the KIB.

Additionally, it is requested that the KIB manages concurrency since two distinct processes need to handle the execution and simulation modules. Finally, it is requested that all the I/O exchanges between the two decision and the process models remain logically correct with respect to the order of the events produced.

Following the classification presented in (Laprie 1992), dependability is denoted as the capability to provide a service. A service is correct when it implements the actual system function and is called improper otherwise. If the service provided by the system doesn't match the correct service, then a system failure occurs. Dependability is characterized by different attributes, notably i) availability (a measure of the alternation between deliveries of proper and improper service), ii) reliability (measure of the continuous delivery of service), iii) safety (the absence of a catastrophic failure), iv) confidentiality (absence of disclosure of confidential information), v) integrity (absence of improper system states) and vi) maintainability (a measure of the time to restoration from last occurred failure.) A failure is defined as a transition from a correct service to a service that doesn't implement the expected system function. As said earlier, a model is an abstraction of a real system and adheres to a formalism (sometimes called modeling language).

The formalisms considered are based on Markovian processes. Therefore, solving a model of this sort is equivalent to apply one of analytical available methods on the model and calculate a set of performance values. The concept of abstraction plays an important role in building modeling frameworks. In (Gholizadeh H. M. and A. 2010), the authors abstract a set of formalism structures in order to build a graph: each node corresponds to a formalism and it is characterized by a set of properties. As a result, the framework built in this way is compatible with a wide collection of formalisms. The developed framework consists of four layers: i) a Meta-formalism layer, ii) a Formalism layer that is described in previous level, iii) a Model class layer, which is described in the Formalism layer and finally iv) a Model layer, representing the models that can be solved. This approach is based on meta-modeling and provides the means to build a modeling framework capable to include different formalisms in an unified fashion.

The value of modeling is well-established. The most notable factors that denote the need of modeling can be found in environments where i) the problem domain is only partially understood, ii) a considerable amount of people need to interact in order to implement a solution, iii) the developed system requires a substantial maintenance and finally iv) the future enhancements of the implemented system will grow significantly. Stochastic modeling and analysis has proven to be a valid approach in order to determine the quantitative measures of systems. Real world offers a wide choice of systems, the most notable being i) real time processes (in this case, the system must be capable of processing the information received and provide a response within a certain time. Failure in accomplishing this may cause catastrophic consequences), ii) business processes (the aim is to understand and align all the aspects of the customers organization) and iii) Discrete Events Dynamic Systems DEDS, see (Bause F., Buchholz P. et al. 1998). This kind of systems are usually asynchronous; the state transitions are triggered by the occurrence of discrete events. Literature offers a wide range of languages used to model stochastic discrete-event systems, including Stochastic Petri Nets, Stochastic Reward Nets SRNs (Muppala J. K., Ciardo G. et al. 1994) and Stochastic Activity Networks SANs (Sanders W. and F. 2002). There are different examples of paradigms used to represent model languages, notably Object Oriented techniques (Booch 1994) provide a modular approach that can be used to represent composition of models based on different formalisms. For example, in OsMoSys it is possible to define a model class and consequently a composed model by including at least one model class. In spite of the wide number of formalisms used in modeling, the

methods to define dependability and performance variables remain unsophisticated. Sometimes it is necessary to add extra components to a model to gather the requested information, resulting in a further change in case new information has to be collected from the model. The advantage of path-based reward variables (Obal W. D. and W. 1999) is two-fold as it extends the performance measure specifications and state-space construction procedures. Specifically, this approach augments current reward variable specification methods with variables including a state and can model behaviors related to sequences of events and states. Additionally, it extends current state-space construction algorithms generating stochastic processes that are suited to the variables studied. A path is defined as a sequence of model states and events; any measure defined on a path is called path-based performance measure. A path can be in one of the following states: i) initialized, when it's in the first state; ii) completed, when last pair in the sequence is satisfied; iii) aborted if the sequence is violate (i.e. if an event occurs in place another one in a model state). Path-set specification is supported by a dedicated automaton (path automata) as there are different possible states that are visited when the sequence of events takes place. The usage of the automaton plays an important role as, together with path-based reward structures (a pair of functions consisting of i) the impulse reward gained when the path automaton is in a particular state and receives a certain input pair and ii) the rate at which reward is gained when the path automaton and the model are in the corresponding states) since it can be used to evaluate path-based performance measures. Finally, reward variables are built considering both the path-based reward structure and the random variables (representing i) the time in which the path automaton is in a certain state, ii) the total time during the interval the automaton was in a particular state and iii) the number of times the automaton is in a certain state) specified on the evolution of the model and the path automaton. As a result, path-based rewards variable can support the investigation related to different questions, i.e. the probability of traversing a path, how long does it take, what the total time in crossing the path within some interval would be and so forth. The authors present also a method to build the state spaces that support these variables by means of a procedure that exploits one or more automata and a model of the system in order to create a state space tailored to the performance variables considered. Questions about the modeled system performance have been investigated also by the means of probes (Clark A. and S. 2008). Firstly, the modeler is requested to define the steady-set, i.e. the set of states considered interesting, and the passage-set, i.e. the set of states specified by the passage-time query. Secondly, it is necessary to define the source states and target states. The former is the set of states belonging to the passage-sets which are the target of those transitions whose source states are outside the passage-set. The latter is the set of states outside the passage-set which are the target of those transitions whose source is in the passage-set. Queries are evaluated according to robustness and portability, meaning that the query specifications preserve correctness in case the model is changed and that the query can be deployed over different models. The eXtended Stochastic Probes (XSP) augments the expressiveness of the classical mechanism for specifying query-sets (state-specifications and activity-specifications) combining state-specifications within an activity probe specification. Informally, a state specification is a predicate including expressions over the multiplicities of the sequential components in a system. An activity-specification is a labeled regular expression denoting the sequence of activities which lead into and out of the query-set. The XSP language is built over the International PEPA Compiler (IPC), a stand-alone modeling tool able to perform steady-state and transient analysis of PEPA models. Firstly, IPC takes in input a PEPA model and an XSP probe and produces in output the translation of the probe specification into a

PEPA component, which is added to the model. Secondly, the new model previously created is passed to IPC that translates it into a Markov Chain. Finally, the resulting Markov Chain is solved for the stationary probability distribution.

STATE OF THE ART

The state of the art presented here aims at describing on the one hand formalisms with respect to the ability to handle the concept of compositionality. On the other hand, frameworks and tools are presented with regard to the capability of supporting a set of key requirements described later.

Formalisms

The classification criterion followed is based on the observation that firstly, there are composition techniques that consider a single formalism. In particular, composition in some formalism, e.g., Stochastic Process Algebra (SPA) and Stochastic Petri Nets (SPN), is somewhat intrinsic to the formalism and it not related to application-specific domains.

Secondly, other approaches consider more than a (well-known) formalism. Finally, more general approaches define composition at higher abstraction levels in order to compose models built using well-known formalisms (that is, formalisms already defined in the literature), user-defined formalisms or both.

Stochastic Process Algebra

Process algebras are abstract languages capable of describing concurrent systems. A system consists of a set of agents that perform actions specifying concurrent behaviors and the synchronization between them. Composability is made explicit with respect to other formalisms, i.e. Stochastic Petri Nets. Classical process algebras such as Communicating Sequential Processes CSP (Hoare 1985) and Calculus of Communicating Systems CCS (Milner 1989) offer a set of primitives for agents: i) prefix, ii) null agent, iii) choice, iv) restriction, v) labeling and vi) parallel composition.

CSP differs from CCS in the way the agents communicate between themselves (there are not complementary actions). Note that composition plays an important role as it specifies the structure of the model denoting the actions that can or cannot be taken. Different extensions have been proposed for the proper study of paradigms such as composability and abstraction. PEPA (Performance Evaluation Process Algebra) is one of the many extensions of Process Algebra. Its novelty consists in the deployment of the concept of duration (an exponentially distributed random variable) of an action that makes explicit the relationship between the Process Algebra model and a Continuous Time Markov Chain.

Different components of a system work together by using cooperation which is characterized by a cooperation set. This set includes a list of actions requesting the simultaneous involvement of the components, resulting in a shared action.

DEDS

The study of Discrete Event (Dynamic) Systems (DES or DEDS) (Bause F., Buchholz P. et al. 1998) describes the dynamic of a system as a sequence of events, which keep evolving in time. Different approaches have been proposed to study the DEDS theory. Firstly, the logical approach (such as Automata and Formal Language Theory) aims to discover either the occurrence of an event or the impossibility for an event to occur (i.e. a deadlock) though no attention is paid to performance issues. Secondly, the quantitative analysis evaluates the number of the occurrences of an event in time, providing the means to measure the performance of the system.

PN-Based Formalisms

Existing literature offers several approaches to composition based on Petri Nets in order to build large models. Since a Petri Net can be regarded as a bipartite graph, it is possible to apply graph transformations. Specifically, Petri Nets transformations (Ehrig H., Hoffmann K. et al. 2006) are based on transformation rules. Each rule is a pair of graphs (L,R) (i.e. left-hand side and right-hand side); applying a rule of this sort corresponds to find a match of L in the source graph (or net) and to replace this match by R. Hierarchical Colored Petri nets (CP-nets) can handle large models as well using mechanisms such as places fusion and transitions fusion. Both techniques can be used also to compose individual CP Nets modules to compute results which can be considered valid for the whole modular CPN. Modules are related to each other by two kinds of relation: i) place fusion and ii) transitions fusion.

In the former, a set of places shares the same tokens; when a transition adds (respectively removes) a token to one of the places in the set, it is added to (respectively removed from) all the places in the set. In the latter, all transitions of a set act as one atomic action sharing the values assigned by a common binding.

Petri Net Algebra (Best E., Devillers R. et al. 2001) is inspired by Process Algebra and Petri Nets: the latter are treated as composable objects and in this way they are embedded in general process algebra. At the same time, a generic process algebra is provided an automatic Petri net semantics in order to apply techniques such as net-based verification techniques, based on structural invariants and causal partial orders. A Petri Nets-based algebra used to model Web Services is introduced in (Hamadi R. and B. 2003). Petri Nets is a convenient formalism as it is quite easy to map a Web Service (considered as a partially ordered set of operations) considering that a Place models the state of the Web Service, a transition models a specific operation and an Arc models a causal relationship.

The proposed algebra contains different operators that combine Web Services in different ways such as i) sequence, ii) choice, iii) unordered sequence, iv) iteration, v) communication, vi) selection and vii) refinement. Each operator corresponds to a Petri Net.

Queueing Petri Nets

Some of the difficulties occurring when trying to study both quantitative and qualitative characteristics of a system have been solved by using different approaches. Since this kind of analysis is typically performed by PNs and QNs respectively, the key idea is to enhance both the formalisms by introducing Queueing Petri Nets QPN (Bause 1993). This formalism integrates the qualitative aspects (boundedness and liveness) and quantitative aspects of a system. QPN uses the concept of timed queueing place defined as a queue and a depository for served tokens that enables transitions in the formalism. Similarly to GSPN, QPN includes immediate queueing places. Every time a Transition fires, the tokens are added to the queue and remain unavailable for Transitions. When the tokens leave the queue, they shift to the depository and become available for the Transitions of the timed queueing place. Quantitative analysis is obtained by studying the Markov chain underlying the QPN stochastic process.

Frameworks

The different frameworks described in literature can be characterized by different properties. Firstly, a framework must be capable to represent multiple and heterogeneous models. If model composition is supported by a tool, then a technique to allow the models to interact and share results must be available.

Secondly, the solution provided must be scalable, i.e. the solution of a model should come at a cost which is lower when compared to the cost of solving an unstructured equivalent model. Thirdly,

a frameworks must be able to support different modeling languages. Furthermore, a framework should be extendible, allowing new formalisms to be implemented without necessarily changing the existing tools. Finally, it is requested to support multiple solution methods (i.e. simulation and numerical analysis).

LARES

Despite the success of stochastic modeling, some criticism has emerged when modeling complex, distributed systems with a high degree of parallelism (leading inevitably to a space state issue). A further problem arises during the modeling phase when the modeler and the system designer need to exchange knowledge.

Decision Diagrams are considered the basis for symbolic approaches which model initially a system using either using GSPN or a SPA to generate in a second phase a compact symbolic representation of the underlying transition system. The advantage of this approach relies in the efficiency in performing further analysis, i.e. i) generating a reachability graph, ii) eliminating the vanishing states and more in general performing the computation of performance measures. An alternative approach consists of LARES (Walter M., Munchen T. U. et al. 2009), a formalism oriented to the modeling of fault-tolerant systems allowing the users to specify different behaviors such as a fault trees, failure propagation, failure with common cause and so forth.

Within LARES, a model is composed of different modules which can be composed in an hierarchy. Each module denotes either a component of the system or an external item determining a sort of influence, i.e. a repairman. The complexity of a behavior ranges from a simple Boolean (i.e. either functioning/not functioning value) to the cross-product of several one-dimensional state spaces. The methodology is structured in three steps: firstly, all the relevant aspects are extracted from the specification and translated in an intermediate language; secondly, the model obtained in this way can be extended by using dependability parameters not included in the original specification and finally, the intermediate model can be translated to a target formalism, either a simulator or a GSPN or a PA.

Möbius

Möbius (Clark G., Courtney T. et al. 2001) allows the user to compose multiformalism models by representing the state of a model using a state variable, which is characterized by a type. A state can be shared among different models according to different modalities. Within equivalence sharing, two state variables become the same variable (though with some limitations due to the type) coexisting in two models at the same time. In functional sharing, it is possible to associate a function with the value of state variables (again with some limitations due to the type value returned by the function).

This approach is suitable when the modeler wants to compose a queueing network (QN) to a stochastic activity network (SAN). A composed model can be built by setting a Place of the SAN model to the value of a function returning the number of customers in a queue of the QN model. It can be seen that the state-sharing framework is general enough to allow the modeler to describe connections and iterations between models. Composition formalisms as the Replicate/Join present an interesting capability as they allow the reduction of the model state space by using symmetries, producing in this way a smaller state space. Moreover, atomic models can be combined to form a composed model organized according to an hierarchy.

Two operations are provided by this composition formalism: Replicate that replicates a model and Join connecting models by using the variable sharing mechanisms presented earlier. To overcome some of the limitation of tree-based representations (for example, they are not suit-

able to model rings present in networks), Möbius exploits the Graph Composed Formalism.

This includes two kinds of nodes called respectively joins and submodels, which can be connected to each other (although combinations like Join to Join and submodel to submodel are not allowed). Specifically, Joins connect submodels by sharing state variables. Graph Composed Formalism models can be regarded as atomic models by using a wrapper, that is a logical (top-level) node and works like an intermediate layer between the parts of the model and the Joins and submodels. Möbius includes both static and dynamic solution integration techniques.

OsMoSys

OsMoSys (Franceschinis G., Gribaudo M. et al. 2002) is a multi-formalism, multi-solution, modeling framework oriented to objects. OsMoSys offers both explicit and implicit multiformalism (respectively occurring when the different modeling languages are specified by the modeler or by the tool/framework) and the capability of composing models within a single-formalism.

The OsMoSys modeling approach consists of a three-layer structure. Firstly, a language called Metaformalism describes any graph-based formalism; secondly, the Model Metaclass (or metaclass in short) is any formal language specified by the metaformalism; finally, the Model Class specifies all those models having a common structure. Metaclasses can be specialized by inheritance (following the is a relationship) in order to build hierarchies.

A Model Class can be either Flat if it is created by using the formalism elements described in the set of element types of a given formalisms or Composed if it contains one or more sub-models. In the latter, the aggregation is said to be weak if it represents the part-of relationship between the metaclass and its sub-models. In order to allow the implementation of reusable submodels, OsMoSys also supports composition by strong aggregation with a mechanism that allows hiding an element of a submodel, so that it is no longer more accessible when it is encapsulated in a new Model class, and consequently the definition of an interface, composed of all the visible elements. The composition of submodels is then performed by their instantiation into a model compliant to a Bridge metaclass, a formalism that composes the Model classes using arcs and operators that describe the solution process.

The main solution mechanism is the exchange of values between submodels by using interface elements: the bridge model is used to generate an OsMoSys business process, that describes the solution process using available solvers as service stations, and the workflow engine implements it, providing in this way multi-solution.

Tools

Atom³

Atom³ (de Lara J. and H. 2002) is a tool using the concept of meta-modeling, a method used to create a model of the modeling language. The advantage of this approach consists in clearly identifying all the structures that a language can define. Furthermore, the meta-modeling formalism can be modeled by a higher abstraction level called meta-meta-model, which provides a clearer aspects of the basic formalism elements. Typical examples of meta-modeling result in Entity-Relationship (ER) diagrams and Unified Modeling Language (UML) class diagrams. Atom³ receives in input a set of meta-specification expressed in the form of ER diagrams and it returns a tool that processes all the models based on the given formalism. All the models must comply with a specific syntax (Abstract Syntax Graph) in order to implement the transformations between formalisms. The tool architecture consists of a processor whose paramount role consists of models creation and manipulation, including the generation of the code.

Every time that Atom³ is executed, a meta-meta-model is loaded to allow the modeling of metamodels. Every formalism element is denoted by a set of attributes. Elements can be connected according to a set of constraints defined at meta-meta-model level. According to these specifications, the Atom³ processor generates a node or a Python class in addition to the classes defined in the semantic space. Graph grammars map a graph on the left-hand side (LHS) to a graph on the right-hand side (RHS), allowing Atom³ to perform formalism transformations.

The graph grammars include a set of rules that may have to be satisfied in order for a certain action to be triggered and executed. A part of formalism transformations, graph grammars can be used by the tool i) to generate the code, ii) to perform model simulation and finally iii) to optimize the model.

SMART

On the one hand, the complexity of discrete-state systems requires that specific properties (i.e. lack of errors in system design) be verified at early stages. On the other hand, the concepts of performance and reliability imply the study of the system behavior from a time perspective. On the basis of these considerations, SMART (Symbolic Model checking Analyzer for Reliability and Timing) (Ciardo G., Jones R. L. et al. 2006) includes both stochastic models and logical analysis. Currently, SMART offers a high level formalism (Petri Nets) and two low level formalisms (discrete-time and continuous-time Markov chains, i.e. DTMC and CTMC) to the modeler who is free to calculate a set of measures for each model and exchange parameters between models.

The logical analysis takes in account the generation of the reachable state space which is implemented either by explicit algorithms or algorithms based on multivalued decision diagrams (MDD). The stochastic analysis is performed by numerical and simulation solvers depending on the underlying process being a CTMC (DTMC) or not. Specifically, SMART provides an on-line component able to classify the underlying stochastic process (this is determined by observing the kind of distributions specified) for a given model. Another interesting feature provided by the tool consists of a strongly typed language that allows considering each object as a (recursive) function.

SHARPE

SHARPE (Symbolic Hierarchical Automated Reliability and Performance Evaluator) is a tool to analyze stochastic models (Trivedi 2002), the most notable being fault trees, product form queueing networks, Markov chains and Generalized Stochastic Petri nets.

The tool provides a set of algorithms and a specification language to build single models or combination of models according to an hierarchy, i.e. the output of a model is regarded as the input of another model.

The information passed between models may be either a number (i.e. the number of tokens in a Petri net's place) or a function with respect to the time (i.e. representing the time to failure). The advantage of using such an hierarchy is twofold as i) it avoids a large state space and ii) it can be used in both model specification and model solution.

The analysis provided by the tool includes reliability, availability and performability.

GRIF

GRIF (GRaphical Interface for reliability Forecasting) is a set of packages developed by Total Research & Development able to determine dependability factors such as i) Reliability, ii) Availability, iii) Performance and iv) Safety. GRIF allows the user to choose the best modeling formalism among block diagrams, fault trees, Markov graphs or Petri nets. Fault Trees are modeled by the Tree module that exploits ALBIZIA, a BDD (Binary Decision Diagram) computation engine

developed by Total. The output provided by the module includes i) Minimal cuts, ii) Unconditional failure intensity, iii) Conditional failure intensity and other notable measures.

ALBIZIA is used also by ETree, a component modeling safety systems (regarded as a set of safety barriers) as an event tree. The Petri module models the behavior of complex dynamic systems using stochastic Petri nets with predicates and assertions (to describe both the dysfunctional parts of an installation such as component failures and the working parts). The provided engine consists of a simulation component based on a high-speed Monte Carlo simulation engine. The dynamic behavior of a system based on a stochastic block diagram is analyzed by the BStok module; again the computation relies on a Monte Carlo simulation engine.

When the modeler creates a block, a Petri Net is generated automatically; in this way, the module can develop a wide library of block configurations to model the different interactions between the elements of the system.

ModHel'X

ModHel'X (Boulanger F. and C. 2008) is a set of tools to provide the semantics specification of a modeling formalism. No reference to any model instance occurs. The approach used is based on component-oriented and hierarchical modeling. The concept of hierarchy describes a way to combine the heterogeneous components of a model and it is regarded as an abstraction mechanism. Every component is regarded as a black box (block); its behavior is visible only at interface level. Every time there is a request to observe a block, a coherent view of its interface at a particular instant of time is returned. This approach provides the capability to embed asynchronous processes in a model without synchronizing their activity. A block can be described by a behavior, i.e. a sequence of observations; each observation of a model is specified as the combination of the observations of its blocks according to a model of computation (MOC, i.e. a set of rules to interpret the relations between the components of a model) at all the levels of an hierarchical model.

The exact state of the interface of each block at a certain instant is a snapshot of the observation of the top-level model. ModHel'X supports all the notions of time used, such as real time, logical clocks and partial order on signal samples. The only notion time that is shared among all the MOCs is the succession of snapshots. Every time that a block state has changed, a snapshot of the model is taken. The meta-model proposed includes the abstract concepts that can be specialized and that represent the element of the model. Pins denote the models and blocks interface; pins relations (which are unidirectional) denote the interactions between blocks, for example they can capture a causal relation between two blocks. Data are represented by tokens.

The algorithm used to compute observations of the model makes a request to the model blocks to update their interface status; these information are propagated to other blocks in a sequential way (as the algorithm is requested to be deterministic). A computation step is composed of different actions: i) it chooses a component (depending on the model state and the available inputs), then ii) it propagates input data to this component, iii) it performs a request to update its state, iv) it selects a component depending on the model state, including the data generated for the update, v) it propagates the data according to the chosen component and vi) it selects a component according to the data which has just been propagated.

Real-Time Systems Modeling

Real-time systems include significative constraints related to the timing behavior, which must be included by the modeler analysis. To this end, more sophisticated extensions of Petri Nets have been proposed.

Oris

Oris (Bucci G., Sassoli L. et al. 2004) is a tool oriented to qualitative verification and quantitative evaluation of reactive timed systems. It can build, simulate, validate and analyze real-time systems characterized by Preemptive Time Petri Nets (PTPS), an extension of Time Petri Nets including a mechanism to assign resources acting as conditions determining the advancement of timers of enabled transitions. PTPS can describe effectively real-time systems working using preemptive scheduling with nondeterministic execution times, synchronization, periodic or sporadic tasks.

Under Oris, a model is built either via a module called Timeline editor or by specifying the tasking set. The latter can be described through a visual formalism that represents i) the type of task-releases, ii) a measure of time for each task denoting the best and the worst completion time, iii) the priorities and finally iv) semaphore synchronization. The model built can be either simulated or analyzed. The simulation process animates the model (moving tokens on the firing of transitions in the so-called "token game") and then generates a file including statistical data (including token distribution, transition firing sequences and other measures) while the analysis is accomplished by a dedicated engine (TPN analyzer engine) whose output is a TPN reachability graph denoting the relations between state classes.

A model checker determines all the symbolic traces compliant with logical sequencing and quantitative timings (the latter being denoted by a set of temporal logic formulae).

SIMTHESys

Following the approaches reviewed earlier, SIMTHESys modeling framework (Barbierato E., Iacono M. et al. 2012) is based on a metamodeling representation of models and formalisms. It includes a CF that accounts for both semantic and syntactic integration aspects and provides a high degree of flexibility.

The basic part of a formalism is the Element, which defines all the atomic primitives that can be used to describe a model. Formalism Elements are used to define submodels, and can contain other elements. An element is characterized by Properties and Behaviors.

The former allows the association of values of given types to the elements of a formalism. The latter defines the actions that the element performs. An element can comply with several Interfaces, each specifying a set of behaviors that the element must define. Behavioral Interfaces allow the creation of families of elements that share similar features, abstracting the characteristics of the evolution of the model. Finally, Solver Interfaces and Solver Helper Interfaces allow the interaction with the solution engines that eventually compute the results of the analysis. The main mechanism for the support of the solution of (multiformalism) models in SIMTHESys is based on the behaviors of the arc elements designed to connect elements belonging to different formalisms.

Such behaviors describe, with the native mechanisms of the formalisms, the action that should performed, thus allowing any kind of semantics in the interaction (included action on whole submodels, that are implemented as special elements): this implicitly specifies how a model should be solved, thus describing the solver to be synthesized for the solution.

Figure 1 represents the architecture of the tool, showing the complete workflow of the solution of a model in a given formalism. The components are described in the following.

- **Solver Interfaces:** A set of interfaces supporting the definition of two formalism families (exponential events and exponential and immediate events based) enabling the access to solving engines.
- **Behavioral Interfaces:** A set of predefined abstract behaviors that formalisms must implement to obtain specific services.
- **FDL Document:** Formalisms are described by the Formalism Description Language (FDL) documents which declare all their modeling primitives. FDL files are XML-based and their definition adheres to the Behavioral and Solver interfaces.
- **FDL Analyzer:** The FDL documents are provided to the FDL Analyzer, which generates the model parser (called MDL parser) able to read models in the specified formalism.
- **DrawNET:** Models are designed with the DrawNET (Gribaudo M., Raiteri-Codetta D. et al. 2005) GUI and saved in the MDL format. The user can invoke the solvers to compute the required solutions.
- **Solution Engines:** Currently SIMTHESys focuses on two formalism families (exponential events and exponential and imme-

Figure 1. SIMTHESys architecture and workflow

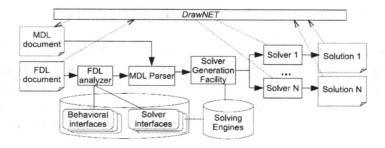

diate events based) and offers six different solution engines called i) S_e, ii) S_g, iii) C_{es}, iv) C_{gs}, v) C_{gt} and vi) C_{et}). Formalisms belonging to these families include SPN, GSPN, Markov Chains (MC), Queuing Networks (QN), Finite Capacity Queuing Networks (FCQN), Fault Trees (FT) and customized multi formalisms based on their composition. Among the solution engines, S_e and S_g evaluate performance indexes by simulation. The other four translate the evolution of the corresponding models into Continuous Time Markov Chains (CTMCs). C_{es} and C_{gs} deal with steady state analysis, while C_{et} and C_{gt} provide a transient solution. S_e, C_{es} and C_{et} consider only exponential events family (i.e. SPNs), and the others support both exponential and immediate transitions (i.e. GSPNs).

- **MDL Document:** It is a file describing the model according to the FDL file in a Model Definition Language, XML-based.
- **MDL Parzser:** The MDL parser is created by the FDL Analyzer and it parses the MDL file received in input. If the process is successful, the parser invokes the Solver Generation Facility.
- **Solver Generation Facility:** It links the MDL parser to the selected Solving Engines to create a set of stand-alone solvers.

Models Composition

Heterogeneous models can be composed in SIMTHESys using a Composition Formalism that includes a set of Elements characterized by properties and behaviors. Compositionality appears in the model description only as the solver studies the underlying CTMC. It is used to connect two well-known formalisms: Finite Capacity Queueing Networks (FCQN) and Stochastic Petri Nets (SPN).

Specifically, it includes an Element called Arc and a set of Behaviors in order to implement the following interactions: SPN place to FCQN queue, SPN transition to FCQN queue, FCQN queue to SPN place and FCQN queue to SPN transition. Other behaviors declared in the ExpEventSolver solving interface must be implemented as well.

An SPN can be connected to an FCQN only through an *Arc* Element starting from a Place or a Transition. In the former case, if the SPN place is marked and the queue has not reached its full capacity, *Arc* enables the execution policy of the queue; in the latter, *Arc* adds a new item in the queue if the queue is not full.

An FCQN can be connected in an SPN ending to a Place or a Transition. In the former case, the end-of-service event inserts a token in the Place; in the latter, the Transition is enabled by the arrival of a new item in the queue server and disabled by a departure. Note that when a Transition fires, an item in the queue is consumed. The behaviors used by the *Arc* Element are depicted in algorithms 2, 3, 4 and 5. Algorithm 1 refers to the *InitEvents* CF behavior, which invokes in turn *InitEvents* behaviors belonging to the formalisms to be composed. Note that *Arc* implements two behaviors, i) Push and ii) Pull that respectively adds and subtracts as many tokens as their weight from the place connected to the other end of the arc using the *AddOccupancy* behavior.

CF has been extended to include more primitives (arcs) used to perform testing conditions: *CheckGE*, *CheckLT* and *CheckCplx*. *CheckGE* and *CheckLT* verify respectively that in performance evaluation formalism, the occupancy (the

Algorithm 1. initEvents behavior for CF

```
1:  for ElementType T in allSubElements do
2:      if T instanceof ExpEventModel then
3:          (ExpEventModel)T .initEvents();
4:      end if
5:  end for
```

Algorithm 2. isActive behavior for Arc

```
1: if from instanceof ElementOccupancy then
2:    return eo.getOccupancy() >= 1;
3: end if
4: return true;
```

Algorithm 3. hasSpace behavior for Arc

```
1: if to instanceof FCQueueEvent) then
2:    return (FCQueueEvent)to.canAccept();
3: end if
4: return true;
```

Algorithm 4. Push behavior for Arc

```
1: if to instanceof ElementOccupancy then
2:    (ElementOccupancy)to.addOccupancy(1);
3: end if
4: return true;
```

Algorithm 5. Pull behavior for Arc

```
1: if from instanceof ElementOccupancy then
2:    (ElementOccupancy)from.addOccupancy(-1);
3: end if
4: return true;
```

Algorithm 6. isTrue for CheckGE

```
1: return from.getOccupancy() >= weight;
```

Algorithm 7. isTrue for CheckLT

```
1: return from.getOccupancy() < weight;
```

Algorithm 8. isTrue for CheckCplx

```
1: if from instanceof CheckIfTrue then
2:    return(CheckIfTrue)from.isTrue();
3: end if
4: return true;
```

CASE STUDY

To illustrate an example of the possible uses of the Composability Formalisms, this section describes a simplified version of a model of the distributed registration system designed for tracking detailed data about transformation and distribution in the agri-food sector .

Data transactions are supported by a communication protocol that implements the well-known two-phase commit (2PC) schema.

The use of a careful exception handling based design can improve the availability of the system. An evaluation of the availability of the system, which is improved by the use of exception handling, is the goal of the study.

The system is composed of three subsystems: an Official Registry (OR), managed by a governmental authority, open to public consultation; a Company Registry (CR), private and managed by a company or a third party, that publishes only the non-confidential part of the stored complete information about the production; and a Tracking Manager (TM), that registers the operations performed on a site. Every registration operation by a TM, operated as a distributed 2PC transition,

number of elements in a queue or the number of tokens in a Place) is greater than or less than the weight attribute of the arc. For example, *CheckGE* and *CheckLT* arcs can interconnect an element from a performance oriented submodel to a Fault Tree (FT) gate. Finally, *CheckCplx* interconnects the TopEvent of a FT to a custom Testing Formalism (TF), which describes a sequence of events that occur in order to achieve a certain state in an automaton-like fashion. For example, a condition that can be verified is if the TopEvent of an FT is true or false.

The *isTrue* behaviors for *CheckGe*, *CheckLT* and *CheckCplx* are shown in algorithms 6, 7 and 8.

involves a CR for internal information computing and an OR for the related certification issues.

A multiformalism availability model of the system is shown in Figure 2. The model has been written using a combined formalism that includes GSPN extended with exception handling to capture the transactional operations, and FT to evaluate the influence of faults. Faults in the TM are neglected. The formalism includes common primitives for immediate and timed transitions, places and related arcs (GSPN), AND, OR gates and events and related arcs (FT).

Some unusual symbols are also used: exception triggering elements (marked with an E in a square), catch elements (ovals), and inter-formalism arcs. Exception triggering elements behave normally, but throw an exception interrupting their usual behavior according to a deterministic (hardware failure, restore in Figure 2) or a probabilistic condition (1stphase in Figure 2). Catch elements act on a submodel (OR, CR, TM) changing the conditions of their internal elements when the related exception is triggered. Interformalism arcs connect elements of different formalisms (e.g. if one of the CPUko places in Figure 2 is marked, the arc transforms this condition into a fault input for the corresponding OR gate). OR and CR are modeled by submodels that present the same structure.

Such submodels are composed of two parts. The left part is modeled by a GSPN that implements the server component of the 2PC protocol. It includes the possibility that a transaction may fail and raise a restore exception in the first phase.

The right part of the submodel, is composed of three GSPNs that represent the working condition of three critical repairable components (HD1, HD2 and CPU), and a FT that throws an exception whenever the combined effect of component failures result in a system fault. TM is modeled by a GSPN that implements the client part of the 2PC protocol which throws a restore exception to handle a failure in the protocol due to a fault in TM or OR. UM represents user requests by a simple GSPN.

The INTERCONNECTION NETWORK allows the proper interconnection between OR, CR and TM, and it is modeled with a proper GSPN.

Evaluation Results

The model has been analyzed using different parameters.

Results were computed by the SIMTHESys analytical solving engine. The rates have been chosen to match typical values collected from various literatures. The parameters marked by a star have been scaled to study the system performance under different rates. In particular, all the marked parameters have been multiplied by the same factor in the different experiments. Figure 3 (left) shows the throughput of the system considering a model M_1 without faults and a model M_2 where software and hardware exceptions can occur during the first phase (Malformed req.).

Both the models use the parameters in Table 1 although for M_1 all the rates of the fault transitions and the probability of the exception throwing nOk have been set to zero. Figure 3 (right) shows the relative distance between the throughput of tUser in models M_1 and M_2. This value has been calculated as $(TM_1 - TM_2)/TM_2$ where TM_1 and TM_2 represent the system throughput in the best case (i.e. no faults occurring) and in the worst case (i.e. both software and hardware faults occurring).

FUTURE RESEARCH DIRECTIONS

Future work will include i) a more user-friendly language to develop the Behaviors (currently, Java-based Behaviors may limit usability), ii) new techniques in order to cope with large state spaces, stiff systems and non-finite CTMC and iii) an extension of the framework in order to support formalism inheritance.

Figure 2. System model

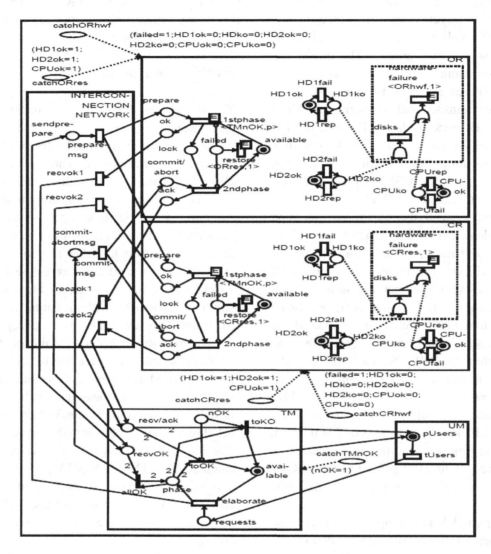

Figure 3. System throughput and unreliability

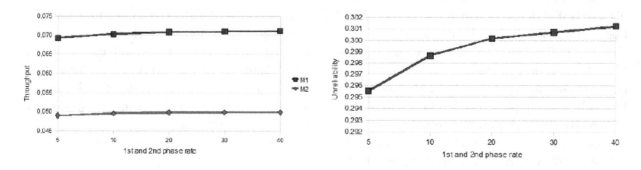

Table 1. Parameters of the agri-food model

Transition	Rate
preparemsg, commitmsg	5.00000E-01
recvok1, recvok2	5.00000E-01
recvack1, recvack2	5.00000E-01
firstPhase*, secondPhase2*	2.00000E+01
CPU Fault	3.12500E-09
HDD Fault	8.33000E-09
CPU Repair	5.55000E-04
HDD Repair	2.77000E-04
Restore	9.25000E-05
tUsers	2.50000E-01

CONCLUSION

This chapter has presented SIMTHESys, a framework for the definition of new formalisms and the generation of related solvers. Its novelty consists of the following aspects: i) it separates the component defining the formalism and implementing the solver for it, from the component solving the model; ii) it provides an open architecture as potentially any kind of formalisms (i.e. not only stochastic) can be added, assuming that a proper solution engine is build; iii) it offers a high degree of flexibility as new formalisms (or extension of the existing ones) can be easily added to the framework by creating a new FDL file, iv) it reduces the code required to specify a new formalism compared with other tools (e.g. SMART, DEDS tool box, Möbius and OsMoSys) and finally v) it clearly separates the syntactic components from the semantic components of a formalism.

With regard of model structure, OsMoSys and SIMTHESys share the main organization: both of them represent a main metaformalims (metametamodel) on which formalisms (metamodels) are based, and that specify the elements included in models; OsMoSys provides formalism inheritance (at formalism and element level, though SIMTHESys doesn't yet), while both of them can extend formalisms by adding new elements.

Both allow model composition by inclusion of submodels, with OsMoSys supporting generic submodels and information hiding. Both support multiformalism models with bridge formalisms, while SIMTHESys also allows Interformalism connection elements and a more flexible interaction. The main difference between OsMoSys and SIMTHESys lays in the description capabilities of the metaformalism, due to the different aims of the two projects.

While OsMoSys metaformalism is a consistent foundation for the description of static aspects of formalisms elements and constraints (mainly syntactical), SIMTHESys metaformalism has been designed to describe both static and dynamic aspects (specially focusing on execution semantics of the elements of a formalism), to allow a further customization of the framework. With regard of the possibility of augmenting the supported formalisms set, adding in SIMTHESys a new formalism just requires the XML description of its elements properties and semantics, in terms of use of one or more elementary solvers (as SIMTHESys is oriented to rapid formalism development). Eventually, the development of a new elementary solver is requested, if the new formalism is based on a completely different logic with respect to the existing ones.

Concerning multiformalism, SIMTHESys and OsMoSys support the creation of multiformalism models by composition of submodels written in different formalisms by using metamodeling. Both OsMoSys and SIMTHESys use a Composition Formalism. However, SIMTHESYS derives the underlying CTMC from the analyzed model; in this way, it is not necessary to consider mechanisms sharing results between sub-models.

Regarding multisolution (i.e. the capability of solving a model by integrating different existing performance evaluation tools), Möbius and SIMTHESys present some similarities in the generation of the final solver. Such solver is synthesized automatically, but in the case of SIMTHESys, a solver that can solve all models based on the same formalisms combination is generated. OsMoSys can solve models by using its workflow engine executing a generated business process describing how external solvers are invoked to generate a solution.

REFERENCES

Barbierato, E., & Iacono, M. et al. (2012). The SIMTHESys multiformalism modeling framework. *Computers & Mathematics with Applications (Oxford, England)*, *64*(12), 3828–3839. doi:10.1016/j.camwa.2012.03.009.

Bause, F. (1993). Queueing petri nets - A formalism for the combined qualitative and quantitative analysis of systems. In *Proceedings of 5th International Workshop on Petri nets and Performance Models*. IEEE Computer Society.

Bause, F. (1994). QPN-tool for qualitative and quantitative analysis of queueing Petri nets. In *Proceedings of the 7th International Conference on Computer Performance Evaluation: Modelling Techniques and Tools*. Vienna, Austria: Springer-Verlag.

Bause, F., Buchholz, P., et al. (1998). A toolbox for functional and quantitative analysis of DEDS. In *Proceedings of the 10th International Conference on Computer Performance Evaluation: Modelling Techniques and Tools*. Berlin: Springer-Verlag.

Best, E., & Devillers, R. et al. (2001). *Petri net algebra*. Berlin: Springer Publishing Company, Incorporated. doi:10.1007/978-3-662-04457-5.

Booch, G. (1994). *Object-oriented analysis and design with applications* (2nd ed.). New York: Benjamin-Cummings Publishing Co., Inc.

Boulanger, F. (2008). Simulation of multi-formalism models with ModHel'X. In *Proceedings of the 2008 International Conference on Software Testing, Verification, and Validation*. IEEE Computer Society.

Bucci, G., Sassoli, L., et al. (2004). ORIS: A tool for state-space analysis of real-time preemptive systems. In *Proceedings of the The Quantitative Evaluation of Systems, First International Conference*. IEEE Computer Society.

Ciardo, G., & Jones, R. L. et al. (2006). Logic and stochastic modeling with SMART. *Performance Evaluation*, *63*(6), 578–608. doi:10.1016/j.peva.2005.06.001.

Ciocchetta, F., & Hillston, J. (2009). Bio-PEPA: A framework for the modelling and analysis of biological systems. *Theoretical Computer Science*, *410*(33-34), 3065–3084. doi:10.1016/j.tcs.2009.02.037.

Clark, A. (2008). State-aware performance analysis with eXtended stochastic probes. In *Proceedings of the 5th European Performance Engineering Workshop on Computer Performance Engineering*. Palma de Mallorca, Spain: Springer-Verlag.

Clark, G., Courtney, T., et al. (2001). The Möbius modeling tool. In *Proceedings of the 9th international Workshop on Petri Nets and Performance Models* (PNPM'01). IEEE Computer Society.

de Lara, J. (2002). AToM3: A tool for multi-formalism and meta-modelling. In *Proceedings of the 5th International Conference on Fundamental Approaches to Software Engineering*. Berlin: Springer-Verlag.

Ehrig, H., & Hoffmann, K. et al. (2006). Transformations of petri nets. *Electronic Notes in Theoretical Computer Science*, *148*(1), 151–172. doi:10.1016/j.entcs.2005.12.016.

Franceschinis, G., Gribaudo, M., et al. (2002). *Towards an object based multi-formalism multi-solution modeling approach*. Paper presented at the Second International Workshop on Modelling of Objects, Components, and Agents (MOCA'02). Aarhus, Denmark.

Gholizadeh, H. M. (2010). A meta-model based approach for definition of a multi-formalism modeling framework. *International Journal of Computer Theory and Engineering*, 2, 87–95.

Gribaudo, M., Raiteri-Codetta, D., et al. (2005). DrawNET, a customizable multi-formalism, multi-solution tool for the quantitative evaluation of systems. In *Proceedings of QEST 2005*. QEST.

Hamadi, R. (2003). A Petri net-based model for web service composition. In *Proceedings of the 14th Australasian Database Conference* (vol. 17). Adelaide, Australia: Australian Computer Society, Inc.

Hoare, C. (1985). *Communicating sequential processes*. Upper Saddle River, NJ: Prentice-Hall, Inc.

Kwiatkowska, M., Gethin, N., et al. (2011). PRISM 4.0: Verification of probabilistic real-time systems. In *Proceedings of the 23rd International Conference on Computer Aided Verification*. Snowbird, UT: Springer-Verlag.

Laprie, J. C. (1992). *Dependability: Basic concepts and terminology*. New York: Springer-Verlag.

Milner, R. (1989). *Communication and concurrency*. Upper Saddle River, NJ: Prentice-Hall, Inc.

Muppala, J. K., & Ciardo, G. et al. (1994). *Stochastic reward nets for reliability prediction*. Communications in Reliability, Maintainability and Serviceability.

Obal, W. D. (1999). State-space support for path-based reward variables. *Performance Evaluation*, 35(3-4), 233–251. doi:10.1016/S0166-5316(99)00010-3.

Sanders, W. (2002). *Stochastic activity networks: Formal definitions and concepts*. New York: Springer-Verlag.

SISC. (2000). *IEEE standard for modeling and simulation high level architecture (HLA) - framework and rules*. Washington, DC: IEEE.

Szabo, C. (2007). On syntactic composability and model reuse. In *Proceedings of the First Asia International Conference on Modelling & Simulation*. IEEE Computer Society.

Total, R., & Development. (2007). *Grif*. Retrieved from http://grif-workshop.com/3

Trivedi, K. S. (2002). SHARPE 2002: Symbolic hierarchical automated reliability and performance evaluator. In *Proceedings of the 2002 International Conference on Dependable Systems and Networks*. IEEE Computer Society.

Walter, M., Munchen, T. U., et al. (2009). Lares: A novel approach for describing system reconfigurability in dependability models of fault-tolerant systems. In *Proceedings of European Safety and Reliability Conference* (ESREL 2009). New York: Taylor and Francis Ltd.

ADDITIONAL READING

Barbierato, E., Bobbio, A., et al. (2012). Multiformalism to Support Software Rejuvenation Modeling. Proceedings of the 2012 IEEE 23rd International Symposium on Software Reliability Engineering Workshops, IEEE Computer Society.

Barbierato, E., Cerotti, D., et al. (2011). A tool suite for modelling spatial interdependencies of distributed systems with markovian agents. Proceedings of the 8th European conference on Computer Performance Engineering. Borrowdale, UK, Springer-Verlag.

Barbierato, E., Gribaudo, M., et al. (2011). Performability modeling of exceptions-aware systems in multiformalism tools. Proceedings of the 18th international conference on Analytical and stochastic modeling techniques and applications. Venice, Italy, Springer-Verlag.

Barbierato, E., & Gribaudo, M. et al. (2011). Defining Formalisms for Performance Evaluation With SIMTHESys. *Electronic Notes in Theoretical Computer Science*, *275*, 37–51. doi:10.1016/j.entcs.2011.09.004.

Barbierato, E., Gribaudo, M., et al. (2011). Exploiting multiformalism models for testing and performance evaluation in SIMTHESys. Proceedings of the 5th International ICST Conference on Performance Evaluation Methodologies and Tools. Paris, France, ICST (Institute for Computer Sciences, Social-Informatics and Telecommunications Engineering).

Barbierato, E., & Gribaudo, M. et al. (2012). *SIMTHESysER: a tool generator for the performance evaluation of multiformalism models*. Caserta, Università degli Studi di Napoli, Belvedere Reale di San Leucio.

Barbierato, E., Iacono, M., et al. (2012). Perfbpel: a graph-based approach for the performance analysis of BPEL SOA applications. 6th International Conference on Performance Evaluation Methodologies and Tools VALUETOOLS.

Clark G., & S. W. H. (2001). Implementing a Stochastic Process Algebra within the Möbius Modeling Framework. Proceedings of the Joint International Workshop on Process Algebra and Probabilistic Methods, Performance Modeling and Verification, Springer-Verlag.

Colom, J. M. (2001). *K. M.* Application and Theory of Petri Nets Springer.

Deavours, D., & Clark, G. et al. (2002). The Möbius Framework and Its Implementation. *IEEE Transactions on Software Engineering*, *28*(10), 956–969. doi:10.1109/TSE.2002.1041052.

Franceschinis G., Gribaudo M., et al. (2004). Compositional modeling of complex systems: Contact center scenarios in OsMoSys. ICATPN'04.

Gribaudo, M., & Sereno, M. (1997). GSPN Semantics for Queueing Networks with Blocking. Proceedings of the 6th International Workshop on Petri Nets and Performance Models, IEEE Computer Society.

Hutton G., & W. J. (2004). Compiling Exceptions Correctly. 7th International Conference on Mathematics of Program Construction, Springer.

Iacono M., & G. M. (2010). Element Based Semantics in Multi Formalism Performance Models. Proceedings of the 2010 IEEE International Symposium on Modeling, Analysis and Simulation of Computer and Telecommunication Systems, IEEE Computer Society.

Nicol, M. D., & Sanders, W. H. et al. (2004). Model-Based Evaluation: From Dependability to Security. *IEEE Transactions on Dependable and Secure Computing*, *1*(1), 48–65. doi:10.1109/TDSC.2004.11.

Pai G. J., & D. J. B. (2002). Automatic Synthesis of Dynamic Fault Trees from UML System Models. Proceedings of the 13th International Symposium on Software Reliability Engineering, IEEE Computer Society.

Raiteri-Codetta, D. I. M., et al. (2004). Repairable Fault Tree for the Automatic Evaluation of Repair Policies. Proceedings of the 2004 International Conference on Dependable Systems and Networks, IEEE Computer Society.

Sanders W. H., Courtney T., et al. (2007). Multiformalism and multi-solution-method modeling frameworks: the Möbius approach.

Steinbauer G. and W. F. (2007). Combining quantitative and qualitative models with active observations for better diagnoses of autonomous mobile robots. 5th Workshop on Intelligent Solutions in Embedded Systems.

Xinhong, H., Hiroshi, M., et al. (2007). A Petri net-based approach to modeling and analysis of component-based distributed real-time systems. Proceedings of the 11th IASTED International Conference on Software Engineering and Applications. Cambridge, Massachusetts, ACTA Press.

KEY TERMS AND DEFINITIONS

Composability: A technique used to compose models in a valid way.

Composition Formalism: A formalism to compose heterogeneous models.

FDL: Within SIMTHESys, Formalisms are described by the Formalism Description Language (FDL).

Interfaces: A component of the SIMTHESys architecture capable to support the definition of the formalism families (exponential events and exponential and immediate events based) in order to enable the access to solving engines.

MDL: Within SIMTHESys, Models are described in a Model Definition Language (MDL) according to the FDL file.

Multiformalism: A sound technique to specify a complex system as the composition of a set of sub-components. Each sub-component is modeled according to the best suited formalism.

SIMTHESys: A framework for the development of modeling languages and the solution of multiformalism models.

Chapter 6

A Meta–Model Based Approach to the Definition of the Analysis Results of Petri Net Models

Simona Bernardi[1]
Centro Universitario de la Defensa, Spain

José Merseguer
Universidad de Zaragoza, Spain

ABSTRACT

Multi-formalism modeling techniques enable the modeling and analysis of different aspects of a system. One of the main issues in the integration of multiple tools to support multi-formalisms is how to provide a common method to report the results of the analysis and how to interchange them between models, based on different formalisms, that often represent the system behavior at different granularity levels. In this chapter, the authors focus on the Petri Net formalism, and they present a preliminary work toward the definition of a common XML-based language for the specification of the results obtained from the analysis of Petri net models. The authors use a meta-model based approach, where first a structured set of meta-models representing the Petri net result concepts and their relationships are defined. Then, model transformation rules enable the mapping of meta-models to XML constructs.

INTRODUCTION

Multi-formalism modeling and solution techniques enable the modeling and analysis of different aspects of a complex system. Two main approaches have been followed for the design and implementation of modeling tools supporting such techniques. One approach consists in building an integrated modeling framework from scratch, that accommodates multiple modeling formalisms, multiple ways to combine models expressed in different formalisms and multiple solution methods (e.g., Sanders et al., 2003; Gribaudo et al., 2006; Vittorini et al., 2004; Barbierato et al., 2011; Iacono et al., 2012). The other approach is based on the integration of multiple tools, each one supporting a single modeling formalism and a set of solution techniques, in a common software environment. For example, in the Software Performance Engineering field (e.g., Smith & Williams, 2002; and many years of activities in the main workshops and conferences in the field, such as

DOI: 10.4018/978-1-4666-4659-9.ch006

WOSP, ICPE, SIGMETRICS or SIGSOFT), most of the works that propose model-2-model (M2M) transformations from semi-formal specifications (e.g., UML, AADL) to performance/dependability formal models (Balsamo et al., 2004; Bernardi et al., 2012b) follow this second approach to provide a tool support for the application of their methods.

The multiple tool integration implies several issues to be tackled; in particular, concerning the results obtained from the model analysis, how to provide a common method for reporting them and how to enable tool interoperability such that the results obtained using one tool can be used as input parameters in another tool.

A common language to express the analysis results can be a solution to the aforementioned issues. In this paper, we focus on the Petri net formalism and we present a preliminary work toward the definition of a common XML-based language for the specification of the results obtained from the analysis of Petri net models.

Although the focus is on a single formalism, it should be observed that different *dialects* of Petri net exists, in the literature, which share common base concepts of the formalism as well as analysis techniques.

Moreover, some Petri net analysis techniques produce results that actually are models expressed in lower-level formalisms (e.g., state space-based techniques developed for Stochastic Petri Net boil down to the generation of Continuous Time Markov Chains). Then a language that supports the specification of such results also support the specification of such lower-level formalisms.

We follow the meta-model based approach described in (Hillah et al., 2009), where reference meta-models for untimed Petri Nets (PN) are defined first, then, using model-to-text transformation rules, the former are mapped to XML constructs (i.e., elements, attributes) which define the syntax of the ISO/IEC standard Petri Net Markup Language (PNML) (ISO/IEC15909-1, 2004; ISO/IEC15909-2, 2011).

As sketched in Figure 1, the *PNResults meta-models*, proposed in this paper, are related to the standard PN meta-models, since some PN concepts represented in the latter are refined in the former. In turn, the proposed XML language obtained by applying the transformation rules, namely *PNRESML*, enables to relate PNRESML documents - that specify the results from the analysis of a concrete Petri Net model - to the PNML documents describing the Petri net models used for the analysis.

The paper is organized as follows. The next Section introduces the meta-model based approach used to define PNML. The third Section describes the structured set of meta-models that represent the results of the analysis of a Petri net model and the mapping of the meta-models to PNRESML is presented. Finally, in the fourth and fifth Sections we discuss future work and draw conclusions.

BACKGROUND

The basic concepts of the Petri net formalism have been defined in (ISO/IEC15909-1, 2004) with meta-models, in terms of UML class diagrams. Figure 2 provides an overview of the Petri net meta-model packages and their *merge* relationships. Currently the standard covers untimed Petri nets, in particular Place/Transition nets (*PT-Net*), symmetric nets and high-level Petri nets (*HLPNG*).

Figure 3 shows the *PNML Core* and *PT-Net* meta-models, the part related to the graphical representation of a Petri Net has been omitted

Figure 1. Meta-model based approach

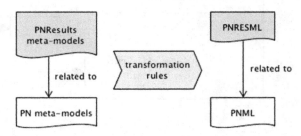

Figure 2. Petri net meta-model package overview

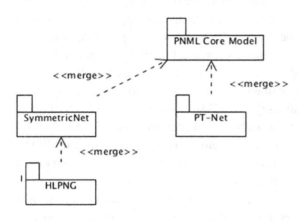

since it is not relevant in this paper. The former defines a *Petri Net document* that contains one or more *Petri Nets*. A *Petri Net* is a labeled directed graph, where all types of specific information of the net is represented by *labels*. There are two kinds of labels: *annotations* and *attributes*. The former are used to represent information typically expressed as text, such as place marking, arc expressions, etc. The latter enable to assign a graphical representation to the labeled object, i.e., arc type. The graph structure of a *Petri Net* is represented by *objects*, which have unique identifiers. An object can be either a *node* or an *arc*. Nodes, i.e., *places* and *transitions*, can be con-

Figure 3. PNML Core and PT-Net meta-models (ISO/IEC15909-1, 2004)

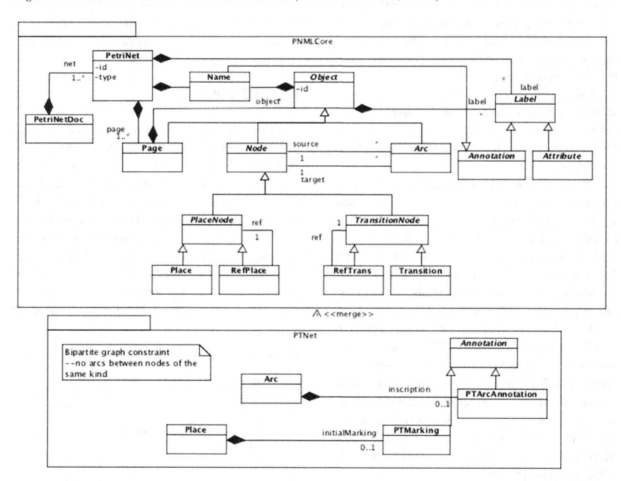

nected by arcs. The concepts of *reference place/transition* are also introduced to enable the specification of a Petri net in different *pages*.

The *PNML Core* meta-model is meant to represent the basic concepts of a Petri net, which have to be refined when specific Petri net classes are considered. Figure 3 (bottom) shows the *PT-Nets* meta-model where concrete annotations are added to *places* and *arcs* that is, respectively, the *initial marking* and the multiplicities (*inscription*). Moreover, the bipartite graph structural restriction (i.e., an arc must not connect a place to a place or a transition to a transition) is also added.

The meta-models are then mapped into a concrete XML syntax, i.e., PNML. In particular, each concrete class corresponds to an XML element, while the attributes and association ends correspond to XML attributes. The composition associations in the meta-models enable to define the tree-structure of the XML document, i.e., the composed classes of a composite class become child XML elements of the XML element. We will use a similar mapping approach in this work. The PNML specification of the Petri net in Figure 4 is shown in Table 1, where the graphical information has been omitted.

META-MODEL AND MODEL-TO-TEXT MAPPING

In this Section, we propose a structured set of meta-models that represent the results coming from the analysis of a Petri net model. Since the results are strictly related to the Petri net model used for the analysis, the new concepts introduced rely on the Petri net meta-models introduced in the previous Section. Figure 5 shows a package overview of the meta-models and their *merge* relationships, which enable to extend already defined concepts in an incremental manner. The green rounded rectangle includes the contribution of this paper. The organization of the packages follows the one introduced by the ISO/IEC stan-

Figure 4. A P/T net model

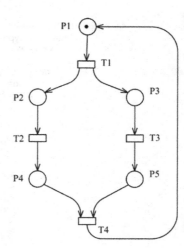

dard: so the *PNResults* package contains the basic concepts and is related to the *Core PNML*. Such concepts are reused, and refined, when considering the analysis results of a P/T net (*PT-NetResults*). In particular, different analysis techniques can be used to prove qualitative properties of a P/T model, such as boundedness, liveness and reversibility. Each technique may produce different kinds of results. The inner packages of *PT-NetResults* reflect the most well-known techniques that are conventionally classified as (Colom et al., 1998):

- **Linear Algebra Techniques:** Based on the computation of P- and T-semiflows.
- **Linear Programming Techniques:** Based on the statement of proper linear programming problems to compute bounds on place markings or transition enablings.
- **Enumeration Techniques:** Based on the construction of a reachability graph which represents the net markings and the single transition firings between them.

Observe that some P/T net techniques have not been considered in the Figure since they do not produce analysis results: for example, simulation of P/T models mainly boils down to play the token game to understand the modeled

Table 1. PNML specification of a P/T model

```
<pnml xmlns="http://www.pnml.org/version-2009/grammar/pnml">
    <net id="net1" type="http://www.pnml.org/version-2009/grammar/ptnet">
        <name>
            <text>example</text>
        </name>
        <page id="page1-net1">
            <place id="P1">
                <initialMarking>
                    <text>1</text>
                </initialMarking>
            </place>
            <place id="P2"> </place>
            <place id="P3"> </place>
            <place id="P4"> </place>
            <place id="P5"> </place>
            <transition id="T1"> </transition>
            <transition id="T2"> </transition>
            <transition id="T3"> </transition>
            <transition id="T4"> </transition>
            <arc id="a0" source="P1" target="T1"> </arc>
            <arc id="a1" source="T4" target="P1"> </arc>
            <arc id="a2" source="T1" target="P2"> </arc>
            <arc id="a3" source="P2" target="T2"> </arc>
            <arc id="a4" source="T2" target="P4"> </arc>
            <arc id="a5" source="T1" target="P3"> </arc>
            <arc id="a6" source="P3" target="T3"> </arc>
            <arc id="a7" source="T3" target="P5"> </arc>
            <arc id="a8" source="P5" target="T4"> </arc>
            <arc id="a9" source="P4" target="T4"> </arc>
        </page>
    </net>
</pnml>
```

Figure 5. Petri Net Results meta-model package overview

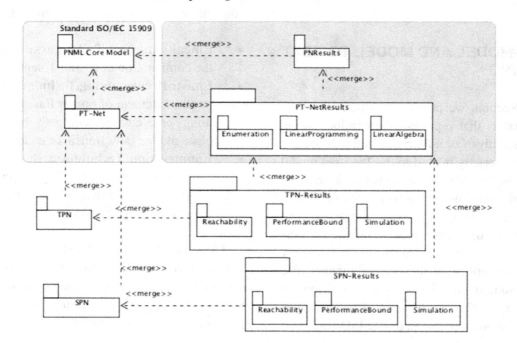

system rather than prove properties. Focusing on some Petri net classes amenable to quantitative analysis purposes, like performance analysis, other packages have been added that reuse the concepts of the *PT-Net* package. Such packages should identify the concepts of Time Petri Nets (Bethomieu & Diaz, 1991) and Stochastic Petri Nets (Florin & Natkin, 1985).

Although they are still not part of the standard, several Petri net tools support PNML-like specifications where timing/stochastic information is captured by specific XML elements (e.g., firing delay intervals for TPN (Berthomieu & Vernadat, 2006), firing rates in SPN (Bonet et al, 2007)). Besides, different but similar analysis techniques can be used for TPN and SPN: packages *TPN-Results* and *SPN-Results* include the concepts related to the analysis results of TPN and SPN, respectively.

In the following we detail the *PNResults* and *PT-NetResults* meta-models.

PN Results Meta-Model

The *PNResults* package contains a single meta-class *ResultDoc* that represents the documents containing the results obtained from the analysis of a Petri net model (see Figure 6.) A concrete document, that is an instance of the *ResultsDoc* meta-class, is associated to the PNML document (*PetriNetDoc*) which specifies the Petri net model

Figure 6. PN results meta-model

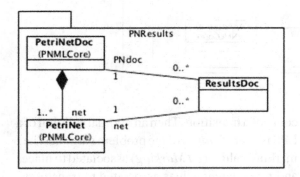

used for the analysis as well as to the *Petri net* itself (since a PNML document can specify more than one Petri net model).

P/T Net Results Meta-Models

We have defined three meta-models (one for each inner package) that capture the concepts related to the results of the analysis carried out on a P/T net model. They are shown in Figures 7, 8 and 9.

Linear algebra techniques mainly consist in the computation of the semiflows of a P/T nets that lead to invariant laws on the possible behavior (i.e., token conservation law and cyclic behavior law). Figure 7 represents the semiflows of a P/T net, that is the integer and non negative solutions of the linear systems of equations: $\mathbf{yC} = \mathbf{0}$ (P-semiflows) and $\mathbf{Cx} = \mathbf{0}$ (T-semiflow), where $\mathbf{C}$ is the incidence matrix of the P/T net. So a PN results document (*ResultsDoc*) may contain the specification of the *semiflows* associated to a P/T net model. Each semiflow has a unique identifier (*id*) and is related either to places (*Psemiflow*) or to transitions (*Tsemiflow*). A P-semiflow $\mathbf{y}$ is a *P*-vector, where *P* is the number of places of the net: the class *Yentry* represents the non null entries of y. Each entry has a positive integer *value* and refers to a place of the P/T net model. Similar consideration holds for T-semiflows.

Linear programming techniques for P/T net models are used to draw conclusions about the net boundedness & liveness. Figure 8 represents the results obtained from the application of linear programming techniques on P/T net models. A PN results document (*ResultsDoc*) may contain solutions of proper linear programming problems stated to compute either *structural bounds* on place marking or transition *enabling bounds*. All the linear programming problems stated for this purpose are characterized by the same set of variables and constraints, while they differ from the objective function (to be maximized). The variables are the marking M of places and the firing count σ of transitions, the set of constraints are the net state equations (i.e., $M - M_0 = C \cdot \sigma$,

Figure 7. P/T net results meta-model: linear algebra

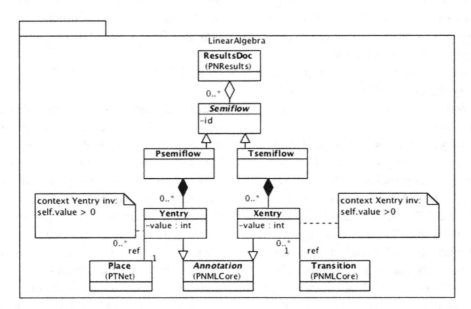

Figure 8. PT-Net results meta-model: linear programming

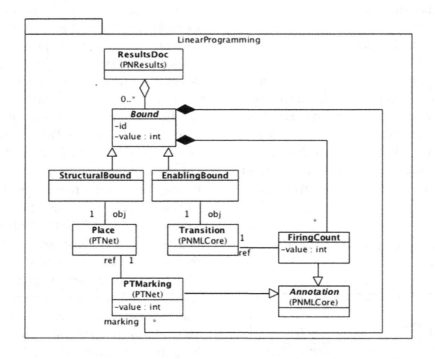

M_0 is the initial marking of the net and **C** is the incidence matrix) and the non negative constraints of the problem variables. The objective function can be either the marking of a place or the firing count of a transition. Then an optimal solution of a LPP is a set of *values* of the problem variables, i.e., marking values (*PTMarking*) associated to places and *firing count* values associated to transitions.

Figure 9. PT-Net results meta-model: enumeration

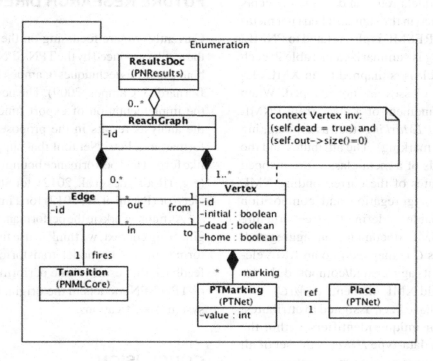

Obviously, we are interested in documenting also the *bound value* associated either to a place (*StructuralBound*) or to a transition (*EnablingBound*), depending on the type of bound.

Enumeration techniques are based on the construction of the reachability graph, in case of bounded P/T nets, or in the coverability graph, in case of unbounded P/T nets. Such graphs are then used to verify qualitative properties (e.g., liveness, mutual exclusion, reversibility, etc.). Figure 9 shows the meta-model representing the reachability graph associated to a P/T net, that is a result of the analysis. A PN results document (*ResultsDoc*) may contain the *reachability graphs* associated to a P/T net model: observe that different reachability graphs can be generated depending on the initial marking set to the P/T net model, so a unique identifier *id* is associated to each graph. A reachability graph is a directed graph that consists of *vertices* and *edges*: a vertex represents a marking of the P/T net (*PTMarking*) while an edge represents the *firing* of a transition *from* a marking where the latter is enabled. The

transition firing lead *to* a new marking. The reachability graph contains at least one vertex, i.e., the *initial* one corresponding to the initial marking of the P/T net. Several properties can be associated to a vertex: a vertex corresponding to a deadlock marking (i.e., marking from which no transition is fireable) is *dead*. A vertex is an *home* state if its corresponding marking can be reached from any other reachable marking of the net.

Model to XML Transformation

The meta-models previously described are the source models in a model-to-text transformation (M2T), where the target is the XML syntax used to generate XML documents specifying the results of the analysis of Petri net models that we call *PNRESML* (Figure 1).

The transformation rules used to map the modelling elements of the Petri net results meta-models to PNRESML are similar to those proposed in (Hillah et al., 2009) to transform Petri Net meta-models to PNML. As the Petri net results meta-models reuse and refine concepts originally defined in the standard Petri net meta-models, the PNRESML is also related to PNML.

The mapping is summarized in Table 2: each concrete meta-class is mapped to an XML element. Abstract classes are not mapped. When a class is a refinement of a class from PNML packages (e.g., *PTMarking*) then a new mapping is defined (e.g. marking). The attributes and the association-ends of a meta-class *C* are mapped to XML attributes of the corresponding XML element *M(C)*. Aggregation and composition associations enable to define the tree-structure of the PNRESML document: an aggregated/composite class *C* is mapped into an XML element *M(C)* and its aggregated/composed classes become the child XML elements of *M(C)*.

Data-types have been assigned to attributes: *ID* is the set of unique identifiers within the document. The data-type *IDRef* is the set of all identifiers, they are used to make reference to identifiers. In particular, the *ref* values correspond to the place/transition identifiers in the PNML document representing the PN model used to get the analysis results. Indeed, a PNRESML document is associated to the PNML document of the Petri net model: *pnresml*, i.e., the root element in the XML tree-structure, has two attributes *PNdoc* and *net* whose values indicate, respectively, the name of the PNML document and the Petri net model identifier within the PNML document. The rest of data-types in Table 2 (column 3) are self-explanatory.

It is useful to show two concrete PNRESML documents, related to the PNML document *example.pnml* in the background Section. Table 3 includes information about the minimal semiflows of the P/T net model of Figure 4, computed using linear algebra techniques:

Table 4 specifies the reachability graph of the running example, generated using enumeration techniques:

FUTURE RESEARCH DIRECTIONS

Currently, we are focussing on the definition of the results produced by the TPN/SPN performance bound analysis techniques (Campos & Silva, 1992; Bernardi & Campos, 2009). The next step will be the implementation of export functionalities of the analysis results in the proposed *PNRESML* format, in a Petri Net tool that supports PNML-like format and performance bounding techniques (e.g., (Rodrigues et al., 2012), for Stochastic Petri Nets, or (Pacini et al., 2012) for Time Petri Nets).

As future work, in the performance software engineering context, we think to use the PNRESML format in text-to-model transformations which feedback the results of the performance analysis of TPN/SPN models in the original UML-based system specifications.

CONCLUSION

We have presented a preliminary work toward the definition of a common XML-based language for specifying the results obtained from the analysis of Petri net models. We have followed a meta-model based approach: first, a set of structured meta-models capturing the concepts of Petri net results and their relationships is defined; then, the XML syntax of the language (*PNRESML*) is derived by applying model-to-text transformation rules.

The definition of the meta-models for Time Petri Nets (TPN) and Stochastic Petri Nets (SPN) is an on-going work; since the analysis result concepts are related to PN concepts, an effort should be made to consider how specific TPN/SPN concepts (e.g., timing and stochastic specifications) are expressed in the proprietary formats of TPN/SPN tools (e.g., Ciardo & Miner; Starke; GreatSPN) in order to use a common terminology in the meta-models.

Table 2. Mapping of the Petri Net results meta-models onto XML

PNResults Package		
Class	**XML Element**	**XML Attribute**
ResultsDoc	<pnresml>	xmlns: anyURI
		PNdoc: PNMLdoc
		net: IDRef (Net)
PT-NetResults::LinearAlgebra Package		
Class	**XML Element**	**XML Attribute**
Psemiflow	<psemiflow>	id: ID
Tsemiflow	<tsemiflow>	id: ID
Yentry	<y>	value: positiveInteger
		ref:IDRef (Place)
Xentry	<x>	value: positiveInteger
		ref:IDRef (Transition)
PT-NetResults::LinearProgramming Package		
Class	**XML Element**	**XML Attribute**
StructuralBound	<structuralbound>	id:ID
		value: nonNegativeInteger
		obj:IDRef (Place)
EnablingBound	<enablingbound>	id:ID
		value: nonNegativeInteger
		obj:IDRef (Transition)
PTMarking	<marking>	value: nonNegativeInteger
		ref: IDRef (Place)
FiringCount	<firingcount>	value: nonNegativeInteger
		ref: IDRef (Transition)
PT-NetResults::Enumeration Package		
Class	**XML Element**	**XML Attribute**
ReachGraph	<rg>	id:ID
Vertex	<vertex>	id:ID
		initial: boolean
		dead: boolean
		home: boolean
Edge	<edge>	id:ID
		from: IDRef (Vertex)
		to: IDRef (Vertex)
		fires: IDRef (Transition)
PTMarking	<marking>	value: nonNegativeInteger
		ref: IDRef (Place)

Table 3. Minimal semiflows of the P/T net model of Figure 4

```xml
<pnresml xmlns="http://cud.unizar.es/bernardi/pnresults" PNdoc="example.pnml" net="net1">
      <psemiflow id="Y1">
                <y value=1 ref="P1"></y>
                <y value=1 ref="P2"></y>
                <y value=1 ref="P4"></y>
      </psemiflow>
      <psemiflow id="Y2">
                <y value=1 ref="P1"></y>
                <y value=1 ref="P3"></y>
                <y value=1 ref="P5"></y>
      </psemiflow>
      <tsemiflow id="X1">
                <x value=1 ref="T1"></x>
                <x value=1 ref="T2"></x>
                <x value=1 ref="T3"></x>
                <x value=1 ref="T4"></x>
      </tsemiflow>

</pnresml>
```

Table 4. Reachability graph of the P/T net model of Figure 4

```xml
<pnresml xmlns="http://cud.unizar.es/bernardi/pnresults" PNdoc="example.pnml" net="net1">
      <rg id="R1">
                <vertex id="M1" initial="true" dead="false" home="true">
                      <marking value=1 ref="P1"></marking>
                </vertex>
                <vertex id="M2" initial="false" dead="false" home="true">
                      <marking value=1 ref="P2"></marking>
                      <marking value=1 ref="P3"></marking>
                </vertex>
                <vertex id="M3" initial="false" dead="false" home="true">
                      <marking value=1 ref="P3"></marking>
                      <marking value=1 ref="P4"></marking>
                </vertex>
                <vertex id="M4" initial="false" dead="false" home="true">
                      <marking value=1 ref="P2"></marking>
                      <marking value=1 ref="P5"></marking>
                </vertex>
                <vertex id="M5" initial="false" dead="false" home="true">
                      <marking value=1 ref="P4"></marking>
                      <marking value=1 ref="P5 "></marking>
                </vertex>
                <edge id="E1" from="M1" to="M2" fires="T1"></edge>
                <edge id="E2" from="M2" to="M3" fires="T2"></edge>
                <edge id="E3" from="M2" to="M4" fires="T3"></edge>
                <edge id="E4" from="M3" to="M5" fires="T3"></edge>
                <edge id="E5" from="M4" to="M5" fires="T2"></edge>
                <edge id="E6" from="M5" to="M1" fires="T2"></edge>
      </rg>
</pnresml>
```

REFERENCES

Balsamo, S., Di Marco, A., Inverardi, P., & Simeoni, M. (2004). Model-based performance prediction in software development: A survey. *IEEE Transactions on Software Engineering, 30*(5), 295–310. doi:10.1109/TSE.2004.9.

Barbierato, E., Gribaudo, M., & Iacono, M. (2011). Defining formalisms for performance evaluation with SIMTHESys. *Electronic Notes in Theoretical Computer Science, 275,* 37–51. doi:10.1016/j.entcs.2011.09.004.

Bernardi, S., & Campos, J. (2009). Computation of performance bounds for real-time systems using time Petri nets. *IEEE Transactions on Industrial Informatics, 5*(2), 168–180. doi:10.1109/TII.2009.2017201.

Bernardi, S., Merseguer, J., & Petriu, D. C. (2012b). Dependability modeling and analysis of software systems specified with UML. *ACM Computing Surveys, 45*(1), 2. doi:10.1145/2379776.2379778.

Berthomieu, B., & Diaz, M. (1991). Modeling and verification of time dependent systems using time Petri nets. *IEEE Transactions on Software Engineering, 17*(3), 259–273. doi:10.1109/32.75415.

Berthomieu, B., & Vernadat, F. (2006). Time petri nets analysis with TINA. In *Proceedings of Third International Conference on the Quantitative Evaluation of Systems (QEST 2006),* (pp. 123-124). Riverside, CA: IEEE Computer Society.

Bonet, P., Llado, C., Puijaner, R., & Knottenbelt, W. (2007). PIPE v2.5: A Petri net tool for performance modelling. In *Proceedings of the 23rd Latin American Conference on Informatics (CLEI 2007).* San Jose, Costa Rica: CLEI.

Campos, J., & Silva, M. (1992). Structural techniques and performance bounds of stochastic Petri net models. *Lecture Notes in Computer Science, 609,* 352–391. doi:10.1007/3-540-55610-9_178.

Ciardo, G., & Miner, A. (n.d.). *Stochastic model checking analyzer for reliability and timing version 1.1.* Retrieved from http://www.cs.ucr.edu/~ciardo/SMART/

Colom, J., Teruel, E., & Silva, M. (1998). Logical properties of P/T systems and their analysis. In Proceedings of Performance Models for Discrete Event Systems with Synchronization: Formalisms and Analysis Techniques, MATCH Human Capital and Mobility CHRX-CT-94-0452. CHRX-CT.

Florin, G., & Natkin, S. (1985). Les reseaux de Petri stochastiques. *Technique et Science Informatiques, 4*(1).

Great, S. P. N. (n.d.). *Graphical editor and analyzer for timed and stochastic Petri nets version 2.0.* Retrieved from www.di.unito.it/~greatspn

Gribaudo, M., Codetta Raiteri, D., & Franceschinis, G. (2006). *The DrawNET modelling system: A framework for the design and the solution of single-formalism and multi-formalism models.* Technical Report TR-INF-2006-01-UNIPMN.

Hillah, L., Kindler, E., Kordon, F., Petrucci, L., & Trèves, N. (2009). A primer on the Petri net markup language and ISO/IEC 15909-2. *Petri Net Newsletter, 76,* 9–28.

Iacono, M., Barbierato, E., & Gribaudo, M. (2012). The SIMTHESys multiformalism modeling framework. *Computers & Mathematics with Applications (Oxford, England), 64,* 3828–3839. doi:10.1016/j.camwa.2012.03.009.

International Electrotechnical Commission. (2004). *ISO/IEC 15909-1: Systems and software engineering – High-level Petri nets - Part 1: Concepts, definitions and graphical notation.*

International Electrotechnical Commission. (2011). *ISO/IEC 15909-2: Systems and software engineering - High-level Petri nets - Part 2: Transfer format.*

Pacini, E., Bernardi, S., & Gribaudo, M. (2009). ITPN-PerfBound: A performance bound tool for interval time Petri nets. [LNCS]. *Proceedings of TACAS*, *5505*, 50–53.

Rodriguez, R. J., Julvez, J., & Merseguer, J. (2012) PeabraiN: A PIPE extension for performance estimation and resource optimisation. In J. Brandt & K. Heljanko (Eds.), *Proceedings of the 12th International Conference on Application of Concurrency to System Designs* (pp. 142-147). Hamburg, Germany: IEEE Computer Society.

Sanders, W., Courtney, T., Deavours, D., Daly, D., Derisavi, S., & Lam, V. (2003). *Multiformalism and multi-solution method modeling frameworks: The Mobius approach*. Academic Press.

Smith, C., & Williams, L. (2002). *Performance solutions: A practical guide to creating responsive, scalable software*. Reading, MA: Addison-Wesley.

Starke, P. H. (n.d.). *Integrated net analyzer version 2.1*. Retrieved from http://www2.informatik. hu-berlin.de/lehrstuehle/automaten/ina/

Vittorini, V., Iacono, M., Mazzocca, N., & Franceschinis, G. (2004). The OsMoSys approach to multi-formalism modeling of systems. *Software & Systems Modeling*, (3): 68–81.

Zimmermann, A., & Knoke, M. (2007). *TIMENET 4.0: A software tool for the performability evaluation with stochastic and colored Petri nets: User manual*. Berlin: Technische Universitat Berlin - Real-Time Systems and Robotic Group.

ENDNOTES

[1]   Simona Bernardi has been supported by the Spanish project TIN2011-24932 of the Ministerio de Economía y Competitividad.

Section 2
Exploiting Multiformalism:
Tool Design Experiences

This section presents design experiences of multiformalism tools.

Chapter 7
A Petri Net–Based Tool for the Analysis of Generalized Continuous Time Bayesian Networks

Daniele Codetta-Raiteri
University of Piemonte Orientale, Italy

Luigi Portinale
University of Piemonte Orientale, Italy

ABSTRACT

A software tool for the analysis of Generalized Continuous Time Bayesian Networks (GCTBN) is presented. GCTGBN extend CTBN introducing in addition to continuous time-delayed variables, non-delayed or "immediate" variables. The tool is based on the conversion of a GCTBN model into a Generalized Stochastic Petri Net (GSPN), which is an actual mean to perform the inference (analysis) of the GCTBN. Both the inference tasks (prediction and smoothing) can be performed in this way. The architecture and the methodologies of the tool are presented. In particular, the conversion rules from GCTBN to GSPN are described, and the inference algorithms exploiting GSPN transient analysis are presented. A running example supports their description: a case study is modelled as a GCTBN and analyzed by means of the tool. The results are verified by modelling and analyzing the system as a Dynamic Bayesian Network, another form of Bayesian Network, assuming discrete time.

INTRODUCTION

We present a software tool for the analysis of *Generalized Continuous Time Bayesian Network* (GCTBN) (Codetta & Portinale, 2010). The tool is based on the model-to-model transformation of a GCTBN into a *Generalized Stochastic Petri Net* (GSPN) (Ajmone et al., 1995).

GCTBN are a particular form of *Bayesian Network* (BN) (Langseth & Portinale, 2007), are characterized by a continuous time dimension, and contain two kinds of variables: delayed variables having a temporal evolution, and immediate variables whose value immediately changes according to the values of the parent variables.

DOI: 10.4018/978-1-4666-4659-9.ch007

The possibilities offered by this generalization, can be exploited in several applications. For example, in system reliability analysis, it is very practical to distinguish between system components (having a temporal evolution) and specific modules or subsystems, whose behavior has to be modeled for the analysis. This is shown by the case study presented in the following sections. Another case concerns *Fault Tree Analysis* (FTA) (Sahner et al., 1996) where basic events represent the system components with their failure rates, while non-basic events are logical gates identifying modules of the system under examination. In *Dynamic Fault Trees* (Bechta Dugan et al., 1992), logical gates identifying sub-modules, can be combined with dynamic gates, modeling time-dependent dependencies (usually assuming continuous time) among components or sub-modules. Also in this case, it is very important to distinguish, at the modeling level, between delayed and immediate entities (see also Portinale et al., 2007). Of course, similar considerations apply in other tasks as well, as in medical diagnosis, financial forecasting, biological process modeling, etc.

GCTBN and GSPN share the same stochastic process composed by tangible states characterized by an actual duration, and vanishing states where the system spend no time. This is the reason why a GCTBN can converted into GSPN. The tool exploits GSPN transient analysis to perform the *inference* of the GCTBN. This means computing the probability distribution of the queried variables at a specific time, conditioned by the observation of the values of other variables at particular times. However, a single transient analysis of the equivalent GSPN is not enough to perform the inference (analysis) of a GCTBN. The inference must take into account the observations (evidences) and their times of occurrence. So, the GSPN model has to be modified and analyzed at each time of interest, in order to represent and consider the observations. The results obtained at each time, must be properly combined in order to return the effective probability distribution of the queried variables.

Solution techniques for GSPN have received a lot of attention, especially with respect to the possibility of solving the underlying state space efficiently (Miner, 2007). For this reason, we exploit GSPN analysis for GCTBN inference. At the moment, this is the only method developed to solve GCTBN models. This method will be useful in the future to verify inference results if a direct solver will be developed for GCTBN. CTBN solution methods (Nodelman et al., 2005) may be extended to deal with GCTBN. However, CTBN solution usually provides approximate results, while the GSPN based approach described in this paper, returns exact results because it exploits GSPN transient analysis.

The presentation of the tool is supported by a running example, and we describe the formalisms involved in the tool (GCTBN and GSPN) in terms of modelling primitives and analysis tasks. In particular, we present the conversion rules from GCTBN to GSPN, and the inference algorithms exploiting GSPN transient analysis. The results obtained for the running example are verified by modelling and analyzing the system as a *Dynamic Bayesian Network* (DBN) (Murphy, 2002).

BACKGROUND

The dependability is a fundamental requirement for critical system and infrastructures, and can be quantified by means of several measures, such as the reliability. A way to compute the reliability is the construction of a probabilistic model of the system. The level of accuracy of the model must be enough to correctly represent the aspects of the system behaviour which are relevant to the computation of the reliability. Traditional modeling approaches in system dependability may be classified as combinatorial or state-space based.

Combinatorial models such as *Fault Trees* (Sahner et al., 1996) and *Reliability Block Dia-*

grams (Sahner et al., 1996) can only represent combinations of component failure events assumed to be independent. Their extensions such as *Dynamic Fault Trees* (Bechta Dugan et al., 1992) and *Dynamic Reliability Block Diagrams* (Distefano & Puliafito, 2009) introduce the possibility to represent dependencies among the failure events, but these models still only focus on the failure propagation ignoring the other aspects of the system behavior.

State-space based models like *Markov chains* (Sahner et al., 1996) or *Petri Nets* (Sahner et al., 1996), rely on the specification of the whole set of the possible system states, so that the stochastic behavior of each component may depend on the state of all the other components. This flexibility is very seldom exploited in practice, and the state space description appears over-specified with respect to the real modeling needs. Furthermore these models incur rapidly in the state space explosion.

An interesting trade-off between combinatorial and state space based models are *Bayesian Networks* (BN) (Langseth & Portinale, 2007) which are a widely used formalism for representing uncertain knowledge in probabilistic systems and have been applied to a variety of real-world problems. BN are defined by a directed acyclic graph (DAG) in which nodes corresponds to discrete random variables having a conditional dependence on the parent nodes. Root nodes are nodes with no parents, and marginal prior probabilities are assigned to them.

BN avoid the generation of the state space which is instead factorized over the variables: a state corresponds to a specific combination of the values of the variables in the BN; the probability of any state can be computed from the conditional probabilities ruling the local dependencies among variables.

Another added value given by BN, with respect to combinatorial and state space based models, is that BN allow not only a forward (or predictive) analysis, but also a backward (diagnostic) analysis, where the posterior probability distribution of any set of variables can be computed, given the observation of the values of other variables. This possibility allows to compute several measures based on conditional probability, such as diagnostic indices and importance (sensitivity) measures (Langseth & Portinale, 2007).

BN have been recently investigated as very promising formalisms for dependability and reliability analysis (Langseth & Portinale, 2007; Portinale et al., 2010): BN allow to easily model probabilistic dependencies, multi-state components, reliability parameteres (like failure rates) depending on the current system state, repair processes, imperfect coverage of failure and repair, noisy Boolean relations (noisy-AND, noisy-OR).

BN models for reasoning about processes that evolve over time have been deeply investigated. When time is taken into account, the main choice concerns whether to consider it as a discrete or a continuous dimension. In the former case, models like *Dynamic Bayesian Networks* (DBN) have become a natural choice (Murphy, 2002); however, there is not always an obvious discrete time unit and, when the process is characterized by several components evolving at different rates, the finer granularity dictates the rules for the discretization (Portinale et al., 2007). Moreover, if evidence is irregularly spaced in time, all the intervening time slices still have to be dealt with (even if no evidence is available at a given time point). For these reasons, models based on BN, but with a continuous time representation of the temporal evolution have started to be investigated. *Continuous Time Bayesian Networks* (CTBN) have been firstly proposed in Nodelman et al., 2005 and then refined in Saria et al., 2007. Extensions have also been proposed both regarding the use of indirect graph models (El-Hay et al., 2008) and the use of Erlang-Coxian distributions on the transition time (Gopalratnam et al., 2005).

In Codetta & Portinale, 2010, another kind of extension is proposed and, in particular, a generalization of the standard CTBN framework, by allowing the presence of nodes which have no explicit temporal evolution; the values of such nodes are, in fact, "immediately" determined, depending on the values of other nodes in the network. This will allow the modeling of processes having both a continuous-time temporal component and a static component capturing the logical/probabilistic aspects determined by specific events occurring in the modeled process. This formalism is called *Generalized Continuous Time Bayesian Network* (GCTBN).

Actually, such a kind of modeling is possible in the framework of DBN, where the notion of temporal arc is used to distinguish nodes having a temporal evolution, from nodes just contributing to the "logic" of the model (Portinale et al., 2007). However, as we have already noticed, since a DBN assumes a discrete dimension of time, this may be problematic for several applications, as well as computationally expensive when absolute time of events are important (Gopalratnam et al., 2005). Then, GCTBN are at the best of our knowledge, the first attempt trying to mix in the same network, continuous-time delayed nodes with standard chance node.

A CASE STUDY

We now consider a case study which can be easily modeled in form of a GCTBN. This is a typical case in the field of reliability analysis, and consists of a small system composed by the main component A and its "warm" spare component B. This means that initially both components are working, but A is active while B is dormant; in case of failure of A, B is activated in order to replace A in its function. We assume that the activation of B occurs with probability *p=0.99*, so in case of failure of A and the contemporary dormant state of B, the component B may keep its state with probability *1-p=0.01*.

The expression "warm" referred to the spare component B indicates that the probability of failure of B is not null while B is dormant, and such value is increased while B is active. So, the spare component B may fail as well, and this can happen before or after the failure of A; if B fails before A, then B can not replace A.

The whole system works if the component A is working, or if A is failed and B is active. The system is considered as failed if A is failed and B is dormant or failed. We suppose that only while the system is failed, the components A and B can undergo repair. As soon as the repair of one of the components is completed, the component re-starts in working state: if A is repaired the system becomes operative again and the repair of B is suspended; if instead B is repaired, this may determine one of these two situations: 1) B may become active with probability *p=0.99* and consequently the system becomes operative again and the repair of A is suspended. 2) B may become dormant with probability *1-p*, so the system is still failed and the repair of A goes on[1].

The time to failure of the components is assumed to be randomly distributed according to the negative exponential distribution whose parameter is called failure rate and is the inverse of the mean time to failure of the component. In the case of the main component A, the failure rate is λ_A=1.0E-06 h^{-1}. The failure rate of B, λ_B, changes according to its current state: if B is active (A is failed), λ_B is also equal to 1.0E-06 h^{-1}. If instead B is dormant (A is not failed), λ_B is equal to 5.0E-07 h^{-1} (i.e. it is discounted by a dormancy factor α=0.5). In other words, the failure rate of B is reduced with respect to the failure of A, while B is dormant; if instead B is active in order to replace A, the failure rate of B is the same as the failure rate of A.

The time to repair of a component is a random variable, still ruled by the negative exponential distribution having as parameter the repair rate equal to the inverse of the mean time to repair the component. A and B have the same repair rate μ_A=μ_B=0.01 h^{-1}.

INVOLVED FORMALISMS

Generalized CTBN (GCTBN)

Following the original paper in Nodelman et al., 2005, a CTBN is defined as follows:

Definition 1: Let $V=\{X_1, ..., X_n\}$ be a set of discrete variables, a CTBN over X consists of two components. The first one is an initial distribution P^0_V over V (possibly specified as a standard BN over V). The second component is a continuous-time transition model specified as: (1) a directed graph G whose nodes are $X_1, ... X_n$ (and with $Pa(X_i)$ denoting the parents of X_i in G); (2) a *Conditional Intensity Matrix* (CIM) $Q_{X_i|Pa(X_i)}$ for every $X_i \in V$. The CIM of a variable X_i provides the transition rates for each possible couple of values of X_i.

We can now introduce the notion of a Generalized CTBN (GCTBN).

Definition 2: Given a set of discrete variables $V=\{X_1,..., X_n\}$ partitioned into the sets D (delayed variables) and I (immediate variables) (i.e. $V = D \cup I$ and $D \cap I = \varnothing$), a *Generalized Continuous Time Bayesian Network* (GCTBN) is a pair $N = \langle P^0_V, G \rangle$ where:

- ○ P^0_V is an initial probability distribution over V;

- ○ G is a directed graph whose nodes are $X_1, ..., X_n$ (and with $Pa(X_i)$ denoting the parents of X_i in G) such that:
  - There is no directed cycle in G composed only by nodes in the set I;
  - For each node $X \in I$ a conditional probability table $P[X|Pa(X)]$ is defined (as in standard BN);
  - For each node $Y \in D$ a conditional intensity matrix $Q_{Y|Pa(Y)}$ is defined (as in standard CTBN).

Delayed (or temporal) nodes are, as in case of CTBN, nodes representing variables with a continuous time evolution ruled by exponential transition rates, and conditioned by the values of parent variables (that may be either delayed or immediate). Delayed nodes have a *Conditional Intensity Matrix* (CIM) of rates associated with them. Immediate nodes are introduced in order to capture variables whose evolution is not ruled by transition rates associated with their values, but is conditionally determined, at a given time point, by other variables in the model. Such variables are then treated as usual chance nodes in a BN and have a standard *Conditional Probability Table* (CPT) associated with them.

Delayed nodes graphically appear as double-circled nodes, while immediate nodes are drawn as circle nodes (Figure 1).

A few words are worth to be spent for the structure of the graph modeling the GCTBN. While it is in general possible to have cycles in

Figure 1. GCTBN model of the case study: A and B are delayed nodes; SYS is an immediate node

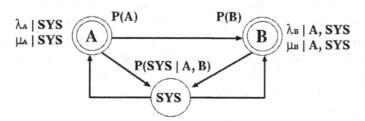

the graph (as in CTBN) due to the temporal nature of some nodes, such cycles cannot be composed only by immediate nodes. Indeed, if this was the case, we would introduce static circular dependencies among model variables.

Finally, it is worth noting that the initial distribution P^0_V can in general be specified only on a subset of V. In particular, let $R \subset I$ be the set of root nodes (i.e. node with no parent in G) which are immediate, then the initial distribution can be computed as:

$$P^0_V = P^0_{R \cup D} \prod_{Y_j \in (I-R)} P\left[Y_j \mid Pa\left(Y_j\right)\right].$$

In fact, while it is necessary to specify an initial distribution over delayed variables, the distribution on the immediate variables can be determined depending on the values of their parents; of course if an immediate variable is modeled as a root node, a prior probability is needed[2].

GCTBN Model of the Case Study

The case study described above can be represented by the GCTBN model in Figure 1 where the variables A, B, SYS represent the state of the component A, of the component B, and of the whole system respectively. All the variables are binary because each entity can be in the working state or in the failed state (for the component B, the working state comprises both the dormancy and the activation). In particular, we represent the working state with the value 1, and the failed state with the value 2.

The variable A influences the variable B because the failure rate of the component B depends on the state of A, as described above. Both the variables A and B influence the variable SYS because the state of the whole system depends on the state of the components A and B, as described above. The arcs connecting the variable SYS to A and B respectively, concern the repair of the components A and B: only while the system is failed, they can be repaired.

The variables A and B in the GCTBN model in Figure 1 are delayed variables and are drawn as double-circled nodes: their value (state of the component) can be equal to 1 or 2, and varies after a random period of time according to the values of the other variables. Both variables implicitly incorporate a *Continuous Time Markov Chain* (CTMC) (Sahner et al., 1996) composed by two states: 1 (working) and 2 (failed). The initial probability distribution reported in Table 1 holds for both variables A and B: the probability to be initially equal to 1 is set to 1, while the probability to be initially equal to 2 is 0. This is due to the assumption that both components are initially supposed to work.

The CTMC incorporated by the variables A and B is shown in Figure 2: the transition from 1 to 2 occurs after a random period of time ruled by the negative exponential distribution according to the failure rate λ. The transition from 2 to 1 is ruled by the same distribution, but according to the repair rate μ.

In the case of A, the current value of the rates λ_A and μ_A depends on the current value of the variable SYS, the only one influencing A. This is shown by the CIM reported in Table 2 where we can notice that the rate μ_A (the repair rate in the

Table 1. Initial probability distribution for the values of the variables A and B in the GCTBN in Figure 1

Value	Prob.
1	1
2	0

Figure 2. The CTMC incorporated in the variables A and B in the GCTBN model in Figure 1

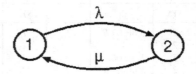

case study) is not null only if the state of *SYS* is 2. The rate λ_A (the failure rate in the case study) instead, is constant (the state of the system influences only the repair of the component A).

In the case of the variable *B*, the current value of the rates λ_B and μ_B depends on the current value of the variables *A* and *SYS*, as shown by the CIM appearing in Table 3 where λ_B (the failure rate of the spare component B) is increased only when *A* is equal to *2* and *SYS* is equal to *1* (this implies that B is active). As in the case of the variable *A*, the rate μ_B is not null only if the value of *SYS* is *2*. Notice that the combination *A=1*, *SYS=2* is impossible, so the corresponding entries are not significant.

The variable *SYS* is immediate and is shown as a circle node in Figure 1. This means that it changes its value as soon as the variables influencing it, change their value. The variable *SYS* depends on both the variables *A* and *B* because the state of the system is determined by the state of both the components *A* and *B*, as described in the case study. The variable *SYS* is characterized by the CPT appearing in Table 4 which expresses the working and failure conditions for the whole system specified in the case study. In particular,

Table 2. CIM for the variable A in the GCTBN model in Figure 1

1→2		2→1	
SYS	λ_A	SYS	μ_A
1	1.0E-06 h^{-1}	1	0 h^{-1}
2	1.0E-06 h^{-1}	2	0.01 h^{-1}

Table 3. CIM for the variable B in the GCTBN model in Figure 1

1→2			2→1		
A	SYS	λ_B	A	SYS	μ_B
1	1	5.0E-07 h^{-1}	1	1	0 h^{-1}
1	2	-	1	2	-
2	1	1.0E-06 h^{-1}	2	1	0 h^{-1}
2	2	5.0E-07 h^{-1}	2	2	0.01 h^{-1}

Table 4. CPT for the variable SYS in the GCTBN model in Figure 1

A	B	SYS	Prob.
1	1	1	1
1	1	2	0
1	2	1	1
1	2	2	0
2	1	1	0.99
2	1	2	0.01
2	2	1	0
2	2	2	1

SYS is surely equal to *1* if *A* is equal to *1*, and surely equal to *2* if both *A* and *B* are equal to *2*. In the case of *A* equal to *2* and *B* equal to *1*, *SYS* assumes the value *1* with probability 0.99 (this implies the activation of the spare component B), or the value *2* with probability 0.01 (this implies that B is still dormant).

Inference

The process to analyze a BN is called inference. Standard inference tasks in a temporal probabilistic model are *prediction* and *smoothing* (Murphy, 2002). Let X_t be a set of variables at time *t* and $y_{\{a:b\}}$ any stream of observations from time point *a* to time point *b* (i.e. a set of instantiated variables). *Prediction* is the task of computing $P(X_{t+h}|y_{1:t})$ for some horizon *h>0*, i.e. predicting a future state taking into consideration the observation up to now (a special case occurs when *h=0* and is called *Filtering* or *Monitoring*). *Smoothing* is the task of computing $P(X_{t-l}|y_{1:t})$ for some *l<t*, i.e. estimating what happened *l* time points in the past, given all the evidence (observations) up to now.

Such tasks can be accomplished, depending on the model adopted, by inference procedures usually based on specific adaptation of standard algorithms for BNs. For instance, in DBN models, both exact algorithms based on junction tree (Murphy, 2002) as well as approximate algorithms exploiting the net structure (Boyen & Koller, 1998) or based on stochastic simulation can be employed. In case of CTBN, exact inference may often be impractical, so approximations through message-passing algorithms on cluster graphs (Nodelman et al., 2005; Saria et al., 2007), or through sampling (El-Hay et al., 2008; Fan & Shelton, 2008) have been proposed.

In the present work, we take advantage of the correspondence between the stochastic processes incorporated by GCTBN and GSPN, in order to propose inference algorithms (both for prediction and smoothing) repeating the update and the transient analysis of the GSPN for each observation or query time, until the final results are obtained. The use of GSPN analysis allows to compute exact results.

Generalized Stochastic Petri Nets (GSPN)

The combination in a single model of entities explicitly evolving over time with entities whose determination is "immediate", is not a novelty; as we have already noticed, in the framework of probabilistic graphical models, DBN provide an example, in case of discrete time. In case of continuous time, a model having such a features can be found in the framework of Petri Nets, namely *Generalized Stochastic Petri Nets* (GSPN) (Ajmone et al., 1995). GSPN are stochastic Petri nets, where there are two different sets of transitions, namely *timed* with an exponentially distributed delay, and *immediate* transitions (with no delay), having priority over temporal ones. This means that, in case both an immediate and a temporal transition are enabled, the firing of the former takes precedence over the firing of the latter.

In a GSPN, two or more immediate transitions may be enabled at the same time; in this case, *weights* and *priorities* can be used to rule the firing of such transitions. A weight and/or a priority can be assigned to an immediate transition. Using weights, given several immediate transitions enabled to fire, higher is the weight of a transition, higher is its probability to fire. Using priorities, given several immediate transitions enabled to fire, the transition with highest priority fires.

In GSPN we have also two types of arcs: oriented arcs and inhibitor arcs. Oriented arcs are used to connect places to transitions and vice-versa, with the aim of moving tokens when transitions fire. Inhibitor arcs connect a place to a transition with the aim of disabling the transition if the place is not empty. A cardinality (multiplicity) can be associated to an arc; in the case of oriented arcs, the cardinality indicates the number of tokens to be moved on that arc when the transition fires; in the case of inhibitor arcs, the cardinality indicates the number of tokens inside the place, necessary to disable the transition.

The stochastic process associated with a GSPN is a homogeneous continuous time semi-Markov process that can be analyzed either by solving the so called *Embedded Markov Chain* or by removing from the set of possible states, the so-called *vanishing states* or *markings* and by analyzing the resulting CTMC (Ajmone et al., 1995).

Vanishing states are the state (or markings) resulting from the firing of immediate transitions; they can be removed, since the system does not spend time in such states. This removal operation has also the advantage of reducing (often in a significant way) the set of possible states to be analyzed.

There are two main analyses that can be performed with a GSPN: *steady state* and *transient analysis*. In the first case, the equilibrium distribution of the states is computed, while in the latter, such a distribution is computed at a given time point. In particular, solving a GSPN (for either steady state or transient analysis) can provide the probability distribution of the number of tokens in each place. This possibility will be exploited in the inference procedures for GCTBN.

GSPN Formal Definition

The GSPN formalism is given by the tuple

$$GSPN = (P, T, A, \#, r, w, \pi, card)$$

Where

- P is the set of the places.
- $T = T_i \cup T_t$ is the set of the transitions; it is the union of two sets:
  - T_i is the set of the immediate transitions;
  - T_t is the set of timed transitions.
- A is the set of arcs; it is the union of two sets:
  - $A_d \subseteq (P \times T) \cup (T \times P)$ is the set of the oriented arcs;
  - $A_h \subseteq P \times T$ is the set of the inhibitor arcs.
- $\# : P \rightarrow \mathbb{N}$ is the function returning the marking of a place.
- $r : T_t \rightarrow \mathbb{R}^+$ is the function returning the firing rate of a timed transition.
- $w : T_i \rightarrow \mathbb{R}^+$ is the function returning the weight of an immediate transition.
- $p : T_i \rightarrow \mathbb{N} - \{0\}$ is the function returning the priority of an immediate transition.
- $card : A \rightarrow \mathbb{N} - \{0\}$ is the function returning the cardinality of an arc.
- Given $t \in T$
  - $\bullet_d t = \{(p, t) \in A_d\}$ is the set of input arcs coming from places and directed to t.
  - $t \bullet_d = \{(t, p) \in A_d\}$ is the set of output arcs coming from t and directed to places.
  - $\bullet_h t = \{(p, t) \in A_h\}$ is the set of inhibitor arcs coming from places and directed to t.
- Given $t \in T$, t is enabled to fire if both the following conditions hold:

- $\forall (p,t) \in \bullet_d t, \#(p) \geq card(p, t)$
- $\forall (p,t) \in \bullet_h t, \#(p) < card(p, t)$

- If m is the marking of $p \in P$ before the firing of $t \in T$, and $\#(p)$ is the marking of p after the firing of t, then the effect of the firing of t is the following:
  - $\#(p) = m - card(p,t)$ if $\exists (p,t) \in \bullet_d t \wedge \nexists (t,p) \in t \bullet_d$
  - $\#(p) = m + card(p, t)$ if $\exists (t,p) \in t \bullet_d \wedge \nexists (p,t) \in \bullet_d t$
  - $\#(p) = m - card(p,t) + card(p, t)$ if $\exists (p,t) \in \bullet_d t \wedge \exists (t,p) \in t \bullet_d$

METHODOLOGIES IMPLEMENTED IN THE SOFTWARE TOOL

Translation Rules from GCTBN to GSPN

This section provides the formal rules to derive the GSPN equivalent to a GCTBN model. First, we introduce the way to convert the delayed variables, then, the way to convert immediate variables.

Conversion of Delayed Variables into GSPN

A delayed variable X of the GCTBN model is converted into several elements of the equivalent GSPN:

- The place X' whose marking represents the value of X; we introduce here the function pl:GCTBN. $(I \cup D) \rightarrow$ GSPN. P returning the GSPN place corresponding to a variable of the GCTBN. In the case of X, $pl(X)=X'$.
- The place X'_init with $\#(X'\_init)=1$, used to set the initial marking of X'.
- The set $T^{init}_{X'}$ of immediate "init" transitions to set the initial marking of X'.

- The set $T^D{}_{X'}$ of timed transitions to change the marking of X'.

The set $T^{init}{}_{X'}$ is created in the following way: given the initial probability distribution $P^0{}_V$ over V, for each possible value x of X such that $P^0(x) \neq 0$ the transition $t_x \in T^{init}{}_{X'}$ is created such that all the following conditions hold:

$$w(t_x) = P^0(x)$$

$$\pi(t_x) = 1$$

$$\bullet_d\, t_x = \{(X'{}_{init}, t_x)\}$$

$$card(X'{}_{init}, t_x) = 1$$

$$\bullet_h\, t_x = \varnothing$$

$$t_x \bullet_d = \{(t_x, X')\}$$

$$card(t_x, X') = x$$

The set $T^{init}{}_{X'}$ will contain an immediate transition for each initial value x of X whose probability is not null. Such transitions are all enabled to fire by the presence of one token inside X'_init: the weight of each transition corresponds to the probability of the corresponding initial value x of X. The effect of the firing of a transition t in $T^{init}{}_{X'}$ consists of removing the token inside X'_init (this disables the firing of the other transitions in $T^{init}{}_{X'}$) and setting the marking of X' to the initial value x of X corresponding to t. Such setting is done by means of the cardinality of the arc (t_x, X') equal to x. Once the initial marking of X' is set, the transitions in $T^{init}{}_{X'}$ can not fire any more because X'_init has become empty.

The set $T^D{}_{X'}$ is created in the following way: for each ordered couple (x_1, x_2) such that $x_1, x_2 \in X$ and $x_1 \neq x_2$, the transition $t \in T^D{}_{X'}$ is created such that all the following conditions hold:

$$\bullet_d\, t = \{(X', t)\}$$

$$card(X', t) \in \bullet_d\, t = x_1$$

$$\bullet_h\, t = \{(X', t)\}$$

$$card(X', t) \in \bullet_h\, t = x_1 + 1$$

$$t \bullet_d = \{(t, X')\}$$

$$card(t, X') = x_2$$

This means that for each possible value transition from x_1 to x_2 by the variable X, a timed transition t is created to model such change of value. Such transition is enabled to fire when the place X' contains exactly x_1 tokens; this is because of the cardinality of the oriented arc $(X', t) \in \bullet_d\, t$ and of the inhibitor arc $(X', t) \in \bullet_h\, t$. The effect of the firing of t consists of setting the marking of X' to x_2, by means of the oriented arc (t, X'). The dependency of the transition rates of X on the values of the parent variables, is modeled in the GSPN by the marking dependent firing rate of t. This rate changes according to the marking of the places representing the parent variables of X. For each combination of the marking values of such places, the firing rate of t assumes a different value.

We introduce now the function Pa: GCTBN. $(I \cup D) \rightarrow$ GCTBN.$(I \cup D)$ which returns the parent variables of a particular variable of the GCTBN. So, $Pa(X)$ returns the variables influencing X; in particular, assuming that such variables are ordered, $Pa_i(X)$ returns the i-th parent variable of X.

The firing rate of t has to be marking dependent:

$$\forall\, c \in \times_i (Pa_i(X)),\ r(t)|cond =$$

$$q_{x\_1,\, x\_2} \mid c \in Q_X|Pa(X)$$

where

$$cond = \wedge_j\, \#(pl(Pa_j(X))) = c_j$$

In other words, if c is a particular combination of the values of the parent variables of X, the firing rate of t, $r(t)|cond$, is set to the value $q_{\{x1,x2\}}|c$ which is the entry in the conditional intensity matrix of X at the row x_1 and the column x_2, for the combination c of the values of the parent variables of X. The condition $cond$ for the firing rate $r(t)|cond$ is the translation of the combination c in terms of markings of the places corresponding to the parent variables of X: $cond$ is the conjunction of several sub-conditions, each requiring that the marking of the place corresponding to the i-th parent of X has to be equal to c_i, where c_i is the value of the i-th parent of X in c.

Let us consider the GCTBN model in Figure 1. Figure 3 shows the GSPN expressing the delayed variable A in the GCTBN. In this GSPN the marking of the place A' represents the value of A, and the place A'_init is used to set the initial marking of A', together with the set of immediate transitions $T^{init}_{A'}=\{A\_init\_1, A\_init\_2\}$, with $w(A\_init\_1)=1$ and $w(A\_init\_2)=0$, according to the initial probability distribution of A (Table 1). The set of timed transitions modifying the marking of A' is $T^D_{A'}=\{A\_1\_2, A\_2\_1\}$. The firing rates of these transitions are marking dependent: the conditions and the values of the rates are reported in Table 5.

Figure 4 shows the GSPN expressing the delayed variable B in the GCTBN in Figure 1. Such GSPN has the same graph structure of the GSPN in Figure 3 because both A and B can be equal to 1 or 2. In Figure 4, the marking of the place B'

represents the value of B, and the place B'_init is used to set the initial marking of B', together with $T^{init}_{B'}=\{B\_init\_1, B\_init\_2\}$, with $w(B\_init\_1)=1$ and $w(B\_init\_2)=0$. The set of timed transitions modifying the marking of B' is $T^D_{B'}=\{B\_1\_2, B\_2\_1\}$. The firing rates of these transitions are marking dependent (Table 6).

Conversion of Immediate Variables into GSPN

An immediate variable Y of the GCTBN model is converted into several elements of the equivalent GSPN:

- The place Y' whose marking corresponds to the values of Y ($pl(Y)=Y'$).
- The set $T^I_{Y'}$ of the immediate transitions used to initialize the value of the marking of Y' and to re-set it whenever the marking of one of the places corresponding to the parent variables of Y' changes.
- The place $empty\_Y'$ used when the marking of the place Y' has to be re-set.
- The set $T^{reset}_{Y'}$ of immediate transitions used to remove the tokens inside Y' when the marking of this has to be re-set.

The set $T^I_{Y'}$ is created in the following way: each $e \in \times_i Pa_i(Y) \times Y$ corresponds to an entry of the CPT of Y, while $P(e)$ is the probability of such entry. Each e is a combination of $n=\sum_i |Pa_i(Y)| + |Y|$ values, where the first $n-1$ values are referred

Figure 3. The GSPN corresponding to the variable A in the CTBN in Figure 1

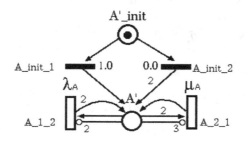
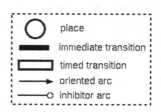

Figure 4. The GSPN corresponding to the variable B in the CTBN in Figure 1

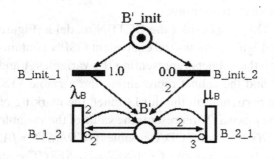

Table 5. Firing rates of the timed transitions in Figure 3

Transition	Condition (*cond*)	Firing Rate (*r*)
A_1_2	#(SYS')=1	1.0E-06 h^{-1}
A_1_2	#(SYS')=2	1.0E-06 h^{-1}
A_2_1	#(SYS')=1	0 h^{-1}
A_2_1	#(SYS')=2	0.01 h^{-1}

Table 6. Firing rates of the timed transitions in Figure 4

Transition	Condition (*cond*)	Firing Rate (*r*)
B_1_2	#(A')=1 ∧ #(SYS')=1	5.0E-07 h^{-1}
B_1_2	#(A')=1 ∧ #(SYS')=2	5.0E-07 h^{-1}
B_1_2	#(A')=2 ∧ #(SYS')=1	1.0E-06 h^{-1}
B_1_2	#(A')=2 ∧ #(SYS')=2	5.0E-07 h^{-1}
B_2_1	#(A')=1 ∧ #(SYS')=1	0 h^{-1}
B_2_1	#(A')=1 ∧ #(SYS')=2	0 h^{-1}
B_2_1	#(A')=2 ∧ #(SYS')=1	0 h^{-1}
B_2_1	#(A')=2 ∧ #(SYS')=2	0.01 h^{-1}

to the parent variables of Y, while the *n-th* one is referred to Y. For each e such that $P(e) \neq 0$, an immediate transition $t \in T'_y$ is created such that the following conditions hold:

$$w(t)=P(e)$$

$$\pi\left(t\right)=1$$

$$\bullet_d t = \cup_i \left(pl\left(Pa_i\left(Y\right) \right), t \right)$$

$$\forall \left(pl\left(Pa_i\left(Y\right) \right), t \right) \in \bullet_d t,$$
$$card\left(pl\left(Pa_i\left(Y\right), t \right) \right) = e_i$$

$$t \bullet = \cup_i \left(t, pl\left(Pa_i\left(Y\right) \right) \right) \cup \left(t, Y' \right)$$

$$\forall \left(t, pl\left(Pa_i\left(Y\right) \right) \right) \in t \bullet_d,$$
$$card\left(t, pl\left(Pa_i\left(Y\right) \right) \right) = e_i$$

$$card(t, Y')=e_n$$

$$\bullet_h t = \cup_i \left(pl\left(Pa_i\left(Y\right) \right), t \right) \cup \left(Y', t \right)$$

$$\forall (pl\left(Pa_i\left(Y\right), t \right) \in \bullet_h t,$$
$$card\left(pl\left(Pa_i\left(Y\right), t \right) \right) = e_i + 1$$

$$card(Y', t)=1$$

In other words, for each entry e of the CPT of Y, the immediate transition t is created. Its effect is setting the value of the marking of Y' to the to value of Y in e. The transition t is enabled to fire when Y' is empty and the markings of the places corresponding to the parent variables of Y assume exactly the values of such variables in e. The weight of t is set to the probability of e in the CPT. In this way, we model in the GSPN the role of each entry e in the CPT of Y.

In the GCTBN, Y directly depends on $Pa(Y)$. However, if the set $Pa(Y)$ contains immediate variables, then the change of such variables is ruled by the change of their parents, eventually being delayed variables. So, what really determines a change in Y is the set of the *"Closest" Delayed Ancestors* (CDA) of Y. Let $CDA(Y)=\{X: X \in D \land \exists$ a path from X to Y with no intermediate delayed node$\}$.

Therefore, each time that the marking of a place in $pl(CDA(Y))$ changes, first, the place Y'

has to become empty, then its marking has to be set according to the current marking of the places in $pl(Pa(Y))$. To set place Y' empty, we introduce the place Y'_empty and the transition set $T^{reset}_{Y'}$; the second step is done by the transition set $T^{I}_{Y'}$ as explained above.

Every time that the marking of a place in $pl(CDA(Y))$ varies, one token has to appear in the place Y'_empty in order to indicate that the place Y' must become empty. Again, let the function $CDA_i(Y)$ returns the i-th closest delayed ancestor of Y; for each $CDA_i(Y)$ and for each $t \in T^{D}_{pl(CDAi(Y))}$, an oriented arc (t, Y'_empty) is added to $t\bullet$. In other words, for each transition modifying the marking of a place corresponding to a CDA variable of Y, we create an arc from such transition to the place Y'_empty. Therefore each time that such transition fires, one token appears in Y'_empty enabling the firing of one of the immediate transitions in the set $T^{reset}_{Y'}$. $T^{reset}_{Y'}$ is created in the following way: for each $y \in Y$, the immediate transition $t \in T^{reset}_{Y'}$ is created such that all the following conditions hold:

$w(t)=1$

$\pi(t)=2$

$\bullet_d t = \{(empty\_Y', t), (Y', t)\}$

$card(empty\_Y', t)=1$

$card(Y', t) \in \bullet_d t = x$

$\bullet_h t = (Y', t)$

$card(Y', t) \in \bullet_h t = x+1$

For each possible marking of Y', one transition in the set $T^{reset}_{Y'}$ is enabled to fire with the effect of removing any token inside Y' and removing the only token inside Y'_empty. When this occurs, some of the transitions in the set $T^{I}_{Y'}$ are enabled to fire in order to set the new marking of Y' according to the current value of place set $pl(Pa(Y))$.

The higher priority (π) of the transitions in $T^{reset}_{Y'}$ determines the correct order of firing of all immediate transitions.

Let us consider the GCTBN model in Figure 1. Figure 5 shows the equivalent GSPN containing the subnets representing the variables A and B and the subnet representing the variable SYS. In particular, in the third subnet, the marking of the place SYS' represents the value of the variable SYS whose set of CDA variables is $CDA(SYS)=\{A, B\}$. In this example, $CDA(SYS)=Pa(SYS)$. The set of places corresponding to $CDA(SYS)$ is $pl(CDA(SYS))=\{A', B'\}$. The set of immediate transitions setting the marking of the place SYS' according to the marking of the places in $pl(Pa(SYS))$ is $T^{I}_{SYS'}=\{set\_SYS\_1, set\_SYS\_2, set\_SYS\_3, set\_SYS\_4, set\_SYS\_5\}$. The weight of each of these transitions is reported in Figure 1, close to the transition. The place $empty\_SYS'$ is used to remove any token inside SYS', together with the immediate transitions in the set $T^{reset}_{SYS'}=\{reset\_SYS\_1, reset\_SYS\_2\}$, with $\pi(reset\_SYS\_1)=\pi(reset\_SYS\_2)=2$. Since $pl(CDA(SYS))=\{A', B'\}$, the place $empty\_SYS'$ is reached by an oriented arc coming from each of the transitions in the set $T^{D}_{A'} \cup T^{D}_{B'}=\{A\_1\_2, A\_2\_1\} \cup \{B\_1\_2, B\_2\_1\}=\{A\_1\_2, A\_2\_1, B\_1\_2, B\_2\_1\}$.

The GSPN Model for the Case Study

According to the conversion rules, the GCTBN of the case study in Figure 1 can be converted into the GSPN model shown in Figure 5 where the places A', B' and SYS' correspond to the variables in the GCTBN model. The value of a GCTBN variable is mapped into the marking (number of tokens) of the corresponding place in the GSPN. Let us consider the place B' in the GSPN: the marking of the place B' can be equal to 1 or 2, the same values that the variable B in the GCTBN can assume. B is a delayed variable and its initialization is modeled in the GSPN by the immediate transitions B_init_1 and B_init_2

Figure 5. GSPN model obtained from the GCTBN in Figure 1

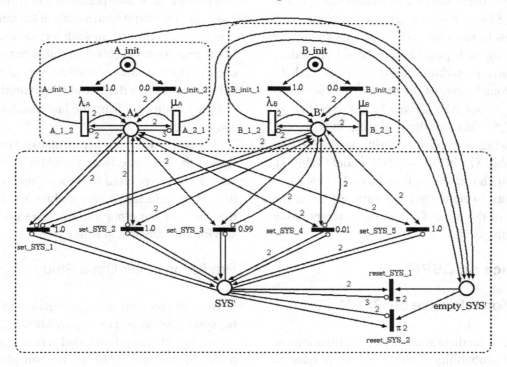

called *"init" transitions*. Such transitions are both initially enabled to fire with the effect of setting the initial marking of the place *B'* to *1* or *2* respectively. The probability of these transitions to fire corresponds to the initial probability distribution of the variable *B* (Table 1)[3].

The variation of the marking of the place *B'* is determined by the timed transitions *B_1_2* and *B_2_1*. The transition *B_1_2* is enabled to fire when the place *B'* contains one token; the effect of its firing is setting the marking of *B'* to *2*.The transition *B_2_1* instead, can fire when the marking of the place *B'* is equal to *2*, and turns it to *1*. The dependency of the transition rate of a variable on the values of the other variables in the GCTBN model, becomes in the GSPN model, the dependency of the firing rate of a timed transition on the markings of the other places. For instance, in the GCTBN model the variable *B* depends on *A* and *SYS*; let us consider λ_B which is the transition rate of *B* from *1* to *2* depending on the values of the variables *A* and *SYS* (Table 3). In the GSPN model,

λ_B becomes the firing rate of the timed transition *B_1_2* whose value depends on the marking of the places *A'* and *SYS'*, and assumes the same values reported in Table 3. The firing rate of the timed transition *B_2_1* instead, will correspond to the rate μ_B reported in Table 3, still depending on the marking of the places *A'* and *SYS'*.

The initialization of the marking of the place *A'* is modeled by the immediate init transitions *A_init_1* and *A_init_2*, while the variation of its marking is modeled in a similar way by the timed transitions *A_1_2* and *A_2_1*, but in this case their firing rate will depend only on the marking of the place *SYS'*, because in the GCTBN model the variable *A* depends only on the variable *SYS*. Such variable is immediate in the GCTBN and depends on *A* and *B*. Therefore in the GSPN, each time the marking of the place *A'* or of the place *B'* is modified, the marking of *SYS'* has to be immediately updated: each time the transition *A_1_2*, *A_2_1*, *B_1_2* or *B_2_1* fires, one token appears in the place *empty_SYS'*; this determines the firing of the immediate transition *reset_SYS_1* or *reset_SYS_2*, with the effect of removing any token inside the place *SYS'*. At this point, the marking of such place has to be set according to the current marking of the places *A'* and *B'*. This is done by one of the immediate transitions *set_SYS_1*, *set_SYS_2*, *set_SYS_3*, *set_SYS_4*, *set_SYS_5*. Each of them corresponds to one entry having not null probability in the CPT of the variable *SYS* in the GCTBN model (Table 4). Each of such immediate transitions has the same probability (weight) and the same effect on the marking of the place *SYS'*, of the corresponding entry in the CPT.

Inference on GSPN

Prediction Inference on GSPN

The task of prediction consists in computing the posterior probability at time t of a set of queried variables $Q \subseteq D \cup I$, given a stream of observations (evidence) $e_{t1}, ..., e_{tk}$ from time t_1 to time t_k with $t_1 < ... t_k < t$. Every evidence e_{tj} consists of a (possibly different) set of instantiated variables.

Prediction can then be implemented by repeatedly solving for transient the corresponding GSPN at the different times corresponding to the observations and the query. Of course, any observation will condition the evolution of the model, so the suitable conditioning operations must be performed before a new GSPN resolution.

Computing the probability of a given variable assignment $X=x_i$ at time t, will correspond to compute the probability of having i tokens in the place modeling X at time t.

Let *Pr{E}* be the probability of the event E, computed from the resulting distribution of a GSPN transient (for instance given a variable X, $P(X=x)=Pr\{\#X'=x\}$ where $\#X'$ is the number of tokens in place X' corresponding to X). The pseudo-code for the prediction procedure is shown in Figure 6.

Notice that, in the special case of *filtering*, the last evidence would be available at the query time (i.e. $t=t_k$ in Figure 6); in such a case, the update of the transition weights (last statement in the *for* cycle) is not necessary, as well as the final transient solution. The procedure would then simply output *Pr{Q|e_t}* computed from the last transient analysis.

In case there is evidence available at time $t_0=0$, then if the evidence is on variables $X \in D \cup R$, then it is incorporated into their "init" distribution; if the evidence is on variables $X \in I-R$, then the "init" of the other variables are updated by solving the transient at time $t_0=0$.

Prediction in the Case Study

Concerning prediction, let us consider to observe the system working at time $t_1=100000\,h$ (*SYS=1* at $t_1=10^5\,h$) and the system failed at time $t_2=200000\,h$ (i.e. *SYS=2* at $t=2*10^5\,h$). By considering the procedure outlined in Figure 6 we can compute the probability of component A being working at time $t=5*10^5\,h$ (conditioned by the observation stream) as follows: (1) we solve the transient at $t=10^5\,h$ and we compute the probabilities of *A* and *B*, conditioned by the observation *SYS=1*; (2) we use the above computed probabilities as the new init probabilities for the places *A'* and *B'* of the GSPN; (3) we solve the transient for another time interval $t=10^5\,h$ and we compute the probabilities of *A* and *B*, conditioned by the observation *SYS=2*; (4) we use the above computed probabilities as the new init probabilities for the places *A'* and *B'* of the GSPN; (5) we solve the transient for a time interval $t=3*10^5\,h$ and we finally compute the probability of the query of *A*.

Table 7 shows the computed value during the above process. The last row shows the required results

Figure 6. The prediction inference procedure

```
Procedure Prediction

INPUT: a set of queried variables Q, a query time t, a set of temporally labeled evidences eₜₗ, ..., eₜₖ
with t₁<...< tₖ<t

OUTPUT: P(Qₜ | eₜₗ, ..., eₜₖ)

- let t₀=0;
  for i=1 to k {
          - solve the GSPN transient at time (tᵢ-tᵢ₋₁);
          - compute from transient, pᵢ(j)=Pr{Xⱼ|eₜᵢ} for Xⱼ ∈ D ∪ R;
          - update the weights of the immediate init transitions of Xⱼ according to pᵢ(j);
  }
- solve the GSPN transient at time (t-tₖ);
- compute from transient, r=Pr{Q};
- output r;
}
```

Table 7. Probabilities for prediction inference in the case study (ev is the current accumulated evidence)

Time (h)	P(A=1|ev)	P(A=2|ev)	P(B=1|ev)	P(B=2|ev)
100000	*0.909228*	*0.090772*	*0.952445*	*0.047555*
200000	0	1	0.071429	0.928571
500000	**0.521855**	**0.478145**	-	-

Smoothing Inference on GSPN

The smoothing task needs a little more attention than prediction; it consists in computing the probability distribution at time t of a set of queried variables $Q \subseteq D \cup I$, given a stream of observations (evidence) $e_{t1}, ..., e_{tk}$ from time t_1 to time t_k with $t < t_1 <... t_k$. As for prediction, the idea is to perform smoothing by repeatedly solving the corresponding GSPN at the different times corresponding to the observations and the query; however, the problem is how to condition on variables observed at a time instant that follows the current one. The idea is then to try to reformulate the problem in such a way that it can be reduced to a prediction-like task. The approach is then based on the application of Bayes rule as follows:

$$P\left(Q_t \mid e_{t1},...,e_{tk}\right) = \alpha P\left(Q_t\right) \ P\left(e_{t1},...,e_{tk\}} \mid Q_t\right) = \alpha P\left(Q_t\right) \ P\left(e_{t1} \mid Q_t\right)... \ P\left(e_{tk} \mid e_{t1},..., \ e_{tk-1}, \ Q_t\right)$$

In this way, every factor in the above formula is conditioned on the past and can be implemented as in prediction. However, the computation of the normalization factor α, requires that a separate computation must be performed for every possible assignment of the query Q. The interesting point is that such computations are independent, so they can be possibly performed in parallel[4].

Once the computation has been performed for every query assignment, then results can be normalized to get the actual required probability values.

Again, let *Pr{E}* be the probability of event E resulting from the current transient analysis; the pseudo-code for the smoothing procedure is shown in Figure 7. The *normalize* operator just divides any entry of the vector A by the sum of all the entries, in order to provide the final probability vector of the query.

Smoothing in the Case Study

Concerning smoothing inference, let us suppose to have observed the system working at time $t_1 = 300000$ h and failed at time $t_2 = 500000$ h. We ask for the probability distribution of component A at time $t = 200000$ h, conditioned by the above evidence. By considering the procedure outlined in Figure 7 we can compute the required probabilities as follows: (1) we first consider the case $A = 1$; (2) we solve the transient at $t = 2 \cdot 10^5$ h and we compute $r1 = P(A=1)$; (3) we condition A and B on $A=1$ and we determine the new init probabilities for A and B; (4) we solve the transient for $t = 10^5$ h (to reach time $3 * 10^5$ h) and we compute $r2 = P(SYS=1)$; we also condition A and B on $SYS=1$ and we use such

Figure 7. The smoothing inference procedure

```
Procedure Smoothing

INPUT: a set of queried variables Q, a query time t, a set of temporally labeled evidences e_{t1}, ..., e_{tk}
with t < t_1 < ... t_k

OUTPUT: P(Q_t | e_{t1}, ..., e_{tk});

{
        - Let N be the cardinality of possible assignments q_i (1 ≤ i ≤ N) of Q;

        - A: array[N];

          for i=1 to N

            //possibly in parallel

            A[i]=Smooth(q_i);

        - output {\bf normalize}(A);

}

Procedure Smooth(q)

{

        - t_0=t;

        - solve the GSPN transient at time t;

        - compute from transient, r=Pr{Q=q};

        - ev=q;

        for i=1 to k {

                - compute from transient, p_{i-1}(j)=Pr{X_j|ev} for X_j ∈ D ∪ R;

                - update the weights of the immediate init transitions of X_j according to p_{i-1}(j);

                - solve the GSPN transient at time (t_i-t_{i-1});

                - compute from transient, p_i(e)=Pr{e_{ti}}

                - r=rp_i(e);

                - ev=e_{ti}; }

        - output r;

}
```

values as new init probabilities for places A' and B'; (5) we solve the transient for $t=2*10^5\,h$ (to reach time $5*10^5\,h$) and we compute $r3=P(SYS=2)$; (6) we compute the un-normalized probability of $A=1$ as $p1=r1*r2*r3$. By performing the above steps also for the case $A=2$ we can similarly compute the un-normalized probability of $A=2$, namely $p2$. A simple normalization over $p1$ and $p2$ will then produce the required results. Table 8 shows the computed value during the above process (partial results $r1, r2, r3$ are shown in bold).

SOFTWARE TOOL ARCHITECTURE

The architecture of the software tool for GCTBN anlysis is depicted in Figure 8: the GCTBN model is built and evaluated following these steps:

1. The user designs the GCTBN including the observations and the query to be evaluated. Then, the user invokes the analysis of the GCTBN. This is done by means of the graphical tool *Draw-Net* (Codetta et al., 2006) (Figure 9) which can be configured for any kind of formalism. In the specific case, the formalisms GCTBN and GSPN are involved. The GCTBN model is passed to the translator from GCTBN to GSPN, called *GCTBN2GSPN*.

2. The GCTBN model is converted into the equivalent GSPN model by means of *GCTBN2GSPN* following and implementing the specific translation rules. The resulting GSPN is passed to the *Inference Solver*.

3. According to the inference procedure (filtering or smoothing) required by the user, the *Inference Solver* updates the GSPN model with the next measures to be computed and the new transition weights. The updated GSPN is passed to the *GreatSPN input filter*.

4. The *GreatSPN input filter* stores the GSPN model in a couple of files (.net, .def) conforming to the *GreatSPN* (Chiola et al, 1995) format. In particular, the .net file contains the specification of places and transitions in the GSPN, while the .def file contains the specification of the measures to be computed.

5. The .net and .def files together with the time of analysis, are passed to the *GreatSPN* transient solver for GSPN.

6. The *GreatSPN* solver performs the transient analysis of the GSPN. The values of the results are stored in the .sta file.

Table 8. Probabilities for smoothing inference in the case study (ev is the current accumulated evidence)

$P(A=1)$ at $t=2\cdot10^5 = \mathbf{0.833086}$				
Time (h)	**P(A=1|ev)**	**P(B=1|ev)**	**P(SYS=1|ev)**	**P(SYS=2|ev)**
200000	*1*	*0.891238*	-	-
300000	*0.913981*	*0.854028*	**0.999988**	-
500000	-	-	-	**0.000022**
p1=0.0000183277				
$P(A=2)$ at $t=2\cdot10^5 = \mathbf{0.166914}$				
Time (h)	**P(A=1|ev)**	**P(B=1|ev)**	**P(SYS=1|ev)**	**P(SYS=2|ev)**
200000	*0*	*0.999922*	-	-
300000	*0.056648*	*0.952429*	**0.999950**	-
500000	-	-	-	**0.000049**
p1=0.0000081784				
$P(A=1\|ev)$ $P(A=2\|ev)$		p1/(p1+p2)=**0.691452** p2/(p1+p2)=**0.308548**		

Figure 8. Scheme of the software tool architecture

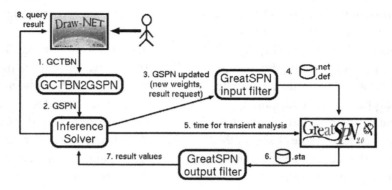

Figure 9. Screenshot of draw-net

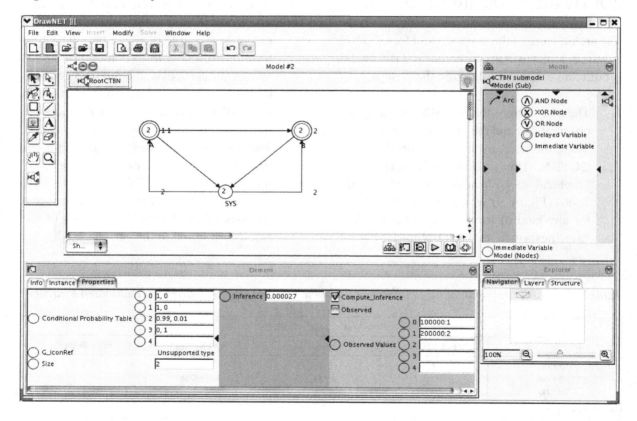

7. The *GreatSPN output filter* loads the results from the .sta file and provides them to the *Inference Solver*. The steps from 3 to 7 are repeated according to the inference procedure requested.

8. The steps from 2 to 7 are repeated according to the inference procedure (filtering or smoothing), the observation times, and the query time. Given all the results returned by *GreatSPN*, the *Inference Solver* generates the result of the query requested by the

user. Such result is passed to *Draw-Net* for the visualization to the user.

All the components of the tool, with the exception of *GreatSPN*, have been developed exploiting the *DNLib* Java library (Codetta et al., 2006). *Draw-Net*, the *GreatSPN input filter* and the *GreatSPN output filter* were previously realized (Codetta et al., 2006). In particular, both filters were realized in order to design and analyze GSPN models by means of *Draw-Net*. The *Inference Solver* and the *GCTBN2GSPN* converter have been specifically developed to deal with GCTBN models.

The GCTBN model designed by means of *Draw-Net*, and the GSPN generated by *GCTBN2GSPN*, are actually objects of the class Model provided by *DNLib,* so it is not necessary to store them into files. The *Inference Solver* and *GCTBN2GSPN* invokes *DNLib* classes and methods in order to manipulate the models. The whole process is transparent to the user. However, the GSPN obtained from the GCTBN can be visualized by means of *Draw-Net*.

VERIFYING INFERENCE RESULTS ON THE DBN MODEL

We presented the procedures to compute prediction and smoothing measures. We applied them to the GSPN corresponding to the GCTBN model of the case study. In order to verify the results reported in Table 7 and 8, now we compare them with the results obtained on the *Dynamic Bayesian Network* (DBN) (Murphy, 2002) in Figure 10 modeling the same case study.

Given a set of time-dependent state variables $X_1, ..., X_n$ and given a BN N defined on such variables, a DBN is essentially a replication of N over two time slices t-Δ and t (being Δ the so called discretization step), with the addition of a set of arcs representing the transition model.

Figure 10. The DBN model of the case study

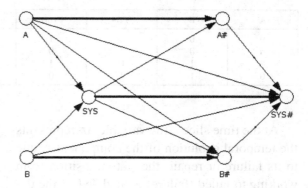

Arcs can connect nodes at different slices or nodes at the same slice. If $X_i^{t-\Delta}$ is the copy of variable X_i at time slice t-Δ, the CPT of $X_i^{t-\Delta}$ specifies the distribution $P[X_i^{t-\Delta}|Y^{t-\Delta}]$ where $Y^{t-\Delta}$ is any set of variables at slice t-Δ different than X_i (possibly the empty set). If X_i^t is the copy of variable X_i at time slice t, the CPT of X_i^t specifies the distribution $P[X_i^t|X_i^{t-\Delta}, Y^{t-\Delta}, Y^t]$ where $Y^{t-\Delta}$ is any set of variables at slice t-Δ different than $X_i^{t-\Delta}$ (possibly the empty set), and Y^t is any set of variables at slice t different than X_i^t (possibly the empty set).

In the DBN depicted in Figure 10, the variables A, B, SYS represent the state of the component A, the component B and the whole system respectively, at the time slice t-Δ. The variables $A\#$, $B\#$, $SYS\#$ have the same role, but at the time slice t. In the DBN of the case study, all the variables are binary: the value 0 is used to model the working state, while the value 1 is used to model the failed state[5].

At the time slice t-Δ, the variables A and B have no parent variables, so their CPT contains the initial probability distribution of their values: since all the components are assumed to be working at the initial time, for both A and B the initial probability to be equal to 0 is null, and the initial probability to be equal to 1 is 1. The variable SYS at the time slice t-Δ depends on A and B: the CPT of SYS expresses the working and failure conditions about the system, and is reported in Table 9[6].

Table 9. CPT for the variable SYS in the DBN model in Figure 10

A	B	SYS	Prob.	A	B	SYS	Prob.
0	0	0	1	1	0	0	0.99
0	0	1	0	1	0	1	0.01
0	1	0	1	1	1	0	0
0	1	1	0	1	1	1	1

At the time slice t, the variable $A\#$ represents the temporal evolution of the component A due to its failure or repair: the state transition from working to failed (failure) is modeled by the dependency of $A\#$ on its copy A at the time slice t-Δ; the state transition from failed to working (repair) is represented by the dependency of $A\#$ on both A and SYS because the repair of the component A is allowed only while the system (SYS) is failed. The time to failure or repair is random and is ruled by the negative exponential distribution; this is reflected in the CPT of the variable $A\#$ (Table 10) according to the time step Δ and the failure and repair rate (λ_A, μ_A).

The variable $B\#$ at the time slice t represents the temporal evolution of the component B. The failure rate of such component changes according to the state of the component A and the eventual activation of B, while the repair of B is allowed only while the system is failed. Therefore $B\#$ depends on A, B and SYS at the time slice t-Δ. The CPT of $B\#$ (Table 11) includes the failure and repair probabilities at time Δ according to λ_B and μ_B.

Finally, the variable $SYS\#$ at the time slice t represents the evolution of the whole system according to the evolution of the components A and B. So, $SYS\#$ depends on SYS, A, B, $A\#$ and $B\#$. The CPT of $SYS\#$ appears in Table 12 and represents the working and failure conditions of the system according to the state of A and B, includ-

Table 10. CPT for the variable A# in the DBN model in Figure 10 (the probabilities of the impossible entries are omitted because they are not significant)

A	SYS	A#	Prob.	A	SYS	A#	Prob.
0	0	0	0.999999	1	0	0	0
0	0	1	0.000001	1	0	1	1
0	1	0	-	1	1	0	0.01
0	1	1	-	1	1	1	0.99

Table 11. CPT for the variable B# in the DBN model in Figure 10 (the probabilities of the impossible entries are omitted because they are not significant)

A	B	SYS	B#	Prob.	A	B	SYS	B#	Prob.
0	0	0	0	0.9999995	1	0	0	0	0.999999
0	0	0	1	0.0000005	1	0	0	1	0.000001
0	0	1	0	-	1	0	1	0	0.9999995
0	0	1	1	-	1	0	1	0	0.0000005
0	1	0	0	0	1	1	0	0	-
0	1	0	1	1	1	1	0	0	-
0	1	1	0	-	1	1	1	0	0.01
0	1	1	1	-	1	1	1	0	0.99

Table 12. CPT for the variable SYS# in the DBN model in Figure 10 (the impossible entries are omitted)

A	B	SYS	A#	B#	SYS#	Prob.		A	B	SYS	A#	B#	SYS#	Prob.
0	0	0	0	0	0	1		1	0	1	0	0	0	1
0	0	0	0	0	1	0		1	0	1	0	0	1	0
0	0	0	0	1	0	1		1	0	1	0	1	0	1
0	0	0	0	1	1	0		1	0	1	0	1	1	0
0	0	0	1	0	0	0.99		1	0	1	1	0	0	0
0	0	0	1	0	1	0.01		1	0	1	1	0	1	1
0	0	0	1	1	0	0		1	0	1	1	1	0	0
0	0	0	1	1	1	1		1	0	1	1	1	1	1
0	1	0	0	1	0	1		1	1	1	0	0	0	1
0	1	0	0	1	1	0		1	1	1	0	0	1	0
0	1	0	1	1	0	0		1	1	1	0	1	0	1
0	1	0	1	1	1	1		1	1	1	0	1	1	0
1	0	0	1	0	0	1		1	1	1	1	0	0	0.99
1	0	0	1	0	1	0		1	1	1	1	0	1	0.01
1	0	0	1	1	0	0		1	1	1	1	1	0	0
1	0	0	1	1	1	1		1	1	1	1	1	1	1

ing the possibility that the component B is not activated in case of failure of A.

The inference of the DBN model of the case study has been performed by means of the *Radyban* tool (Portinale et al., 2007)[7]. We have computed the same inference measures. First, the prediction task assuming to observe $SYS=0$ at time $t_1=100000$ h and $SYS=1$ at time $t_2=200000$ h, has been performed on the DBN model in Figure 10, querying the node $A\#$. The results appear in Table 13: we can observe that the probabilities computed at time 500000 h are very close to the values obtained for the same measure on the GSPN model in Figure 5, as reported in Table 7. In this way, we verify the correctness of the prediction procedure in Figure 6.

Then, we have performed the smoothing task on the DBN model assuming the observation that $SYS=0$ at time $t_1=300000$ h and $SYS=1$ at time $t_2=500000$ h. We have queried again the node $A\#$ at several mission times obtaining the results appearing in Table 14. We can notice that the probabilities at time 200000 h are very similar to those obtained on the GSPN model (Table 8) by means of the smoothing inference procedure specified in Figure 7. This confirms the correctness of such procedure.

FUTURE RESEARCH DIRECTIONS

Analyzing a GCTBN by means of the underlying GSPN is only one possibility that does not take

Table 13. Prediction inference results for the variable A# in the DBN model in Figure 10. ev={ SYS=0 at time t_1=100000 h, SYS=1 at time t_2=200000 h }

Time (h)	$P(A=0|ev)$	$P(A=1|ev)$
100000	0.909251	0.090749
200000	0.000000	1.000000
300000	0.532266	0.467726
400000	0.527495	0.472497
500000	**0.524189**	**0.475810**

Table 14. Smoothing inference results for the variable A# in the DBN model in Figure 10. ev={ SYS=0 at time t_1=300000 h, SYS=1 at time t_2=500000 h }

Time (h)	$P(A=0|ev)$	$P(A=1|ev)$
100000	0.831101	0.168900
200000	**0.689048**	**0.310946**
300000	0.569523	0.430477
400000	0.468789	0.531207
500000	0.000000	1.000000

explicit advantage of the structure of the graph as in CTBN algorithms (Nodelman et al., 2005; Saria et al., 2007). Our future works will try to investigate the possibility of adopting cluster-based or stochastic simulation approximations, even on GCTBN models, and in comparing their performance and quality with respect to GSPN-based solution techniques. In particular, since Petri Nets are a natural framework for event-based simulation, it would be interesting to investigate how simulation-based approximations can be actually guided by the underlying GSPN model. Finally, since symbolic representations (based on matrices or decision diagrams) have been proved very useful for the analysis of GSPN models, it would also be of significant interest to study the relationships between such representations and the inference procedures on probabilistic graphical models in general, since this could in principle open the possibility of new classes of algorithms for BN-based formalisms.

CONCLUSION

We have presented a software framework for the analysis of GCTBN which allow one to mix in the same model continuous time delayed variables with standard "immediate" chance variables. The usefulness of this kind of model has been discussed through an example concerning the reliability of a simple component-based system. The analysis of GCTBN is based on their conversion into GSPN and exploits well established GSPN analysis techniques, in order to perform standard prediction or smoothing inference. In particular, adopting GSPN solution algorithms as the basis for GCTBN inference, allows one to take advantage of specialized methodologies for solving the underlying stochastic process, that are currently able to deal with extremely large models; in particular, such techniques (based on data structures like matrices or decision diagrams) allows for one order of magnitude of increase in the size of

the models, to be solved exactly, with respect to standard methods, meaning that models with an order of 10^{10} tangible states can actually be solved (Miner, 2007). Exact inference of CTBN model may be impractical if the model size grows, so approximate algorithms are applied. The GSPN based analysis of GCTBN models provide exact results and can be applied to CTBN models as well.

ACKNOWLEDGMENT

The authors thank the students Valentina Zogno and Simonetta Busatta for implementing the *GCTBN2GSPN* converter and the *Inference Solver*, respectively.

REFERENCES

Ajmone-Marsan, M., Balbo, G., Conte, G., Donatelli, S., & Franceschinis, G. (1995). *Modelling with generalized stochastic Petri nets*. Hoboken, NJ: J.Wiley.

Bechta-Dugan, J., Bavuso, S. J., & Boyd, M. A. (1992). Dynamic fault-tree models for fault-tolerant computer systems. *IEEE Transactions on Reliability*, *41*, 363–377. doi:10.1109/24.159800.

Boyen, X., & Koller, D. (1998). Tractable inference for complex stochastic processes. In *Proceedings of Conference on Uncertainty in Artificial Intelligence* (pp. 33–42). AUAI.

Chiola, G., Franceschinis, G., Gaeta, R., & Ribaudo, M. (1995). GreatSPN 1.7: Graphical editor and analyzer for timed and stochastic Petri nets. *Performance Evaluation*, *24*(1-2), 47–68. doi:10.1016/0166-5316(95)00008-L.

Codetta-Raiteri, D., Franceschinis, G., & Gribaudo, M. (2006). Defining formalisms and models in the draw-net modelling system. In *Proceedings of International Workshop on Modelling of Objects, Components and Agents* (pp. 123–144). University of Hamburg.

Codetta-Raiteri, D., & Portinale, L. (2010). Generalized continuous time Bayesian networks and their GSPN semantics. In *Proceedings of European Workshop on Probabilistic Graphical Models* (pp. 105-112). HIIT.

Distefano, S., & Puliafito, A. (2009). Dependability evaluation with dynamic reliability block diagrams and dynamic fault trees. *IEEE Transactions on Dependable and Secure Computing*, *6*(1), 4–17. doi:10.1109/TDSC.2007.70242.

El-Hay, T., Friedman, N., & Kupferman, R. (2008). Gibbs sampling in factorized continuous time Markov processes. In *Proceedings of Conference on Uncertainty in Artificial Intelligence*. AUAI.

Fan, Y., & Shelton, C. (2008). Sampling for approximate inference in continuous time Bayesian networks. In *Proceedings of International Symposium on AI and Mathematics*. Springer.

Gopalratnam, K., Kautz, H., & Weld, D. S. (2005). Extending continuous time bayesian networks. In *Proceedings of AAAI Conference on Artificial Intelligence* (pp. 981–986). AAAI.

Langseth, H., & Portinale, L. (2007). Bayesian networks in reliability. *Reliability Engineering & System Safety*, *92*, 92–108. doi:10.1016/j.ress.2005.11.037.

Miner, A. S. (2007). Decision diagrams for the exact solution of Markov models. *Applied Mathematics and Mechanics*, *7*(1).

Murphy, K. (2002). *Dynamic Bayesian networks: Representation, inference and learning.* (PhD Thesis). UC Berkeley, Berkeley, CA.

Nodelman, U., Shelton, C. R., & Koller, D. (2005). Expectation propagation for continuous time Bayesian networks. In *Proceedings of Conference on Uncertainty in Artificial Intelligence* (pp. 431–440). AUAI.

Portinale, L., Bobbio, A., Codetta-Raiteri, D., & Montani, S. (2007). Compiling dynamic fault trees into dynamic Bayesian nets for reliability analysis: The RADYBAN tool. In *Proceedings of CEUR Workshop*. CEUR.

Portinale, L., Codetta-Raiteri, D., & Montani, S. (2010). Supporting reliability engineers in exploiting the power of dynamic bayesian networks. *International Journal of Approximate Reasoning*, *51*(2), 179–195. doi:10.1016/j.ijar.2009.05.009.

Sahner, R. A., Trivedi, K. S., & Puliafito, A. (1996). *Performance and reliability analysis of computer systems: An example-based approach using the SHARPE software package.* Boston: Kluwer Academic Publisher. doi:10.1007/978-1-4615-2367-3.

Saria, S., Nodelman, U., & Koller, D. (2007). Reasoning at the right time granularity. In *Proceedings of Conference on Uncertainty in Artificial Intelligence* (pp. 421–430). IEEE.

ADDITIONAL READING

Balbo, G., Chiola, G., Franceschinis, G., & Molinari-Roet, G. (1987). On the efficient construction of tangible reachability graph of GSPN. *Workshop on Petri Nets and Performance Evaluation* (pp. 136–145).

Codetta-Raiteri, D., Franceschinis, G., Iacono, M., & Vittorini, V. (2004). Repairable fault tree for the automatic evaluation of repair policies. *International Conference on Dependable Systems and Networks* (pp. 157–159).

Dean, T., & Kanazawa, K. (1989). A model for reasoning about persistence and causation. *Computational Intelligence*, *5*(3), 142–150. doi:10.1111/j.1467-8640.1989.tb00324.x.

Jensen, F. V., & Nielsen, T. D. (2007). *Bayesian Networks and Decision Graphs* (2nd ed.). Springer. doi:10.1007/978-0-387-68282-2.

Kjaerulff, U. (1995). dHugin: a computational system for dynamic time-sliced Bayesian networks. *International Journal of Forecasting*, *11*, 89–101. doi:10.1016/0169-2070(94)02003-8.

Miner, A. S. (2004). Implicit GSPN reachability set generation using decision diagrams. *Performance Evaluation*, *56*(1-4), 145–165. doi:10.1016/j.peva.2003.07.005.

Miner, A. S., & Parker, D. (2004). Symbolic representation and analysis of large probabilistic systems. In *Validation of Stochastic Systems* (pp. 296–338). Springer. doi:10.1007/978-3-540-24611-4_9.

Nodelman, U., Shelton, C. R., & Koller, D. (2002). Continuous Time Bayesian Networks. *Conference on Uncertainty in Artificial Intelligence* (pp. 378–387).

Portinale, L., & Codetta-Raiteri, D. (2009). Generalizing Continuous Time Bayesian Networks with Immediate Nodes. *Workshop on Graph Structures for Knowledge Representation and Reasoning*.

Schneeweiss, W. G. (1999). *The Fault Tree Method*. LiLoLe Verlag.

Weber, P., Medina-Oliva, G., Simon, C., & Iung, B. (2012). Overview on Bayesian Networks applications for dependability, risk analysis and maintenance areas. *Engineering Applications of Artificial Intelligence*, *25*(4), 671–682. doi:10.1016/j.engappai.2010.06.002.

KEY TERMS AND DEFINITION

BN: Bayesian Network.
CDA: Closest Delayed Ancestor.
CIM: Conditional Intensity Matrix.
CPT: Conditional Probability Table.
CTBN: Continuous Time Bayesian Network.
CTMC: Continuous Time Markov Chain.
DAG: Directed Acyclic Graph.
DBN: Dynamic Bayesian Network.
FTA: Fault Tree Analysis.
GCTBN: Generalized Continuous Time Bayesian Network.
GSPN: Generalized Stochastic Petri Net.
MRF: Markov Random Field.

ENDNOTES

[1] Notice that, in principle, different repair policies can be adopted (Portinale et al., 2010); the one proposed in this example is a kind of subsystem local policy, with the repair of the minimal set of necessary working components.

[2] Actually, since prior probabilities on immediate root nodes are a special case of CPT, then we could also simply write $P^0_V = P^0_D \prod_{Yj \in I} P[Y_j | Pa(Y_j)]$, to emphasize the fact that, for the specification of the temporal evolution of the model, the only initial distribution is on delayed nodes (the other parameters are actually a fixed specification on the network).

[3] In case of transitions having weights (or rates) equal to *0*, they can be omitted from the model; in Figure 5 they are shown, for the sake of generality.

[4] An alternative can be to directly compute the denominator of the Bayes formula (i.e. the probability of the evidence stream); however, this requires a larger number of

transient solutions if the length of observation stream is greater than the number N of assignments of Q (i.e. if $k>N$), as is usually the case.

[5] This differs from the GCTBN model where the value *1* stands for the working state, while the value *2* stands for the failed state.

[6] This CPT corresponds to the CPT reported in Table 4 and concerning the variable *SYS*

in the GCTBN model in Figure 1, but with the difference that the working state is represented as *1*, and the failed state as *2*.

[7] Because of the time discretization in DBN models, the results obtained on such models suffer from some approximation. The approximation degree is proportional to the time step Δ used to discretize the mission time.

Chapter 8
GPA:
A Multiformalism, Multisolution Approach to Efficient Analysis of Large–Scale Population Models

Jeremy T. Bradley
Imperial College London, UK

Marcel C. Guenther
Imperial College London, UK

Richard A. Hayden
Imperial College London, UK

Anton Stefanek
Imperial College London, UK

ABSTRACT

This chapter discusses the latest trends and developments in performance analysis research of large population models. In particular, it reviews GPA, a state-of-the-art Multiformalism, Multisolution (MFMS) tool that provides a framework for the implementation of various population modelling formalisms and solution methods.

1 INTRODUCTION

A decade ago Sanders (Sanders 1999) noted that in spite of research advances in the performance modelling and analysis field, the work of performance analysts has by no means become easier since both the expectation in their work as well as the complexity of systems to be evaluated have also grown considerably. To equip performance analysts with expressive modelling formalisms and

efficient solution methods, Sanders suggested a multiformalism, multisolution (MFMS) paradigm that would not only allow modellers to model systems in a natural composite manner using different formalisms in the same model, but also provide them with different analysis options for such heterogeneous composite models.

While MFMS research and tools development have led to a better range of software products for performance analysts, there are still quite a lot of open research challenges in the performance

DOI: 10.4018/978-1-4666-4659-9.ch008

community with regards to improving formalisms and their solution techniques. Population models, which are the focus of this chapter, are one such area that has recently received a lot of attention in the literature due to the growing need to model and analyse crowd behaviour (Massink et al. 2011), biological systems (Ciochetta & Hillston 2009) as well as large, distributed communication systems with thousands of network participants (Stefanek et al. 2010). The challenge in analysing these models is the fact that the state-space of population models increases exponentially in the number of interacting individuals/agents, making it computationally expensive to solve such models using traditional Monte Carlo simulation techniques. Moreover, even moderate population models with only a few hundred agents often exceed the capabilities of traditional numerical state-space avoidance and largeness tolerance solution methods. As a consequence, novel mean-field analysable formalisms have been developed, which can efficiently handle models with large populations. The efficient mean-field/fluid analysis techniques look at the models from a macroscopic point of view instead of treating every component at an individual level. By aggregating the behaviour of individual components, it is often possible to derive a set of Ordinary Differential Equations (ODEs) whose solution expresses the evolution of probabilistic measures such as the means and higher order moments of populations.

Grouped PEPA Analyser (GPA) (Stefanek et al. 2010) is an advanced software solution for population modelling and mean-field analysis. Originally developed for the analysis of the Grouped PEPA process algebra (GPEPA) (Hayden & Bradley 2010, Hillston 2005) in 2009, the tool has since been extended to support a range of different population modelling formalisms and solution methods. As this change continues, the tool is slowly embracing more and more MFMS principles, with a strong focus on population modelling formalisms. In this chapter we give an overview of mean-field analysable population

models and describe how the architecture of GPA facilitates the implementation of new formalisms and solution techniques for such models. The chapter is organised as follows; In Section 2 we define population modelling, introduce different classes of mean-field analysable formalisms in Section 2.1 and formally describe a Population CTMCs, the central intermediate representation used by GPA, in Section 2.2. In addition to this, Section 2.3 reviews related MFMS and population modelling tools. Section 3 and 4 describe the architecture of GPA and show how different formalisms and solution techniques were implemented. Finally, Section 5 discusses future extensions for GPA and we present our conclusions in Section 6.

2 BACKGROUND

Population models describe interactions between individuals, which are grouped into populations. Individuals can represent a number of different entities or agents such as people, telecommunication equipment or vehicles to name but a few. While the individual behaviour of agents can be described using a small set of rules, the simulation of population models becomes infeasible when looking at the interaction of thousands or millions of individuals. However, when grouping a large number of individuals into populations, it is possible to evaluate the effects of interactions using efficient mean-field analysis techniques rather than simulation.

2.1 Mean-Field Analysable Population Models

Before we discuss the population model classes that are currently supported by GPA, we would like to give a brief overview of different population model classes and measures that can be calculated with mean-field fluid techniques. To distinguish between different classes of population models, we consider different possibilities of

- Agent state-space.
- State sojourn time distribution.
- Distribution of the next state after each transition.
- The method of accumulation and feedback.

From the perspective of an individual, the state-space can be discrete, continuous or mixed. For instance, if we were to model a single mobile device, its state-space might consist of a continuous variable for the remaining battery charge, as well as a set of discrete states to keep track of whether the device is idle or in communication mode. Thus the state of an individual with discrete modes from a set D and continuous attributes can be expressed as a tuple in $D \times \mathbb{R}^c$ or a state-space of $(D \times \mathbb{R}^c)^n$ for a population of n devices. The abstraction from individual to population specific measures enables us to use a more compact state-space representation of $(\mathbb{N} \times (\mathbb{R}^c \to \mathbb{R}))^d$. Then each state is a d tuple with the i-th element being a tuple (n_i, f_i) where n_i is the number of devices in state d_i and $f_i(x_1,...,x_c)$ is the distribution function over the continuous quantities.

Throughout this chapter, we consider models that evolve in continuous time. The sojourn time is the time it takes for an agent to transit from one discrete mode to another. Traditionally, this is an exponentially distributed random variable, enforcing the Markov property and enabling various efficient analysis techniques. Furthermore these can be readily be generalised to the cases where the sojourn time follows a phase type distribution. However, realistic examples often require further distributions that cannot be efficiently represented as a phase type distribution. For example, deterministic and uniformly distributed delays and delays from distributions with heavy tails would require intractably large phase type representations. This forms a distinction between individual agents being represented by a Continuous Time Markov Chain (CTMC) in the exponential/phase type case and by a Generalised Semi-Markov Process (GSMP) in the general case. Moreover, in some models the sojourn time for an individual agent is undefined and only determined globally when the agent is synchronised with another agent.

After each transition, an agent changes its state from one mode to another. The second mode could follow a deterministic, probabilistic or a non-deterministic choice. In this framework, we directly represent only a deterministic choice. However, the probabilistic choice can in some cases be emulated by adding additional transitions with appropriately weighted rates.

In case the agent state space contains continuous variables, the way these evolve over time has to be defined. Traditionally, each of the individual agent continuous variables accumulates linearly over time, with rate depending on its current mode. These could also evolve in a different way, such as with non-linear rates or with added stochastic noise. In addition to individual agent continuous variables, models can feature global continuous variables, for example representing temperature, the total cost of the system etc. Both local and global continuous variables may also feed back into the sojourn time distribution parameters and affect the distribution of agent transitions. Time-inhomogeneous behaviour can be seen as a special case, with time being represented by a continuous variable evolving linearly with rate .

Not all the combinations of the above possibilities have been considered, especially in the context of mean-field/fluid analysis. Some examples of existing work include:

1. The agent state space is discrete, sojourn times are exponential and next mode chosen deterministically. Examples include the PEPA/GPEPA process algebras, chemical equations, BioPEPA, MASSPA spatial process algebra, Stochastic Petri Nets. It is possible to derive ODEs describing means (Hillston 2005) and higher moments (Hayden & Bradley 2010) of populations.

2. Additionally, the discrete state space is extended with global continuous state space, where the continuous variables accumulate in between discrete transitions according to a system of ODEs. It is possible to extend the ODEs for the discrete model with additional equations capturing the means and higher moments of the continuous variables - both in case of no feedback (Stefanek, Hayden & Bradley 2011) and feedback from the continuous variables (Stefanek et al. 2012).

3. The sojourn times can be deterministic in addition to exponential. It is possible to derive Delay Differential Equations for the mean of populations (Hayden 2012a, Bortolussi & Hillston 2012a).

4. Individual agents can contain continuous variables. It is possible to derive Partial Differential Equations (PDEs) for the mean populations and distribution of the values of the continuous quantities (Hayden 2012c, Chaintreau et al. 2009).

The GPA tool generalises techniques listed in (i) and (ii). It uses an intermediate representation, so-called Population Continuous-Time Markov Chains (PCTMCs), that capture features of the formalisms mentioned in (i). This representation is augmented with continuous variables to capture the formalisms in (ii). GPA implements the efficient mean-field/fluid techniques for PCTMC models. In this chapter we will provide an overview of how different formalisms can be translated into this intermediate representation and how the techniques can be used to answer additional questions about the models.

2.2 PCTMC

Population Continuous-Time Markov Chains (PCTMCs) consist of a finite set of populations S, $n = |S|$ and a set E of transition classes. States are represented as an integer vector

$\vec{P}(t) = (P_1(t), ..., P_n(t)) \in \mathbb{N}^n$, with the i-th component being the current population level of species $S_i \in S$ at time t. A transition class $e \in E$ is a tuple $(\mathrm{r}_e, \vec{\mathrm{c}}_e) \in \mathrm{E}$ that describes a transition with negatively exponentially distributed delay D at rate $r_e : \mathbb{Z}^n \to \mathbb{R}$, which sets the population vector $\vec{P}(t + D)$ to $\vec{P}(t) + \vec{c}_e$. The analogue to PCTMCs in the systems biology literature are Chemical Reaction Systems, were $\vec{P}(t)$ describes a molecule count vector and transition classes represent chemical reactions between the molecules with being the reaction rate function and $\vec{c}\_e$ the stoichiometric vector for a specific reaction. For notational convenience we write a transition class (or an event) as:

$$\underbrace{S_{i_1} + ... + S_{i_k}}_{in} \to \underbrace{S_{j_1} + ... + S_{j_l}}_{out} \text{ at } r_e\left(\vec{P}(t)\right)$$

(1)

where $S_* \in S$ represent different species that are involved in the event - of them on left hand side and 1 on the right hand side of the above equation. The corresponding change vector is $\vec{c}_e = \left(s_1^{out} - s_1^{in}, ..., s_n^{out} - s_n^{in}\right) \in \mathbb{Z}^n$ where s_i^{in} represents the number of occurrences of a particular species on the left hand side of the event and the number of its occurrences on the right hand side. The rate of each transition depends on the current population level $\vec{P}(t)$ and is equal to:

$$\begin{cases} r_e(\vec{P}(t)) & \text{if } P_i(t) \geq s_i^{in} \text{ for all } i - 1, ..., n. \\ 0 & \text{otherwise} \end{cases}$$

(2)

An important feature of PCTMC models is that approximations to the evolution of population moments of the underlying stochastic process can be represented by the following system of ordinary differential equations (ODEs) (Hayden & Bradley 2010, Hillston 2005, e.g.)

$$\frac{d}{dt}\mathbb{E}\Big[T\big(\vec{P}(t)\big)\Big] = \sum_{e \in E} \mathbb{E} \qquad (3)$$

$$\Big[\big(T\big(\vec{P}(t) + \vec{c}_e\big) - T\big(\vec{P}(t)\big)\big) r_e\big(\vec{P}(t)\big)\Big]$$

where $T : \mathbb{Z}^n \to \mathbb{R}$ is a real valued function defined on the populations.

To obtain the ODEs describing the evolution of the mean of a population , all we need to do is to substitute $T(\vec{P}(t)) = P_i(t)$ in the above system of equations, where $P_i(t)$ is the random variable representing the population count of species at time . The right hand side of this ODE can depend on further means (after some approximating assumptions are considered) which have to be included in the final system of ODEs. In the literature the resulting system of ODEs is often referred to as the mean-field approximation. Similarly, ODEs for higher joint moments can be obtained by choosing adequate $T(\vec{P}(t))$, e.g. $T(\vec{P}(t)) = P_i(t) - \mathbb{E}[P_i(t)]^2$ for the variance of $P_i(t)$. Alternatively stochastic simulation (Gillespie 1977) can be used to evaluate PCTMCs. Like discrete event simulation for low-level protocol models, this latter simulation technique captures the stochastic behaviour of PCTMCs exactly, but does not scale for models with larger populations.

2.3 Related Tools

Before describing the features and architecture of GPA in detail, we ought to review existing population and multiformalism modelling and analysis tools. In doing so we also provide a high-level comparison between GPA and other popular tools that have been developed by the research community over the last decade. In their purest form, multiformalism modelling and solution tools should allow modellers to compose models build from smaller sub-models, each of which may have been defined in its own specific formalism (Sander 1999). Subsequently the composite model is analysed by the software in order to work which solution methods can be used to evaluate the performance measures selected by the user. Currently, the most sophisticated tool that follows this paradigm is Möbius (Deavours et al. 2002). Similar tools, although less well-known and versatile, are DrawNET++ (Gribaudo et al. 2005), SHARPE (Sahner et al. 1997) and SMART (Ciardo & Miner 1996). Tools such as GPA (Stefanek et al. 2010) and PRISM (Kwiatkowska et al. 2011) belong to a slightly less generic class of multiformalism, multisolution (MFMS) tools, as their focus is less on the evaluation of compositional models containing sub-models expressed in different formalisms. Instead, they provide a modelling and evaluation framework that easily allows programmers to add a range of formalisms and re-use existing solution methods. The reason for this difference is mainly because both GPA and PRISM were designed as specialised frameworks with a focus on large population models and probabilistic model checking, respectively. What is interesting though is that the current evolution of GPA is currently moving into the direction of the original multiformalism, multisolution modelling paradigm, suggested by Sanders (Sanders 1999).

To see why this is the case we need to briefly review the architecture of the Möbius framework. Möbius is currently the most powerful MFMS tool because of its well-defined, generic Abstract Functional Interface (AFI) (Deavours et al. 2002) in which virtually any low-level formalism, e.g. CTMCs, GSMPs, Coloured Stochastic PetriNets, can be implemented. Through the AFI, any two sub-models written in a formalism that is implemented using the interface, can be combined into a larger composite model and analysed using a single solver. This is made possible by properties, i.e. a form of meta-data, which are added to each formalism implementation of the AFI. Depending on its underlying formalism and nature, a sub-model exposes properties that determine suitable solution methods. Naturally, any model expressed in any formalism can be analysed using stochastic simulation techniques. However, other, more efficient solvers, can be used on models that satisfy certain properties, for instance models that translate to CTMCs. When analysing composite models with two or more sub-models, Möbius can algorithmically find all suitable solvers by taking into account the nature of the composition and the individual properties of the sub-models. While this maximises the re-use of solvers for different formalisms, it also means that any novel properties required by newly implemented solution algorithms have to be added to the existing formalisms supported by Möbius.

While the PCTMC formalism that represents the current low-level interface of GPA is much less abstract than the AFI, it is still true to say that the low-level population formalism of GPA is slowly becoming more generic. While Möbius was designed to be a multiformalism, multisolution tool from the very beginning, the growing abstractness of GPA's low-level formalism is an evolutionary development that is driven by the recent surge in research on fluid analysis techniques for large population models in the performance community. GPA started as a tool for the evaluation of the GPEPA formalism (Hayden & Bradley 2010) and was only later extended to cater for other formalisms such as MASSPA (Guenther & Bradley 2011), the Chemical Reaction style formalism (Section 2.2) and Unified Stochastic Probes defined over the GPEPA process algebra (Kohut et al. 2012). Ultimately, future versions of GPA will feature even more generic population formalisms than PCTMCs in order to support a range of non-Markovian population formalisms (Section 5) as well as composite models. As part of this change, a Möbius inspired property metadata language for efficient application of different solution methods across different formalisms, is likely to be added.

Having discussed different MFMS tools, we also need to look at other population modelling and analysis frameworks that support similar models as GPA does. Most notable are the tools that were written for the evaluation of Bio-PEPA (Ciocchetta & Hillston 2009), SCCP (Bortolussi & Policriti 2008) and Markovian Agent Models (MAM) (Gribaudo et al. 2008).

Bio-PEPA is an evolution of the PEPA process algebra aimed towards modelling of biological systems at various levels of abstraction, such as bio-chemical networks (Ciochetta et al. 2010), epidemiological models (Ciocchetta & Hillston 2010) and emergent behaviour in crowd dynamics (Massink et al. 2011). The Bio-PEPA language is supported by the Bio-PEPA tool suite (Ciochetta et al. 2009), consisting of the Bio-PEPA Eclipse plugin and the Bio-PEPA workbench. The Bio-PEPA Eclipse plugin contains a full tool chain that allows modellers to specify Bio-PEPA models and analyse them with fluid analysis and simulation. The Bio-PEPA workbench is an experimental tool that provides researchers with a way to export Bio-PEPA models into further representations that can be used with a range of simulators and ODE solvers, or for example the PRISM model checking tool. Some work has been done to show how Bio-PEPA can be used as an intermediate formalism, thus allowing the solution techniques provided by the Bio-PEPA tool suite to be applied to a wider range of models. For example, a subset of the models specified in the Systems Biology Graphical Notation Process Description can be translated into Bio-PEPA (Loewe et al. 2011).

While some of the tools like Bio-PEPA offer additional solution methods for PCTMCs that are currently not available in GPA, these could be added in principle. Moreover, much like it was shown how the MAM formalism can be implemented in GPA (Guenther & Bradley 2011), it would also be possible to add Bio-PEPA and SCCP grammars.

3 POPULATION MODEL DEFINITION AND ANALYSIS IN GPA

The high level architecture of GPA is shown in Figure 1. The central representation is based on the PCTMC formalism introduced in Section 4.2, to which all the other supported formalisms are translated. Currently, the supported formalisms are: a simple language similar to chemical equations, the GPEPA process algebra and MASSPA algebra for spatial models.

All formalisms use a common specification interface which defines the format of the input to GPA. The initial section contains a definition of all the parameter constants in the model. This is followed by the model definition which is spe-cific to the formalisms. Defined models can be analysed using different explicitly specified solution techniques, described in Section 4. The analysis can compute various metrics of interest that are based around the moments of the populations in the model. In case of the GPEPA formalism, GPA additionally provides and implementation of the Unified Stochastic Probes formalism. This allows modellers to specify complex passage time measures based on the model behaviour. The GPEPA model is automatically augmented with additional states that are translated into new PCTMC populations.

Moments of these populations are then implicitly used to produce the desired passage time

Figure 1. Architecture of the GPA tool. The input file format supports different model formalisms. Models are translated into a PCTMC intermediate representation. Each type of analysis generates an abstract representation from the PCTMC model. This is translated into a specific implementation and solved with a numerical solver. The implementation can be passed into further secondary solvers that allow parameter exploration, compute complex passage time probabilities or compute the distributions of various metrics over time.

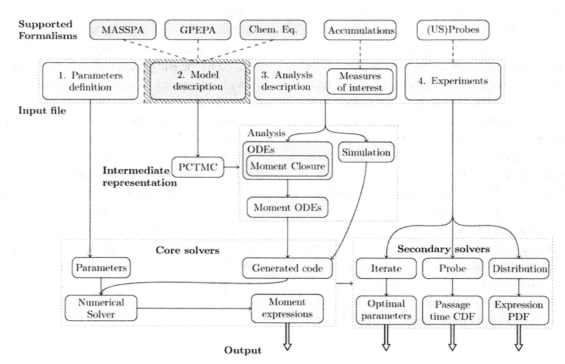

probabilities. We describe the USP formalism and the extended analysis process in Section 4.2.2.

Furthermore, GPA extends the solution techniques to allow the analysis to produce metrics based around accumulations defined on the population levels. These can be useful when modelling continuous quantities such as energy consumption or temperature.

Finally, the metrics from the analysis can form objective functions and constraints in parameter optimisation experiments introduced in Section 4.2. In general, the resulting global optimisation problems are hard and computationally not feasible. However, when the mean-field analysis solution method is chosen, even naive sweeping algorithms can explore a large range of parameters. The architecture shown in Figure 1 is designed to support future extensions of PCTMCs (Section 5) such as population models with deterministically (Hayden 2012a) or generally timed delays (Hayden 2011) or rates that depend on a feedback from reward measures (Stefanek et al. 2011). As shown in Figure 1, the input of GPA starts with a declaration of all used parameters. These are of the form:

```
alpha=0.1;
beta=0.2'
...
```

3.1 Simple Chemical Equations

GPA supports a formalism that directly represents PCTMCs in form of equations as in Equation (1). Each model is defined by a set of such equations and a list of initial population values. The population names used in the equations, rates and initial values definitions are uppercase strings enclosed in braces, such as {S}. Figure 2 shows a GPA definition of a model of a circadian clock (Engblom 2006). There are populations and equations (transition classes). At time t=0, all the populations are except for {Da} and {Dr} equal to .

After the definition, various types of analysis can be performed on the model. For example, the underlying PCTMC can be simulated to obtain sample traces of population evolution or statistics from a large number of simulation traces. Figure 3 shows an example of a single trace and a mean of populations of species and obtained from simulation traces.

Alternatively, GPA implements efficient fluid analysis solution techniques introduced in Section 4.1.2. Figure 4 shows the means of species and for the same parameter values as the simulation analysis in Figure 3a. This model is an example where the first order mean-field analysis is not sufficient to capture oscillations in the populations and a second order analysis is required.

Figure 2. GPA syntax of a simple chemical equations model of a circadian clock

```
{Da_} -> {Da}    @ {Da_}*theta_a;              -> {A} @ {Ma}*beta_a;
{Da} + {A} -> {Da_} @ {Da}{A}*gamma_a;          -> {A} @ {Da_}*theta_a;
{Dr_} -> {Dr}    @ {Dr_}*theta_r;              -> {A} @ {Dr_}*theta_r;
{Dr} + {A} -> {Dr_} @ {Dr}{A}*gamma_r;    {A} ->     @ {A}*delta_a;
                                     {A} + {R} -> {C} @ {A}{R}*gamma_c;
        -> {Ma}    @ {Da_}*alpha_a_;
        -> {Ma}    @ {Da}*alpha_a;                 -> {R} @ {Mr}*beta_r;
   {Ma} ->         @ {Ma}*delta_ma;        {R} ->     @ {R}*delta_r;
                                           {C} -> {R} @ {C}*delta_a;
        -> {Mr}    @ {Dr_}*alpha_r_;
        -> {Mr}    @ {Dr}*alpha_r;     {Da} = 1;
   {Mr} ->         @ {Mr}*delta_mr;    {Dr} = 1;
```

Figure 3. Single trace and a mean of populations of species R and C obtained from simulation traces

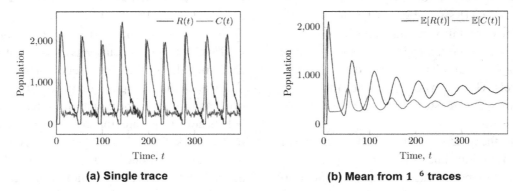

(a) Single trace **(b) Mean from 1 ⁶ traces**

Figure 4. Means of species R and C for the same parameter values as the simulation analysis in Figure 3 (a)

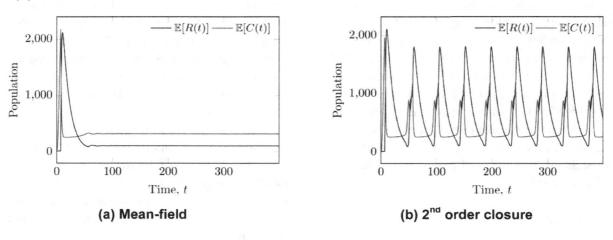

(a) Mean-field **(b) 2ⁿᵈ order closure**

3.2 GPEPA

GPA has originally been developed as an implementation of the higher order fluid techniques in (Hayden & Bradley 2010). GPA models can be described in the Grouped PEPA (GPEPA) process algebra. The input file syntax closely follows the formal definition of GPEPA. Processes can be defined as a choice between a number of actions (the operator) or synchronised in parallel by the operator where is a set of actions:

$$S ::= (\alpha,r).S \mid S + S \mid C_S$$
$$P ::= P \underset{L}{\triangleright\triangleleft} P \mid C$$

The initial part of the model definition contains a number of component definitions, written as equations with the component label on the left hand side and the corresponding PEPA process on the right.

The system equation is defined as a composition of different labeled groups. Each group contains a large number of identical components that do not directly communicate. Different types of components in the group are separates by the operator. Groups can be composed in parallel with the PEPA operator:

$$G : \boldsymbol{G}\{P[n] \mid ... \mid P[n]\}$$
$$M : M \underset{L}{\triangleright\triangleleft} M$$

Figure 5. Simple client/server model

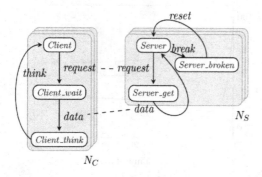

```
Client          = (req, rreq).Client_waiting;
Client_waiting  = (data, rdata).Client_think;
Client_think    = (think, rthink).Client;

Server          = (req, rreq).Server_get
  + (break, rbreak).Server_broken;
    Server_get     = (data, rdata).Server;
    Server_broken  = (reset, rreset).Server;

Clients{Client[N_c]}<req,data>Servers{Server[N_s]}
```

(a) **Diagram of the system equation.** (b) **GPA definition using GPEPA syntax.**

where n is an integer and G a group label. For example, Figure 5 shows a simple Client/Server model. The model consists of a large number of clients and servers. Each client repeatedly requests some data from the group of servers and subsequently receives the data and performs an independent operation on the data. The servers answer requests and provide the data and are susceptible to occasional failures.

Figure 6 shows the means and standard deviation of some of the populations in the Client/Server model. This example demonstrates an improvement in accuracy when a second order closure based on the normal distribution is used. We can inductively define a PCTMC semantics of the GPEPA process algebra. The set of populations of a GPEPA model M is:

$$S\left(\boldsymbol{G}\left\{P_1[n_1] \mid \ldots \mid P_m[n_m]\right\}\right) = \left\{(\boldsymbol{G}, P_1), \ldots, (\boldsymbol{G}, P_m)\right\}$$
$$S(M_1 \underset{A}{\bowtie} M_2) = S(M_1) \cup S(M_2)$$

In order to inductively define the set of PCTMC transitions for composed GPEPA models, we label the transitions with the GPEPA actions. For a simple labeled GPEPA group $\boldsymbol{G}\left\{P_1[n_1] \mid \cdots \mid P_m[n_m]\right\}$ the resulting PCTMC has a (labelled) transition class for each PEPA transition $P_i \xrightarrow{(\alpha, r)} P_i'$

$$(\boldsymbol{G}, Pi) \to (\boldsymbol{G}, P_i') \qquad \text{at rate } N_{G, P_i \cdot r}, \text{label} : \alpha$$

Now let the model M be a cooperation of two GPEPA models $M_1 \bowtie_A M_2$ and let be the transition classes of PCTMCs corresponding to the models M_i respectively (Hayden & Bradley).

The set of transition classes for the PCTMC of M consists of:

1. All transition classes in C_1 and C_2 not labelled by an action in the cooperation set A.
2. For each combination of transition classes in C_1 and C_2 labelled by an action α in the cooperation set.

$$\sum_{i=1}^{k} \boldsymbol{G}_i, P_i \mapsto \sum_{i=1}^{k'} \boldsymbol{G}_i, P_i' \qquad \text{at rate } R_1, \text{label } \alpha$$

$$\sum_{i=1}^{l} \boldsymbol{H}_i, Q_i \mapsto \sum_{i=1}^{l'} \boldsymbol{H}_i, Q_i' \qquad \text{at rate } R_2, \text{label } \alpha$$

The transition class defined as:

$$\sum_{i=1}^{k} \boldsymbol{G}_i, P_i + \sum_{i=1}^{l} \boldsymbol{H}_i, Q_i \to \sum_{i=1}^{k'} \boldsymbol{G}_i, P_i' + \sum_{i=1}^{l'} \boldsymbol{H}_i, Q_i'$$
$$\text{at rate } R, \text{label } \alpha$$

Figure 6. Means and standard deviation of some of the populations in the client/server model

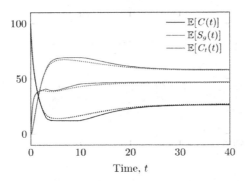

(a) Means from mean-field analysis.

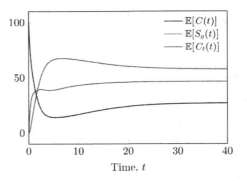

(b) Means from second order closure.

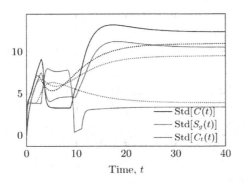

(c) St. dev. From mean-field analysis.

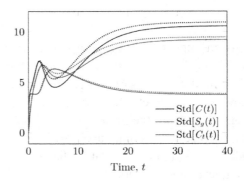

(b) St. dev. From second order closure.

where the rate R is:

$$\frac{R_1}{r_\alpha\left(M_1\right)} \cdot \frac{R_2}{r_\alpha\left(M_2\right)} \cdot \min(r_\alpha\left(M_1\right), r_\alpha(M_2))$$

where $r_\alpha(M_i)$ is the GPEPA apparent rate of the action α in the model M_i:

$$r_\alpha\left(M_i\right) = \sum\nolimits_{...,at\ r,\ label\ \alpha \in c_i} r$$

3.3 MASSPA

Similarly to GPEPA we can also inductively define a PCTMC semantics of the MASSPA process algebra. The MASSPA grammar presented here was changed slightly from the one used in (Guenther & Bradley 2011) in order to make it easier for the reader to compare it with the GPEPA grammar discussed above.

$$P :|:= (r).P\big|!(m, g_m, r).P\big|?(m, a_m).P\big|P + P\big|C_P \mid \varnothing$$

$$M :|:= M \underset{c}{\triangleright\!\!\triangleleft} M \mid P @ l[N]$$
where $\mathcal{C} = \{\text{Channel}\left(P @ l, P @ k, m, u\right),...\}$

where P is a generic agent component, whose definition, \eg transition rates, may be location dependent (the location placeholder x in the model shown in Figure 7). The (r) transitions represent local transitions within an agent that occur at rate r, !(m,g$_m$,r) local transitions, which fire g$_m$ messages of type m?(m,a$_m$) are message induced transitions that execute with probability a$_m$ when the agent receives a message of type m. The set of all message types defined among the components is M. A MASSPA model M consists of a finite composition of local agent component instances $P@l[N]$ where local components are like component groups in GPEPA. A local agent component $P@l$ inherits the definition from the generic agent component P but it can override message labels and transition rates to make them location dependent. The finite set of all locations is denoted $\mathcal{L}$ and for each $P@l[N]$ we have $l \in \mathcal{L}$. Model instances of local components such as $P@l[N]$ operate in parallel subject to channel constraints defined in the set C We say that a local agent $P@l$ can send a message of type $m \in \mathcal{M}$ to Q@K iff Channel$(P@l, Q@k, m, u) \in C$. When translating a MASSPA model into a PCTMC the local agent component P@l associated with the population P@l.

$$S(P@l[N]) = D(P@l)$$

where D(P@l) is the set derivative populations of local agent component P@l, i.e. the set of populations associated with local agent components that can be reached from P@l through transitions. This might well be a subset of all components that are theoretically reachable according to the generic agent component definition P since some local transition rates at location l could be zero, thereby disabling potential transitions. Like in GPEPA the set of populations of a composite model is simply:

$$S(M_1 \underset{c}{\rhd\!\lhd} M_2) = S\left(M_1\right) \cup S\left(M_2\right)$$

Next we need to inductively define the set of PCTMC transitions for a MASSPA model. We start by deriving the local PCTMC transitions. In a MASSPA model the occurrence of any ! (m,g$_m$,r).P'@1 and (r).P'@1 transitions in the definition of a local agent component P@1 creates the following PCTMC transition for a model instance $P@l[N]$.

$$P@l \rightarrow P'@l \quad \text{at rate } N_{P@l} \cdot r$$

While the behaviour of a local transition is similar to a silent transition in GPEPA, the translation of message emission transitions semantically

Figure 7. Location placeholder x

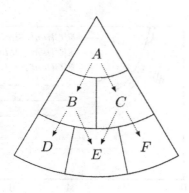

(a) Diagram of the system equation.

```
Client_stale@x    = ?(m, 0.25).Client_updated@x +
                     ?(m, 0.75).Client_stale@x;
Client_updated@x  = (r_stale@x).Client_stale@x;

Server@x          = !(r_rx, m, 0.1).Server@x +
                     (r_stale@x).Server_refresh@x;
Server_refresh@x  = ?(m, 0.1).Server@x +
                     ?(m, 0.9).Server_refresh@x;


Server@A[N_A]<>Server_refresh@B[N_B]<>
Server_refresh@C[N_C]<>Client_stale@D[N_D]<>
Client_stale@E[N_E]<>Client_stale@F[N_F];

Channel(Server@A,Server_refresh@B,m,2);
Channel(Server@A,Server_refresh@C,m,1);
Channel(Server@B,Client_stale@D,m,3);
Channel(Server@B,Client_stale@E,m,1);
Channel(Server@C,Client_stale@E,m,2);
Channel(Server@C,Client_stale@F,m,2);
```

(b) GPA definition using GPEPA syntax.

implies that broadcast messages are only sent while an agent is sojourning in a particular state. To express a broadcast message that is sent as part of a state transition, the translation to PCTMC level would become significantly harder, despite the fact that the resulting first-order moment mean-field ODEs would not change.

If M is a composite of two MASSPA models $M_1 \rhd\lhd_c M_2$ and T_i the set of PCTMC transitions of the PCTMCs corresponding to the models M_i the set of transitions for the PCTMC of M is the union of $T_1 \cup T_2 \cup T_{12}$, where T_{12} where T_{12} represents the set of message induced transitions that occur when other agent states receive messages on channels that they listen to.

For each Channel(P@l, Q@k, m, u), $k, l \in \mathcal{L}, m \in \mathcal{M}$ for which exist valid transitions $!(m, g_m, r).P'@l$ in the definition of local agent component P@l and $?(m, a_m).Q'@k$ in the definition of Q@k there is a PCTMC transition:

$$P@l + Q@k \rightarrow P@l + Q'@k$$

at rate $N_{P@l} \cdot N_{Q@k} \cdot r \cdot g_m \cdot a_m \cdot u$

To illustrate the MASSPA grammar, Figure 7 shows a simple spatial content distribution model implemented in MASSPA. The diagram conceptually shows the available message channels described by the process algebra definition. Due to space restrictions we did not include all constant definitions. While choosing any non-zero rate for r_stale will suffice for most locations, in location A we have to have r_stale@A = 0 to reflect that there is a reliable source of information in the network. Figure 8 shows the ODE mean-field analysis results (Section 4.1.2) for a particular configuration of the model.

4 SOLVING PCTMC MODELS IN GPA

Figure 9 outlines the input and steps GPA takes to evaluate PCTMC models. Having defined a model in a PCTMC translatable formalism, modellers can specify the measures that they are interested in, for instance central moments and distributions of a population or passage time distribution bounds. The choice of solution method then depends on the chosen measures and the rates in the model. GPA currently does not assist modellers by suggesting the most suitable evaluation method given

Figure 8. ODE mean-field analysis results

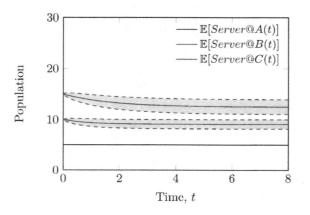

(a) Servers in the distribution MASSPA model.

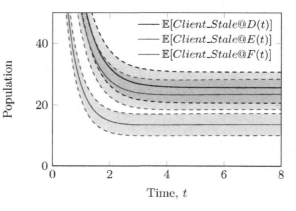

(b) Stale clients.

Figure 9. The process of solving a PCTMC model in GPA

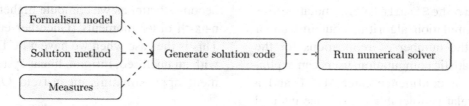

a PCTMC model and the desired measures, but this feature could easily be added.

Given the model, measures and the solution method, GPA first translates the model into an internal PCTMC representation and consequently generates a source code for the model to speed up its evaluation. The nature of the generated code depends on the solution method, for instance for the mean-field solution (Section 4.1.2) the source code represents the system of ODEs, which can be integrated using standard ODE solvers. One important aspect of the code generation is that the source code for the solution method only needs to be generated once, even when multiple experiments are conducted with different start conditions and parameters. Moreover, while GPA supports generated Java code natively, users can alternatively choose other output languages such as Matlab and C++.

4.1 Solution Methods

In a GPA analysable model, the solvers are defined below the model definition using the syntax in Table 1.

Each solver can take pre- and post-processor arguments. Pre-processor options have an impact on how source code is generated for the PCTMC model and the chosen metrics, whereas post-processor arguments are passed to the solution algorithm, for instance to define numerical accuracy and the stop time for the evaluation.

4.1.1 Simulation

GPA provides two variants of the stochastic simulation technique that is also known as Gillespie's simulation technique (Gillespie 1977). The syntax for the solution methods is shown in Table 2.

Simulation uses replications many traces from time to stopTime and records the

Table 1.

```
SOLVER[(<PREPROC_OPTION>,)*]((<POSTPROC_OPTION>,)*) {
    ((<MEASURE>,)+ (-> <OUTPUT_FILE>)? ;)+
}
```

Table 2.

```
Simulation (stopTime = <FLOAT>, stepSize = <FLOAT>, replications = <INT>) {...}

AccurateSimulation (stopTime = <FLOAT>, stepSize = <FLOAT>, CI = <FLOAT>,
                    maxRelCIWidth = <FLOAT>, batchSize = <INT>) {...}
```

ensemble statistics for every interval of stepSize width. `AccurateSimulation` simulation uses the same simulation algorithm, but instead of specifying the number of replications for the ensemble statistic computation, users can explicitly specify a confidence interval `CI` and a maximum relative tolerable confidence interval width `maxRelCIWidth` which is checked for all measures every `batchSize` many replications. The simulation only stops once the confidence interval is tight enough (Guenther et al. 2012) The Gillespie implementation is generic, but for efficiency reasons the reaction rate computation and the population state update functions are automatically generated from the model definition, compiled and passed to the Gillespie evaluator. To speed up simulation even further, we are also currently looking into implementing a -leaping simulator (Gillespie & Petzold 2003).

4.1.2 Mean-Field Analysis

Mean-field ODE analysis of population moments using GPA can be done by adding the following code to the solver section (see Table 3.)

In contrast to the simulation solvers, the ODE solution allows the user to provide optional preprocessor commands such as `maxOrder`, the order of the highest moment that is to be computed and the `momentClosure` method that is to be used. By default `maxOrder` is equal to the highest order among the moments defined in the measures section of the solver … and the default moment closure is the normal moment closure.

The default value for `maxOrder` is intuitive, since we generally need to compute at least the first *n* moments if we are interested in an *n-th* moment population measure. Occasionally, how-ever, the accuracy of the n-th moment estimation becomes better as we compute higher-order, say n+x-th order moments (Guenther et al. 2012). This is the case when we have a PCTMC model with an unclosed, infinite, linear systems of moment approximating mean-field ODEs. This happens when there exist evolution rates $r_e\left(\vec{P}\right)$ (Section 2.2) with non-linear polynomials in the population counts, such as $r_e\left(\vec{P}\right) = P_i P_j$. This quadratic reaction rate, is commonly referred to as a mass-action type reaction and can often be found in PCTMCs representing biological systems, but also in the MASSPA and MAM formalisms. When expanding Equation (3) for such PCTMCs, moment ODEs will depend on higher-order moment ODEs. In a simple example with a transition class:

$$S_1 + S_2 \rightarrow S_3 + S_4 \qquad \text{at rate} \, r(\vec{P}) = P_1 P_2$$

the ODE describing the mean of P_1, $\mathbb{E}\left[P_1\left(t\right)\right]$ depends on a second order moment $\mathbb{E}[P_1\left(t\right) P_2\left(t\right)]$ the ODE for this moment depends on third order moments and so on. To solve such infinite systems of coupled ODEs numerically, we need to approximate higher-order moments of some order using moments with order no larger than the order of the highest moment we wish compute, i.e. we close the system of moment ODEs at a particular order. By applying such a moment closure, we are changing a linear but infinite system of moment ODEs into a finite non-linear system of ODEs. While allowing us to solve the closed system, there are two drawbacks to applying a

Table 3.

```
ODEs [momentClosure = <STRING> , maxOrder= <INT>]?
     (stopTime = <FLOAT>, stepSize = <FLOAT>, density = <FLOAT>) { ... }
```

closure. Firstly, to compute specific non-linear replacement terms for all higher-order moments that exceed maxOrder, we have to make a decision as to which family of distributions the population random variables belong to. Secondly, adding non-linear terms makes the numerical integration more expensive and sometimes less stable. Before moving on to our description of GPA's ODE generation and moment closure application, we briefly review the mean-field and the normal moment closure (Whittle1957). For a detailed overview of moment closures that have been implemented in GPA please refer to (Guenther et al. 2012).

Mean-field analysis (Opper & Saad 2001) methods investigate the evolution of the mean of population vectors. The mean-field closure approximates higher-order moments such as $\mathbb{E}\left[P_i\left(t\right)P_j\left(t\right)\cdots P_k\left(t\right)\right]$ by the product of the individual expectations $\mathbb{E}\left[P_i\left(t\right)\right]\mathbb{E}\left[P_j\left(t\right)\right]\ldots\mathbb{E}[P_k\left(t\right)]$. In other words, the mean-field approach ignores the covariance between any two populations. This produces good approximations for population means, especially when the populations are high. However in some model, for instance in the circadian clock model the mean-field closure does not perform well (Engblom 2006, Stefanek, Guenther & Bradley 2011). Note that the approximation of population moments using fluid analysis is generally referred to as mean-field analysis in the literature irrespective of both the moment closure that is applied and the order of the moments that are approximated.

The *normal moment closure* (Whittle, 1957) can be applied to any system of ODEs originating from a PCTMC for which we want to find 2nd or higher-order moments. It assumes that the populations at each point in time are approximately multivariate normal and therefore all third- and higher-order moments can be expressed in terms of means and covariances. This relationship is captured by the Isserlis' theorem (Isserlis 1918):

For $\vec{P}$ multivariate normal with mean $\vec{i}$ and covariance matrix o'_{ij} we have:

$$\mathbb{E}\left[(\vec{P}-\vec{\mu})^{\vec{m}}\right] = \mathbb{E}[(P_1-\mu_1)^{m_1}\ldots(P_n-\mu_n)^{m_n}] = 0,$$
if $o(\vec{m})$ is odd

$$\mathbb{E}\left[(\vec{P}-\vec{\mu})^{\vec{m}}\right] = \sum\prod\mathbb{E}[(P_i-\mu_i)(P_j-\mu_j)],$$
if $o(\vec{m})$ is even
(4)

where sums through all the distinct partitions of $1,\ldots,n$ into disjoint sets of pairs i,j. If some elements in $\vec{m}$ are greater than one, then certain pairs i,j will appear multiple times in the resulting sum. To obtain the raw moment, we need to expand the central moment in Equation (4) first and subsequently rearrange the equation. For example, instead of including an ODE for the third order joint raw moment $\mathbb{E}[P_1(t)P_2(t)^2]$ we can close the expansion at second order by using the approximation:

$$\mathbb{E}\left[P_1\left(t\right)P_2\left(t\right)\right] \approx 2\mathbb{E}\left[P_2\left(t\right)\right]\mathbb{E}\left[P_2\left(t\right)P_1\left(t\right)\right] +$$
$$\mathbb{E}\left[P_1\left(t\right)\right]\mathbb{E}\left[P_2\left(t\right)^2\right] - 2\mathbb{E}\left[P_1\left(t\right)\right]\mathbb{E}\left[P_2\left(t\right)\right]^2$$

which yields
$$\mathbb{E}\left[\left(P_1\left(t\right)-\mu_1\left(t\right)\right)\left(P_2\left(t\right)-\mu_2\left(t\right)\right)^2\right] = 0 \text{ as required, since the multivariate normal distribution is not skewed.}$$

For efficient ODE generation, GPA generates only those ODEs that are actually required for the evaluation of the measures. Having parsed the moments required for the measures specified for the solver, GPA first generates all right-hand side terms of these moments. Before being added to the right-hand side, each term is first closed using the chosen moment closure method and any previously unknown population moments are added to the list of ODEs that still need to be generated. When there are no more new population moments, the generation algorithm terminates and returns a system of ODEs, which can then be translated to Java, C++ or Matlab source code. Subsequently GPA fetches the post-processor parameters `stopTime`, `stepSize` and `density` and passes them to the integration algorithm along with the compiled version of the ODE source code. While, `stopTime` and `stepSize` have the same meaning as for the simulation solver explained in Section 4.1.1, the `density` argument currently defines the integration interval size of explicit Runge-Kutta method used by GPA. Naturally, it would be possible to provide other integration methods such as Euler's method or potentially a parallel algorithm. To do this, all developers would need to do is implement the algorithm using the provided post-processor interface and further add another option such as `algoName = <STRING>` to enable users to choose between all available integration methods.

4.1.3 Computing Accumulated Rewards

In case of the previously mentioned Client/Server model, a useful metric of interest would be the total power consumption of all the servers throughout the analysed time interval. For example, we can assume that each server consumes c_1 and c_2 units of energy per unit of time in the states `Server` and `Server_get` respectively and none in the `Server_broken` state. In that case, the total energy can be written as an integral over the population processes:

$$E\left(t\right) = c_1 \int_0^t S\left(u\right)\ du + c_2 \int_0^t S_g\left(u\right)\ du$$

In general, other useful quantities can be expressed as linear combinations of the integrals of populations over time. It can be shown (Stefanek

et al. 2012) that the system of ODEs from the fluid analysis can be extended with additional ODEs describing the evolution of means and higher moments of these integrated processes. GPA implements this extension for both ODE and simulation solvers. The syntax for $\int_0^t P(u)du$ is `acc(P)`, so for example to plot the mean energy consumption above, the following expression can be used (see Table 4).

4.2 Experiments

The flexible architecture of GPA allows analysis methods to be combined, compared or repeated in a number of secondary experiment solvers.

4.2.1 Optimisation

Fluid analysis is often much more computationally efficient than an equivalent stochastic simulation. This makes it possible to repeat the analysis for a large number of parameter configurations. GPA provides a command that can iterate over a range of values of the parameters and evaluate complex reward and constraint expressions. For example, in the client / server model, we can define a reward as the total income from running the system. We can define this as a combination of the number of completed client requests minus the energy above and the initial cost of servers where #data is the syntax for the number of times the data action has taken place and income is the units of income for each request, e_cost the cost of consuming a unit of energy per unit time and S_cost the cost of each server (see Table 5.) Using techniques from (Hayden et al. 2012) we can also define an expression that captures the probability that a client finishes each request within a given time. A

Table 4.

```
E[c_1 * acc(Servers:Server) + c_2 * acc(Servers:Server_get)]
```

Table 5.

```
$reward = #data * income
  - e_cost * c_1 * acc(Servers:Server) - e_cost * c_2 * acc(Servers:Server_get)
  - N_S * S_cost
```

Figure 10. Parameter exploration/optimisation in the client/server model. The reliability (break rate) of the servers and the number of servers is varied. The configuration with the highest achieved reward that satisfies passage time based service level agreements is chosen.

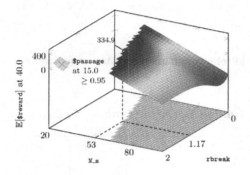

```
Iterate N_s from 1.0 to 100.0 with step 1.0
        rb from 0.0 to 2.0 in 100 steps
   ODEs(stopTime=40.1,stepSize=0.1,density = 10)
   plot{
     E[$reward] at 40.0
        when $passage at 15.0 >= 0.95
        -> "tmp/scalability/reward";
}
```

(a) Expected reqard for the parameters where the passage time SLA is satisfied.

(b) Definition of the sweeping intervals and the objective function with constraints.

service level agreement could be that this probability has to be higher than an agreed constant (say at a given point in time, e.g. after units of time. A possible optimisation problem for a provider of such a system would be to explore the number of servers that are needed to satisfy the SLA. Additionally, we could assume that the provider can obtain cheaper servers at the expense of reliability, making the cost S_cost inversely proportional to the break rate of servers. Figure 10 shows how this problem could be specified in GPA.

4.2.2 Unified Stochastic Probes for GPEPA

In case of model specification in GPEPA, GPA implements the Unified Stochastic Probes (USP) framework (Hayden et al. 2013). This allows modellers to observe additional passage times without explicitly modifying the GPEPA system model.

The USP language can express a variety of passage time measures. For example, in the Client/Server model, a measure of interest could be the time it takes an individual client to execute its first think action. This can be achieved by defining a probe attached to a single client component. This probe starts its clock at the initial time and finishes when the observed client fires a think action. Probes are defined in a regular expression like language and multiple probes can be composed together. To define the placement of the probe (in this example attaching the probe to a single client), USP accepts a simple GPEPA model transformation language. Figure 11 shows the GPA definition of the probe and the respective model transformation.

This probe definition shows an example of an individual passage time measurement. Additionally, the framework defines so-called global passage times. These can use clocks triggered by a mixture of actions and conditions on the global

Figure 11. An example of passage time specification and calculation using the Unified Stochastic Probes formalism. The local probe LProbe·tracks the time between t=0 and the first think action of the client it is attached to. The Clients group is modified with a probe attached to one of the clients.

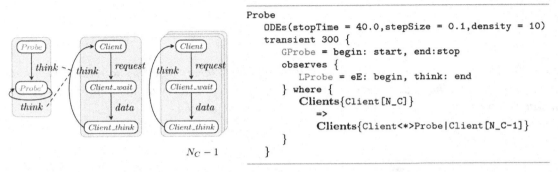

(a) Diagram of the modified Clients group.

```
Probe
    ODEs(stopTime = 40.0,stepSize = 0.1,density = 10)
    transient 300 {
        GProbe = begin: start, end:stop
        observes {
            LProbe = eE: begin, think: end
        } where {
            Clients{Client[N_C]}
                =>
                Clients{Client<*>Probe|Client[N_C-1]}
        }
    }
```

(b) Probe definition and system modification.

Figure 12. Computation of passage time CDFs via the Unified Stochastic Probes

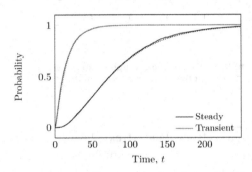

(a) Individual passage time CDF.

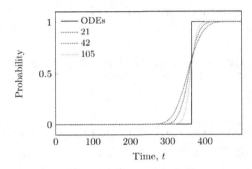

(b) Global passage time CDF.

state space. For example, a measure of interest could be the time it takes for half of the total N_C clients to execute their first think action.

Internally, GPA follows the algorithms defined by the USP framework. Using the model transformation and definitions of probes, the original GPEPA model is translated into an intermediate GPEPA model that also allows passive cooperation. This is then translated into a standard GPEPA model so that the execution chain of GPA can be applied. As shown in Figure 1, the generated core for the primary solvers is re-used and the respective analysis executed to calculate certain expressions required by the USP algorithms. Finally, the re-

sults are transformed to provide approximations of various passage time measures. Figure 12 plots an example of an individual passage time and a global passage time computed by GPA.

4.2.3 Distribution Calculation

To give further insight into the behaviour of the underlying PCTMC of a model, GPA can calculate the probability distribution of population and reward based expressions. The example in Table 6 shows the syntax to calculate the distribution of the population of servers and the server utilisation at each time within the interval of the analysis.

Table 6.

```
Distribution
  Simulation(stopTime=40.0, stepSize=12.5, replications=10000)
  computes {
    Servers:Server into 60 bins;
    acc(Servers:Server_get) /(acc(Servers:Server) + acc(Servers:Server_get))
      into 100 bins;
  }
```

Figure 13. Example of distributions form the Client/Server model

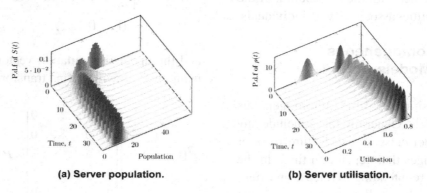

(a) Server population.　　　(b) Server utilisation.

GPA generates the code for primary solvers and then adds additional routines to keep track of the sample values of the given expressions. In the end, it displays the distributions, Figure 13.

5 FUTURE GPA EXTENSIONS

While the current version of GPA supports a large range of PCTMC specific analysis techniques and modeling features, our ultimate goal is to extend GPA's capabilities to other types of population models. In this section we will discuss some planned future extensions to GPA, which will capture a number of population model classes that were mentioned in Section 2.

5.1 Population Models with Continuous States

One such extension is to consider models which are governed by some continuous quantities evolving over time in addition to the discrete populations. These can represent energy, temperature, continuous location in a space etc. One line of work has further extended the accumulated reward described in Section 4.1.3. Instead of considering the rewards as additional measures obtained from the analysis, they can be treated as part of the state space of the system. The population vector of the PCTMC can be augmented with a number of global continuous quantities that evolve over time as defined by a set of ODEs (Stefanek et al. 2012). These ODEs can depend on the population vectors and the transition rates of the PCTMC part of the model can in turn depend on the continuous quantities. It can be shown that the ODE techniques can be extended to provide means and higher moments of both populations and continuous quantities in such models. The current version of GPA supports this to some extend by allowing rates to depend on expressions that involve accumulated populations. In future, we plan to extend this to general accumulations defined by a set of additional ODEs.

Another line of work adds continuous quantities at individual rather than at global level. For example, Hayden et al. (Hayden 2012c) look at a wireless sensor network model where each of the large number of nodes in addition to the discrete state space contains a continuous value representing the current battery level. In such cases, the fluid analysis comes down to a system of Partial Differential Equations that capture the mean populations together with the distribution of the continuous quantities associated with individuals.

5.2 Time-Inhomogeneous Population Models

Another extension are time inhomogeneous population models. Generally these include any population model class, which feature rates or population changes that depend on time. In the near future we are intending to release an extension for GPA, which will allow modellers to define and evaluate a range of time-inhomogeneous PCTMCs (IPCTMCs) that were shown to be useful in (Guenther & Bradley 2013, Stefanek et al. 2013). A IPCTMC is a PCTMC that also features deterministic rate and population changes, which occur at deterministic times. More formally for rates this means that any reaction rate $r_e\left(\vec{P}(t)\right)$ (Section 2.2) is now time dependent, i.e. $r_e\left(\vec{P}(t),t\right)$ becomes:

$$\begin{cases} r_e(\vec{P}(t),t_1) & \text{if } P_i(t) \geq s_i^{in}\forall i=1,...,n \wedge t < t_1 \\ r_e(\vec{P}(t),t_2) & \text{if } P_i(t) \geq s_i^{in}\forall i=1,...,n \wedge t_1 \leq t < t_2 \\ ... & \\ 0 & \text{otherwise} \end{cases}$$

where t_1, t_2,...are deterministic times at which reaction rate changes occur. Moreover, we allow deterministically timed events that result in an affine transformation of the population vector $\vec{P}(t)$. In the following let us assume that if a deterministic population change occurs at time t_d then no population changes occur due to random

PCTMC events between $t_d - \delta t$ and t_d. Should no such interval exist then we informally assume that the deterministic event is triggered immediately after the random event. Let D denote the set of all deterministic events, s.t. $(t_d, M) \in D$, where:

$$M_{n,n+1} = \begin{pmatrix} \lambda_1 & 0 & \cdots & 0 & c_1 \\ 0 & \lambda_2 & \cdots & 0 & c_2 \\ \vdots & \vdots & \ddots & \vdots & \vdots \\ 0 & 0 & \cdots & \lambda_n & c_n \end{pmatrix}$$

and the updated population vector is computed using the following affine transformation:

$$\vec{P}(t_d) = M \times \left(\begin{pmatrix} 1 & 0 & \cdots & 0 \\ 0 & 1 & \cdots & 0 \\ \vdots & \vdots & \ddots & \vdots \\ 0 & 0 & \cdots & 1 \\ 0 & 0 & \cdots & 0 \end{pmatrix} \times \vec{P}(t_d - \delta t) + \begin{pmatrix} 0 \\ 0 \\ \vdots \\ 0 \\ 0 \end{pmatrix} \right)$$

that way we can describe a reset of population 1 to c_1 and a population jump of population 1 by c_1 as:

$$Reset_{n,n+1} = \begin{pmatrix} 0 & 0 & \cdots & 0 & c_1 \\ 0 & 1 & \cdots & 0 & 0 \\ \vdots & \vdots & \ddots & \vdots & \vdots \\ 0 & 0 & \cdots & 1 & 0 \end{pmatrix}$$

$$Jump_{n,n+1} = \begin{pmatrix} 1 & 0 & \cdots & 0 & c_1 \\ 0 & 1 & \cdots & 0 & 0 \\ \vdots & \vdots & \ddots & \vdots & \vdots \\ 0 & 0 & \cdots & 1 & 0 \end{pmatrix}$$

To use IPCTMCs in (Guenther & Bradley 2013, Stefanek et al. 2013) we had to implement new GPA post-processors for both the simulation and the ODE solver. Although we are presently improving these methods, here is a brief description of the solution algorithm that we intend to release in a GPA version later this year. In IPCTMC simulation runs, deterministic events can be immediately applied to the current population vector at the time they occur. Thus a IPCTMC simulation can be build on top of the existing simulation code, the difference being that we need to apply the affine transformation of the population vector and rate changes every time a deterministic event occurs. Similarly, when using mean-field ODEs to estimate the moments of the IPCTMC process, we need to integrate the ODEs stepwise between subsequent events. This means that we can also reuse existing ODE integration algorithms and simply have to take care of applying the deterministic events. However, unlike individual simulation runs, mean-field ODEs keep track of population moments, which have to be recomputed whenever a deterministic event occurs at time t_d. For instance assuming that we a have two populations and and that the following deterministic population change occurs at

$$t_d ; x(t_d) = \lambda_x x(t_d - \delta t) + c_1 \text{ and } Y(t_d - \delta t)$$

then

$$\mathbb{E}\left[X\left(t_d\right) Y\left(t_d\right)\right] \begin{vmatrix} = \mathbb{E}\left[\left(\lambda_x \ X\left(t_d - \delta t\right) + c_1\right) Y\left(t_d - \delta t\right)\right] \\ = \lambda_x \mathbb{E}\left[\ X\left(t_d - \delta t\right) Y\left(t_d - \delta t\right)\right] \\ + c_1 \mathbb{E}\left[Y\left(t_d - \delta t\right)\right] \end{vmatrix}$$

and similarly for

$$\mathbb{E}\left[X\left(t_d\right)^2\right]$$

or any other uncentred joint moment. Since the transformation of the population vector is affine, we do not have to use moment closures (Guenther et al. 2012) in order to compute the new values of the moments at time t_d. However, an important issue that is subject to future research are solution methods that can handle boundary conditions for populations. For instance, if we had to ensure that a population must always stay positive, we would need to change our population vector update method for the simulation. Moreover, for the ODE solution of IPCTMCs such boundary conditions

are even harder to achieve, as we would have to apply moment closures to estimate the probability that a deterministic IPCTMC event leaves the population vector within its legal boundaries before updating the population vector.

5.3 Population Models with Non-Markovian Delays

So far the population models supported by GPA all have an underlying CTMC representation. However, models often require deterministic or other non-exponentially distributed delays that cannot easily be approximated using phase-type distributions. Under these circumstances we require a population GSMP model (Section 2.1). It was recently shown that first order mean-field analysis can be used to solve a subclass of PGSMP models that supports deterministic delays (Bortolussi & Hillston 2012a, Hayden 2012b). Moreover, both papers hint at how the solution technique could be applied to PGSMPs with generally-timed delays. While incorporating PGSMPs into GPA is a straightforward task, it would ideally lead to a novel, more general abstraction layer between population formalisms, low-level state-space representations and available solution methods, thus helping GPA to embrace the MFMS paradigm further.

5.4 Model Checking

In Section 4.2.2 we illustrated how Unified Stochastic Probes (Hayden et al. 2013, Kohut et al. 2012) were integrated into GPA. While mean-field ODEs for population dependent global passage times can only be used to derive bounds of the underlying distribution, it was shown that passages time distributions of individuals can be computed exactly if the individual is assumed to be interacting with a mean field regime (Hayden et al. 2012). In the literature this is also occasionally referred to as fast simulation (Darling & Norris 2007). The efficient mean-field computation of both global passage time bounds as well as individual passage time distributions, could help to address model checking problems for population models that were previously confined to the realm of simulation techniques, due to their vast state spaces. As an example Bortolussi et al. (Bortolussi & Hillston 2012b) show how mean-field passage time computations can be used to cover a subset of the Constraint Stochastic Logic (CSL) formalism. Fluid analysable subsets of CSL or similar model checking formalisms would make a useful extension to GPA. Moreover, if general model checking formalisms were to be added to GPA, it would be possible to write an algorithm that determines whether individual queries can be solved using mean-field analysis or if simulation techniques or state space exploration techniques are needed. This would then enable us to compare the performance of different solution techniques for various types of models and model checking queries and possibly help us to assist modellers in their choice of solver.

6 CONCLUSION

Our examples of mean-field analysable model classes in Section 2.1 show that recent research in the field has vastly increased the expressiveness of tractable formalisms. However, the popularity of tools such as Möbius and PRISM illustrates that only the availability of user-friendly software tools, truly brings theoretical advances to the modelling community. In view of the ever increasing size and complexity of systems, it is thus important to offer modellers a powerful population modelling and analysis framework. Even though GPA was initially designed as an evaluation tool for GPEPA, the intention was to provide modellers with the means that would encourage them to move away from simulation based analysis of large population models towards more efficient mean-field analysable formalisms. As the family of mean-field analysable population modeling continues

to extend, we aim to implement new formalisms and solution techniques in GPA. However, the transformation from a single formalism tool into a general multiformalism multisolution population model analysis framework is ongoing work, as the examples in Section 2.1 show. Ultimately, we hope that future development will help to make GPA accessible to an even wider group of modellers and become the framework of choice for implementing future population modelling formalisms.

REFERENCES

Bortolussi, L., & Hillston, J. (2012a, September). Fluid approximation of CTMC with deterministic delays. In Proceedings of 2012 Ninth International Conference on Quantitative Evaluation of Systems (pp. 53–62). London: IEEE.

Bortolussi, L., & Hillston, J. (2012b, March). Fluid model checking. Retrieved from http://arxiv.org/abs/1203.0920

Bortolussi, L., & Policriti, A. (2008). Modeling biological systems in stochastic concurrent constraint programming. *Constraints*, *13*(1-2), 66–90. doi:10.1007/s10601-007-9034-8.

Chaintreau, A., Boudec, J.-Y. L., & Ristanovic, N. (2009). The age of gossip: Spatial mean field regime. In Proceedings of Joint International Conference on Measurement and Modeling of Computer Systems. IEEE.

Ciardo, G., & Miner, A. (1996). SMART: Simulation and Markovian analyzer for reliability and timing. In Proceedings of IEEE International Computer Performance and Dependability 20 Symposium. IEEE.

Ciocchetta, F., Degasperi, A., Heath, J. K., & Hillston, J. (2010). Modelling and analysis of the NF-kB pathway in Bio-PEPA. *Transactions on Computational Systems Biology*, *12*, 229–262. doi:10.1007/978-3-642-11712-1_7.

Ciocchetta, F., Duguid, A., Gilmore, S., Guerriero, M. L., & Hillston, J. (2009, September). The Bio-PEPA tool suite. In Proceedings of 2009 Sixth International Conference on the Quantitative Evaluation of Systems, (pp. 309–310). IEEE.

Ciocchetta, F., & Hillston, J. (2009). Bio-PEPA: A framework for the modelling and analysis of biological systems. *Theoretical Computer Science*, *410*(33-34), 3065–3084. doi:10.1016/j.tcs.2009.02.037.

Ciocchetta, F., & Hillston, J. (2010). Bio-PEPA for epidemiological models. *Electronic Notes in Theoretical Computer Science*, *261*, 43–69. doi:10.1016/j.entcs.2010.01.005.

Darling, R. W. R., & Norris, J. R. (2007). Differential equation approximations for Markov chains. *Probability Surveys*, *5*, 37–79.

Deavours, D. D., Clark, G., Courtney, T., Daly, D., Derisavi, S., & Doyle, J. M. et al. (2002). The Mobius framework and its implementation. *IEEE Transactions on Software Engineering*, *28*(10), 956–969. doi:10.1109/TSE.2002.1041052.

Engblom, S. (2006). Computing the moments of high dimensional solutions of the master equation. *Applied Mathematics and Computation*, *180*(2), 498–515. doi:10.1016/j.amc.2005.12.032.

Gillespie, D. T. (1977). Exact stochastic simulation of coupled chemical reactions. *Journal of Physical Chemistry*, *81*(25), 2340–2361. doi:10.1021/j100540a008.

Gillespie, D. T., & Petzold, L. R. (2003). Improved leap-size selection for accelerated stochastic simulation. *The Journal of Chemical Physics*, *119*(16), 8229. doi:10.1063/1.1613254.

Gribaudo, M., Cerotti, D., & Bobbio, A. (2008). Analysis of on-off policies in sensor networks using interacting markovian agents. In Proceedings of 6th IEEE International Conference on Pervasive Computing and Communications PerCom (2008), (pp. 300–305). IEEE.

Gribaudo, M., Codetta-Raiteri, D., & Franceschinis, G. (2005). Draw-net, a customizable multi-formalism, multi-solution tool for the quantitative evaluation of systems. In Proceedings of Second International Conference on the Quantitative Evaluation of Systems (QEST'05) (pp. 257–258). Torino, Italy: IEEE.

Guenther, M. C., & Bradley, J. T. (2011). Higher moment analysis of a spatial stochastic process algebra. In Proceedings of 8th European Performance Engineering Workshop - EPEW 2011. EPEW.

Guenther, M. C., & Bradley, J. T. (2013). Journey data based arrival forecasting for bicycle hire schemes. In Proceedings of Twentieth International Conference on Analytical & Stochastic Modelling Techniques & Applications ASMTA. ASMTA.

Guenther, M. C., Stefanek, A., & Bradley, J. T. (2012). Moment closures for performance models with highly non-linear rates. In Proceedings of 9th European Performance Engineering Workshop (EPEW). Munich, Germany: EPEW.

Hayden, R. (2012). Mean field for performance models with deterministically-timed transitions. In Proceedings of 9th International Conference on Quantitative Evaluation of Systems (QEST 2012). London: IEEE.

Hayden, R. A. (2011). *Mean-field approximations for performance models with generally-timed transitions*. ACM SIGMETRICS Performance Evaluation Review. doi:10.1145/2160803.2160877.

Hayden, R. A. (2012a, September). Mean field for performance models with deterministically-timed transitions. In Proceedings of 2012 Ninth International Conference on Quantitative Evaluation of Systems (pp. 63–73). London: IEEE.

Hayden, R. A. (2012b). Mean-field models for interacting battery-powered devices. In *Proceedings of Imperial College Energy and Performance Colloqium*. London: Imperial College..

Hayden, R. A., & Bradley, J. T. (2010). A fluid analysis framework for a Markovian process algebra. *Theoretical Computer Science, 411*(22-24), 2260–2297. doi:10.1016/j.tcs.2010.02.001.

Hayden, R. A., Bradley, J. T., & Clark, A. (2013). Performance specification and evaluation with unified stochastic probes and fluid analysis. *IEEE Transactions on Software Engineering, 39*(1), 97–118. doi:10.1109/TSE.2012.1.

Hayden, R. A., Stefanek, A., & Bradley, J. T. (2012). Fluid computation of passage-time distributions in large Markov models. *Theoretical Computer Science, 413*(1), 106–141. doi:10.1016/j.tcs.2011.07.017.

Hillston, J. (2005). Fluid flow approximation of PEPA models. In Proceedings of Second International Conference on the Quantitative Evaluation of Systems (QEST'05) (pp. 33–42). IEEE.

Isserlis, L. (1918). On a formula for the product-moment coefficient of any order of a normal frequency distribution in any number of variables. *Biometrika, 12*(1/2), 134–139. doi:10.2307/2331932.

Kohut, M., Stefanek, A., Hayden, R., & Bradley, J. T. (2012). Specification and efficient computation of passage-time distributions in GPA. In Proceedings of Ninth International Conference on Quantitative Evaluation of Systems (QEST'12). London: IEEE.

Kwiatkowska, M., Norman, G., & Parke, D. (2011). PRISM 4.0: Verification of probabilistic real-time systems. In Proceedings of the 23rd International Conference on Computer Aided Verification (CAV) (LNCS), (Vol. 6806, pp. 585–591). Berlin: Springer.

Loewe, L., Guerriero, M., Watterson, S., Moodie, S., Ghazal, P., & Hillston, J. (2011). Translation from the quantified implicit process flow abstraction in SBGN-PD diagrams to bio-PEPA illustrated on the cholesterol pathway. *Transactions on Computational Systems Biology, 13*, 13–38. doi:10.1007/978-3-642-19748-2_2.

Massink, M., Latella, D., Bracciali, A., Hillston, J., & Faedo, I. A. (2011). Modelling non-linear crowd dynamics in bio-PEPA. In D. Giannakopoulou, & F. Orejas (Eds.), *Fundamental approaches to software engineering* (Vol. 6603, pp. 96–110). Berlin: Springer Berlin Heidelberg. doi:10.1007/978-3-642-19811-3_8.

Opper, M., & Saad, D. (2001). *Advanced mean field methods: Theory and practice*. Cambridge, MA: The MIT Press..

Sahner, R., Trivedi, K., & Puliafito, A. (1997). Performance and reliability analysis of computer systems. *IEEE Transactions on Reliability, 46*(3), 441. doi:10.1109/TR.1997.664017.

Sanders, W. H. (1999). *Integrated frameworks for multi-level and multi-formalism modeling*. Washington, DC: IEEE Computer Society. doi:10.1109/PNPM.1999.796527.

Stefanek, A., Guenther, M. C., & Bradley, J. T. (2011). Normal and inhomogeneous moment closures for stochastic process algebras. In Proceedings of 10th Workshop on Process Algebra and Stochastically Timed Activities (PASTA'11). PASTA.

Stefanek, A., Hayden, R. A., & Bradley, J. T. (2010). A new tool for the performance analysis of massively parallel computer systems. In Proceedings of Eighth Workshop on Quantitative Aspects of Programming Languages QAPL. QAPL.

Stefanek, A., Hayden, R. A., & Bradley, J. T. (2011). Fluid analysis of energy consumption using rewards in massively parallel Markov models. In Proceedings of ICPE'11 - Second Joint WOSP/SIPEW International Conference on Performance Engineering. ACM Press.

Stefanek, A., Hayden, R. A., & Bradley, J. T. (2013). Mean-field analysis of large scale Markov fluid models with fluid dependent and time-inhomogeneous rates. Technical report.

Stefanek, A., Hayden, R. A., Gonagle, M. M., & Bradley, J. T. (2012). Mean-field analysis of Markov models with reward feedback. In Proceedings of ASMTA (pp. 193–211). ASMTA.

Whittle, P. (1957). On the use of the normal approximation in the treatment of stochasticprocesses. *Journal of the Royal Statistical Society. Series B. Methodological, 19*(2), 268–281.

Chapter 9
A Symbolic Approach to the Analysis of Multi–Formalism Markov Reward Models

Kai Lampka
Uppsala University, Sweden

Markus Siegle
Bundeswehr University Munich, Germany

ABSTRACT

When modelling large systems, modularity is an important concept, as it aids modellers to master the complexity of their model. Moreover, employing different modelling formalisms within the same modelling project has the potential to ease the description of various parts or aspects of the overall system. In the area of performability modelling, formalisms such as stochastic reward nets, stochastic process algebras, stochastic automata, or stochastic UML state charts are often used, and several of these may be employed within one modelling project. This chapter presents an approach for efficiently constructing a symbolic representation in the form of a zero-suppressed Binary Decision Diagram (BDD), which represents the Markov Reward Model underlying a multi-formalism high-level model. In this approach, the interaction between the submodels may be established either by the sharing of state variables or by the synchronisation of common activities. It is shown that the Decision Diagram data structure and the associated algorithms enable highly efficient state space generation and different forms of analysis of the underlying Markov Reward Model (e.g. calculation of reward measures or asserting non-functional system properties by means of model checking techniques).

DOI: 10.4018/978-1-4666-4659-9.ch009

1 INTRODUCTION

Motivation: Due to the complexity of today's systems, performance and dependability models should be built in a structured, i.e. Modular and hierarchical fashion. Employing different modelling formalisms within the same overall model can greatly assist the modeller in describing different aspects of the system in a clear and concise way. (generalised) stochastic petri nets, stochastic activity neworks, stochastic automata, stochastic process algebras, stochastic extensions of uml state charts and other modelling formalisms may thus be employed in an overall multi-formalism model. There are two basic forms of interaction between the submodels of an overall model, both well understood in the theory of concurrent processes: one of them is the sharing of state variables, which is a very general concept supported by literally every modelling formalism mentioned above. In this approach, a subset of the state variables of a submodel is shared with one or more other submodels, so these state variables can be considered as global variables. The other form of interaction is synchronisation of common activities, which means that a designated subset of events may only take place jointly between two or more submodels. The consequence is that submodels have to wait for each other to perform these synchronised activities and are blocked as long as the partners are not ready to proceed. For the analysis, the high-level model description needs to be transformed into its low-level counterpart, of which this chapter assumes that it can be formalised as a Markov Reward Model (MRM), widespread in the performance and dependability literature. MRMs are continuous-time Markov chains augmented by reward (or cost) functions which enable the description and computation of a wide range of interesting performance and dependability measures. Examples for such measures are the expected accumulated reward gained during the mission of a spacecraft or the mean energy consumption per unit time of a production system.

A well-known drawback of state-based analysis is the problem of state space explosion, which means that the number of reachable states may grow exponentially in the number of concurrent activities of the high-level model. Among the techniques devised for coping with this problem, symbolic, i.e. decision diagram based approaches have shown to be particularly effective.

(Reduced Ordered Binary) Decision Diagrams (DD) are very useful for efficiently constructing and compactly representing the MRM underlying a high-level model description. Among the tools which successfully employ DD-based techniques are stochastic model checkers like PRISM (PRISM web page), CASPA (Kuntz et al. 2004) and SMART (SMART web page). These tools are able to analyse models with hundreds of millions of states. However, when it comes to tools which support multiple modelling languages, e.g. the Moebius performance analysis framework (Moebius web page), it is important that the DD-based analysis of MRMs is independent of the concrete model description method. This is not only because different entities of a system model might be described in a different method, but future extensions of the set of modelling formalisms should not require a re-implementation of the analysis engine. Independence of modelling formalism and DD-based analysis can be achieved by carrying out standard state space traversal and step-wise augmentation of the DD encoding the MRM. It is important, however, to note that these steps cannot practically be performed in a state-by-state manner, since this would lead to an unacceptable runtime overhead. Instead, operations which process sets of states and sets of transitions within one step are needed. Such operations can be provided by a DD environment, but they need to be used with great care and insight into the structure of the high-level model. Otherwise, negative effects[1] may compromise the efficiency of the approach.

Contribution: In order to address these problems, this chapter introduces a scheme for efficiently constructing a DD-based representation of a high-level model's underlying MRM. The proposed technique does not depend on a specific modelling method and is therefore very well suited for multi-formalism models. This implies that the method needs to support different model composition schemes, where the paper discusses model composition via shared state variables and via synchronization of activities, both applicable within the same overall model. The state space generation method and the method for handling reward variables have been described before (Lampka et al. 2006a, Lampka et al. 2006b, Lampka 2007), but they are here placed for the first time in the context of a multi-formalism modelling environment.

Organisation of the Chapter: Sec. 2 recapitulates basics of Markov Reward Modelling, introduces zero-suppressed Multi-terminal Binary Decision Diagrams (ZDDs) and shows how they can be employed for representing Markov Reward Models. This prepares the ground for a generation and analysis scheme which is independent of the used modelling formalisms. Sec. 3 elaborates on the part which constructs the Continuous Time Markov Chain underlying a high-level model description. Sec. 4 presents the algorithms for constructing ZDD-based representation of reward functions and computing the performance metrics for the modelled system. Throughout the paper, we employ a simple running example, specified as a multi-formalism MRM, to illustrate the concepts.

2 BACKGROUND MATERIAL

Finite state Markov models constitute the common base for a wide range of different stochastic modelling formalisms. In the following, we briefly review the fundamentals of Markov Reward Models (MRM). This will be followed by a very brief introduction to high-level modelling techniques and composition schemes, i.e. methods for constructing high-level models in a hierarchic and compositional style. This will be followed

by introducing zero-suppressed Multi-terminal Binary Decision Diagrams (ZDD) and showing how they can be used in a straight-forward manner to represent Markov reward models. Overall, this provides the background for the discussion on how to derive symbolic model representations in the context of a multi-formalism high-level modelling environment efficiently.

2.1 Markov Reward Models

A (finite state) Markov Reward Model (MRM) consists of a Continuous Time Markov Chain (CTMC) and a set of reward functions defined for the states and the state-to-state transitions of the CTMC. In the following we detail on the relevant concepts.

Continuous Time Markov Chain (CTMC): A CTMC is a stochastic process $\{X(t) \mid t \in \mathbb{R}\}$ where $X(t)$ is interpreted as the state of the system at time t. In the context of this chapter, the state space is assumed to be a finite set of vectors $(s \in S)$ of dimension n, where n is the number of state variables. Where appropriate, we will also employ indices like i and j in order to denote states. The distinctive property of Markov chains is the fact that they are memoryless, which means that the future evolution depends only on the current state and not on the past history. The memoryless property implies that a Markov chain is not only independent of the sequence of visited states in the past, but also that the sojourn time T_i to be spent in the current state i is independent of the sojourn time already elapsed. Randomly distributed continuous sojourn times satisfying this property have exponential distribution: $\text{Prob}(T \leq t) = 1 - e^{-\lambda t}$. We formally define Continuous Time Markov chains (CTMC) as follows:

Definition 1: A finite continuous time Markov chain (CTMC) is a triple C:= (S, T, $\pi(0)$) where S is the finite set of system states. T is the matrix of transition rates among states, i.e. a mapping $S \times S \to \mathbb{R}_0^+$ where $\forall i \in S : T(i, i) = 0$. Vector $\pi(0)$ defines an initial probability distribution on S.

In the context of this chapter, we are only concerned with time-homogeneous CTMCs, i.e. CTMCs where the transition rates are constant over time.

Reward Functions: In addition to the CTMC, which captures the system behaviour, reward functions constitute the other important part of a Markov reward model. Rate rewards depend on the system state of the CTMC, i.e. the value of the state variables, while impulse rewards are associated with the completion of transitions in the CTMC. A rate reward defines the reward gained per unit time by the model in a specific state. In contrast, an impulse reward defines the reward obtained by executing a specific activity in a specific state (Sanders et al. 1991).

A set of rate and impulse reward functions, defined by the user on the high-level model, can be combined to form complex performance variables, i.e. the value of a performance variable p is assumed to be the sum of a set of rate or impulse reward functions. In the context of this chapter, the specific state- and/or transition-dependent reward values are assumed to be time-independent and we define them as follows:

Definition 2: A rate reward r defined on a CTMC is a function $R_r : S \to \mathbb{R}$. The set of all rate rewards defined for a given CTMC is denoted R.

Definition 3: An impulse reward a of a CTMC is a function $I^a : S \times S \to \mathbb{R}$. The set of all impulse rewards defined for a given CTMC is denoted I.

With these definitions we can now define:

Definition 4: A Markov reward model (MRM) is a triple M := (C, I, R), where C is a CTMC, I is a set of impulse reward functions and R a set of rate reward functions.

2.2 Numerical Solution of (Low-Level) Markov Reward Models

The numerical solution of a Markov reward model involves the computation of state probability distributions and, on top of this, the computation of measures w. r. t. reward functions.

Computing State Probability Distributions: The state probability distribution of the Markov reward model (both for the transient and – if it exists – the stationary case) can be computed by standard numerical techniques for CTMC analysis. For the scope of this paper, we assume that the CTMC at hand is irreducible, as this simplifies the presentation. However, the methods presented are also applicable to the general case of finite Markov chains with more than one bottom strongly connected components. Numerical methods for calculating steady-state or transient probabilities can be found in the literature, e.g. (Stewart 1994, Fox et al. 1988) and for their BDD-based variants (Parker 2002, Kwiatkowska et al. 2002, Zimmermann 2005, Hermanns et al. 1998a, Lampka et al. 2007, Schuster et al. 2008).

Computing Performability Measures: From the state probability distribution, measures related to the reward functions can be computed. Examples of such measures are the expected instant-of-time reward at steady-state, or the mean number of transitions of a certain type (i.e. their throughput) per unit time. For simplicity we defined rate and impulse rewards as being state-/activity-dependent functions. In the following we briefly discuss the concept of rate and impulse rewards, details can be found e.g. in (Sanders 1988, Sanders et al. 1991, Ciardo et al. 1993).

Handling of Rate Rewards: A rate reward is the cost or gain obtained while being in a state *i*.

Thus the rate reward obtained in a specific state i at time point t can be computed as follows:

$$R^r(i,t) := \pi_i(t) \cdot R^r(i) \tag{1}$$

where $\pi_i(t)$ is the probability of being in state i at time point t and $R^r(i)$ is the time-independent rate reward value of state i concerning rate reward r (cf. Definition 2). The probability $\pi_i(t)$ can be computed by standard numerical methods, namely the uniformisation algorithm for finite time points and iterative steady-state solvers for the limit $t \to \infty$. Since each state $i \in S$ has its own rate reward value with respect to reward function r, one must simply sum the reward values over all states yielding the state-independent reward value $Rr(t)$ at time-point

$$R^r(t) := \sum_{i \in S} R^r(i,t) = \sum_{i \in S} \pi_i(t) R^r(i) \tag{2}$$

In addition to instant-of-time rewards, also interval-of-time and time-averaged interval-of-time rewards are important. A rate reward obtained for a time interval [t, t + Δt] can be computed as follows:

$$R^r\left(t, t + Dt\right) := \sum_{i \in S} R^r(i) \tilde{\pi}_i\left(t, t + \Delta t\right) \Delta t \tag{3}$$

where $\tilde{\pi}_i\left(t, \ t + \Delta t\right)$ is the average state probability for being in state i during time interval [t, t + Δt]. It can be computed as follows:

$$\tilde{\pi}_i\left(t, t + \Delta t\right) := \frac{1}{\Delta t} \int_{\tau=0}^{t+\Delta t} \pi_i\left(\tau\right) \ d\tau$$

By norming the computed value to the time period analysed $\left(1 / \Delta t\right)$, the above interval-of-time reward measure can be converted into a

time-averaged value. For the case $t \to \infty$ (steady-state), $\pi_i(t, t + \Delta t)$ is simply replaced by the steady-state distribution π_i. Note that due to the above Definition of rate rewards, only those states contribute to R^r which have a state probability different from 0. We will come back to this issue in the next section, where SG reduction techniques are addressed.

Handling of Impulse Rewards: An impulse reward associated with a specific transition is obtained, each time the respective transition is taken by the system, i.e. $i \xrightarrow{\lambda_{i,j}} j$ may contribute to the overall value of an impulse reward I^a. The impulse obtained during the time interval $(t, t + \Delta t)$ by a single transition is computed as follows:

$$I^a(i,j,t,t+\Delta t) := \tilde{\pi}_i\left(t, t + \Delta t\right) \Delta t \ I^a\left(i,j\right) \lambda_{i,j} \tag{4}$$

where $\tilde{\pi}_i\left(t, t + \Delta t\right)$ is defined as above and $\lambda_{i,j}$ is the transition rate between state i and j and $I^a(i, j)$ is the impulse reward associated with this transition. Since there might be more than one transition emanating form state i and contributing to impulse reward I^a it follows:

$$I^a\left(i,t,t+\Delta t\right) := \tilde{\pi}_i\left(t, t + \Delta t\right) \Delta t \sum_{j \in S} I^a\left(i,j\right) \lambda_{i,j} \tag{5}$$

In order to obtain the "state-independent" impulse reward one simply needs to sum over all states, yielding:

$$I^a\left(t, t + \Delta t\right) := \sum_{i \in S} \sum_{j \in S} I^a\left(i, j, t, t + \Delta t\right) \tag{6}$$

So far we only computed an interval-of-time impulse reward. By norming the computed values to the length of the time-interval (t), the above interval-of-time reward measures can be converted into time-averaged values. In the steady-state case, we restrict the discussion to time-averaged impulse rewards, so that $\tilde{\pi}_i\left(t, t + \Delta t\right)$ in Equation 4 can be replaced with the steady-state distribution π_i, where a subsequent norming to the length of the time interval of interest must follow. This yields the steady-state impulse reward rate from state i to state j:

$$\tilde{I}^a\left(i, j\right) := \pi_i \, I^a\left(i, j\right) \lambda_{i,j} \tag{7}$$

If this is employed in Equation 5 and Equation 6 one obtains:

$$\tilde{I}^a\left(i\right) := \sum_{i \in S} \tilde{I}^a\left(i, j\right) = \pi_i \sum_{j \in S} I^a\left(i, j\right) \lambda_{i,j}$$
$$and \quad \tilde{I}^a := \sum_{i \in S} \sum_{j \in S} \tilde{I}^a\left(i, j\right) \tag{8}$$

which is the average impulse reward (value) obtained in steady-state for impulse reward a.

2.3 High-Level System Modelling

In the following we will briefly introduce the aspects of high-level system modelling. This introduction starts with the description of (sub-)models in a concise way, takes us through mechanisms for composing models in a hierarchical way and ends with the specification of performability measures.

2.3.1 High-Level Model Description Techniques

High-level modelling is a key to state based system analysis, as it supports the compact, human readable system description, opposed to the error-prone specification of CTMCs with a huge number of states. All high-level model specification methods discussed in the sequel have in common that a model M consists of a finite ordered set of discrete state variables (*S*) and a finite set

of activities (*Act*). We use the term "activity" when referring to the high-level constructs (such as an action in a process algebra or an arrival in a queuing network) and the term "transition" when referring to the underlying Markov reward model. Thus, the execution of an activity in the high-level model is reflected by a state-to-state transition in the low-level model, i.e. in the CTMC.

Stochastic Automata Networks: Stochastic automata networks (Plateau 1985, Buchholz 1991, Stewart 1994) are a relatively low-level modelling approach, since the high-level model description resembles activity-labelled CTMCs. For compactly specifying complex systems, the modeller may combine sets of stochastic automata by activity synchronization (cf. Sec. 2.3.2). This leads to a network of stochastic automata which describes the behaviour of a system in a compositional way. Since the individual stochastic automata do not contain any local variables, the state of a stochastic automata network is naturally described by a set of local state counters, each referring to the state of a specific stochastic automaton.

Stochastic State Charts: In recent years, state charts like the ones employed in UML have been extended to the Markovian case. In its simplest form, a stochastic state chart consists of a set of states, additional variables and transitions among these states, whose execution may modify the variables. Thus, a state of the state chart can be described by the current values of the local variables and an additional state counter, where the latter is employed for tracking the active state of the state charts. In order to specify timed behaviour, activities of the state charts are labelled with rates, which specify an exponentially distributed execution delay. For modelling case distinctions, it is also possible to make use of a special "decision" node which is connected to one source state and possibly many successor states. The incoming edge of this node defines a Markovian activity, i.e. an activity which is executed after an exponentially distributed delay. The outgoing edges are equipped with probabilities, such that they allow the modelling of a probabilistic choice among the successor states.

By introducing the concept of initial and terminal states and referencing of (sub-) state charts, state charts can be organised in a modular fashion. It seems to be straight-forward to also allow the composition of state charts via the sharing of variables and/or the joint execution of activities (cf. Sec. 2.3.2). A stochastic extension of UML state charts is described in (Jansen 2003).

Generalized Stochastic Petri Nets: A generalized stochastic Petri Net (GSPN) is a bi-partite directed graph, which consists of a set of activities (called "transitions" in the usual Petri net terminology) and a set of places. The current state of the system is given by the current marking, i.e. the number of tokens contained in each place, which means that each place of the GSPN can be regarded as a state variable of the overall model. The dynamic behaviour is specified by the activity firing rule. For specifying timed behaviour, activities are either executed after an exponential delay or instantaneously, where the race condition among competing activities must be resolved. A profound overview of GSPNs can be found in (Balbo 1995). In order to enable the specification of complex GSPNs, it is possible to combine different (sub-) nets via the sharing of places. Furthermore, concepts known from stochastic automata and stochastic process algebras have been extended to the area of GSPNs, such that the composition via activity-synchronization is also applicable, see e.g. (Ciardo et al. 1996, Hermanns et al. 1997).

Stochastic Activity Networks: Stochastic Activity Networks (SAN), introduced in (Sanders et al. 1991), resemble GSPNs. A state of a SAN can also be described as a tuple of state variables, each of which refers to a specific place of the net. In addition to GSPNs, SANs allow the use of so called input and output gates. These gates can be seen as an enrichment of the enabling predicates (guards) and the execution functions of the connected activities. SANs also allow the association of each activity with a set of "cases", where the individual execution probability is determined by the specific case-individual weight. SANs allow the use of not only exponential distributions but also general distributions for the delay of activities. However, in the context of this chapter, we are occupied with Markovian models, thus we only consider Markovian and non-delayed activities. The SAN modelling formalism includes operators for composing submodels via the sharing of places (a general Join and a special Replicate operator). Furthermore, it is also possible to compose submodels via the joint execution of activities.

Stochastic Process Algebras: A stochastic process algebra (SPA) specification is built with the help of operators for action prefix (guarded) choice, (implicit or explicit) recursion, parallel composition, hiding, etc.. Consequently, the state of the process may be described by the values of the local process variables and a process counter. Actions can be timed, i.e. they are equipped with rates, or in some cases also non-delayed, i.e. instantaneous. Examples of stochastic process algebras can be found in (Götz 1994, Hillston 1994, Hermanns et al. 1998a, Hermanns et al. 1998b, Kuntz et al. 2004).

An important concept of process algebras is constructivity: (a) Similar to stochastic automata, a system can be built in a compositional manner, where activity-synchronization (cf. Sec. 2.3.2) is employed for combining the individual process instances. (b) Process algebras are equipped with notions of equivalence of processes, which allows one to replace processes with simpler ones, such that the overall system becomes smaller, but exhibits the same functional and timed behaviour. In recent years, aspects of constructivity have been adopted to other high-level model description methods, where especially the compositional construction of high-level models plays an important role (Hermanns et al. 1997).

Remark: Timed and untimed activities. Most high-level Markov modelling methods feature the use of Markovian activities, i.e. activities whose execution delay is sampled from an exponential distribution, and the use of non-delayed, i.e. instantaneous activities. Therefore, after transformation of the high-level model into its underlying Markov reward model, two kinds of transitions between pairs of states exist: immediate and timed ones. Timed transitions are taken with an exponential delay, whereas instantaneous transitions are taken immediately. It is is evident that within states with outgoing immediate and timed transitions, the latter will never be taken, known as the maximum progress assumption. The system will spend non-zero time only in states which can exclusively be left via outgoing timed transitions. States of such kind are denoted as tangible, whereas states to be left via immediate transitions are denoted as vanishing. In case a vanishing state can be left via more than one immediate activity, the non-determinism has to be resolved. This is done by assigning probabilities to each immediate transition. The result is a transition matrix T, where some entries refer to transition probabilities and some to transition rates. As known from the literature, e.g. (Balbo et al. 1995, Ciardo et al. 1993), T can be converted into a pure transition rate matrix by eliminating all entries referring to vanishing states. This elimination can be done either at the level of the high-level model or at the level of the state space (Bachmann et al. 2009). For simplicity we only consider high-level model descriptions with timed activities.

2.3.2 Composition of High-Level Model Descriptions

The high-level model is constructed in a modular and hierarchic way by specifying the type of interaction between a given set of submodels.

Sharing of State Variables: If a high-level modelling formalism employs (local) variables, it is possible to compose submodels by merging sets of local variables. This technique is commonly denoted as sharing or joining of state variables. In the following, we assume that (global) variables are shared among submodels. Local variables with the same name are consequently overloaded by the global definitions. Sanders 1988) presents a composition scheme, where on top of the sharing re-model instantiation takes place. The induced symmetry can be exploited on-the-fly, leading to substantially smaller CTMCs to be analysed.

Joint Activity Execution: When composing submodels via joint activity execution, they are executed in parallel, but a subset of dedicated activities has to be executed jointly by all participating partners. Different approaches concerning the type of synchronizing activities exists, with different schemes for computing the rate of synchronised activities. In the following we will employ the operator $S_1 \parallel_{SAct} S_2$ over all activities appearing on the set *SAct*, which means that activities with the same label are executed synchronously. In general, the synchronization operator is not associative.

Pure Interleaving: If no interaction among the submodels takes place, one speaks of pure interleaving. In this case, the submodels are in fact (disjoint) partitions of the overall model executing concurrently. Pure interleaving is the special case of joint activity execution and sharing of state variables, in case the set of objects over which the submodels interact is empty. In this case we write $S_1 \parallel S_2$.

Running Example

Throughout this chapter, we employ a running example to illustrate the concepts. In the example system, two users generate requests which are served by a processor, either individually or together. The maximum number of requests generated per user is two, and once this number has been reached by both, an exception handling activity may empty the system. The example does not model a particular real system, it is just for demonstration purposes. The high-level description of the example is shown in Figure 1. It is a multi-formalism model, where the overall model consists of two SPN submodels and three SPA

Figure 1. Running example: A high-level model composed from heterogenous submodels by sharing variables and synchronizing activities

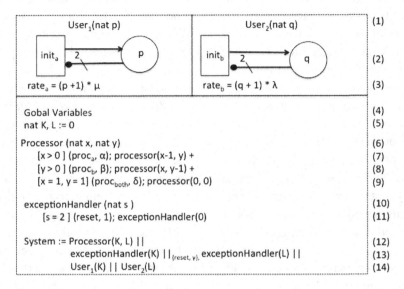

submodels. Using SPA notation, the overall model is given by the expression defined in line (12) to (14) in Figure 1. The submodels interact via the global variables K and L, as they are passed by name into the instances of the submodels. The notation $\|_{reset,\gamma}$ means that the two instances of submodel *exceptionHandler(.)* interact by synchronizing the execution of activity reset, with γ as the resulting transition rate of the synchronised activities. An example of a performance variable w. r. t. this high-level model is given in Figure 6. There, we define a performance variable *Avail* which consists of the sum of two rate reward functions, r_1 and r_2 respectively (defined in a pseudo C notation). We obtain a rate reward value of 1 for each state where either K or L are 0 and a rate reward value of 2 for the initial system state (where K and L are 0).

2.4 Symbolic Representation of Markov Reward Models

In this chapter we make use of zero-suppressed Multi-terminal Binary Decision Diagrams (ZDDs)

(Lampka et al. 2010) which we introduce in the following, together with their use for encoding MRMs.

The ZDD Data Structure and its Associated Algorithms: ZDDs are directed acyclic graphs with a dedicated root node. If they are ordered and reduced, they allow (weakly) canonical representations of pseudo-Boolean function, i.e. of functions of the kind $f : \mathbb{B}^{|V|} \to \mathbb{R}$ with $V :=\{v_1,...v_n\}$ as finite set of (Boolean) function variables.

A Binary Decision Tree (BDT) (Lee 1959) is a binary tree

$B := \{V, K, value, var, then, else\}$, where:

- $V := \{v_1,...v_n\}$ is a finite and non-empty ordered set of boolean variables

- $K := K_T \cup K_{NT}$ is a finite non-empty set of nodes, consisting of the disjoint sets of terminal nodes K_T and non-terminal nodes K_{NT},

- The mappings *var*: $K_{NT} \to V$ and *value*: $K_{NT} \to \mathbb{B}$ are defined,

Figure 6. ZDD-based representation of performance variables

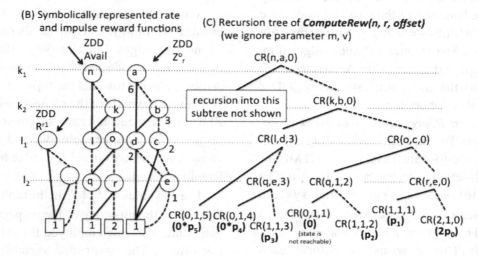

- The functions *else, then*: $K_{NT} \to K$ and the function *getroot*: $B \to K$ are defined.

For the BDT to be ordered the following constraint must hold: $\forall u \in K_{NT}$:

- $then(u) \in K_{NT} : var\big(then(u)\big) \succ var(u)$
- $else(u) \in K_{NT} : var\big(else(u)\big) \succ var(u)$

where $\succ V \times V$ is a fixed ordering relation.

The BDT becomes a Multi-terminal BDT (Formal Methods in System Design 1997) if we allow the terminal nodes to also hold other values than 0 and 1, which can be easily achieved by extending the Definition of function value accordingly. In the following we are only concerned with the ordered multi-terminal case.

A Multi-terminal BDT becomes a Multi-terminal zero-suppressed BDD (ZDD for short) by applying the following two reduction rules:

1. Non-terminal nodes whose 1-successor is the terminal 0-node are skipped.
2. Isomorphic subgraphs are merged.

The first rule is the one originally proposed for zero-suppressed BDDs by Minato (Minato 1993), and the second rule is the same as for standard BDDs.

For a ZDD it is important to know the set of Boolean variables on which it depends (since skipping a Boolean variable level means that the corresponding variable takes the value 0). This is especially important in multi-rooted DD environments as implemented in packages such as CUDD (Somenzi 1998). Here, ZDD-nodes lose their uniqueness if the represented functions have different sets of input variables. We define ZDDs to be partially shared if they do not necessarily have identical sets of Boolean variables, leading to different semantics of skipped levels while traversing the ZDDs. For this reason, we developed an algorithm for efficiently manipulating partially shared ZDDs, denoted as ZApply-algorithm, which is an extension of Bryant's famous Apply-algorithm (Bryant 1986). Our algorithm, which is described in (Lampka et al. 2010), allows to apply Boolean and arithmetic operators to ZDDs, where the operators mainly differ in the handling of the terminal nodes; we exploit the dualities $+ = \vee$ and $\cdot = \wedge$ in our notation from now on. Apart from the ZApply-algorithm, we also employ the algorithm Abstract($\cdot$, S, Z) which allows the all quantification of a ZDD Z w. r. t. variables of set S.

ZDD-Based Representation of Markov Reward Model: By explicitly generating system states and state-to-state transitions, a CTMC for a given high-level model can be constructed. The CTMC defines a transition system $T \subseteq (S \times Act \times \mathbb{R}^+ \times S)$. Each transition of T can be encoded by applying a binary encoding function *Encode*. This allows us to transforms each transition of the CTMC $i \xrightarrow{\lambda} j$ into a bit-vector. The individual bit positions correspond to the input variables of the ZDD, where we have the following convention: **s**-variables hold the encodings of source states, *t*-variables hold the encodings of target states and the transition rate is stored in the terminal node.

Following a widely used heuristics, the variables are ordered in an interleaved fashion: $s_1 < t_1 \ldots < s_n < t_n$. This encoding yields a pseudo-Boolean function for each finite state CTMC.

In a similar fashion one may encode the set of reachable states, the rate and impulse reward functions. In these cases, the corresponding ZDDs take solely the s-variables as input.

Running Example

For the high-level model specified in Figure 1, Figure 2.A – C sketches the above encoding scheme: The CTMC underlying the high-level model is depicted in Figure 2.A. An example of a binary encoded (pseudo-) Boolean function

and the corresponding ZDD-based representation is provided by Figure 2.B and C. Dashed (solid) lines in the ZDDs indicate the value assignment 0 (1) to the corresponding Boolean variable on the respective path. The ZDDs are ordered, i.e. they have the same variable ordering one each path. As the order is from top to bottom, we omit the arrow heads on the node connecting edges. For clarity we also omitted the terminal 0-node and its incoming edges. The arrows pointing towards the top node of a ZDD signal the root node of the respective ZDD. The ZDDs are reduced and zero-suppressed, i.e. we do not show isomorphic nodes and we do not show nodes whose outgoing 1-edge leads to the terminal 0-node.

The variables k_i, k_i', l_i, l_i' in the table of Figure 2.B report the bit-value of the respective Boolean (state) variable employed for encoding the transitions. The un-primed variables refer to the values of the bit positions of the encoded state variables before the transition has taken place, i.e. they refer to the s-variables in the above encoding scheme. The primed variables refer to the target state, i.e. the t-variables. Figure 2.B and C also show the binary encodings and ZDD based representation of a reward function w. r. t. the variables K and L of the high-level model, where we specified the reward function in Figure 6. A and in a C-like expression.

3 SCHEME FOR CONSTRUCTING A CTMC FROM ITS MULTI-FORMALISM MODEL DESCRIPTION

The scheme presented in the following makes it possible to treat different high-level modelling formalisms in a more or less black-box manner. The scheme only builds on some basic properties derived from the structure of any high-level model making use of variables and activities.

Figure 2. Running example: CTMC and ZDD-based representation of the underlying Markov Reward model

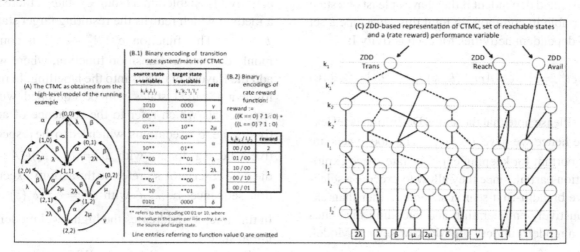

3.1 Structural Properties of High-Level Models-Level Models

We define a high-level model as a quadruple $(\mathbb{S}, s^\epsilon, Act, Con)$, with:

- $\mathbb{S} := \{s_1, ..., s_n\}$ is an ordered set of state variables. As each state variable can take values from a finite domain, the states of a high-level model can be written as a vector of integers $s \in S \subset N_0^{|\mathbb{S}|}$.
  - s^ϵ is the high-level model's initial state, i.e. it provides the initial value assignment for the state variables.
  - $Act := \{n, l, ..., z\}$ refers to the set of activities, the execution of which allows the model to evolve from state to state.
  - With $Con \subseteq (\mathbb{S} \times Act) \cup (Act \times \mathbb{S})$ we address a connection relation, where we define a state variable s_i and an activity l as connected iff s_i influences the behaviour of l or s_i changes its value when activity l is executed.

Based on the connection relation, we define the set of dependent state variables for each activity l:

$$\mathbb{S}_l^D := \{s_i \mid (s_i, l) \in Con \vee (l, s_i) \in Con\}$$

The complementary set $\mathbb{S}_l^I := \mathbb{S} \setminus \mathbb{S}_l^D$ denotes the independent state variables, i.e. the ones which neither influence the behaviour of activity nor change their values when is executed. Based on the above Definition we define a projection function $\chi_l : \mathbb{N}_0^{|\mathbb{S}|} \to \mathbb{N}_0^{|\mathbb{S}_l^D|}$ for each activity $1 \in Act$. This function extracts the subvector w. r. t. activity's set of dependent state variables and w. r. t. a state, where for simplicity we use the shorthand notation: $s_{d_1} := \chi_1(s)$. The partial state vector s_{d_1} is called the activity-local marking of state s (w. r. t. activity l). The above Definition of dependent state variables enables one furthermore to define a reflexive and symmetric dependency relation $Act^D \subseteq Act \times Act$ where:

$$(k, l) \in Act^D \Leftrightarrow \mathbb{S}_k^D \cap \mathbb{S}_l^D \neq \varnothing ? \qquad (9)$$

According to this, two activities $1, k \in Act$ are called dependent if they have at least one state variable in common. In total this gives one a set of dependent activities for each activity l:

$$Act_l^D := \{k \in Act \mid (l, k) \in Act^D\} \qquad (10)$$

Please note that the above Definition is reflexive hence we have $l \in Act_l^D$. The above sets are important for keeping explicit state space exploration partial, since they allow to execute a selective breadth-first search scheme, rather than exhaustively enumerating and encoding the states of a model's underlying Markov Reward Model.

Running Example

For the example of Figure 1 we have $Act := \{init_a,$ $init_b, proc_a, proc_b, proc_{both}, reset_1, reset_2\}$ as set of activities, where according to the above concept each activity possesses its individual sets of dependent and independent state variables, e.g. activity $init_a$ only contains variable in its set of dependent state variable $\left(\mathfrak{S}_{init_a}^D := \{K\}\right)$. As state variable is shared among different submodels, we also have that is in a dependency relation with $proc_a, proc_{both}$, and $reset_1$ which yields

$$Act_{(init_a)}^D := \{proc_a, proc_b, reset_1\}.$$

The operational semantics of a modelling formalism is irrelevant for the discussion to follow. This is because the proposed scheme relies on (partial) standard state space exploration, which makes it applicable for any kind of (state-based) high-level modelling formalism. The only three things which matter are the following:

Guard Functions: For a given state s and a given activity l, a test method (aka guard) has to be available which decides whether or not l is executable in state s. Formally: $guard_l$: $\mathbb{N}_0 \to \{true, false\}$, where for $guard_l(s) = $ true one says that activity l is enabled in state s.

Transitions Generating Functions: In case activity l is enabled in a (source) state s, there is a method which returns the resulting target state $t \in \mathbb{N}_0^{|\mathfrak{S}|}$. This function $\delta_l : \mathbb{N}_0^{|\mathfrak{S}|} \to \mathbb{N}_0^{|\mathfrak{S}|}$ is commonly denoted as transition function, where we add the flavour of events into the labelling. In the following, target states will be equipped with superscripts which refer to the sequence of activities, i.e. δ_1 executions, which led to the respective state, e.g. for s^ω with $\omega := (\alpha, ..., \zeta) \in Act^*$ the state descriptor s^ω refers to the activity execution sequence $\alpha, ..., \zeta$ with $s^\omega := \delta_\zeta(..\delta_\alpha(s)..)$. In this line, s^ε addresses the high-level model's initial state.

Rate Returning Functions: When executing l in a state s one needs a method which returns the execution rate of l. This function $\eta_l : N_0^{(|\mathfrak{S}|)} \to \mathbb{R}^+$ is addressed as rate returning function. It is evaluated for the source state, i.e. a priori to the execution of the respective δ_l-function.

The concrete implementations of δ_l, $guard_l$ and η_l are irrelevant for the discussion to follow. It is only required, that the evaluation of these functions solely depends on the dependent SVs of the respective activity. Employing all implementations of the δ_l, $guard_l$ and η_l functions of a high-level model in a fixed point computation allows one to construct the activity-labeled CTMC for a given high-level model, the stochastic activity-labeled transition system $T \subseteq \left(S \times Act \times \mathbb{R}^+ \times S\right)$ respectively, where $S \subset \mathbb{N}_0^{|\mathfrak{S}|}$ addresses the model's set of (reachable) states.

Running Example

For the example of Figure 1, the guard function $guard_{proc_a}$ is given by the following (C-like) expression $(K > 0)$? true : false. At model construction time, the local variable x of the instance of submodel *Processor* is bound to global variable

K, whereas local variable y is bound to global variable L (see Figure 1). As another example, one may consider activity $init_a$, with the expression $(K < 2)$? true : false as guard function. For $proc_a$ we also have δ_{proc_a} defined by the expression $K = K - 1$ and η_{proc_a} by the constant expression α. In case of activity $init_a$, we obtain the expressions $K = K + 1$ and $(K + 1) \cdot \mu$ for the δ and η-function respectively.

As already pointed out, we use joint variables and/or activity synchronization for constructing models in a hierarchic manner. We assume that all state variables have a unique identifier throughout all submodels. Hence, sharing of state variables is realised by (re-)using the same (global) variable in different submodels. This naming convention is sufficient when it comes to the construction of the overall model's MRM at the level of decision diagrams. Dealing with activity-synchronization also makes it necessary to define a naming convention. We assume that activities to be synchronised carry the same (main) label which we prime and index accordingly. The index refers to the respective instance of a submodel participating in the synchronization. Moreover, hierarchic use of synchronization operators yields a multiset *SAct* of activity labels, where each of its elements refers to a set of (sub-) activities to be jointly executed, i.e. synchronised. However, sets of synchronizing (sub-) activities referring to the same (main) label and which are directly adjacent within the model description need to be merged. E.g., $X\|_a Y\|X\|_a Y$ results in the multiset $SAct := \{a,a\}$ where each symbol references its set of (sub-) activities, here: $\{a'_{X_1}, a'_{Y_1}\}$ and $\{a'_{X_2}, a'_{Y_2}\}$.
In case of $X\|_a Y\|_a X\|_a Y$ we would need to merge the sets accordingly, yielding the (multi-) set *SAct* $:= \{a\}$ and the set $\{a'_{X_1}, a'_{Y_1}, a'_{X_2}, a'_{Y_2}\}$ of (sub-) activities. In terms of the model of Figure 1, we have a single element on the multiset *SAct* $:= \{reset\}$ and a single set of sub-activities $\{reset'_a, reset'_b\}$.

Beyond the naming convention and as far as the explicit exploration procedure is concerned, the handling of activities which take part in a synchronisation is straight-forward: the (sub-) activities are treated just like any other activity. Synchronization is only considered when carrying out the ZDD-based computations for constructing a high-level model's CTMC.

3.2 The Scheme at Glance

As main goal we aim at limiting the number of explicit state enumerations and individual encodings of transitions as far as possible, as this is computationally expensive. The vast majority of transitions will be obtained by ZDD-based computations, where we generate all possible transition interleavings by customised cross-product computations. In a nutshell, the proposed technique is round-based, where a round is made of (a) explicit state space exploration steps, (b) individual encoding of the generated state-to-state transitions, (c) pure symbolic, i.e. BDD-based manipulations of the generated transition system and (d) a re-initialization procedure for preparing the next round. Carrying out these steps in a fixed point computation, ultimately delivers the complete set of reachable states and transitions of the high-level model under analysis. These steps will be briefly sketched in the following paragraphs.

Explicit Generation and Encoding of Transitions: For generating symbolic representations of the state-to-state transition functions we employ the activity-local scheme as presented in (Lampka et al. 2006a). This scheme constructs a ZDD for each activity which we denote ZDD Z^l in case of a non-synchronizing activity l, and ZDD Z^{l_i} for a synchronizing activity l_i. It is important to note that the number of executions of synchronizing activities may not be bounded when exploring them in isolation. This situation can be easily caught by simply limiting the number of explicit state explorations to be executed at once, i.e. per round.

Symbolic Manipulations for Obtaining Set of States and Transitions: For obtaining a symbolic representation of the model's set of reachable states we employed a symbolic composition scheme which generates supersets of transitions. These potential transition functions are employed in a (standard) symbolic reachability analysis which at termination delivers a ZDD Z_R which is the symbolic representation of a model's set of reachable states.

The algorithms implementing the above steps are shown in Figure 3. In the following we detail on selected aspects of the scheme.

3.3 Implementation Details

For convenience we introduce the following sets:

$$D_l := \left\{ \boldsymbol{s}^i, \boldsymbol{t}^i \mid s^i \in \mathbb{S}_l^D \right\} \text{ and } I_l := \left\{ \boldsymbol{s}^i, \boldsymbol{t}^i \mid s^i \in \mathbb{S}_l^I \right\}$$
(11)

where $\boldsymbol{s}^i$ and $\boldsymbol{t}^i$ in D_l refer to those Boolean variables which encode the value of dependent state variable s_i in the source and target state of a transition with respect to activity l. Analogously, the set I_l refers to l's set of independent SVs, i.e. their Boolean counterparts, respectively. In case it is required we will make use of the symbols D_l^s, I_l^s and D_l^t, I_l^t when referring to the sets restricted to the s or t-variables.

In lines 1-3 of the top-level algorithm (Figure 3.A) some data initialization is done: ZDD Z_R is set to the initial state s^e and the exploration and encoding buffers *StateBuffer* and *TransBuffer* are allocated. The buffer *StateBuffer* is used for holding tuples of states and activities, where the activities are supposed to be executed in the state. The buffer *TransBuffer* holds transitions to be explicitly encoded and inserted into a ZDD. Routine *Initialize()* fills *StateBuffer* with the (initial) elements to be explored, i.e. with tuples

consisting of the initial state and an activity to be executed in this state, where we have a tuple for each activity enabled in the initial state.

Explicit Generation of States and Transitions: Routine *Explore()* generates a symbolic representation Z_l for each activity, including the sub-activities l_i. The symbolic structure is generated by explicitly exploring and individually encoding the detected transitions. This step is repeated until no new transition can be detected or a predefined maximum on the explicit state exploration steps is reached. This latter maximum is necessary, as the exploration steps of any synchronizing (sub-) activity may not be finite when considered in isolation. The most distinguished feature of function *Explore* is the selective breadth-first-search (bfs) exploration and encoding of transitions. A selective bfs scheme is obtained by executing activity k in a state $s^{\omega l}$ if and only if activity k depends on the last activity whose execution led to the state $s^{\omega l}$ (here l) and the activity-local marking of the current state $s_{d_k}^{\omega l}$ has not been tested for enabling activity k before ($k \in Act_l^D \wedge s_{d_k}^{\omega l} \notin E_k$). Note that we do not need to expand all sequences of activity executions, as this is done on the level of symbolic reachability analysis. For simplicity we store the activity markings which have already been tested on activity k in a symbolic structure denoted E_k.

The above ideas are implemented with the help of two complementary while-loops of the algorithm of Figure 3.C. The upper loop fetches states and lists of activities $\left(s, F_s^l \right)$ from the (exploration) *StateBuffer* (line 3) and computes for each activity $k \in F_s^l$ the successor state s^k and the transition rate w. r. t. the given source state s (lines 5 and 6). The thereby established (stochastic) transition is inserted into the (encoding) buffer *TransBuffer* (line 7) and these steps are repeated until all activities of F_s^l have been processed. This inner for-loop is repeated until all tuples of

Figure 3. Algorithms for the exploration scheme

(A) Main routine

`ConstructMRM()`
/* *Encode the initial system state as ZDD* */
(1) $Z_R := \text{Encode}(s^\epsilon)$

/* *Initialize data structures* */
(2)   StateBuffer $:= empty$
(3)   TransBuffer $:= empty$
(4) $Initialize()$

/* *Fixed point computation for* */
/* *Constructing set of reachable states* */
(5)   WHILE StateBuffer $\neq \emptyset$ DO

/* *Explicit exploration and encoding step* */
(6) $Explore()$

/* *Symbolic composition and reachability scheme* */
(7) $Z_R := \text{SymbReach}()$
/* *Re-initialization of scheme* */
(8) $Initialize()$

(B) (Re-)initialization procedure

`Initialize()`
(1) FOR $l \in Act$ DO
(2) $Z_{new} := Z_R - E_l$
(3)   WHILE $Z_{new} \neq \emptyset$ DO

/* *Extract random state from ZDD and* */
/* *turn into state vector* */
(4) $Z_s := \text{ExtractState}(Z_{new})$
(5) $s := \text{Encode}^{-1}(Z_s)$

/* *Test activity l for enabledness in this new state* */
(6)   IF $guard_l(s)$ THEN
        push(StateBuffer, $(s, \{l\})$)
(7)   ENDIF

/* *Remove all states with equivalent markings* */
/* *w.r.t. activity l from set of new states* */
(8) $Z_{new} := Z_{new} - \text{Abstract}(+, l_i^*, Z_s)$

(C) Exploration and encoding Routine

`Explore()`
(0) $fireCnt := 0;$
(1)   DO$\{ fireCnt$ ++
(2)   WHILE StateBuffer $\neq empty$ DO

/* *Fetch state and set of activities* */
/* *from buffer of unexplored states* */
(3)   pop($(s, \mathcal{F}_s^l)$, StateBuffer)

/* *Execute each activity and obtain rate info* */
(4)   FOR $k \in \mathcal{F}_s^l$ DO
(5) $s^{lk} := \delta_k(s)$
(6) $\lambda := \eta_k(s^l)$
(7)   push(TransBuffer, (s, k, λ, s^k))

/* *Encode detected transitions and* */
/* *prepare next explicit exploration step* */
(8)   WHILE TransBuffer $\neq empty$ DO
(9)   pop(TransBuffer, $(s, l, \lambda s^l)$)
(10) $Z_l := Z_l + \text{Encode}(s_{d_l}, \lambda, s_{d_l}^l)$

/* *Did we already reach the max number of exploration step* */
(11)   IF $fireCnt \leq MAX$ THEN
(12) $\mathcal{F}_{s\,l}^l := \emptyset$

/* *Check all dependent activities of t* */
/* *if the state was not already tested* */
/* *and if the activity, here k is executable* */
(13)   FOR $k \in Act_l^D$ DO
(14)   IF $(\text{Encode}(s_{d_k}^l) \times E_k = 0) \wedge$
            $guard_k(s^l)$ THEN
(15) $\mathcal{F}_{s\,l}^l := \mathcal{F}_{s\,l}^l \cup \{k\}$
(16) $E_k := E_k + \text{Encode}(s_{d_k}^l)$
(17)   ENDIF
(18)   IF $\mathcal{F}_{s\,l}^l \neq \emptyset$ THEN
(19)   push(StateBuffer, $(s^l, \mathcal{F}_{s\,l}^l)$)
(20)   ENDIF
(21)   ENDIF
(22) $\}$ WHILE StateBuffer $\neq \emptyset \wedge FireCnt \leq MAX$

(D) Symbolic Reachability analysis

`SymbReach()`
(1) $Z_{unex} := Z_R$
(2) $Z_T := \sum_{k \in Act \setminus Act_S} Z_k \times \mathbf{1} <l_k>$
(3)   FOR $l \in Act_S$ DO
(4) $Z_l := \prod_{\forall l_i'} Z_{l_i'}$
(5) $Z_T := Z_T + \sum_{l \in Act_S} Z_l \times \mathbf{1} <l>$
(6)   DO$\{$
(7) $Z_R := Z_{unex} + Z_R$

/* *Execute symbolic transition functions* */
(8) $Z_T' := Z_{unex} \times Z_T$
(9) $Z_{unex} := \text{Abstract}(Trans', s, +) \{t \longleftarrow s\}$

/* *Extract newly reached states* */
(10) $Z_{unex} := Z_{unex} \setminus Z_R$
(11) $\}$ WHILE $Z_{unex} \neq \emptyset$ DO
(12) RETURN Z_R

---

states and activities lists have been fetched from the exploration buffer *StateBuffer*.

Now we execute the lower while-loop which reads the individual transitions from the encoding buffer, individually encodes them and inserts the symbolically represented transition into the respective (activity-local) ZDD, where the encoding is implemented by function *Encode* (line 8 and 10). As long as the maximum number of exploration steps has not been reached (line 11), one computes the set of those activities which need to be considered for being explored in the state under consideration. The obtained set F_s^l of activities is a subset of those activities which are in the dependency relation with the activity whose execution led to the target state (line 13), here l, and whose enabledness w. r. t. the state under consideration, here s has not been tested yet in a previous round (line 14). For testing if an activity k was already considered for execution we

exploit symbolic structure E_k. As pointed out above, this structure represents all activity-local markings the resp. activity was already tested or explored with. It is updated in line 16. The obtained set of enabled activities, together with the state under consideration is then inserted into the exploration buffer *StateBuffer* (line 19). Note that we only explore activities on states if the respective activity was not already tested in that state and if the activity is enabled (line 14). As we also only test activities which are on the dependency set of the activity whose execution led to the currently considered target state s^l, here l, we implement a selective breadth-first search scheme. Both while-loops of the algorithm of Figure 3.C are executed sequentially until we reach a fixed point, i.e. *StateBuffer* $= \varnothing \wedge FireCnt > MAX$ holds (line 22). Now, we have visited all states reachable from the initial state(s) of this round through sequences of dependent activities. In case the maximum number of state enumerations has been reached, i.e. *FireCnt > MAX* holds, we resume with state enumeration and transition encoding in the next round of partition-local explorations only, if re-initialization (*Initialize*) indicates the necessity of doing so. As already mentioned, this catches the case that possible exploration of (sub-) activities in isolation is unbounded a priori to their synchronization. Once routine *Explore*() has terminated, routine *SymbReach()* for obtaining a model's set of reachable states is executed.

Symbolic Reachability Analysis: SymbReach() (Figure 3.D) executes a symbolic reachability analysis in a fixed point iteration, organised here as a breadth first search; a more sophisticated scheme can be found in (Lampka et al. 2006a). At first the symbolic transition functions are extended by identity structures, assigned to those positions referring to the independent state variables of the respective activity. Building the union over all the extended symbolic transition functions yields the superset of transitions (line 2-9). Note that the synchronizing activities need to be combined via product-building before insertion of the identity structure, in order to implement their synchronised execution at the level of ZDDs. Once the symbolic transition function of the overall model is constructed (line 5), the actual symbolic reachability analysis can start.

Symbolic reachability analysis begins with the known states, i.e. either with the system's initial state or the states generated in previous rounds, realised by the initialization of Z_{unex} in line 1. In line 8 we compute the set of transitions emanating from the symbolically represented set of (currently) reachable states, whereas line 9 restricts these transitions to the encodings of target states and does a relabelling of the *t*- into *s*-variables. The latter operation, denoted $\{t \leftarrow s\}$, shifts the target states to source states. In fact, the above steps yield the set of newly reached states, which serve as input to the next iteration of the surrounding do-while-loop (line 6-7). Once a fixed point

is reached, the set of (currently) reachable states has been generated.

The paper (Lampka 2008) introduces optimizations which make the symbolic composition procedure (line 2-5) a priori to symbolic reachability analysis unnecessary. At the bottom-line, that paper introduces a ZDD-operator *Execute* to be used in the do-while-loop of routine *SymbReach()*. This operator computes a symbolic image w. r. t. partial transition functions and for ZDD-based state representations. Moreover, instead of applying a pre-computed synchronisation product of the synchronizing activities in a single step, they can simply be executed sequentially. For conciseness, we do not discuss this any further, the interested reader is referred to (Lampka 2008) for details.

At termination, routine *SymbReach()* has constructed the set of all currently reachable states. This may include states which result from the interleaved execution of independent activities. These states must be tested if they trigger new explicit model behaviour, not covered by the symbolic transition functions encoded by Z_T. For detecting such states we (re-)execute routine *Initialize()*.

Re-Initialization: A re-initialization of the scheme is necessary, as the routine *Explore()* only extracts traces of dependent activities. Interleaving with independent activities is only done at the level of the symbolic representations. Therefore, states which are reached on execution traces consisting of the interleaved execution of independent activities may result in new model behaviour. The re-initialisation is realised by re-executing routine *Initialize()* which fills *StateBuffer* with the new elements, i.e. here with tuples consisting of a state and an activity. An activity *l* and a state *s* are considered by routine *Initialize()* for exploration if and only if the activity-local marking of state *s* has not already been tested for enabledness by this activity (cf. line 2 of the algorithm of Figure 3.B) and if the activity is enabled in this state (cf. line 6). If such states exist, the complete state space construction scheme must be re-executed. In case routine *Initialize( )* as called in line 8 of the main routine does not find states triggering new transitions, a global fixed point has been reached and the scheme terminates.

Construction of the CTMC: At termination, the above scheme delivers a set of (activity-local) transition systems, each induced by a dedicated activity and represented by a respective ZDD Z_l. Together with the ZDD-based representation of the set of reachable states Z_R this allows us to construct the ZDD-based representation of the CTMC as follows:

$$Z_R \left(\sum_{l \in SAct} \left(\prod_{\forall l_i} Z_{l_i} \right) * \rho_l * 1_{<I_l>} \right) + \sum_{\{k \in Act \setminus SAct\}} Z_k * 1_{<I_l>}$$

$1_{<I_l>}$ is an identity structure over the set of activity l's set of independent SVs, their Boolean counterparts respectively. The insertion of identity structures accounts for the fact that the independent variables maintain their values when the respective activity is executed. The rate ρ_l denotes the transition rate of the synchronised activities. The above composition scheme resembles the Kronecker-operator-based approach of (Plateau 1985). However, as the BDD operators can cope with partition-wise nested variable orderings, the composition scheme of BDDs is much more flexible and can therefore be applied to almost arbitrarily structured high-level models, which makes the here presented scheme extremely flexible.

Running Example

Figure 4.A-F illustrates the steps taken for the running example. Figure 4.A shows the ZDD encoding the set of reachable states at the beginning (when only the initial state (0,0) is known), and at the end of round 1. In Figure 4.B, the fraction of the CTMC generated after the first round of the main routine is depicted. It contains only those transitions which can be reached on paths of dependent activities, i.e. the activities executed on the different paths have at least pair-wise non-disjoint sets of variables. In part C of the figure, the transitions generated in the second round are shown, which are enabled due to the execution of independent activities. All of the respective (interleaved) execution sequences are generated on the level of ZDDs, rather than doing this explicitly. The transitions resulting from the synchronisation of activities are also solely generated at the level of ZDDs. Non-synchronised executions are automatically discarded, due to the symbolic composition scheme. The remaining parts of Figure 4 (D - F) depict the ZDDs encoding the activity-local transition functions, where part E shows where identity structures are inserted to reflect the fact that state variables not affected by a particular activity remain unchanged. The resulting transition system and set of reachable states has already been given in Figure 2C.

4 SCHEME FOR THE ZDD-BASED HANDLING OF PERFORMANCE VARIABLES

Performance variables, consisting of rate reward and/or impulse reward definitions, enable the modeller to define complex performability measures on the basis of the high-level model, rather than on the level of the underlying CTMC.

Structural Properties of Rate Reward Returning Functions: Each rate reward function $R^r(s)$ has a set of input variables which is the set of state variables on which the computation of the rate reward value actually depends. Analogously to activities, we can extend this set to the Boolean variables used for encoding the respective state variables within the ZDD structures, denoted by the sets D_r^s and I_r^s, (containing the rate reward dependent/independent Boolean variables). Here

Figure 4. Running Example: From a multi-formalism model to he ZDD-based presentation of the activity-local transition functions

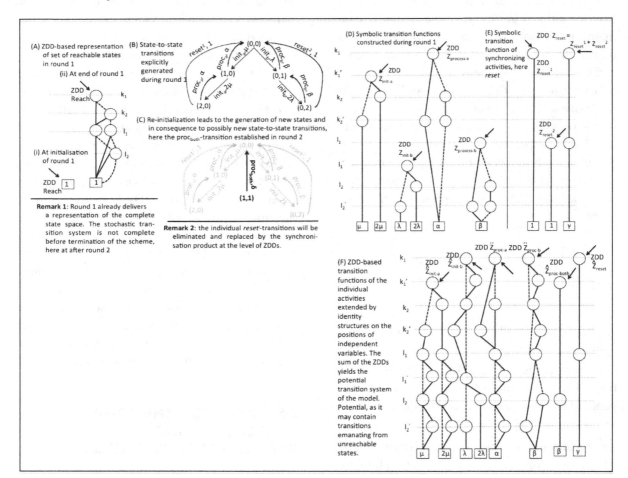

we are only dealing with state encodings and not transition encodings, hence the above sets of Boolean variables are restricted to the set of *s*-variables. Analogously to the δ-functions, the concrete implementation of a reward returning function R_r is irrelevant.

Structural Properties of Impulse Reward Returning Functions: An impulse reward *i* is generated each time an activity k from the impulse reward's set of activities Act_i is executed. The value of the impulse reward can be constant or state-dependent. This allows us to define the impulse reward returning function for impulse reward *i* as follows:

$$I^i(s) := \sum_{\{k \in Act_i \cap A_s\}} I^i_k(s) * \eta_k(s)$$

where A_s is the set of activities enabled in state *s*, and η_k is the rate returning function, both introduced earlier. I^i_k is the impulse reward returning function of impulse reward *i* and w. r. t. activity k. This allows for greater flexibility, as an impulse reward can be associated with different activities. Moreover, an activity may produce different reward values for different impulse reward definitions. In the following, we assume that the computation of the impulse reward returning function I^i_k solely depends on those positions of s which actually correspond to state variables of $\mathfrak{S}_k^D$, otherwise $\mathfrak{S}_k^D$ needs to be adapted accordingly. Such an adjustment would be irrelevant for the scheme for generating the state space, as the generation of reward values for transitions and states only takes place once state space construction has terminated. Analogously to rate rewards, we derive the sets D_k^s and I_k^s which contain the dependent and independent variables.

For computing the mean and variance of the user-defined performance variables, the top-level routine *ComputePV()* defined in Figure 5.A exploits the following algorithms.

1. Algorithm *ComputeStateProbabilities()* for computing the state probability distribution. This algorithm is not explained here. An overview of numerical solution methods can be found e.g. in (Stewart 1994). The adaptations of the numerical solution methods to the case of BDD-based matrix representations will be briefly sketched.
2. Algorithms *MakeRateRewards()* and *MakeImpulseRewards()* which generate the ZDD-based representations of the user-defined rate and impulse reward functions.
3. Algorithm *ComputeRew()* which combines reward information with the computed state probabilities.

In the following we will explain the algorithms.

4.1 Computing State Probabilities

Function *ComputeStateProbabilities()* (line 3 of the algorithm of Figure 5.A) delivers the vector of state probabilities. The iterative solvers follow an approach in which the generator matrix is represented by a symbolic data structure and the probability vectors are stored as arrays. For details please refer to (Parker 2002, Zimmermann 2005, Lampka et al. 2007).

If n Boolean variables are used for state encoding, there are 2^n potential states, of which only a small fraction may be reachable. Allocating entries for unreachable states in the vectors would waste memory space, thereby severely restricting the applicability of the algorithms. Therefore a dense enumeration scheme for the reachable states is implemented via the concept of offset-labelling, as first suggested in (Parker 2002) for the MTBDD data structure. While traversing the MTBDD representation of a matrix, in order to extract a matrix entry, the row and column index in the dense enumeration scheme can be determined from the offset values, basically by adding the offsets of those nodes where the *then*-Edge is taken. In other words, the offsets are used to map the s and t vectors to a pair (r, c) of dense row and column indices. Using ZDDs we adapted the concept of offset-labelling:

- With standard Multi-terminal Binary Decision Diagrams (MTBDDs), skipped nodes (corresponding to don't cares) must be reinserted, because they carry an offset (which is relevant if their then-edge is followed). With ZDDs, skipped nodes correspond to zero-valued variables for which the offset is irrelevant. Therefore, in the ZDD case, skipped nodes do not have to be reinserted, which keeps the symbolic data structure compact.
- Similar to the MTBDD case, a ZDD node may have to be duplicated if the offset of a shared node is different on different paths (also called "offset-clash").

The space efficiency of ZDD-based matrix representation comes at the cost of computational overhead, caused by the recursive traversal of the DD during access to the matrix entries. Analogously to (Parker 2002), we replace the lower levels of the ZDDs by explicit sparse matrix representations, which works particularly well for block-structured matrices. We call the resulting

Figure 5. Algorithms for the handling of performance variables

(A) Top level algorithm

ComputePV()
(1) $Z_T = Z_T \cdot Z_R$
(2) $Z_R^o := \text{OffsetLabel}(Z_R)$
(3) $prob := \text{ComputeStateProbabilities}(Z_R^o, Z_T)$
(4) $\text{MakeRateRewards}(Z_R)$
(5) $\text{MakeImpulseRewards}(Z_R)$
(6) for $p \in PV$
(7) $Z_{rate} := \sum_{r \in \mathcal{R}^p} R^r$
(8) $Z_{imp} := \sum_{i \in \mathcal{I}^p} I^i$
(9) $n := \text{getRoot}(Z_{rate}), r := \text{getRoot}(Z_R^o)$
(10) $\text{ComputeRew}(n, r, 0, p.r\_mean, p.r\_var)$
(11) $n := \text{getRoot}(Z_{imp})$
(12) $\text{ComputeRew}(n, r, 0, p.i\_mean, p.i\_var)$
(13) $p.r\_var := p.r\_var - p.r\_mean^2$
(14) $p.i\_var := p.i\_var - p.i\_mean^2$
(15) end for

(B) Generating symbolic rate reward functions

MakeRateRewards(Z_R)
(1) for $r \in \mathcal{R}$
(2) $R^r := \emptyset, Z_U := Z_R$
(3)   while $Z_U \neq \emptyset$
(4) $Z_s := \text{ExtractState}(Z_U)$
(5) $s := \text{Encode}^{-1}(Z_s)$
(6) $Z_s := \text{Abstract}(Z_{tmp}, I_r^s, +)$
(7) $rew := \mathcal{R}_r(s)$
(8)   IF $(rew \neq 0)$ THEN
(9) $R^r := R^r + rew \cdot (Z_s \cdot Z_U)$
(10) $Z_U := Z_U \setminus Z_s$
(11)   end while
(12) end for

(C) Generating symbolic impulse reward functions

MakeImpulseRewards(Z_R)
(1) for $i \in \mathcal{I}: \widetilde{Z}_T := \text{ZDD2zBDD}(Z_T)$
(2)   for $k \in \mathcal{A}ct_i$
(3) $I_k^i := \emptyset$
(4) $Z_U := \text{Abstract}(\widetilde{Z}_T \cdot Z_k, \mathcal{V}_t, +)$
(5)   while $Z_U \neq \emptyset$
(6) $Z_s := \text{ExtractState}(Z_U)$
(7) $s := \text{Encode}^{-1}(Z_s)$
(8) $Z_s := \text{Abstract}(Z_{tmp}, I_k^s, +)$
(9) $imp := \mathcal{I}_k^i(s)$
(10)   IF $(imp \neq 0)$ THEN
(11) $I_k^i := I_k^i + imp \cdot (Z_s \cdot Z_U)$
(12) $Z_U := Z_U \setminus Z_s$
(13)   end while
(14)   end for
(15) $I^i := \sum_{k \in \mathcal{A}ct_i} I_k^i$
(16) end for

(D) Computing Rewards

ComputeRew(n, r, off, m, v)
(1) IF $n \in \mathcal{K}_T$ THEN
(2) $m := m + prob[off] * \text{value}(n)$
(3) $v := v + prob[off] * \text{value}(n)^2$
(4) ELSE IF $\text{var}(n)_\pi > \text{var}(r)$ THEN
(5) $\text{ComputeRew}(n, \text{else}(r), off, m, v)$
(6) ELSE
(7) $\text{ComputeRew}(\text{then}(n), \text{then}(r),$
             $r.offset + off, m, v)$
(8) $\text{ComputeRew}(\text{else}(n), \text{else}(r),$
             $off, m, v)$

data structure hybrid offset-labelled ZDD (HO ZDD). The level from where one replaces the remaining ZDD-levels by sparse matrices is called sparse level. It depends on the available memory space, i.e. there is a typical time/space trade-off. For numerical analysis, the Gauss-Seidel (GS) method and its over-relaxed variant typically exhibit much better convergence than the power method, Jacobi (JAC) or Jacobi-Over-relaxation (JOR). However, Gauss-Seidel requires row-wise access to the matrix entries, which unfortunately cannot be realised efficiently with DD-based matrix representations. As a compromise, we adapt the so-called pseudo-Gauss-Seidel (PGS) iteration scheme (Parker 2002) to the case of HO ZDDs. For doing so, the overall matrix is partitioned into blocks (not necessarily of equal size, due to unreachable states). Within each block, access to matrix entries is in arbitrary order, but the blocks are accessed in ascending order. PGS requires only one complete iteration vector and an additional vector whose size is determined by the maximal block size. Given a HO ZDD which represents the matrix, each inner node at a specific level corresponds to a block. Pointers to these nodes can be stored in a sparse matrix, which means that effectively the top levels of the HO ZDD have been replaced by a sparse matrix of block pointers. The level at which the root nodes of the matrix blocks reside is called block level. Overall, this yields a memory structure in which some levels from the top and some levels from the bottom of the HO ZDD have been replaced by sparse matrix structures. The choice of adequate sparse and block levels for converting the ZDD into sparse matrix structures is an optimization problem. In general, increasing the number of top ZDD levels improves convergence of the PGS scheme, and replacing more levels at the bottom of the ZDD, i.e. turning the terminal nodes into sparse matrix structures, improves speed of access. Since ZDDs are often more compact than MTBDDs, their processing requires less CPU-time. Due to their lower memory requirements they furthermore allow the removal of more levels, resulting in an additional speed-up. If the block-level meets the sparse-level, as has been described in (Mehmood 2004) and (Zimmermann 2005), all DD levels have disappeared and the PGS scheme becomes a proper GS scheme, but in most interesting cases this situation cannot be realised since memory is at a premium. Our experiments, carried out in (Zimmermann 2005), showed that using ZDDs an optimal choice for the block-levels to be removed often lies beyond half of the DD-levels. For comparison, the heuristic developed in (Parker 2002) for MTBDDs suggested one third.

4.2 Generating ZDD-Based Representations of Rate Rewards

Once the state probabilities are computed, we call the functions *MakeRateRewards* and *MakeImpulseRewards* for computing symbolic representations of the rate reward and impulse reward functions associated with the user-defined performance variables. Again, our algorithms exploit locality, such that the explicit evaluation of reward functions is limited to a small fraction of states, rather than evaluating a reward function for each state.

Algorithm *MakeRateRewards()* as specified in Figure 5.B consists of two nested loops. The outer for-loop processes each rate reward Definition contained in a user-defined performance variable, whereas in the inner while-loop sets of states are processed. Z_U, initialised with the set of reachable states in line 2, contains all those states which still need to be considered for reward computation. First, an arbitrary state is extracted from the set of reachable states (line 4). This state is reduced to the positions referring to the rate reward-dependent state variables by an abstraction operation. Next, r's rate reward is calculated w.

r. t. the extracted state vector, which can be done by executing the respective rate reward function $R_r(s)$ (line 6). In case the obtained reward *rew* is not equal to zero, Z_S, Z_R and *rew* are multiplied. The newly obtained pairs of full (!) states and rate rewards are then added to the previously computed pairs as represented by ZDD R'(line 8). Note that the operation $Z_R * Z_U$ in line 8 yields the set of reachable states which are all equivalent concerning the variables of D_r^s. Line 9 removes all these states from the set of states represented by Z_U. Once all rate reward-dependent partitions of Z_R are processed, i.e. once Z_U is empty, the reward computation proceeds with the next rate reward (outer for-loop). At termination, a ZDD-based representation for each rate reward function is generated.

4.3 Generating ZDD-Based Representations of Impulse Rewards

Figure 5.C. shows the algorithm *MakeImpulseRewards()* for calculating impulse reward functions. Each activity may generate different impulse rewards for different impulse reward definitions, thus the algorithm iterates over three nested loops. The two outer for-loops process each impulse reward Definition and its respective sets of activities. The inner while-loop processes one state for each activity-local marking in which the activity is enabled and calculates the respective impulse reward (line 5-12). In case the obtained impulse reward for a state is not equal to zero, the ZDD-based representation of all equivalent states (i.e. those with the same activity-local marking) is multiplied with the impulse reward *imp* (line 10-11). Due to the construction of Z_U (line 4), the obtained pairs of states and impulse rewards are automatically weighed by the execution rate of the activity. The newly obtained pairs of full states and weighed impulse rewards are then added to the set of previously computed impulse rewards. This procedure is repeated until all "activity-local" markings are processed, i.e. until ZDD Z_U is empty.

4.4 Computing the Performability Measures

From the symbolic representations Z_{rate}, Z_{imp} and the probability vector, the first and second moment of performance variable p is computed by simultaneously traversing the offset-labelled *ZDD* Z_r^o and Z_{rate}, Z_{imp} respectively. This is the idea behind algorithm *ComputeRew()* of Figure 5.D: while traversing the ZDDs, the state index of the traversed path is obtained by summing over the offsets of nodes (line 7-8 of algorithm of Figure 5.D). Once a terminal non-zero node for Z_r^o is reached, the index of the state currently under consideration is determined, here contained in variable off (offset). The index allows one to fetch the respective probability value from the vector of state probabilities and compute (successively) the mean and second moment of the user-defined reward (line 2-3).

4.5 The Top-Level Algorithm

Routine *ComputePV()* puts everything together: in line 1, we restrict the CTMC to its reachable portion. This is followed by applying the offset-labelling scheme, thereby generating ZDD Z_r^o. Depending on the employed solution method, the state probability vector refers either to the steady-state probability distribution or to the transient state probabilities at time t. In line 4 and 5 our algorithm generates the symbolic representation for each rate and impulse reward function as contained in the user-defined performance variables. The for-loop of lines 6-15 processes each of the user-defined performance variables, where in lines 7-8 the respective reward functions are aggregated and where the call to ComputeRew delivers the mean and second moment of the reward function under consideration. After using

these values for computing the variances of the rate and impulse reward (lines 13-14), the algorithm resumes with the next performance variable, until all user-defined performance variable have been processed.

Running Example

Continuing our running example, the ZDD-based representation of the user-defined performance variable *Avail* (already introduced earlier) is depicted in Figure 6. It consists of the sum of two rate reward functions, r_1 and r_2 respectively (see Example in Sec. 2.3). Figure 6.B depicts the ZDDs obtained for the rate reward functions R_{r_1} where the skipping of the variables k_1, k_2 refers to the fact that they are not in the support of rate reward function R_{r_1}. The combined rate reward, i.e. a ZDD-based representation of performance variable *Avail*, is also given in Figure 6.B, together with the offset-labelled ZDD Z_{reach}. As the latter encodes the set of reachable states, it allows a dense numbering of the state space via the concept of offset-labelling as already mentioned above. Figure 6.C shows parts of the recursion tree of algorithm *ComputeRew* when executed on ZDDs Z_{Avail} and Z_{reach}. The return values are indicated at the bottom-line. For conciseness, the parameters m and v are omitted, as they are only used for propagating the return values (mean and second moment of the reward function).

5 CONCLUSION

This chapter reviewed an efficient semi-symbolic technique for constructing a compact, ZDD-based representation of a high-level model's reachable state space, as well as its underlying Markov Reward Model. As its key feature, the presented approach is independent of the modelling formalism, which makes it applicable in the context of multi-formalism modelling environments (as shown by a small running example). Our implementations were carried out in the Moebius performance analysis framework (Moebius web page), but the method could easily be adapted to a wide range of tools. The independence of the modelling formalism has its price, namely it comes with explicit enumeration and encoding of states and transitions, and reward evaluations for individual states. In order to keep this overhead as low as possible, the presented technique exploits the dependency relation among activities, reward returning functions and state variables of the high-level model. This features a selective handling of individual states, thereby effectively limiting CPU-time and peak memory consumption. Without such a feature, any BDD-based technique handling individual states could not succeed, since the peak number of BDD-nodes and the related memory requirements easily exceed the capacity of today's computers.

REFERENCES

Bachmann, J., Riedl, M., Schuster, J., & Siegle, M. (2009). An efficient symbolic elimination algorithm for the stochastic process algebra tool CASPA. In *Proceedings of the 35th Int. Conf. on Current Trends in Theory and Practice of Computer Science* (SOFSEM'09) (LNCS), (vol. 5404, pp. 485–496). Berlin: Springer.

Balbo, G., Conte, G., Donatelli, S., Franceschinis, G., & Ajmone Marsan, G. (1995). *Modelling with generalized stochastic petri nets*. Hoboken, NJ: John Wiley & Sons.

Bryant, R. E. (1986). Graph-based algorithms for Boolean function manipulation. *IEEE Transactions on Computers, C-35*(8), 677–691. doi:10.1109/TC.1986.1676819

Buchholz, P. (1991). *Die strukturierte analyse Markovscher modelle*. (PhD thesis). Universität Dortmund, Dortmund, Germany.

Ciardo, G., Blakemore, A., Chimento, P. F. J., Muppala, J. K., & Trivedi, K. S. (1993). Automated generation and analysis of Markov reward models using stochastic reward nets. *IMA Volumes in Mathematics and its Applications, 48*, 145–191.

Ciardo, G., & Tilgner, M. (1996). *On the use of Kronecker operators for the solution of generalized stochastic Petri nets* (Technical Report 96-35). Institute for Computer Applications in Science and Engineering.

Fox, B. L., & Glynn, P. W. (1988). Computing Poisson probabilities. *Communications of the ACM, 31*(4), 440–445. doi:10.1145/42404.42409

Formal Methods in System Design (1997). Special Issue on Multi-Terminal Binary Decision Diagrams, 10(2-3).

Götz, N. (1994). *Stochastische prozessalgebren – Integration von funktionalem entwurf und leistungsbewertung verteilter systeme*. (PhD thesis). Universität Erlangen-Nürnberg, Erlangen, Germany.

Harwarth, S. (2006). *Computation of transient state probabilities and implementing Moebius' state-level abstract functional interface for the data structure ZDD*. (Master Thesis). University of the Federal Armed Forces, Munich, Germany.

Hermanns, H., Herzog, U., Klehmet, U., Mertsiotakis, V., & Siegle, M. (1998). Compositional performance modelling with the TIPPtool. In *Proceedings of 10th International Conference on Modelling Techniques and Tools for Computer Performance Evaluation* (TOOLS'98) (LNCS), (vol. 1469, pp. 51– 62). Berlin: Springer Verlag.

Hermanns, H., Herzog, U., & Mertsiotakis, V. (1998). Stochastic process algebras – Between LOTOS and Markov chains. *Computer Networks and ISDN Systems, 30*(9-10), 901–924. doi:10.1016/S0169-7552(97)00133-5

Hermanns, H., Herzog, U., Mertsiotakis, V., & Rettelbach, M. (1997). Exploiting stochastic process algebra achievements for generalized stochastic Petri nets. In *Proceedings of the 6th International Workshop on Petri Nets and Performance Models*. Washington, DC: IEEE Computer Society.

Hillston, J. (1994). *A compositional approach to performance modelling*. (PhD thesis). University of Edinburgh, Edinburgh, UK.

Jansen, D. (2003). *Extensions of statecharts: With probability, time, and stochastic timing*. (PhD thesis). University of Twente, Enschede, The Netherlands.

Kuntz, M., Siegle, M., & Werner, E. (2004). Symbolic performance and dependability evaluation with the tool CASPA. [LNCS]. *Proceedings of EPEW*, *3236*, 293–307.

Kwiatkowska, M., Mehmood, R., Norman, G., & Parker, D. (2002). A symbolic out-of-core solution method for Markov models. *Electronic Notes in Theoretical Computer Science*, *68*(4), 589–604. doi:10.1016/S1571-0661(05)80394-9

Lampka, K. (2007). *A symbolic approach to the state graph based analysis of high-level Markov reward models*. (PhD thesis). Universität Erlangen-Nürnberg, Erlangen, Germany.

Lampka, K. (2008). A new algorithm for partitioned symbolic reachability analysis. In *Proceedings of ENTCS 223, Workshop on Reachability Problems*. ENTCS.

Lampka, K., Harwarth, S., & Siegle, M. (2007). Can matrix-layout-independent numerical solvers be efficient? In *Proceedings of the International Workshop on Tools for solving Structured Markov Chains*, (vol. 2, pp. 1–9). Nantes, France: ACM.

Lampka, K., & Siegle, M. (2006). Activity-local state graph generation for high-level stochastic models. In *Proceedings of 13th GI/ITG Conf. on Measuring, Modelling and Evaluation of Computer and Communication Systems* (MMB'06), (pp. 245–264). GI/ITG.

Lampka, K., & Siegle, M. (2006). Analysis of Markov reward models using zero-supressed multi-terminal decision diagramms. In *Proceedings of VALUETOOLS 2006*. VALUETOOLS.

Lampka, K., Siegle, M., Ossowski, J., & Baier, C. (2010). Partially-shared zero-suppressed multi-terminal BDDs: Concept, algorithms and applications. *Formal Methods in System Design*, *36*, 198–222. doi:10.1007/s10703-010-0095-8

Lee, C. Y. (1959). Representation of switching circuits by binary-decision programs. *The Bell System Technical Journal*, *38*, 985–999. doi:10.1002/j.1538-7305.1959.tb01585.x

Mehmood, R. (2004). *Disk-based techniques for efficient solution of large Markov chains*. (PhD thesis). University of Birmingham, Birmingham, UK.

Minato, S. (1993). Zero-suppressed BDDs for set manipulation in combinatorial problems. In *Proceedings of the 30th Design Automation Conference* (DAC), (pp. 272–277). Dallas, TX: ACM / IEEE.

Moebius. (n.d.). *Page*. Retrieved from www.mobius.uiuc.edu

Parker, D. (2002). *Implementation of symbolic model checking for probabilistic systems*. (PhD thesis). University of Birmingham, Birmingham, UK.

Plateau, B. (1985). On the stochastic structure of parallelism and synchronization models for distributed algorithms. [New York: ACM Press.]. *Proceedings of SIGMETRICS*, *85*, 147–154. doi:10.1145/317786.317819

PRISM. (n.d.). *Web page*. Retrieved from www. prismmodelchecker.org

Sanders, W. H. (1988). *Construction and solution of performability models based on stochastic activity networks*. (PhD thesis). University of Michigan, Ann Arbor, MI.

Sanders, W. H., & Meyer, J. F. (1991). A unified approach for specifying measures of performance, dependability, and performability. *Dependable Computing and Fault-Tolerant Systems: Dependable Computing for Critical Applications, 4*, 215–237. doi:10.1007/978-3-7091-9123-1_10

Schuster, J., & Siegle, M. (2008). A symbolic multilevel method with sparse submatrix representation for memory-speed-tradeoff. In *Proceedings of 14th GI/ITG Conference on Measurement, Modeling and Evaluation of Computer and Communication Systems*, (pp. 191-205). VDE-Verlag.

SMART. (n.d.). *Web page*. Retrieved from www. cs.ucr.edu/~ciardo/SMART

Somenzi, F. (1998). *CUDD: Colorado university decision diagram package, release 2.3.0: User's manual and programmer's manual*. Boulder, CO: Colorado University.

Stewart, W. J. (1994). *An introduction to the solution of Markov chains*. Princeton, NJ: Princeton University Press.

Zimmermann, D. (2005). *Implementierung von Verfahren zur lösung dünn besetzter linearer gleichungssysteme auf basis von zero-suppressed multi-terminalen binären entscheidungs-diagrammen*. (Master Thesis). Universität der Bundeswehr München, Munich, Germany.

ENDNOTES

[1] For example, the size of intermediate DD stuctures may increase dramatically during the incremental insertion of states / transitions, even if the final result is very compact.

Chapter 10
Designing User–Defined Modeling Languages with SIMTHESys

Mauro Iacono
Seconda Università degli Studi di Napoli, Italy

ABSTRACT

The availability of modeling languages that best suit the needs of modelers from case to case can enhance the applicability and immediateness of a model-based approach in the design and evaluation of systems, and can meet the modelers' expertise and customs. The goal of SIMTHESys is to enable the design and implementation of user-defined modeling languages (dubbed formalisms) and their native integration in multiformalism models, so that it is possible to develop language enhancements for existing formalisms, domain-oriented languages, extensions for existing languages, and abstraction tools to empower the modeling process. The key of this feature relies on the SIMTHESys metamodel and the description framework that is founded onto it. This chapter presents the foundation of SIMTHESys formalisms and demonstrates the possibilities it offers by examining a complete modeling example of a classical problem and a number of different formalisms, chosen to suggest how to exploit the framework.

INTRODUCTION

Abstractions are the key tool by which the essential aspects of a problem to be solved can be isolated from the richness of complex but negligible details characterizing reality. Such essential aspects can

be explored at different level of detail, to help dominating the problem in different phases of its analysis or in different perspectives of is nature. The mean by which abstractions are practically used to support reasoning, analysis and solution of a problem are usually proper representations, formal or informal, textual, mathematical or graphical, called models. A model describes a part of a real problem, materializing an abstraction of it

DOI: 10.4018/978-1-4666-4659-9.ch010

to allow the modeler to focus on that specific part and dominate it by understanding its explicit and implicit properties, evolution and characteristics.

A modeler can identify the causes and effects that are important for the evolution of a model, and describe them by appropriate modeling languages. The advantages resulting from the correct choice of a modeling language (a formalism) for a certain part of the system are twofold. From point of view of the modeler, it is possible to model each subsystem using the most appropriate language; from point of view of the analysis, the right (combination of) formalism(s) results in a proper mapping of the model concepts onto the primitives in which the analysis tool (a solver) is articulated.

The correctness criteria of the choice are a matter of the specific problem to be faced, and should be determined case by case by the modeler: the point is to provide a modeler with the right language, whichever the criteria. A possible, reference, general interpretation of what a right language is can be given by ease of use, where ease of use can result e. g. from:

- Ease of representation: choice of a language the constructs of which are semantically or syntactically close to the objects that are relevant in the domain of the problem that the modeler wants to represent: an example (furtherly detailed in this chapter) can be given by designing a language to support modeling of software aging and rejuvenation problems that represents by specific constructs a critical error due to accumulation of errors over time, a rejuvenation strategy, a degradation condition.
- Ease of learning and application: choice of a language in which new aspects of a problem are represented by additional elements for an existing language with which the modeler is already familiar: an example is given in (Codetta Raiteri et al. 2004) where a language able to analyze reliabil-

ity and availability of repairable systems (Repairable Fault Trees) is defined by extending the common Fault Trees language with a state-space component, namely Repair Box, that hides all repair-related aspects and transparently applies them for the analysis[1] of the resulting model.

- Time efficiency in modeling: choice of a language that allows rapid development of models from parts of the real world problem: an example is given by the SIMTHESysHQL language (Barbierato et al. 2013c), that allows the direct use of queries defined in a Big Data applications query language in performance models, thus enabling an immediate modeling of complex operations such as massively distributed data retrieval operations.

Width of choice possibility is thus a factor that can improve the overall efficiency of the modeling process: the problem is the availability of a multitude of modeling languages, or, better, the availability of a mean to extend the possibility of designing, experimenting and customizing specialized modeling languages to meet the needs that every case will manifest; and, consequently, the availability of a mean to rapidly develop proper analysis algorithms for the needed modeling languages. A further, desirable characteristic is the possibility of defining models in which different parts are modeled with different modeling languages, to ensure flexibility in the approach.

SIMTHESys (Structured Infrastructure for Multiformalism modeling and Testing of Heterogeneous formalisms and Extensions for SYStems (Gribaudo & Iacono 2011a, Iacono & Gribaudo 2010, Iacono et al. 2012)) is a framework for the definition and solution of multiformalism models. It is based on the automatic generation of implementations of specific analysis algorithms (solvers), starting from the rules contained in the definitions of modeling languages (formalisms).

Figure 1. SIMTHESys metamodeling stack

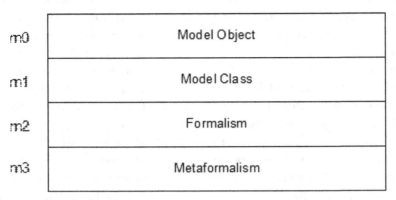

Both formalisms and models are written in XML language.

Models and formalisms are based on the SIMTHESys metamodel, which is inspired by Os-MoSys (Franceschinis et al. 2002a, Franceschinis et al. 2002b, Franceschinis et al. 2004, Vittorini et al. 2004, Moscato et al. 2007, Franceschinis et al. 2009) (and DrawNet (Gribaudo et al. 2005)), the framework that supplies the visual front-end and part of the data structures of both). The metamodeling stack is composed of four layers: metaformalism (M3), formalisms (M2), model classes (M1) and model objects (M0), as in Figure 1. The metaformalism defines the grammar used to describe formalisms; formalisms are the modeling languages available for models; model classes denote parametric submodels used to compose models; finally, model objects represent solvable models. Note that OsMoSys metaformalism describes the static aspects of formalisms elements and constraints (mainly syntactical), while SIMTHESys metaformalism has been defined to specify both static and dynamic aspects (focusing on execution semantics of the elements of a formalism).

Solvers for models that use combinations of SIMTHESys formalisms can be automatically generated by SIMTHESys*ER*. SIMTHESys*ER* is a tool based on the SYMTHESys framework. Although several tools with similar goals exist (see Möbius (Clark et al. 2001, Courtney et al. 2009), Sharpe (Trivedi 2002), SMART (Ciardo & Miner 2004, Ciardo & Miner 2009), the DEDS toolbox (Bause et al. 1998) and OsMoSys (Vittorini et al. 2004)), the innovation of SIMTHESys*ER* consists of i) rapid prototyping of new formalisms and solution techniques, ii) the capability of deploying new solvers without modifying existing ones; its open architecture (the possibility to define new interfaces that can be used to characterize different classes of formalisms). SIMTHESysER main goals aim at simplifying the definition of new variants of existing formalisms, and allowing the creation of new formalisms without the development of specific solver tools. The main users of the tool are thus the formalism developers. However other categories of users can benefit from it: model developers can exploit more favorable modeling primitives in their modeling activity; model users can use existing models by simply changing their parameters. The main functionalities, including their dependencies and their relations with the user categories are shown in the UML use case diagram in Figure 2.

The aspects regarding the efficiency of the solving engines or their optimization, e.g. solving stiff Markov models, models with infinite state spaces, or the analysis of the performance of automatic generated solvers vs. manually designed

Figure 2. SIMTHESysER use case diagram

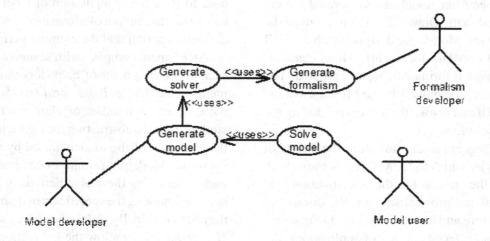

Figure 3. SIMTHESysER architecture and workflow

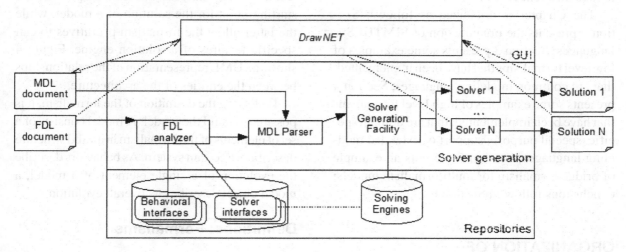

solvers are not in the aims of SIMTHESysER. Figure. 3 represents the architecture of the tool by showing the complete workflow of the solution of a model in a given formalism.

The input given to SIMTHESysER is the description of the formalism, while the output is a tool, based on the DrawNET GUI, that can be used to design and analyze models computing required performance indexes. The tool can generate several solution engines for the same formalisms, which can then be selected by the user via the GUI. Formalisms are described by Formalism Description Language (FDL) documents, that are organized as shown in the next Section, while models are described by Model Description Language (MDL) documents, also presented in the next Section. To define a new formalism, the user creates a FDL file that declares all its modeling primitives. The FDL documents are provided to the FDL Analyzer, that builds the final solver and its GUI in several steps. First it generates the model parser (called MDL parser), that can read models in the specified formalism. Then the Solver Generation Facility links the model parser to the selected Solving Engines to produce a set of solver functionalities. Generated solvers are inserted in the DrawNET GUI to produce the user interface. Models are designed with the GUI and saved in MDL documents, where elements of the provided formalism are instantiated. The user can store the models in the MDL format using the GUI and invoke the solvers producing the required solutions.

This Chapter presents in details the system of languages by which the SIMTHESys framework provides the means for the specification and analysis of multiformalism models, discussing their structure and how they are used to generate solvers, and offers a number of applications, describing the formalisms that have been developed to face different cases[2].

The Chapter is organized as follows: Section 2 presents the organization of SIMTHESys languages; Section 3 presents some examples of low level formalisms that have been implemented, that are common modeling languages; Section 4 presents some examples of high level formalisms that have been implemented, that are domain specific, special purpose, support or extended modeling languages; Section 5 presents an example of bridge formalism for multiformalism models; conclusions follow in Section 6.

ORGANIZATION OF SIMTHESYS LANGUAGES

The basic part of a SIMTHESys formalism is the *Element*, that de>ines all the atomic elements of a formalism (i.e. in a Stochastic Petri Net (Kartson et al. 1994), SPN, the elements are the places, the transitions, and the arcs). *Formalism Elements* are used to define entire formalisms, and can contain other elements. An element is characterized by *Properties* and *Behaviors*. The former allows the modeler the association of values of given types to the elements of a formalism. A Property value can be a constant (i.e. a label associated to an element),

a variable (i.e. the number of tokens in a place) or used to store the computation of a performance index (i.e. throughput of a transition). A Behavior defines an action that the element performs.

An Element complies with several *Interfaces*, each specifying a set of behaviors that the element should define. *Behavioral Interfaces* allow the creation of families of elements that share similar features, abstracting the characteristics of the evolution of the model caused by a specific primitive. Modeling primitives can interact with each other using these abstractions, without the need for knowing the specific formalism to which they belong. Finally, *Solver Interfaces* and *Solver Helper Interfaces* allow the interaction with the solution engines that eventually compute the results of the analysis. The former provide the starting point for the solution of a model, while the latter allow the formalism primitives to call specific features of a solution engine. Figure 4 shows an UML representation of the relationships between the entities of the architecture.

Following the definition of the formalism, it is possible to build the model. A model consists of a set of elements of the formalism in a valid structure describing a certain system. As behaviors describe the evolution of a single element of a model, a model object describes its overall evolution.

Definitions: Formalisms

Both FDL and MDL are languages derived by XML. A FDL document describes a formalism as a sequence of elements. The formal specification (as a XML schema fragment) of a FDL description is given by[3]:

```
<xs:element name="fdl">
<xs:complexType>
<xs:sequence>
<xs:element ref="elementType"/>
</xs:sequence>
</xs:complexType>
</xs:element>
```

Figure 4. Description of the SIMTHESys metaformalism

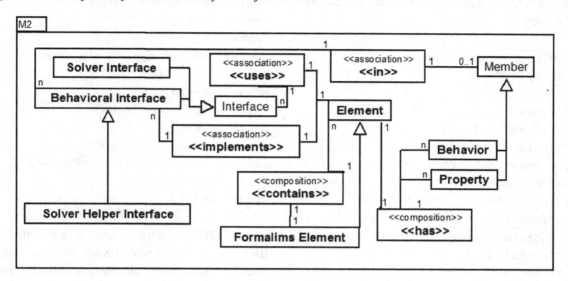

Elements are defined by an elementType declaration. An elementType can represent either a single formalism[4] (i.e. a SPN) or a construct of a formalism (i.e. a Place, a Transition, an Arc or an Inhibitor Arc in a SPN). Each elementType has a name, that identifies it in the formalism, and is characterized by a set of contained elements, indentified by the elementType tag, a set of behaviors, indentified by the behavior tag, a set of implemented interfaces, indentified by the implements tag, a set of properties, indentified by the propertyType tag, a set of used interfaces, indentified by the uses tag:

```
<xs:element name="elementType">
<xs:complexType mixed="true">
<xs:choice minOccurs="0"
maxOccurs="unbounded">
<xs:element ref="elementType"/>
<xs:element ref="behavior"/>
<xs:element ref="implements"/>
<xs:element ref="propertyType"/>
<xs:element ref="uses"/>
</xs:choice>
<xs:attribute name="name"
use="required" type="xs:NCName"/>
</xs:complexType>
</xs:element>
```

A property is specified by a name that caracterizes it into its Element, a type (that can be an elementType, String, double, int or Result, a custom type), a default value and a storage that can be in turn static (i.e. a value that does not change in time, like a label), dynamic (a value that changes over time, i. e., in a SPN, the number of tokens in a Place) or computed (a performance measure, i. e., in a SPN, the Transition throughput or the average number of tokens in a Place):

```
<xs:element name="propertyType">
<xs:complexType>
<xs:attribute name="default"/>
<xs:attribute name="name"
use="required" type="xs:NCName"/>
<xs:attribute name="storage"
use="required" type="xs:NCName"/>
<xs:attribute name="type"
use="required" type="xs:NCName"/>
</xs:complexType>
</xs:element>
```

A behavior is a description of an algorithm stating how an elementType evolves in time and eventually interacts with other elements. A behavior is characterized by a name, a type denoting the returned value, a sequence of optional parameters and a body[5]:

```
<xs:element name="behavior">
<xs:complexType>
<xs:sequence>
<xs:element minOccurs="0"
maxOccurs="unbounded"
ref="parameter"/>
<xs:element ref="code"/>
</xs:sequence>
<xs:attribute name="name"
use="required" type="xs:NCName"/>
<xs:attribute name="return"
use="required"/>
</xs:complexType>
</xs:element>
```

A behavior body is simply defined as a string that contains its description[6]:

```
<xs:element name="code"
type="xs:string"/>
```

A parameter plays the role of an input or output variable with respect to a behavior, and is carachterized by a name and a type (similarly to a property):

```
<xs:element name="parameter">
<xs:complexType>
<xs:attribute name="name"
use="required" type="xs:NCName"/>
<xs:attribute name="type"
use="required" type="xs:NCName"/>
</xs:complexType>
</xs:element>
```

The implements statement and uses statement allow to bind the formalism description to the SIMTHESys solving engines and to reuse mechanisms, by means of SIMTHESys*ER*. Both statements are carachterized by the indication of an interface name:

```
<xs:element name="implements">
<xs:complexType>
<xs:attribute name="ref"
use="required" type="xs:NCName"/>
</xs:complexType>
</xs:element>
<xs:element name="uses">
<xs:complexType>
<xs:attribute name="ref"
use="required" type="xs:NCName"/>
</xs:complexType>
</xs:element>
```

SIMTHESys interfaces are defined in interface files, also specified with a XML schema syntax. Interface files can contain uses and behavior statements, already presented, and formally specify interfaces[7]:

```
<xs:element name="interface">
<xs:complexType>
<xs:sequence>
<xs:element maxOccurs="unbounded"
ref="uses"/>
<xs:element maxOccurs="unbounded"
ref="behavior"/>
</xs:sequence>
</xs:complexType>
</xs:element>
```

Definitions: Models

In SIMTHESys, a model is a MDL document adhering to a FDL document definition. A MDL specification is carachterized by a list of element, that represent the structure of the model, a reference to the formalism to which the model conforms, an unique identifier, an optional list of imported information (contained in different documents), and is formally specified as from the following XML schema fragment:

```
<xs:element name="mdl">
<xs:complexType>
<xs:sequence>
<xs:element ref="ModelName"/>
</xs:sequence>
<xs:attribute name="fdl"
use="required" type="xs:NCName"/>
<xs:attribute name="id"
use="required" type="xs:NCName"/>
<xs:attribute name="import"
use="optional" type="xs:NCName"/>
</xs:complexType>
</xs:element>
```

The specification of the elements that compose the model cannot be given in a general form, as the related XML schema fragment depends on the chosen formalism.

MDL documents admit the specification of parameters in place of values, to allow parametric solution campaigns whenever it is necessary to measure the performance of a multiformalism model by varying the value range of a set of static properties. For example, the modeler could design a sequence of tests where in a SPN a Transition rate is magnified by a certain factor during each test case. This is allowed by using labels denoting constants instead of explicit values, that will be properly managed by SIMTHESys*ER*. Labels are formally defined and instantiated in IPT documents as a sequence of constants[8]:

```
<xs:element name="constants">
<xs:complexType>
<xs:sequence>
<xs:element maxOccurs="unbounded"
ref="constant"/>
</xs:sequence>
</xs:complexType>
</xs:element>
```

Each constant is characterized by a name and a value:

```
<xs:element name="constant">
<xs:complexType>
<xs:attribute name="name"
use="required" type="xs:NCName"/>
<xs:attribute name="value"
use="required" type="xs:decimal"/>
</xs:complexType>
</xs:element>
```

Formalisms and Solver Generation

Besides being the foundation of MDL documents, FDL documents are also the cornerstone of the solver generation process, as enacted by SIMTHESys*ER*. The key of the process is the fact that the binding between a formalism and one or more of the solving engines available in the framework is suggested by the corresponding FDL document by means of the behaviors of the formalism element it describes. This is obtained by implementing special interfaces, namely the solver interfaces and the solver helper interfaces, that provide bidirectional interaction between the models that use the formalism and the engines used to build the solver for the formalism. Similarly, in case of multiformalism models the solver is built by exploiting the same mechanism, but involving more formalism elements to build the binding.

Once a FDL multi or single formalism document is produced, the FDL Analyzer component of SIMTHESys*ER* takes it in input and produces in output a MDL parser that can handle all possible models based on that document. Note that the latter is composed of i) a pre-existing set of software components (including the solution engines) and ii) a set of software components created on-the-fly by the FDL Analyzer. The process performed by the FDL Analyzer relies on the following prerequisites to be satisfied:

Pre-requisites: The initial set of Java files representing the foundation of the solution engines is available.

The FDL document is handled by the SIMTH-ESys*ER* FDL Parser according to an algorithm composed of the following steps:

INPUT: A FDL document:

1. Retrieve the configuration files and apply the configuration parameters chosen by the user;
2. Parse the FDL document in two phases:
   a. **First Phase:**
      i. The interfaces invoked by the FDL document are used to generate the related code.
      ii. The MDL parser pre-existing software components are expanded by adding the code of custom software components referring to the elements of the input formalism[9].
      iii. The main MDL parser code is initially created, including all the references to existing and custom software components and the actual parser for the formalism elements[10].
   b. **Second Phase:**
      i. In this phase, the symbol table built during the first phase is used to resolve all the references that were eventually suspended during the first phase.
      ii. The custom code invoking the solvers is generated.
      iii. The custom code that generates the performance measures is generated[11].

OUTPUT: The MDL parser.

In turn, the generated MDL Parser handles MDL documents according to an algorithm that composed of the following steps:

INPUT: solver name S, MDL document f

1. Retrieve the configuration files and apply the configuration parameters chosen by the user;
2. Parse the MDL document f ;
3. Create an instance of the custom code corresponding to the model;
4. Create an instance s of the custom code corresponding to the solver name S ;
5. Invoke the solver s on f ;
6. Generate the performance indices.

OUTPUT: The performance indices.

The generated solver will be built, according to the solver interfaces and the solver helper interfaces implemented and used in the FDL document, by exploiting solving engines from one or more of the extensible set of SIMTHESys formalism families. A formalism family is a set of formalisms that share a common elementary solution method, on top of which more sophisticated solvers can be built[12].

A Running Example

In this Section we provide a FDL document that describes the implementation of the SPN formalism in SIMTHESys, and a MDL document that represents the classical five dining philosophers problem using the SPN model presented in Figure 5.

The analysis of the FDL document is presented in the following, interlaved with the comments about its design, to punctually guide the readers in the generic specification process of a user defined formalism. Readers that are not familiar with SPN can refer to (Karston et al. 1994) for more details about how it is formally specified and its execution semantics.

As for any other FDL document, all the elements of a formalism have to be defined inside their formalism element, that represents a model using the formalism: in the following, their definitions will be presented separately and anticipated to facilitate the analysis and follow the design process.

Figure 5. The SPN model for the classical five dining philosophers problem

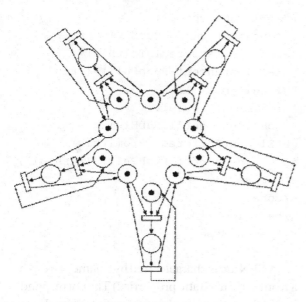

A SPN place is characterized by a name (a static property) and a number of tokens it contains in a certain marking (a dynamic property). The performance measure over places is the mean number of tokens by which they are marked (a computed property). The corresponding FDL element implements an interface, ElementOccupancy, that is an utility to standardize the access to elements that logically contain a positive discrete or continuous number of items, or nothing. The description of these features in the Place elementType is:

```
<elementType name="Place">
<implements ref="ElementOccupancy"/>
<propertyType name="id" type="String"
default="" storage="static"/>
<propertyType name="Tokens"
type="int" default="0"
storage="dynamic"/>
<propertyType name="MeanTokens"
type="Result" storage="computed"/>
```

The ElementOccupancy interface requires the implementation of the getOccupancy, setOccu-pancy and addOccupancy behaviors, that operate on the Tokens property:

```
<behavior name="getOccupancy"
return="int">
<code>
return getTokens();
</code>
</behavior>
<behavior name="setOccupancy"
return="void">
<parameter name="i" type="int"/>
<code>
setTokens(i);
</code>
</behavior>
<behavior name="addOccupancy"
return="void">
<parameter name="i" type="int"/>
<code>
setTokens(getTokens() + i);
</code>
</behavior>
</elementType>
```

A SPN transition is characterized by a name and a rate (static properties). The performance measure over transitions is their throughput (a computed property). The corresponding FDL element implements an interface, Active, that is an utility to standardize the interaction of the solver with the element that play an active role in the execution semantics of a model; moreover, it uses two interfaces: PushPull, that standardizes the implementation of flow-like mechanisms between properties of different interacting elements, and CapacityCheck, that standardizes the implementation of a check over an element implementing the ElementOccupancy interface (or similar interfaces):

```
<elementType name="Transition">
<implements ref="Active"/>
<uses ref="PushPull"/>
```

```
<uses ref="CapacityCheck"/>
<propertyType name="id" type="String"
default="" storage="static"/>
<propertyType name="Rate"
type="double" default="1.0"
storage="static"/>
<propertyType name="Throughput"
type="Result" storage="computed"/>
```

The Active interface requires the implementation of the isActive and fire behaviors, that are used by the solver to verify if an element is able to perform a fire action in the current state and to execute the action that characterizes the evolution of the state in a formalism by the elements that can play an active role.

The isActive behavior of the Transition elementType applies the verification of SPN transition activation condition, by exploiting the Active interface[13]; note that the isActive behavior performs three type of checks: enabling of the transition in the model; enabling of the transition if the transition is part of a submodel and has input arcs coming from outside the submodel; and the ability of the output elements outside the submodel to receive the effects of the firing:

```
<behavior name="isActive"
return="boolean">
<code>
for(ElementType el:
 _container.getAllSubElements().
getElementReferredInTo(this))
{if(el instanceof Active)
if(! ((Active)el).isActive()) return
false;
}
return true;
</code>
</behavior>
```

The fire behavior implements the SPN transition firing rule by exploiting the PushPull interface[14]:

```
<behavior name="fire" return="void">
<code>
for(ElementType el:
 _container.getAllSubElements().
getElementRefferedInTo(this))
if(el instanceof PushPull) ((Push-
Pull)el).pull();
for(ElementType el:
 _container.getAllSubElements().
getElementRefferedInFrom(this))
if(el instanceof PushPull)((PushPull)
el).push();
</code>
</behavior>
</elementType>
```

A SPN arc is characterized by a name, a weigth, a from and a to (static properties) The corresponding FDL element implements an interface, Edge, that is an utility to standardize arc-like elements, and the Active, PushPull and ElementOccupancy interfaces, to support the behaviors of Transition:

```
<elementType name="Arc">
<implements ref="Edge"/>
<implements ref="PushPull"/>
<implements ref="Active"/>
<uses ref="ElementOccupancy" />
<propertyType name="id" type="String"
default="" storage="static"/>
<propertyType name="Weight"
type="int" default="1"
storage="static"/>
<propertyType name="from"
type="ElementType" default=""
storage="static"/>
<propertyType name="to"
type="ElementType" default=""
storage="static"/>
```

The isActive behavior evaluates if the SPN enabling rule is satisfied by the input place of the arc (this is a requirement to support Transition isActive behavior):

```
<behavior name="isActive"
return="boolean">
<code>
if(from instanceof ElementOccupancy)
{ElementOccupancy eo = (ElementOccu-
pancy)from;
 return (eo.getOccupancy() >=
Weight);
}
return true;
</code>
</behavior>
```

Push and Pull (implementing PushPull) determine token consumption and production in consequence of the activation of the Transition fire behavior:

```
<behavior name="push" return="void">
<code>
if(to instanceof ElementOccupancy)
{ElementOccupancy eo = (ElementOccu-
pancy)to;
 eo.addOccupancy(Weight);
}
</code>
</behavior>
<behavior name="pull" return="void">
<code>
if (from instanceof ElementOccupancy)
{ElementOccupancy eo = (ElementOccu-
pancy)from;
 eo.addOccupancy(-Weight);
}
</code>
</behavior>
</elementType>
The InhibitorArc definition is simi-
larly to the definition of Arc:
<elementType name="InhibitorArc">
<implements ref="Edge"/>
<implements ref="Active"/>
<uses ref="ElementOccupancy"/>
<propertyType name="id" type="String"
default="" storage="static"/>
<propertyType name="weight"
type="int" default="1"
storage="static"/>
<propertyType name="from"
type="ElementType" default=""
storage="static"/>
<propertyType name="to"
type="ElementType" default=""
storage="static"/>
The only behavior, isActive, negates
activation of the depending Transi-
tion if the Place from which it de-
pends has a sufficient marking
<behavior name="isActive"
return="boolean">
<code>
if(from instanceof ElementOccupancy)
{ElementOccupancy eo = (ElementOccu-
pancy)from;
 return (eo.getOccupancy() <=
Weight);
}
return false;
</code>
</behavior>
</elementType>
```

Finally, the formalism element has the duty of describing all that is needed to support the solver generation process: consequently, it has to use at least one of the solver interfaces for a formalism family (in this case, the ExpEventSolver family), and provide implementations for the behaviors described in the related solver helper interface (in this case, ExpEventModel), to allow the solver to properly examine the model during the solution process; moreover, other utility interfaces can be implemented, to reuse useful mechanisms or to implement useful features (in this case, hasSub-Elements enables the formalism to support SPN composed models):

```
<fdl>
<elementType name = "SPN">
<uses ref = "ExpEventSolver"/>
<implements ref = "ExpEventModel"/>
<implements ref = "hasSubElements"/>
```

The formalism element also should have properties that describe it (static properties) and represent global results computed on a model (computed properties):

```
<propertyType name="id" type="String"
default="" storage="static"/>
<propertyType name = "description"
type = "String" default = "An SPN
model" storage = "static"/>
<propertyType name = "bounded" type =
"boolean" storage = "computed"/>
```

The ExpEventModel solver helper interface requires the implementation of the InitEvents, ComputeStateRewards, countStateRewards, setStateRewards, listImpulseRewards and set-ImpulseReward behaviors.

InitEvents allows the solver to understand what should be done in the next solution step, given the current state of the model. In SPN, the evolution of a model is determined by the set of Transition elements that are enabled in the given state, that will produce a change of the state of the model by transforming it with an operation called firing: consequently, the InitEvents behavior checks all Transition elements in the model and schedules their fire behavior:

```
<behavior name = "InitEvents" return
= "void">
<code>
for(Transition T: sub_Transition)
{if(T.isActive()) {
final Transition _T = T;
BehaviorAdapter ba = new BehaviorA-
dapter() {public void execBehavior()
{_T.fire();}};
```

```
if(getModel().getSolver() instanceof
ExpEventSolver)
{ ((ExpEventSolver)getModel().get-
Solver()).schedule(ba, T.getRate(),
T.getId(), 1.0);
};
}
}
</code>
</behavior>
```

The other behaviors allow the solver to account for results when executing the run schedule. This is done by using two different kinds of reward variables, for the state and for the counts. The solver obtains the reward variables by querying the model:

```
<behavior name="countStateRewards"
return="int">
<code>
return sub_Place.size();
</code>
</behavior>
<behavior name="listImpulseRewards"
return="String[]">
<code>
String[] out = new String[sub_Transi-
tion.size()];
int i = 0;
for(Transition T: sub_Transition)
{out[i++] = T.getId();}
return out;
</code>
</behavior>
```

State rewards are computed by describing the SPN firing rule by the computeStateRewards behavior:

```
<behavior name="computeStateRewards"
return="double[]">
<code>
double[] out = new double[sub_Place.
```

```
size()];
int i = 0;
for(Place P: sub_Place)
{out[i++] = P.getTokens();}
return out;
</code>
</behavior>
```

In this way, the execution semantics of SPN is captured and described to SIMTHESys*ER*, that exploits it to build up the SPN solver from generic Exponential Events Family (EEF) solving engines.

Behaviors are also needed to provide the solver with the means to set and update them:

```
<behavior name="setStateRewards"
return="void">
<parameter name="r" type="Result[]"/>
<code>
int i = 0;
for(Place P: sub_Place)
{ P.setMeanTokens(r[i++]);}
</code>
</behavior>
<behavior name="setImpulseReward"
return="void">
<parameter name="N" type="String"/>
<parameter name="r" type="Result"/>
<code>
Transition T = sub_Transition.get(N);
T.setThroughput(r);
</code>
</behavior>
```

The formal description of the formalism is completed by the descriptions of its elements, that have been anticipated:

```
<!Sub Elements descriptions are list-
ed in place of this placeholder-->
</elementType>
</fdl>
```

According to this FDL document, the presented 5 dining philosopher problem can be described by the following MDL document (that is highly symmetrical, and will be presented in a compact form):

```
<mdl id="Philosophers" fdl="SPN.fdl">
<SPN id="5Philosophers" descrip-
tion="5 dining philosophers">
```

Each of the philosophers can either be thinking or eating at a time, and is initially thinking:

```
<Place id="P1Eat" Tokens="0" />
...
<Place id="P5Eat" Tokens="0" />
<Place id="P1Think" Tokens="1" />
...
<Place id="P5Think" Tokens="1" />
```

Between each couple of philosophers there is one available chopstick, and a philosopher will need to get both the one on the left and the one on the right to be able to eat:

```
<Place id="Chopstick1" Tokens="1" />
...
<Place id="Chopstick5" Tokens="1" />
```

Each of the philosopher will decide to start eating according to an own rate:

```
<Transition id="P1StartEat"
Rate="1.0" />
... (Rates: P2StartEate=2.0, P3Start-
Eat=2.5, P4StartEat=1.5)
<Transition id="P5StartEat"
Rate="2.0" />
```

and will similarly decide to stop eating, when satisfied:

```
<Transition id="P1StopEat" Rate="2.0" />
... (Rates: P2StopEat=1.0, P3StopE-
```

```
at=1.0, P4StopEat=3.0
<Transition id="P5StopEat" Rate="1.5" />
```

Arcs describe the connections between Places and Transitions:

```
<Arc id="A1" from="P1Think"
to="P1StartEat" Weight="1" />
...
<Arc id="A5" from="P5Think"
to="P5StartEat" Weight="1" />
<Arc id="B1" from="Chopstick1"
to="P1StartEat" Weight="1" />
...
<Arc id="B5" from="Chopstick5"
to="P5StartEat" Weight="1" />
<Arc id="C1" from="Chopstick2"
to="P1StartEat" Weight="1" />
...
<Arc id="C5" from="Chopstick1"
to="P5StartEat" Weight="1" />
<Arc id="D1" from="P1StartEat"
to="P1Eat" Weight="1" />
...
<Arc id="D5" from="P5StartEat"
to="P5Eat" Weight="1" />
<Arc id="E1" from="P1Eat"
to="P1StopEat" Weight="1" />
...
<Arc id="E5" from="P5Eat"
to="P5StopEat" Weight="1" />
<Arc id="F1" from="P1StopEat"
to="P1Think" Weight="1" />
...
<Arc id="F5" from="P5StopEat"
to="P5Think" Weight="1" />
<Arc id="G1" from="P1StopEat"
to="Chopstick1" Weight="1" />
...
<Arc id="G5" from="P5StopEat"
to="Chopstick5" Weight="1" />
<Arc id="H1" from="P1StopEat"
to="Chopstick2" Weight="1" />
...
```

```
<Arc id="H5" from="P5StopEat"
to="Chopstick1" Weight="1" />
</SPN>
</mdl>
```

DEFINING LOW LEVEL FORMALISMS WITH SIMTHESYS

SIMTHESys has been used to define many formalisms, to experiment special features or to face specific case studies. Part of the formalisms are implementations or reimplementations of classical formalisms, to which the possibility of use in multiformalism models has been added. In this Section some examples of classical formalisms are presented, to show how the main aspects of their logic can be captured by the SIMTHESys methodology and stimulate the readers to experiment with their own variations and their own ideas.

Tandem Finite Capacity Queuing Networks

Queuing Networks (QN) is a classical performance oriented formalism, that is widely used in literature and in the practice to analyze systems composed by a number of servers that provide a service to a number of customers, passing from one server to another to complete their overall services and waiting into queues to access every server. A QN formalism has two kinds of elements: the queue and the arc. If the same N customers move from one queue to another the resulting queuing network is said to be closed, otherwise it is said to be open (with some customers joining and leaving the network according to a given interarrival time distributions).

In Tandem Finite Capacity Queuing Networks (TFCQN) (Gribaudo & Sereno, 1997) every queue has a finite number of places for customers waiting for the service (Finite Capacity hypothesis) and only a single arc departs from each queue (Tandem Network hypothesis). When the maximum capacity of a queue is reached, the queue from which the new customer is coming stops serving (Blocking hypothesis), until the customer will be able to take a place in the queue, when an existing customer will be served.

Blocking can happen according to several blocking policies, the three most common of which are: Blocking After Service (BAS), Blocking Before Service (BBS) and Repetitive Service (RS). The BAS policy states that the customer who could not find a place in the next queue if processed by the blocked queue is processed anyway, to be blocked right after service completion. The BBS policy states that the customer who could not find a place in the next queue if processed by the blocked queue is blocked before being processed: in this case, either the customer enters the server, that will become occupied (BbsSoQueue case), or it does not, leaving the server not occupied (BbsSnoQueue), and consequently the number of places in the queue is set to M-1 until it is unblocked. The RS policy states that the customer who could not find a place in the next queue if processed by the blocked queue is processed anyway and reinserted in the same queue to be served again later (RSqueue).

In the hypothesis of exponential distribution of the service time, the difference between the BAS case and the others is significant for the choice of the formalism family to which TFCQN variants belong: in the other cases, when the queue is unblocked the customer is processed, and consequently moved into the destination queue after an exponentially distributed time; in the BAS case, the customer has already been processed when the destination queue is unblocked, and consequently must be immediately moved into it. For this reason, the BAS queue requires the formalism to belong to the EIEF formalism family, while fot the implementation of the others the EEF formalism family is sufficient. The BAS case will be ignored in the rest of this example.

To shape the SIMTHESys TFCQN formalism (that has been presented, together with a case study, in (Barbierato et al. 2011a)), it is possible to design the formalism element, a queue element for each of the three residual blocking policies and the Arc element. Each queue element is characterized by two static properties: the maximum capacity of the queue and the rate of the exponential distribution corresponding to the service time. The dynamic property that represent the state is its current number of occupied places in the queue (its length). Each queue element has two computed properties representing its performance indices: the mean queue length and the throughput. The elements, properties and behaviors that define a TFCQN in SIMTHESys are summarized in Table 1. All the queues have the same attributes and behaviors, but the latter have different implementations to account for the different blocking policies.

The Arc element implements the PushPull interface, and consequently has a Push behavior that transfers a customer to its own destination queue by its AddOccupancy behavior:

- to.AddOccupancy(1)

The HasSpace just transfer the requests to the destination queue by the algorithm:

- return to.CanAccept()

All queue elements are active elements, as they all perform a change of state when activated, and consequently implement the Active interface. Their IsActive behavior checks if their length is greater than 0, as an empty queue cannot process any customer, thus cannot change its state.

The blocking condition is checked by the CanSend behavior. In an RSQueue, the behavior always returns true (because it is always enabled to service, and continuously services its customers in turn if the destination node is full). In the other cases the CanSend behavior implements the algorithm:

1. for all incoming Arc elements a do

Table 1. Elements of the TFCQN SIMTHESys definition

TFCQN			
Property	**Type**	**Modifier**	**Behaviors**
			ComputeStateRewards InitEvents CountStateRewards SetStateRewards ListImpulseRewards SetImpulseReward
BbsSnoQueue			
Property	**Type**	**Modifier**	**Behaviors**
Length MeanLength Capacity Rate Throughput	integer float integer float float	dynamic computed static static computed	IsActive Fire AddOccupancy CanSend CanAccept
BbsSoQueue			
Property	**Type**	**Modifier**	**Behaviors**
Length MeanLength Capacity Rate Throughput	integer float integer float float	dynamic computed static static computed	IsActive Fire AddOccupancy CanSend CanAccept
RSQueue			
Property	**Type**	**Modifier**	**Behaviors**
Length MeanLength Capacity Rate Throughput	integer float integer float float	dynamic computed static static computed	IsActive Fire AddOccupancy CanSend CanAccept
Arc			
Property	**Type**	**Modifier**	**Behaviors**
From To	element element	static static	Push HasSpace

2.　if NOT a.HasSpace() then
3.　return false;
4.　end if
5.　end for
6.　return true

Note that this algorithm is more general than needed, as for the tandem hypothesis there is only one destination queue. The algorithm checks the state of the destination queue by exploiting the HasSpace behavior of the Arc element.

The CanAccept behavior returns true if a queue can accept a customer. For the RSQueue and the BbsSoQueue this means verifying that the current value of the length property is less than the value of the capacity property:

- return length <= capacity;

while for the BbsSnoQueue also the concurrency with a blocking has to be considered:

1.　if length < capacity − 1 then

2. return true;
3. else
4. return CanSend() ∧ length < capacity;
5. end if

The fire behavior implements the end of the service of a customer in a queue. In the case of the BbsSoQueue and BbsSnoQueue it is implemented according the algorithm:

1. for all a ∈ Arc where a.from = this do
2. a.Push();
3. end for
4. length = length - 1

while in the case of RSQueue, since the same behavior has to be rescheduled in case of blocking, it is implemented according to the algorithm:

Algorithm 16 Fire RSQueue

1. for all a ∈ Arc where a.from = this do
2. if a.HasSpace() then
3. a.Push();
4. length = length - 1;
5. end if
6. end for

Note that rescheduling is not explicitly performed, as it is sufficient to keep the element active to automatically have it rescheduled.

The formalism element uses the ExpEventSolver solver interface and implements the ExpEventModel solver helper interface, as it belongs to the EEF. Its InitEvents behavior implements the algorithm:

1. for all q ∈ RSQueue ∪ BbbSoQueue ∪ BbsSnoQueue do
2. if q.IsActive() ∧ q.CanSend() then
3. solver.Schedule(q.rate, "q.Fire()", q.id, 1);
4. end if
5. end for

The firings of the enabled queues are scheduled with the solver if active and not blocked. Scheduling needs four parameters, that are: the rate of the exponential distribution that characterizes the firing time; the piece of code that must be executed when the event occurs; the name of the impulse reward that is associated to the event; the increment of the reward. Since every queue has an associated throughput, the name of the queue is used as the name of the corresponding reward. Due to the fact that throughput counts the number of services in a queue, its corresponding reward increment is always 1.

The behaviors of the solver helper interfaces are implemented as follows:

- CountStateRewards returns the number of queues in the model.
- ListImpulseRewards returns a list of their indentifiers.
- SetImpulseReward sets the T hroughput property.
- SetStateRewards fills the meanLength property.
- ComputeStateRewards returns a vector with the length of the queues.

Gordon and Newell Queueing Networks

Gordon and Newell Queueing Networks (GNQN) (Gordon & Newell 1967) are closed networks in which every queue processes customers with service time according to the EEF property and first come first served policy, but Finite Capacity, Tandem Network and Blocking hypotheses are removed. Due to the removal of the Tandem hypothesis, every queue can have more destination queues, to which the processed customers are sent by choosing between them according to a probability. The Arc element in this case has a static property prob that holds this probability.

Due to the similarities, the design of the SIMTHESys formalism (that has been presented, together with a case study, in (Barbierato et al. 2011a)) follows the logic presented in the previous Section. The elements of the formalism are summarized in Table 2.

The behaviors of the Arc element are the same as in the TFCQN case; the behaviors of the Queue element differ in the implementation of the fire behavior, as it must account for the choice of the destination queue according to the algorithm:

1. a.Push()
2. length = length 1

In which the arc to be fired is determined during the scheduling phase.

The formalism element also implements and uses the same interfaces as the TFCQN formalism element, as they belong to the same formalism family, but has a different implementation of the InitEvents behavior:

1. for all q ∈ Queue do
2. if q.IsActive() then
3. for all a ∈ Arc where a.from = q do

4. solver.Schedule(a.prob • q.rate, "q.Fire(a)", q.id, 1);
5. end for
6. end if
7. end for

Since GNQN are characterized by the choice of the next queue either at the end of a service or at its beginning, the scheduling considers that, given the probability p_i of choosing the i-destination for a queue serving at rate λ, exponential distribution of the serving times guarantees that scheduling a service at rate λ first and then choosing the destination with probability pi is equivalent to scheduling one service for each possible destination i at rate pi • λ. The Fire behavior of a queue is thus scheduled for all destinations, weighting it with the probability of each destination, obtaining a rate a.prob • q.rate.

Repairable Fault Trees

Fault Trees (FT) (Codetta Raiteri et al 2004) is a formalism dedicated to the qualitative and quantitative reliability or availability of a given system.

Table 2. Elements of the GNQN SIMTHESys definition

GNQN			
Property	**Type**	**Modifier**	**Behaviors**
			ComputeStateRewards InitEvents CountStateRewards SetStateRewards ListImpulseRewards SetImpulseReward
Queue			
Property	**Type**	**Modifier**	**Behaviors**
Length MeanLength Rate Throughput	integer float float float	dynamic computed static computed	IsActive Fire AddOccupancy
Arc			
Property	**Type**	**Modifier**	**Behaviors**
From To Prob	element element float	static static static	Push

Given the structure of a system, a FT describes how an undesirable event (Top Event, TE) can occur because of a combination of elementary faults (Basic Events, BE). The fault probability of the TE is obtained as a combination of the fault probabilities of the BEs by means of AND and OR operators[15], that produce intermediate events describing what happens at a subsystem level. Repairable Fault Trees (RFT) is a variant of FT that allows the evaluation of repairable systems, that are systems in which a fault of a component can be solved (by fixing or replacing it)[16]. In the RFT formalism that is presented here (that has been already presented, together with a case study, in (Barbierato et al. 2011c)) repairing is allowed at the level of a BE, and happens without the need for any detection at subtree level or system-level intervention. The elements of the SIMTHESys RFT formalism are presented in Table 3. A BE is described by a BasicEvent element. Each BasicEvent element has two static properties that specify an exponential failure time (break rate), and an exponential repair time (repair rate, which can be set to 0 if the represented component is not repairable). BasicEvent elements also have a broken dynamic property that checks whether a component is currently in failed mode, and implement the Fire and the isTrue behaviors. The TopEvent element has a prob computed property that describes its fault probability. The structure of the tree is built by using Arc elements, And elements and Or elements, all of which implement a IsTrue behavior to check and propagate the state of the subtree they are connected to.

The TopEvent and And elements isTrue behaviors, required by CheckIfTrue, implement the algorithm:

1. for all Arc elements a do
2. if NOT a.isTrue() then
3. return false
4. end if
5. end for
6. return true

The Or element isTrue behavior, required by CheckIfTrue, implements the algorithm:

1. 1: for all Arc elements a do
2. 2: if a.isTrue() then
3. 3: return true
4. 4: end if
5. 5: end for
6. 6: return false

The BasicEvent Fire behavior simply replaces the value of its broken property with its negate, the isTrue returns the negate of the value of the broken property, while the getRate behavior implements the algorithm:

1. if broken then
2. return repair_rate
3. else return break_rate
4. end if

The InitEvent behavior of the formalism element implements the algorithm:

1. for all BasicEvent elements b do
2. b.Fire()
3. schedule b at rate b.getRate() and with reward increment 1.0
4. end for

DEFINING HIGH LEVEL FORMALISMS WITH SIMTHESYS

Besides being able to support modeling with traditional formalisms, SIMTHESys expresses at best its nature in enabling the design of domain oriented formalisms and custom formalisms, the extension of existing formalisms with special features and formalisms that provide additional possibilities in multiformalism modeling. In this Section this aspect is presented, by means of the description of the implementation of several new formalisms.

Table 3. Elements of the FT SIMTHESys definition

FT			
Property	**Type**	**Modifier**	**Behaviors**
			ComputeStateRewards InitEvents CountStateRewards SetStateRewards ListImpulseRewards SetImpulseReward
TopEvent			
Property	**Type**	**Modifier**	**Behaviors**
Prob	float	computed	IsTrue
BasicEvent			
Property	**Type**	**Modifier**	**Behaviors**
Prob Broken BreakRate RepairRate	float boolean float float	computed dynamic static static	IsTrue Fire GetRate
Arc			
Property	**Type**	**Modifier**	**Behaviors**
From To	element element	static static	IsTrue
Or			
Property	**Type**	**Modifier**	**Behaviors**
			IsTrue
And			
Property	**Type**	**Modifier**	**Behaviors**
			IsTrue

The first formalism is PerfBPEL. PerfBPEL is designed to support performance modeling of Service Oriented Architecture (SOA) complex applications based on BPEL workflows. The approach is to mimic BPEL, a workflow specification language for the specification of composed web services: the formalism has been designed to be as close as possible to BPEL to lower the semantic gap between the skills that are typical of BPEL developers and the skills that are needed to develop performance models.

The second and the third formalisms are designed to allow the implementation of submodels that offer services to other submodels. The second formalism, Test, shows how it is possible to design general-oriented service formalisms for multiformalism applications. Test submodels enable the verification of complex conditions over other submodels, written in other formalisms, with no limitation on the nature of the conditions, by offering proper interfaces that can be implemented by the other formalisms to exploit the verification features. This allows the reuse of any formalism in combination with Test if the support is implemented by the bridge formalism.

The third formalism, Rejuvenation, shows how it is possible to design domain-oriented service formalisms for multiformalism applications. Rejuvenation submodels enable the application of software aging and rejuvenation over other submodels representing the evolution of software systems, written in other formalisms, similarly to how it is done in Test. This allows the reuse of any performance oriented formalism in combination with Rejuvenation if the support is implemented by the bridge formalism.

The fourth proposal presented in this Section is actually not a formalism but a software extension. The exception enabled formalism extension describes how any formalism can be given support for software-like exception features, to implement the modeling of special conditions without the need to explicitly design complex (and potentially error prone) models.

PerfBPEL

PerfBPEL is a domain oriented formalism (that has been already presented, together with a case study, in (Barbierato et al 2012b)) designed to implement performance models of complex SOA applications written in BPEL. PerfBPEL submodels can be integrated with other submodels to represent with the most appropriate formalisms the effects of the substanding architecture or the network. The evaluation of performances of a SOA based application since the early phases of the design cycle simplifies the choice between alternatives and verification of QoS policies: consequently, PerfBPEL is designed to represent all performance related aspects of BPEL while keeping the structure of models as similar as possible to BPEL workflow s, by rendering each BPEL construct with a PerfBPEL equivalent, that captures the same semantics and enrich it with performance related annotations. The main advantages of using PerfBPEL for such a task contributions of this approach are the minimal syntactical difference with respect to BPEL workflow s, the possibility of obtaining automatic generation of PerfBPEL models from BPEL workflow s, the integrability in multiformalism comprehensive models.

BPEL is a complex language with a complex syntax and a complex execution policy, as it offers concurrency, synchronization, message-based communication, exception handling and the use of variables: thus modeling approaches based on low level formalisms (such as Petri nets like in (Holanda et al 2010) and (Lohmann et al 2009)) imply that the modeler should produce very large models to represent even small BPEL workflows, complicating the analysis and affecting its complexity, if all details of it should be captured for a faithful evaluation: e. g. consider that BPEL supports fault handling, that is heavily used to manage quite frequent problems that show up with connections.

The solution of PerfBPEL models is based on the generation of an equivalent Markov chain, to minimize the state space. PerfBPEL belongs to the EIEF formalism family.

The version of PerfBPEL presented in this Section is limited by several assumptions: variables are managed by collapsing the virtually unlimited set of possible values in relevant subsets, each one determined according to the combination of conditions present in a given workflow, to reduce the original number of possible values of a variable during the execution of the workflow to a finite and generally small number of states; variables that do not assume a limited and deterministic set ov values are modeled by a stochastic characterization of their states, obtained by profiling analogous workflow s, analyzing the specifications or setting proper hypotheses; synchronization inside Flow constructs is not covered; the reference implementation is WS-BPEL 2.0[17]; the details of real service invocations (not necessarily available in the first phases of the cycle) have been ignored in favor of a simplified and generalized approach. Moreover, only the design of the main elements is described.

BPEL constructs are divided in Basic Activities and Structured Activities. Basic activities are atomic operations of the language, while Structured Activities describe its control flow.

Besides the elements that correspond to BPEL constructs (and include properties describing the parameters needed to evaluate execution time in terms of deterministic and exponentially distributed duration), additional elements have been added to connect PerfBPEL elements in a graph structure and implement the interactions that represents the BPEL execution paths. PerfBPEL and BPEL related elements share the same name (taken from the WS-BPEL reference). The PerfBPEL elements are summarized in Table 4.

The Start and the End elements define the beginning and the end of the model. They have a name static property and there must be a single Start and a single End element in the submodel. The Start element cannot have any incoming arc; the End element cannot have any outgoing arc.

The IsEnabled behavior (Enable interface), common to all PerfBPEL elements, determines if all incoming arcs that could eventually block the activity (also in multiformalism models) are enabled according to the algorithm:

1. for all incoming Arc elements a implementing Active do
2. if NOT a.isActive() then
3. return false
4. end if
5. end for
6. return true

The Start Fire behavior updates the currentAction property of the submodel to the value of the to property of the Next arc element that has the Start in its from property; the End Fire behavior cleans the variableValues property of the submodel and sets the currentActivity to the only Start element of the submodel.

The Sequence element represents the start of a sequence of actions. It has a name static property. The use of it in PerfBPEL is pleonastic, as a PerfBPEL model is inherently a graph: thus notwithstanding, for the sake of formal correctness and for future use it has been included.

The element has the isEnabled behavior to implement the Enable interface.

The Sequence Fire behavior updates the currentAction property of the submodel to the value of the to property of the Next arc element that has the Sequence in its from property.

The Assign element represents a variable valorization action. It has the name static property, the variable static property, that represents the BPEL variable set by the activity, and the value dynamic property, that represents the value that it is going to be assigned. When this activity is executed, the given variable is set to the specified value.

The element has the isEnabled behavior to implement the Enable interface.

The Assign Fire behavior updates the variableValues property of the submodel updating it with the value of its value property in correspondence with the value of its variable property in the variables property of the submodel, and updates the currentAction property of the submodel to the value of the to property of the Next arc element that has the Assign in its from property.

The Reply element represents the response of a service after its invocation. It has a name static property, a service static property, that represents the name of the service that is being performed, and a rate static property, that optionally represents the mean exponential time needed to issue the reply.

The element has the isEnabled behavior to implement the Enable interface.

The communication protocol between PerfBPEL submodels is implemented by means of properly defined Connection arc elements in the bridge formalism in which the model hosting the submodels is written. The Reply Fire behavior looks for all the Connection arc elements of the model that start from the submodel in which the Reply element is contained. For all the arcs whose service property matches the one contained in the corresponding property of the Reply element, it executes a Push behavior to send this event to other submodels. It also changes the currentActivity property of the BPEL submodel containing the Reply element to its getNext().to element.[18]

Table 4. The elements of PerfBPEL

PerfBPEL			
Property	**Type**	**Modifier**	**Behaviors**
variableValues	string	dynamic	ComputeStateRewards
currentActivity	element	dynamic	InitEvents
waitingForEvent	string	dynamic	CountStateRewards
valueSet	string	static	SetStateRewards
variableType	string	static	ListImpulseRewards
			SetImpulseReward
Start			
Property	**Type**	**Modifier**	**Behaviors**
			Fire
			IsEnabled
End			
Property	**Type**	**Modifier**	**Behaviors**
			Fire
			IsEnabled
Sequence			
Property	**Type**	**Modifier**	**Behaviors**
			Fire
			IsEnabled
Assign			
Property	**Type**	**Modifier**	**Behaviors**
variable	string	static	Fire
value	string	dynamic	IsEnabled
Reply			
Property	**Type**	**Modifier**	**Behaviors**
service	string	Static	Fire
			IsEnabled
Receive			
Property	**Type**	**Modifier**	**Behaviors**
service	string	static	Fire
waiting	string	dynamic	IsEnabled
Invoke			
Property	**Type**	**Modifier**	**Behaviors**
service	string	static	Fire
waiting	string	dynamic	IsEnabled
If-Else			
Property	**Type**	**Modifier**	**Behaviors**
condition	string	static	Fire
probability	float	static	IsEnabled
While			
Property	**Type**	**Modifier**	**Behaviors**
condition	string	static	Fire
probability	float	static	IsEnabled

continued on following page

Table 4. Continued

For-each			
Property	**Type**	**Modifier**	**Behaviors**
variable set currentValue	string string string	static static dynamic	Fire IsEnabled
Next			
Property	**Type**	**Modifier**	**Behaviors**
From To	element element	static static	Fire IsActive getNext
Else			
Property	**Type**	**Modifier**	**Behaviors**
From To	element element	static static	Fire IsActive getNext

The Receive element represents the wait for a response from a service after its invocation. It has a name static property, a service static property, that represents the name of the service that is being performed, and a waiting dynamic property, defining the state of the element with respect to communication synchronization.

The element has the isEnabled behavior to implement the Enable interface.

The Receive Fire behavior sets the waitingForEvent property of the submodel to the value of its own service property and sets its own waiting property.

When the Connection arc of the bridge formalism that has the submodel containing the Receive element in its to property executes a push behavior, it checks if the submodel containing the Receive is waiting for the event specified in the service property of the arc. If it matches, the waiting property of the Receive and the waitingForEvent property of the submodel are unset and the getNext().to.Fire() behavior of the Receive is scheduled.

The Invoke element represents the invocation of an external service. It has a name static property, a service static property, that represent the name of the element and the name of the service to execute, a waiting dynamic property, defining

the state of the element with respect to communication synchronization, and a rate static property, that optionally represents the mean exponential waiting time needed to issue the request.

The element has the isEnabled behavior to implement the Enable interface.

The Invoke Fire behavior is implemented similarly to a sequence of a Reply and a Receive Fire behaviors, and the same considerations over Connection arc interactions hold.

The If-Else element represents a conditional choice. It has a name static property and two mutually exclusive static properties, namely condition and probability, to be used in the case in which an explicit If condition to be checked on the model variables is present, or in the case in which the choice is probabilistic between the two alternative bodies of the choice. The syntax for an If-Else element prescribes that it must have exactly two outgoing arcs: a Next arc (towards the first element to be executed if the condition is true) and an Else arc (towards the first element to be executed if the condition is true).

The element has the isEnabled behavior to implement the Enable interface.

The If-Else Fire behavior implements the algorithm:

1.   if condition is set then
2.   if condition then set currentActivity to this. getNext().to
3.   else set currentActivity to this.getElse().to
4.   end if
5.   else if getNext().isEnabled() then
6.   if getNext().to has the rate property then
7.   r= getNext().to.rate
8.   else r = 0
9.   end if
10. schedule getNext().to with rate r • probability
11. schedule getElse().to with rate r • (1 – probability)
12. update variableValues
13. update currentActivity
14. end if

The While element represents a conditional loop. It has a name static property and two mutually exclusive static properties, namely condition and probability, to be used as for the If-Else element. The syntax for a While element prescribes that the flow of the actions in the body of the element is required to form a closed loop back to it.

The element has the isEnabled behavior to implement the Enable interface.

The While Fire behavior is similar to the Else-If Fire behavior.

The For-each element represents a serial or parallel iterative construct (currently approximated in PerfBPEL as serial). It has a name static property, a variable static property, that represents the variable used to identify the iterations and to parameterize, in case, the action executions and the service invocations in each iteration, a set static property that represents the possible values for the variable property, a currentValue dynamic property, that represent current value of the iteration variable. The syntax for the For-each element prescribes a Next and a Else element outgoing arcs, similarly to the case of the While element.

The element has the isEnabled behavior to implement the Enable interface.

The For-each Fire behavior assigns the current value to the variable, and then sets its own currentValue property to the next element of the set (defined in the corresponding property). It schedules the Fire behavior of the element in the to property of its Next arc element if there are other elements in the set, or schedules the Fire behavior of the element in the to property of its Else arc if there are no new values to be assigned.

The Next element and the Else element have a name static property and implement the Active and the Edge interfaces.

The formalism element BPEL. has a name static property, a variables static property, an array of labels that represents all the variables used in the model, the valueSet static property that defines the range of possible values for each variable, a variableType static property that associates to each variable its type, a currentActivity dynamic property, tracking the currently running activity, a waitingForEvent dynamic property, that tracks if the submodel is waiting for an event from another submodel, by its name, and. a variableValues dynamic property that tracks the current value for each variable.

The InitEvents behavior mimics the execution of the represented BPEL workflow by a workflow engine, to produce the corresponding Markov chain by scheduling its events with the solver, implementing the algorithm:

1.   if this.isEnabled()
2.   if NOT waitingForEvent then
3.   for all PerfBPEL elements e do
4.   if e.isEnabled() then
5.   if e has the rate property then
6.   r=e.rate
7.   else r = 0
8.   end if
9.   schedule e.Fire() with rate r
10. update variableValues
11. end if
12. end for
13. end if
14. end if

Test

Test is a custom formalism (that has been already presented, together with a case study, in (Barbierato et al. 2011b)) designed to verify complex conditions over other submodels in multiformalism models. Test is used to define submodels that describe the condition to be checked in an automaton-like style. The condition is described in the form of a sequence of subconditions that should be satisfied in a certain order. The formalism is designed to measure the probability of occurrence of the desired condition. To make it a formalism of general use, conditions are not stored into local testing elements but materially composed by special checking arcs coming to the local testing elements from elements of the submodels on which a subcondition has to be checked. This allows the reuse of Test submodels in combination with submodels written in any other formalism, simply redesigning the checking arcs to handle the characteristics of the formalisms and couple them with Test logic. All types of checking arcs have to implement the CheckIfTrue interface to be recognized as valid.

In order to design the FDL description of the formalism, consider that, besides the formalism element, four types of element are needed: one to represent the verification of the desired condition, one to represent the verification of an intermediate condition, one to test an intermediate condition and one arc element that defines the relations between the others.

Sat is the element that represents the verification of the desired condition. Besides a name static property, that identifies it within the model, it has a prob computed property that will contain the verification probability and no behavior.

State is the element that represents the verification of an intermediate subcondition. Besides a name static property it has a prob computed property, that will contain the state probability, and a getNext behavior, that computes the next state to switch to by implementing the algorithm[19]:

1. for all Next elements n departing from this do
2. if n.IsTrue() then
3. return n.getDestination()
4. end if
5. end for

Check is the element that represents a check over a desired subcondition. It has a name static property and an isTrue behavior (to implement the CheckIfTrue interface), that tests the subcondition it guards according to the incoming testing arcs by the algorithm:

1. for all arc elements c directed to this that implement CheckIfTrue and do not belong to Next elementType
2. if NOT c.IsTrue() then
3. return false
4. end if
5. end for

The Next element is the only arc type element of the formalism: consequently, it implements the Edge interface, and additionally it implements the CheckIfTrue interface and uses the same CheckIfTrue and the.ElementOccupancy interface. It has a name, a to and a from static properties, and two behaviors, getDestination, that returns the arc destination, and isTrue, that implements the algorithm:

1. for all outgoing Next arc elements n
2. return n.to.isTrue()
3. end for

The Test element of the Test formalism has a dynamic property currentState (that is preset to the initial state of the automaton). This property is used to track the state of the Test formalism. As Test belongs to the EEF formalism family, it implements the ExpEventModel (and consequently InitEvents and the five reward behaviors.), hasSubElements and canPerformTest (and consequently the PerformTest behavior) interfaces. Since its evolution depends on the interactions with other submodels rather than on the presence of active elements[20], initEvents is just a placeholder, while PerformTest is used to offer to the solvers a way to invoke the check of the model by means of the incoming text arcs, by implementing the algorithm

- currentState.getNext()

Consequently, the Test formalism evolution depends on the GetNext behavior of the State element, invoked by the solver. The behavior uses the IsTrue behavior of the Next arc elements to verify if some of the conditions (specified by the incoming testing arcs to the Check elements) are verified. If this is true, the formalism uses the GetDestination behavior to update the current state. Solving a Test automaton requires the accumulation of probability of the Sat event(s) in a Test submodel. Due to the probabilistic nature of the approach, instead of developing a separate dedicated solving engine it has been decided to exploit the existing exponential events solving engines. At every state change, the conditions are evaluated and the probability of every Sat state is updated, according to the evolution of the events detected by the Check elements. The behaviors of the elements describe how to call the solving engines in order to get to the final result. The testing arc elements of the bridge formalism transfer the condition verified by the elements of the other submodels to the Test submodel, achieving the final effect of verifying the given model.

In a valid Test submodel Next elements connect either a State element and a Check elements or a Check element and a State or a Sat element. A summary of the elements is presented in Table 5.

Software Rejuvenation

Software Rejuvenation is a custom formalism (that has been already presented, together with a case study, in (Iacono et al. 2012) and (Barbierato et al. 2012a)) designed to add software aging and rejuvenation (Avritzer & Weyuker 1997, Cotroneo et al. 2011, Huang et al. 1995) effects to multiformalism models that represent systems in which there is some software. Software Rejuvenation is used to define submodels that describe the effects of the aging process and the rejuvenation strategies chosen to restore a normal operational condition after the system degradation phase. The aging and rejuvenation process is described in the form of a set of elements meant to influence the elements of the submodel representing the software system without the need for any modification in them, by exploiting proper arcs in the bridge formalism: this allows reuse and independent design. The formalism is designed to alter the ordinary execution policy of the influenced formalism element, by interdiction of their habilitation or modification of their properties.

The possibility of adding such features to models is a significant tool when designing software, as the most of the problems that cause performance degradation, hangs and crashes in computer systems are caused by software problems. The proposed solution allows to model independently the system and any proactive or reactive recovery technique and couple them with a simple compositional approach. Generally, rejuvenation strategies consist in a periodical restore of the system to a known state, that could be considered as a snapshot of the system taken before any failure emerges as a consequence of software aging.

From the point of view of the evaluation of submodels, the Software Rejuvenation formalism has been built to fit into the EEF family as well, even if it is necessary to take into consideration the fact that aging problems are typically characterized by non-Markovian behaviors: in fact, modeling and evaluating aging problems is a mathematically complex problem, generally managed by means of ad-hoc solutions, derived case by case[21]. The choice of a generalized, approximated approach has been done because of the goals of SIMTHESys: ad hoc approaches would not enable reuse

Table 5. Elements of the TEST SIMTHESys definition

Test			
Property	**Type**	**Modifier**	**Behaviors**
CurrentState	string	dynamic	PerformTest ComputeStateRewards InitEvents CountStateRewards SetStateRewards ListImpulseRewards SetImpulseReward
Sat			
Property	**Type**	**Modifier**	**Behaviors**
Prob	float	computed	
State			
Property	**Type**	**Modifier**	**Behaviors**
Prob	float	computed	GetNext
Next			
Property	**Type**	**Modifier**	**Behaviors**
From To	element element	static static	IsTrue GetDestination
Check			
Property	**Type**	**Modifier**	**Behaviors**
			IsTrue

and formalisms combination. The compromise solution that keeps coherence with the framework is the use of phase-type distributions (O'Cinneide 1990) to represent rejuvenation techniques based on application restarts.

Besides the formalism element, the formalism offers three elements, to represent the three main conditions of aging and rejuvenation processes and their effect: the Degradation, the Crash and the Rejuvenation[22]. With respect to a generic submodel representing the software portion of a system, the Degradation affects the operations of one of its elements by diminishing its effectiveness, the Crash blocks its evolution and the Rejuvenation recovers with a certain policy the normal operations of it, while the RateControl arc element connects one of the other three elements with the element on which it acts.

To be as faithful as possible to what literature describes the action of aging is, the effect of a Degradation element is implemented as a sequence of exponential events according to a Markov Chain, in which each state represents a different level of degradation, each of which slows down of a certain factor the exponential firing time of the element to which it is connected by a RateControl arc. The mean sojourn time in each state of the chain is exponentially distributed. At the end of each degradation state in the chain the degradation gets to a maximum degradation level in which the influenced element remains until a crash or a rejuvenation happen.

The Degradation element has a name static property, the Phase dynamic property describing the current phase of the element, the nPhases static property describing the number of degradation phases, the phaseRate static property, describing the rate at which the element switches from one phase to the next one, the phaseDeg static property, describing the degradation factor it applies to its influenced element, the degMeasure computed property, describing the current overall degradation to be applied to its influenced element. The getPhaseDegr behavior returns the current value of Phase, the getPhRate behavior returns the value of phaseRate, the getNextPhase behavior returns the next degradation phase.

A Crash element is implemented as having two states, one to represent the conditions in which the influenced element is working and one to represent the conditions in which the influenced element is under repair. The mean sojourn time in the first state (Mean Time To Failure, or MTTF) is distributed according to a n phase type distribution with constant jump rate between phases; the mean sojourn time in the second state (Mean Time To Repair, or MTTR) is also distributed according to a m phase type distribution.

The Crash element implements the ElementOccupancy interface and has a name static property, the Phase dynamic property describing the current phase of the element, the Ok dynamic property describing if it is in a phase in which its influenced element can work or not, the nPhasesOk static property describing how many phases of the degradation over the influenced element let it work even if with a degradation of its performances, the eventRateOk static property, describing the rate at which the element switches from one working condition phase to the next one, the phaseRateOk static property, describing the rate to which it exits a working condition, the nPhasesKo static property describing how many phases of the degradation over the influenced element do not let it work, the eventRateKo static property, describing the rate at which the element switches from one non working phase to the next one, the phaseRateKo static property, describing the rate to which it exits a non working condition, the crashMeasure computed property, describing the current overall crash condition with respect to its

influenced element. The getOccupancy behavior (Occupancy interface) returns the current value of the Ok property, the getPeOk behavior returns the current value of Phase if the element is in a working phase, the getPeKo behavior returns the current value of Phase if the element is in a non working phase, the getPhRateOk behavior returns the value of phaseRate if the element is in a working phase, the getPhRateKo behavior returns the value of phaseRate if the element is in a non working phase, the getNextPhaseOk behavior returns the next working condition phase, the getNextPhaseKo behavior returns the next non working condition phase.

A Rejuvenation element is implemented as having two states, one to represent the normal operation and one to represent the time during which the rejuvenation process is being performed. The sojourn time in both states is also respectively n and m phase type.

The Rejuvenation element implements the ElementOccupancy interface and has a name static property, the Phase dynamic property describing the current phase of the element, the Ok dynamic property describing if it is in a phase in which its influenced element can work or not, the nPhasesOk static property describing how many phases of the rejuvenation over the influenced element let it work even if with a degradation of its performances, the eventRateOk static property, describing the rate at which the element switches from one working condition phase to the next one, the phaseRateOk static property, describing the rate to which it exits a working condition, the nPhasesKo static property describing how many phases of the degradation over the influenced element do not let it work, the eventRateKo static property, describing the rate at which the element switches from one non working phase to the next one, the phaseRateKo static property, describing the rate to which it exits a non working condition, the rejMeasure computed property, describing the current overall rejuvenation condition with respect to its influenced element. The getOccupancy behavior (Occupancy interface) returns the current value of the Ok property, the getPeOk behavior returns the current value of Phase if the element is in a working phase, the getPeKo behavior returns the current value of Phase if the element is in a non working phase, the getPhRateOk behavior returns the value of phaseRate if the element is in a working phase, the getPhRateKo behavior returns the value of phaseRate if the element is in a non working phase, the getNextPhaseOk behavior returns the next working condition phase, the getNextPhaseKo behavior returns the next non working condition phase.

The formalism element belongs to the EEF formalism family, so it implements the ExpEventModel solver helper interface and uses the ExpEventSolver solving interface. Moreover it implements the hasSubelements interface and uses the CheckIfTrue interface. It has only one name static property. As it is in charge of keeping the interactions between all the elements in a Software Rejuvenation submodel, its behaviors require a deeper examination. The interactions between the elements of a Software Rejuvenation submodel are mainly regulated by the formalism element InitEvents behavior. When a crash occurs[23], the system identifies its cause and proceeds to a system restart: in the while the system is in a non working state, and degradation or rejuvenation are blocked; after a restart, the evolution of Degradation and Rejuvenation elements is reset to the initial state; during a rejuvenation, the a Degradation element is reset to its initial state; the occurrence of a crash during a rejuvenation does not reset a Crash element and does not block the corresponding event, but the rate at which the phase of a Crash can change (and the event can occur in a phase) is inversely proportional to the Degradation element phase, so that crashes are more likely in a degraded system[24]. Consequently, the InitEvents behavior is in charge of enabling these relations. The InitEvents behavior can be

divided into three sections: the first section implements the algorithm

1. for each Crash element c do
2. if c is in a working state in a phase different from the last one or c is in a non working state different from the last one then
3. if a rejuvenation occurred then
4. c.setPhase(0)
5. c.setOk(true)
6. else if (for each incoming arc a directed to c holds that a.CheckIfTrue()) then
7. if c is in a working state
8. schedule the switch to the next phase of the current state with rate phRateOk
9. else schedule the switch to the next phase of the current state with the rate of the current degradation phase
10. end if
11. end if
12. else if c is in the last working state
13. schedule the switch to the non working state with the proper rate
14. set phase to 0
15. end if
16. end for

This section is responsible for the evolution of Crash elements. Line 2 partitions the control flow between the cases in which there is not a state change or a state change is required. Line 3 applies to the case in which a Rejuvenation element has been activated and generated a rejuvenation: consequently the Crash element is reset in phase 0 and in the working state. Line 6 evaluates if the element is active with respect to the state of all the elements (from other submodels) that can influence it and consequently enables the cases of line 7 or 9, that schedule the phase switch according to the current situation. Line 12 accounts for the case in which it is necessary to change state.

The second section similarly deals with the evolution of Rejuvenation elements according to the algorithm

17. for each Rejuvenation element r do
18. if r is in a working state in a phase different from the last one or c is in a non working state different from the last one then
19. if a crash occurred then
20. r.setPhase(0)
21. 2r.setOk(true)
22. else if (for each incoming arc a directed to r holds that a.CheckIfTrue()) then
23. if r is in a working state
24. schedule the switch to the next phase of the current state with rate phRateOk
25. else schedule the switch to the next phase of the current state with the rate of the current degradation phase
26. end if
27. end if
28. else if r is in the last working state
29. schedule the switch to the non working state with the proper rate
30. set phase to 0
31. end if
32. end for

The third section drives the evolution of Degradation elements, that is simpler, as the various phases are all relative to a single state and the maximum degradation state has no direct consequence. The element only evolves if not in the last phase and is reset in consequence of the evolution of a Crash or a Rejuvenation element: the element evolves between its phases if enabled. Evolution happens according to the algorithm

33. for each Degradation element d do
34. if r is in a phase different from the last one
35. if a crash or a rejuvenation occurred then
36. d.setPhase(0)
37. else if (for each incoming arc a directed to d holds that a.CheckIfTrue()) then
38. if d is not in the last phase
39. schedule the switch to the next phase at the proper rate
40. end if
41. end if
42. end if
43. end for

The getDegRate behavior updates the current degradation rate for each element in the model as the product of its degradation phase and a memory factor tracking its past evolution; the hasCrashOccurred and hasRejuvenationOccured behaviors evaluate if at least one Crash or Rejuvenation element are in a working state; the computeStateRewards, countStateRewards, setImpulseReward and setStateRewards behaviors update the internal state of the formalism element with the current parameters related to its contained elements.

A summary of the elements is presented in Table 6.

A variant of this formalism, based on the SIMTHESys Labeled Fluid Exponential Formalism Family (LFEF), has also been implemented by means of the framework. The Fluid Rejuvenation Formalism (that has been already presented, together with a case study, in (Barbierato et al. 2012a)) extends the presented one to include continuous time aging related processes, and offers four elements: Degradation, Crash, Rejuvenation and SelfRestoration. The Degradation element represents the aging process by a fluid (continuous) time dependent variable, called Degradation Factor (DF), that varies according to a static property (describing a function with saturation) and is reset at each repair; the Crash and Rejuvenation elements are similar to the one of the Software Rejuvenation formalism; the SelfRestoration element represents a self-healing process with a DF dependent start rate and duration and

Table 6. Elements of the Software Rejuvenation formalism

SR			
Property	**Type**	**Modifier**	**Behaviors**
			ComputeStateRewards
			InitEvents
			CountStateRewards
			SetStateRewards
			ListImpulseRewards
			SetImpulseReward
			getDegRate
			hasCrashOccurred
			hasRejuvenationOccurred
Degradation			
Property	**Type**	**Modifier**	**Behaviors**
Phase	integer	dynamic	getPhaseDegr
nPhases	integer	static	getPhRate
phaseRate	float	static	getNextPhase
phaseDeg	float	static	
degMeasure	float	computed	
Crash			
Property	**Type**	**Modifier**	**Behaviors**
Phase	integer	dynamic	getOccupancy
Ok	boolean	dynamic	getPeOk
nPhasesOk	integer	static	getPeKo
eventRateOk	float	static	getPhRateOk
phaseRateOk	integer	static	getPhRateKo
nPhasesKo	integer	static	getNextPhaseOk
eventRateKo	float	static	getNextPhaseKo
phaseRateKo	integer	static	
crashMeasure	float	computed	
Rejuvenation			
Property	**Type**	**Modifier**	**Behaviors**
Phase	integer	dynamic	getOccupancy
Ok	boolean	dynamic	getPeOk
nPhasesOk	integer	static	getPeKo
eventRateOk	float	static	getPhRateOk
phaseRateOk	integer	static	getPhRateKo
nPhasesKo	integer	static	getNextPhaseOk
eventRateKo	float	static	getNextPhaseKo
phaseRateKo	integer	static	
rejMeasure	float	computed	

a working rate that decreases to account for the self-healing workload, that reduces the DF according to a static property (describing a function with saturation). Further details on the formalism and its solution strategy, that is based on the generation of a mixed continuous-discrete state, continuous time Markov chain, is omitted for the sake of brevity (details can be found in (Barbierato et al. 2012a)).

Exceptions Enabling

Exceptions Enabling is a custom formalism extension (that has been already presented, together with a case study, in (Barbierato et al. 2011c)) designed to add exception management to existing formalisms. Exceptions Enabling is used to define submodels that closely describe systems or subsystems characterized by hardware or software exceptions, or similar mechanisms in other application fields (e. g. rush orders in production chain scheduling applications), or submodels that use exception features as a tool to model complex system behaviors in a more compact way.

Exceptions handling, that inspired the development of the Exceptions Enabling extension, is a typical feature of object oriented languages and of computer architectures. It is a technique that allows the interruption of the current evolution of the system to switch to a different execution path and handle another task (eventually to resume the previous operations), widely used in both software and hardware to manage unexpected situations (e. g. generated by the environment in which a system is evolving), or expected situations that need to be managed with a higher priority with respect to normal operations (e. g. depending on some expected event characterized by long and stochastic dynamics), or desired situations that require an interruption of current operations to be managed with efficiency (e. g. the handling of fixable errors). Exceptions can be generated as synchronous, when intentionally used and explicitly invoked, or asynchronous, when originated by uncontrolled causes; they can be generated by an event or by a state of the system; they can be generated during the evolution of a system according to a deterministic process or stochastic process. Once an exception is activated (thrown), the control of the system is passed to a proper subsystem, the handler.

Exceptions can be implemented as event triggered or state triggered. In the hypothesis of a mechanism based on the element, in the first case, the firing of a given active event can throw an exception; in the second case, the exception is activated by a certain combination of the values of the properties of an element. Exploiting multiformalism, the second case can be implemented

by exploiting the first mechanism, as it is possible to properly specify an ancillary formalism (e. g. FT) to identify and combine different events that generate an artificial state, that in turn throws the desired state-based exception: consequently, in the design of Exception Enabling the choice has been to implement an event based approach. This solution allows the same exception handler to be used by more elements of different formalism by throwing the same exception, the name of which identifies the handler.

To show how it is possible to extend an existing SIMTHESys formalism to support exceptions, SPN has been extended. The extension requires a formalism to include a new Catch element, that handles an exception, and its elements that should be enabled to throw exceptions must be extended with a Throws static property, declaring the name of the exception(s) to be thrown, and a ThrowsProb static property, that contains the probability by which the exception is thrown if the element becomes active (the value is 1 to implement synchronous exception, or a probability for asynchronous exceptions). Moreover, the bridge formalism should define a proper Effect arc element that connects a Catch element to the submodels affected by the execution of the exception, a new RaiseException behavior, that is executed with a probability ThrowsProb every time the behavior representing the execution of an active element is performed, and a new CheckExceptions behavior, that examines all existing exceptions to determine which should be executed by RaiseException.

As already seen, the Transition element is the only element of the formalism that implements the Active interface, consequently it has to be augmented with the static properties Throws and ThrowsProb. The InitEvents behavior of the formalism element has to be modified to check for pending exceptions by invoking the CheckExceptions behavior of the bridge element, according to the algorithm

1. for each Transition t do
2. if t.isActive() then
3. if t.ThrowsProb <> 1.0 then
4. schedule t.fire() and call CheckExceptions on the bridge formalism element of the main model with rate t.Rate * (1.0 − t.ThrowsProb)
5. else
6. schedule t.fire() and call ThrowExceptions(t.Throws) and checkExceptions on the bridge formalism element of the main model with rate t.Rate
7. end if
8. end if
9. end for

A reference implementation of a CheckExceptions behavior is given by the algorithm

1. for all active elements of exception enabled submodels a do
2. if a throws an exception e then
3. ThrowException(e)
4. end if
5. end for

while a reference implementation for a ThrowException behavior is given by the algorithm

1. for all Catch elements c do
2. if the name of c is coincident with the thrown exception name
3. c.CatchException()
4. end if
5. end for

A Catch element has a name static property, uses the Raise interface and has a CatchException behavior that follows the algorithm

1. for all incoming Effect arc elements e do
2. e.RaiseException()
3. end for

A reference Effect arc element has a name static property, uses the hasSubElements interface and should implement the Edge and the Raise interface by means of a RaiseException behavior, capable to correctly signaling the exception at its destination formalism element.

DEFINING BRIDGE FORMALISMS FOR MULTIFORMALISM MODELS IN SIMTHESYS

Designing a bridge formalism in SIMTHESys is not conceptually different from designing any other formalism. Bridge formalisms can freely introduce any additional element that can be useful for the desired application, but should at least include proper elements (generally arc elements) to implement the interactions between submodels. In the most of the cases, this is done by exploiting the interfaces that are typical of arc elements (e. g. Edge) together with the interfaces that are typical of each formalism, coupling these last ones according to the couple of formalisms that should interact. In this Section a bridge formalism is presented to give an example of how to obtain multiformalism.

Tester Bridge Formalism

The Tester bridge formalism (that has been already presented, together with a case study, in (Barbierato et al. 2011b)) allows the interaction between the Test, the RFT, the SPN and the GNQN formalisms. Tester has five arc elements: Arc, CheckGE and CheckLT, CheckTrue and CheckFalse. The semantics of Arc (SPN Place element to GNQN Queue element) is analogous to the semantics of a SPN arc element, as it obtains that a place marked with a number of tokens equal to the weight property of Arc, enables the destination queue, that processes the requests. The semantics of CheckGE and CheckLT (GNQN Queue element or SPN Place element to RFT Gate element) is

Table 7. Elements of the Tester SIMTHESys definition

Tester			
Property	**Type**	**Modifier**	**Behaviors**
			InitEvents ComputeStateRewards CountStateRewards SetStateRewards ListImpulseRewards SetImpulseRewards
Arc			
Property	**Type**	**Modifier**	**Behaviors**
From To	element element	static static	IsTrue
CheckLT			
Property	**Type**	**Modifier**	**Behaviors**
From To Weight	element element float	static static static	IsTrue
CheckGE			
Property	**Type**	**Modifier**	**Behaviors**
From To Weight	element element float	static static static	IsTrue
CheckTrue			
Property	**Type**	**Modifier**	**Behaviors**
From To	element element	static static	IsTrue
CheckFalse			
Property	**Type**	**Modifier**	**Behaviors**
From To	element element	static static	IsTrue

analogous to the semantics of a normal RFT Arc element that connects an event to a gate, as it feeds the gate with the result of a check over the number of units waiting in the queue or the number of tokens in a place with respect to a property of CheckGE or CheckLT, that defines a reference value. The semantics of CheckTrue and Check-False (RFT event element to Test check element) checks if the current probability of the Top Event element satisfies the specified condition (true or false) and consequently enable the evolution of the destination Check element. Tester elements are summarized in Table 7.

The Arc element has a name static property and the From and To static properties, representing the origin and the destination it connects, implements the Edge and PushPull interfaces, to allow typical arc interactions, the Active interface to support the abilitation of active elements, and the CapacityCheck interface, to offer tests on the availability of the destination, and uses the FC-QueueEvent and ElementOccupancy interfaces to offer tests on the availability of the destination. The isActive behavior tests if the occupancy of the origin is more than 0; the hasSpace behavior tests if a destination queue has free places by the canAccept Queue behavior; the Push and Pull behavior add one item to the destination occupancy and subtract one item from the origin occupancy.

The CheckGE and CheckLT elements have a name property, the From and To static properties and the Weight static property, to store the value against which destination occupancy should be tested, implement the Edge and CheckIfTrue interfaces, and use the ElementOccupancy interface. The isTrue behavior (CheckIfTrue interface) tests if the occupancy of the origin is not less than 0r less than Weight.

The CheckTrue and CheckFalse elements are similar to CheckGE and CheckLT.

The formalism element has a name static property, implements the hasSubElements, ExpEventModel and canPerformTest, and uses the ProbWeight, PushPull, Activeand FCQueueEvent interfaces. The InitEvents behavior just calls the InitEvent behavior of every contained submodel: the scheduling of the active elements events in the submodels is thus simply executed by their formalism elements, and has as a consequence the proper activation of the elements of the bridge formalism, that in turn will transport significant influences and activations between the submodels. Note that the mechanism is formally independent by the involved formalism families, as it only depends on the interfaces implemented by the arc elements of the bridge formalism: in case of multiformalism models that involve different formalism families together, the design of arc elements could be more complex but will anyway follow the same general framework.

CONCLUSION

In this Chapter the general framework and a comprehensive application of SIMTHESys to formalism design have been given, together with some significant examples of formalisms, that have been introduced and examined, chosen between the ones used to analyze various case studies to provide guidelines for a wide set of potential applications. The examples have been graduated to step from demonstrating the implementation of classical formalisms up to high level, custom, domain oriented, specially featured cases, and finally a multiformalism application. For complete specific applications of the example formalisms to performance evaluation of systems, the Chapter provides proper references.

REFERENCES

Avritzer, A., & Weyuker, E. J. (1997). Monitoring smoothly degrading systems for increased dependability. *Empirical Software Engineering*, 2, 59–77. doi:10.1023/A:1009794200077

Barbierato, E., Bobbio, A., Gribaudo, M., & Iacono, M. (2012a). Multiformalism to support software rejuvenation modeling. In *Proceedings of ISSRE Workshops* (pp. 271-276). IEEE.

Barbierato, E., Dei Rossi, G., Gribaudo, M., Iacono, M., & Marin, A. (2013a). Exploiting product form solution techniques in multiformalism modeling. In *Proceedings of Sixth International Workshop on Practical Applications of Stochastic Modelling*. London: Elsevier.

Barbierato, E., Gribaudo, M., & Iacono, M. (2011a). Defining formalisms for performance evaluation with SIMTHESys. *Electronic Notes in Theoretical Computer Science*, 275, 37–51. doi:10.1016/j.entcs.2011.09.004

Barbierato, E., Gribaudo, M., & Iacono, M. (2011b). Exploiting multiformalism models for testing and performance evaluation in SIMTHESys. In *Proceedings of the 5th International ICST Conference on Performance Evaluation Methodologies and Tools*. Paris, France: ICST (Institute for Computer Sciences, Social-Informatics and Telecommunications Engineering).

Barbierato, E., Gribaudo, M., & Iacono, M. (2013b). A performance modeling language for big data architectures. In *Proceedings of HiPMoS 2013 – ECMS 2013*. HiPMoS.

Barbierato, E., Gribaudo, M., & Iacono, M. (2013c). *Performance evaluation of NoSQL big-data applications using multi-formalism models.* Fut. Gen. Comp. Sys.

Barbierato, E., Gribaudo, M., Iacono, M., & Marrone, S. (2011c). Performability modeling of exceptions-aware systems in multiformalism tools. In K. Al-Begain, S. Balsamo, D. Fiems, & A. Marin (Eds.), *Proceedings of ASMTA* (pp. 257-272). Berlin: Springer.

Barbierato, E., Iacono, M., & Marrone, S. (2012b). PerfBPEL: A graph-based approach for the performance analysis of BPEL SOA applications. In *Proceedings of VALUETOOLS* (pp. 64-73). IEEE.

Bause, F., Buchholz, P., & Kemper, P. (1998). A toolbox for functional and quantitative analysis of DEDS. In R. Puigjaner, N. N. Savino, & B. Serra (Eds.), *Computer Performance Evaluation (Tools)* (pp. 356–359). Berlin: Springer. doi:10.1007/3-540-68061-6_32

Bobbio, A., Garg, S., Gribaudo, M., Horvath, A., Sereno, M., & Telek, M. (2008). Compositional fluid stochastic petri net model for operational software system performance. In *Proceedings of IEEE 1st Intl Workshop Software Aging and Rejuvenation* (WoSAR) (pp. 1–6). IEEE.

Castiglione, A., Gribaudo, M., Iacono, M., & Palmieri, F. (2013). Exploiting mean field analysis to model performances of big data architectures. *Future Generation Computer Systems*. doi:10.1016/j.future.2013.07.016

Ciardo, G., Jones, R. L., Miner, A. S., & Siminiceanu, R. I. (2006). Logic and stochastic modeling with SMART. *Performance Evaluation*, *63*(6), 578–608. doi:10.1016/j.peva.2005.06.001

Ciardo, G., & Miner, A. S. (2004). SMART: The stochastic model checking analyzer for reliability and timing. In *Proceedings of QEST* (pp. 338-339). IEEE Computer Society.

Ciardo, G., Miner, A. S., & Wan, M. (2009). Advanced features in SMART: The stochastic model checking analyzer for reliability and timing. *SIGMETRICS Performance Evaluation Review*, *36*, 58–63. doi:10.1145/1530873.1530885

Clark, G., Courtney, T., Daly, D., Deavours, D., Derisavi, S., & Doyle, M. ... Webster, P. (2001). The Möbius modeling tool. In *Proceedings of the 9th International Workshop on Petri Nets and Performance Models* (PNPM'01). IEEE Computer Society.

Codetta Raiteri, D., Iacono, M., Franceschinis, G., & Vittorini, V. (2004). Repairable fault tree for the automatic evaluation of repair policies. In *Proceedings of DSN* (pp. 659-668). IEEE Computer Society.

Cotroneo, D., Natella, R., Pietrantuono, R., & Russo, S. (2011). Software aging and rejuvenation: Where we are and where we are going. In *Proceedings of IEEE 3rd Int Workshop Software Aging and Rejuvenation* (WoSAR). IEEE.

Courtney, T., Gaonkar, S., Keefe, K., Rozier, E., & Sanders, W. H. (2009). Möbius 2.3: An extensible tool for dependability, security, and performance evaluation of large and complex system models. In *Proceedings of DSN* (pp. 353-358). IEEE.

Franceschinis, G., Gribaudo, M., Iacono, M., Marrone, S., Mazzocca, N., & Vittorini, V. (2004). Compositional modeling of complex systems: Contact center scenarios in OsMoSys. In J. Cortadella & W. Reisig (Eds.), *Proceedings of ICATPN* (pp. 177-196). Berlin: Springer.

Franceschinis, G., Gribaudo, M., Iacono, M., Marrone, S., Moscato, F., & Vittorini, V. (2009). Interfaces and binding in component based development of formal models. In G. Stea, J. Mairesse, & J. Mendes (Eds.), *Proceedings of VALUETOOLS* (p. 44). ACM.

Franceschinis, G., Gribaudo, M., Iacono, M., & Vittorini, V. (2002a). Towards an object based multi-formalism multi-solution modeling approach. In *Proceedings of Second International Workshop on Modelling of Objects, Components, and Agents* (MOCA'02). Aarhus, Denmark: MOCA.

Franceschinis, G., Gribaudo, M., Iacono, M., Vittorini, V., & Bertoncello, C. (2002b). DrawNet++: A flexible framework for building dependability models. In *Proceedings of DSN* (p. 540). IEEE Computer Society.

Garg, S., Puliafito, A., Telek, M., & Trivedi, K. (1995). Analysis of software rejuvenation using Markov regenerative stochastic Petri nets. In *Proceedings of the 6-th International Symposium on Software Reliability Engineering*. Toulouse, France: IEEE.

Gordon, W., & Newell, G. (1967). Closed queueing systems with exponential servers. *Operations Research*, *64*(2), 254–265. doi:10.1287/opre.15.2.254

Gribaudo, M., Codetta-Raiteri, D., & Franceschinis, G. (2005). DrawNET, a customizable multi-formalism, multi-solution tool for the quantitative evaluation of systems. In *Proceedings of QEST 2005*. IEEE.

Gribaudo, M., Iacono, M., Mazzocca, N., & Vittorini, V. (2003). The OsMoSys/DrawNET XE! languages system: A novel infrastructure for multi-formalism object-oriented modelling. In *Proceedings of ESS 2003: 15th European Simulation Symposium And Exhibition*. ESS.

Gribaudo, M., & Sereno, M. (1997). GSPN semantics for queueing networks with blocking. In *Proceedings of the 6th International Workshop on Petri Nets and Performance Models*. Washington, DC: IEEE Computer Society.

Holanda, H., Merseguer, J., Cordeiro, G., & Serra, A. (2010). Performance evaluation of web services orchestrated with WS-BPEL4People. *International Journal of Computer Networks & Communications*, *2*(11), 18.

Huang, Y., Kintala, C., Kolettis, N., & Fulton, N. D. (1995). Software rejuvenation: analysis, module and applications. In *Proceedings of Fault Tolerant Computing Symp* (FTCS-25) (pp. 381–390). FTCS.

Iacono, M., Barbierato, E., & Gribaudo, M. (2012). The SIMTHESys multiformalism modeling framework. *Computers & Mathematics with Applications (Oxford, England)*, *64*, 3828–3839. doi:10.1016/j.camwa.2012.03.009

Iacono, M., & Gribaudo, M. (2010). Element based semantics in multi formalism performance models. In *Proceedings of MASCOTS* (pp. 413-416). IEEE.

Kartson, D., Balbo, G., Donatelli, S., Franceschinis, G., & Conte, G. (1994). *Modelling with generalized stochastic Petri nets*. New York, NY: John Wiley & Sons, Inc.

Koutrasa, V., Platisa, A., & Gravvanisb, G. (2007). On the optimization of free resources using non-homogeneous Markov chain software rejuvenation model. *Reliability Engineering & System Safety*, *92*, 1724–1732. doi:10.1016/j.ress.2006.09.017

Lohmann, N., Verbeek, H., Ouyang, C., & Stahl, C. (2009). Comparing and evaluating Petri net semantics for BPEL. *International Journal of Business Process Integration and Management*, *4*(1), 60–73. doi:10.1504/IJBPIM.2009.026986

Moscato, F., Flammini, F., Di Lorenzo, G., Vittorini, V., Marrone, S., & Iacono, M. (2007). The software architecture of the OsMoSys multisolution framework. In P. W. Glynn (Ed.), *VALUETOOLS* (p. 51). ACM. doi:10.4108/valuetools.2007.1913

O'Cinneide, C. A. (1990). Characterization of phase-type distributions. *Communications in Statistics: Stochastic Models*, 6(1), 1–57. doi:10.1080/15326349908807134

Trivedi, K. S. (2002). SHARPE 2002: Symbolic hierarchical automated reliability and performance evaluator. In *Proceedings of DSN* (p. 544). IEEE Computer Society.

Trivedi, K. S., Vaidyanathan, K., & Goseva-Popstojanova, K. (2000). Modeling and analysis of software aging and rejuvenation. In *Proceedings of the 33rd Annual Simulation Symposium*, (p. 270). IEEE Computer Society.

Vittorini, V., Iacono, M., Mazzocca, N., & Franceschinis, G. (2004). The OsMoSys approach to multi-formalism modeling of systems. *Software & Systems Modeling*, 3, 68–81. doi:10.1007/s10270-003-0039-5

ENDNOTES

1 Note that the extension is not merely a syntactic addition: while Fault Tree models can be quantitatively evaluated by combinatorial algorithms, a Repairable Fault Tree model behaves differently according to the state (repaired/damaged) of each repairable component, and must consequently be analyzed by state space based algorithms.

2 The interested reader can find for a comparison in (Gribaudo et al. 2003) a presentation of a version of the OsMoSys/Drawnet family of languages, that deals with similar problems with a stronger orientation to element, formalism and model reuse.

3 A complete example of definition of a formalism and a model based on the formalism is given later in this chapter: consequently, for the sake of brevity, in this Section examples will be given in footnotes only for the definitions that are not used in the complete example.

4 This is the previously mentioned case of formalism elements, that are used to represent submodels in composed models. Also *bridge formalisms*, that are special formalisms designed to enable multiformalism models, are declared exactly in the same way, as they are just formalisms in which some elements can interact with elements from other formalisms.

5 The following example shows how the InitEvents behavior, that enables model solution, is implemented:

```
<behavior name="InitEvents"
return="void">
<code>
for(ElementType T: allSubElements) {
if(T instanceof ExpEventModel)
{ ((ExpEventModel)
T).InitEvents();}
}
</code>
</behavior>
```

6 Currently, a behavior body is manually written by the modeler in Java. This choice presents some limitations, notably i) the modeler is bound to have a good working knowledge of Java and ii) the effort requested to test a behavior can be significant. Future work aims at providing an easier to use proprietary language.

7 An example of interface definition is:

```
<interface>
<behavior name="push"
return="void"/>
```

```
<behavior name="pull"
return="void"/>
</interface>
```

8 Consider a SPN formalism that has a Place element and a Transition element (the complete definition will be presented later in this Chapter). An example of use of labels for a fictionary SPN MDL fragment, with four labels denoted as StartTokens, EndTokens, TransfRate and Transf2Rate is:

```
<mdl id="SPN" fdl="spn.fdl"
import="SPNconstants.ipt">
<Place id="Start"
Tokens="StartTokens" />
<Place id="End"
Tokens="EndTokens" />
<Transition id="Transf"
Rate="TransfRate" />
<Transition id="Transf2"
Rate="Transf2Rate" />
...
</mdl>
```

The fragment can be bound to desired values by the IPT document fragment:

```
<constants>
<constant name="StartTokens"
value="3" />
<constant name="EndTokens" val-
ue="0" />
<constant name="TransfRate" val-
ue="0.5" />
<constant name="Transf2Rate"
value="2" />
</constants>
```

that will produce the instantiated MDL elements:

```
<Place id="Start" Tokens="3" />
<Place id="End" Tokens="0" />
<Transition id="Transf"
Rate="0.5" />
<Transition id="Transf2" Rate="2"
/>.
```

9 For example, if the input is a FDL document representing a SPN, the FDL Analyzer will add the code for Place, Transition, Arc and Inhibitor Arc components.

10 . Note that some elements that have behaviors that interact with other elements, i. e. SPN Arcs, may refer to an elementType which currently is unknown as it could be defined later in the FDL document: in this case, the parser builds a symbol table, storing the details about every elementType.

11 The code also manages result storage by means of XML files, that will not descrive in this Chapter.

12 E. g.: SPN, Markov Chains (MC), Queuing Networks (QN), Fault Trees (FT) belong to the Exponential Events based formalism Family (EEF), as they all rely on solution algorithms based on exponentially distributed interarrival stochastic processes; Generalized Stochastic Petri Nets (GSPN) and Finite Capacity Queuing Networks (FCQN) belong to the Exponential and Iimmediate Events based formalism Family (EIEF), as they rely on solution algorithms that need the evaluation of events with zero duration before evaluating the effects of exponentially distributed interarrival stochastic processes. For these two families six different solution engines exist (called Se, Sg, Ces, Cgs, Cgt and Cet), designed to be the cores to build solvers for multiformalism models based on the families, with analytic steady state, analytic transient or simulative techniques. All the solution engines supports the execution of snapshots of the state of a model, including all the properties containing state information. The snapshots are then used by solvers to back track to a previous state: for example, the simulation based solvers reschedule all the events after each firing then repeat the analysis for a fixed number of runs. Each run is executed until a global maximum time is reached; statistics are collected only after a transient time of fixed length. Initially

a snapshot of the first state is taken, and then, after each run has finished, the snapshot is used to start a new simulation from the same initial state. The execution of each run calls a behavior to find all the enabled events, and then draws exponentially distributed samples for each of them.

13 Each elementType that represents a SPN arc in the SPN FDL implements Active to support this behavior.

14 Each elementType that represents a SPN arc in the SPN FDL implements PushPull to support this behavior.

15 This is the most elementary formulation of the FT formalism: there are more complex variants of it that allow more operators to be used.

16 There are different versions of RFT in literature, with different purposes: an example is given in (Codetta Raiteri et al 2004), in which the purpose is the evaluation of the effects of different repairing strategies on a system by means of a multiformalism approach based on OsMoSys (Vittorini et al. 2004).

17 Web Services Business Process Execution Language Version 2.0. OASIS Standard," 2007. Available at docs.oasis-open.org/wsbpel/2.0/wsbpel-v2.0.pdf

18 Connection arcs can be designed to handle communications between a PerfBPEL submodel and a submodel written in another formalism: to handle such a case, if the to value of the Connection arc is not a PerfBPEL submodel, the Push behavior of the Connection arc checks that its destination element implements the Occupancy interface. If this is the case, it uses the addoccupancy behavior to increase of one unity the occupancy of the destination element, e. g. to increase the number of tokens in a GSPN place, or the jobs in a FCQN queue.

19 Note that it is required that only the condition related to one Check element can be satisfied

at a given time: otherwise, the Test formalism will evolve following the specification associated to the first Next arc element as listed in the MDL document.

20 Note that the isActive interface is not implemented.

21 Some of the analytical techniques that have been applied to evaluate the performance impact of rejuvenation policies are Continuous Time Markov Chains (Huang et al. 1995), Non-Homogeneous Markov Chains (Koutrasa et al. 2007), Markov Regenerative Processes (Trivedi et al. 2000), Markov Regenerative Stochastic Petri Nets (Garg et al. 1995), Fluid Petri Nets (Bobbio et al. 2008).

22 The reader will notice that in this formalism there is no arc element: in a Software Rejuvenation model the relations between the elements are rather implemented by the formalism element, so they depend on the fact that some elements belong to a given sub model and consequently interact with each other. An important role is taken in this formalism by the bridge formalism, that must offer proper interformalism arc elements that do the trick. The Software Rejuvenation formalism basically offers as a tool, on which the design of interactions with the controlled models should be founded, that is a progressively numbered sequence of phases per each internal state of its components, that can be exploited by interformalism arcs by forcing elements of the performance submodel to check it against one or more reference level or by reòying on it to activate actions on elements of the performance model, generally oriented to modify some of their internal parameters according to a dedicated property.

23 During a system restart crashes cannot happen.

24 As a consequence, the rejuvenation also implicitly influences the probability of a crash event by reducing the rate at which it can happen.

Section 3
Applying Multiformalism:
Case Studies

This section presents modeling experiences coming from industrial applications.

Chapter 11
A Unified Modelling and Operational Framework for Fault Detection, Identification, and Recovery in Autonomous Spacecrafts

Andrea Bobbio
University of Piemonte Orientale, Italy

Daniele Codetta-Raiteri
University of Piemonte Orientale, Italy

Luigi Portinale
University of Piemonte Orientale, Italy

Andrea Guiotto
Thales Alenia Space, Italy

Yuri Yushtein
ESA-ESTEC, The Netherlands

ABSTRACT

Recent studies have focused on spacecraft autonomy. The traditional approach for FDIR (Fault Detection, Identification, Recovery) consists of the run-time observation of the operational status to detect faults; the initiation of recovery actions uses static pre-compiled tables. This approach is purely reactive, puts the spacecraft into a safe configuration, and transfers control to the ground. ARPHA is an FDIR engine based on probabilistic models. ARPHA integrates a high-level, a low-level, and an inference-oriented formalism (DFT, DBN, JT, respectively). The off-board process of ARPHA consists of the DFT construction by reliability engineers, the automatic transformation into DBN, the manual enrichment of the DBN, and the JT automatic generation. The JT is the on-board model undergoing analysis conditioned by sensor and plan data. The goal is the current and future state evaluation and the choice of the most suitable recovery policies according to their future effects without the assistance of the ground control.

DOI: 10.4018/978-1-4666-4659-9.ch011

INTRODUCTION

In autonomous spacecraft operations, both the system behavior and the environment can exhibit various degrees of uncertainty; control software must then provide the suitable and timely reaction of the system to changes in its operational environment, as well as in the operational status of the system. The operational status of the system depends on the internal system dependability factors (e.g. sub-system and component reliability models), on the external environment factors affecting the system reliability and safety (e.g. thermal, radiation, illumination conditions) and on system-environment interactions (e.g. stress factors, resource utilization profiles, degradation profiles, etc.). Combinations of these factors may cause mission execution anomalies, including mission degradations and system failures. To address possible system faults and failures, the system under examination must be provided with some form of health management procedures, usually relying on the *Fault Detection, Identification and Recovery* (FDIR) process.

The goal of the VERIFIM (*Verification of Failure Impact by Model-checking*) study is an innovative approach to on-board FDIR: the FDIR engine exploits an on-board probabilistic graphical model which must take into account the system architecture, the system environment, the system-environment interaction, and the dynamic evolution in presence of uncertainty and partial observability. Moreover, the on-board FDIR engine must provide the system with diagnosis (fault detection and identification) and prognosis (fault prediction) on the operational status to be taken into account for autonomous reactive or preventive recovery actions. To this aim, inside VERIFIM, we developed the software prototype called ARPHA (*Anomaly Resolution and Prognostic Health management for Autonomy*).

Before the execution of ARPHA (on-board process), the on-board model must be prepared. Since several aspects have to be represented by the on-board model, the modelling phase (off-

board process) integrates a high level modeling formalism (*Dynamic Fault Tree* (DFT) (Dugan et al., 1992)), a low level modeling formalism (*Dynamic Bayesian Network* (DBN) (Murphy, 2002)) and an inference oriented formalism (*Junction Tree* (JT) (Huang & Darwiche, 1996)). Basic notions about these formalisms are reported in the next section. The on-board model (JT) is obtained through a sequence of model conversions and model enrichment. We present a case study concerning the power supply subsystem of a Mars rover. This case study provides a running example for the off-board process (modelling phase) and the on-board process (diagnosis, prognosis and recovery of the system, conditioned by sensor data and plan data).

BACKGROUND

Currently employed state-of-the-art of the FDIR is based on the design-time analysis of the faults and failure scenarios (e.g. *Failure Mode Effect Analysis* (FMEA), *Fault Tree Analysis* (FTA) (Schneeweiss, 1999)) and run-time observation of the system operational status (health monitoring). The goal is in general to detect faults in a timely manner and to start a predefined recovery procedure (by using look-up tables), having the goal of putting the spacecraft into a known safe configuration and transfer control to the ground operations for troubleshooting and planning actual recovery.

Standard FDIR approaches have multiple shortcomings which may significantly reduce effectiveness of the adopted procedures:

- The system, as well as its environment, is only partially observable by monitoring procedures; this introduces uncertainty in the interpretation of observations in terms of the actual system status, which is often disregarded in choosing the possible recovery.

- Recovery is essentially triggered following a reactive approach, a post-factum operation, not capable of preventive measures and that cannot provide and utilise prognosis for the imminent failures.

The main source of such limits is recognized to be the fact that knowledge of the general operational capabilities of the system (that should potentially be expressed in terms of causal probabilistic relations) is not usually represented on-board, making impossible to estimate the impact of the occurred faults and failures on these capabilities. Several studies have tried to address these problems, some by restricting attention to manned systems (Schwabacher et al., 2008) or to systems requiring heavy human intervention (Robinson et al., 2003), some others by emphasizing the prognostic phase and relying on heuristics techniques to close the FDIR cycle (Glover et al., 2010).

BASIC NOTIONS ABOUT DFT, DBN, JT

Dynamic Fault Trees

Fault Tree (FT) (Schneeweiss, 1999) is the most diffused and popular model in Reliability analysis. A FT is a *directed acyclic graph* (DAG) representing how several combinations of *Basic Events* lead to the occurrence of a particular event called *Top Event*. Each basic event (component failure) has a certain probability to occur according to its failure rate. So, it is possible to compute the probability of occurrence of the top event (system failure). In FT, basic events are assumed to be independent and the combinations of basic events leading to the top event can only be expressed by means of *Boolean gates* (AND, OR, etc.) (Figure 1). Therefore the modeling power of FT is rather limited, so several extensions have been proposed in the literature (Dugan et al., 1992; Bobbio et al., 2003; Codetta et al., 2004).

Figure 1. Boolean gates: (a) AND, (b) OR

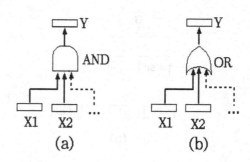

In particular, *Dynamic Fault Trees* (DFT) (Dugan et al., 1992) introduce *dynamic gates* representing dependencies: a dependency arises when the failure behavior of a component depends on the state of another component or subsystem. Dynamic gates represent several kinds of dependencies: functional dependencies, dependencies concerning the events order, and the presence of spare components. In particular, DFT introduce four dynamic gates: the *Warm Spare* (WSP), the *Sequence Enforcing* (SEQ), the *Functional Dependency* (FDEP) and the *Priority AND* (PAND) gate.

WSP Gate

A WSP dynamic gate models one primary component that can be substituted by one or more backups (spares), with the same functionality (see Figure 2 (a)), where spares are connected to the gate by means of "circle-headed" arcs). The WSP gate fails if its primary component fails and all of its spares have failed or are unavailable (a spare is unavailable if it is shared and being used by another spare gate). Spares can fail even while they are dormant, but the failure rate of an unpowered (i. e. dormant) spare is lower than the failure rate of the corresponding powered one. More precisely, being λ the failure rate of a powered spare, the failure rate of the unpowered spare is $\alpha\lambda$, with $0 \leq \alpha \leq 1$ (α is called the dormancy factor). Spares are more properly called "*hot*" if $\alpha=1$, and "*cold*" if $\alpha=0$.

Figure 2. Dynamic gates: (a) WSP, (b) FDEP, (c) PAND

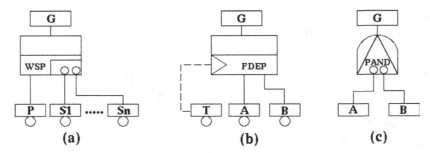

SEQ Gate

A SEQ gate forces its inputs to fail in a particular order: when a SEQ is found in a DFT, it never happens that the failure sequence takes place in a different order. SEQ gates can be modeled as a special case of a cold spare (Manian et al., 1999).

FDEP Gate

In the FDEP gate (Figure 2 (b)), one trigger event *T* (connected with a dashed arc in the figure) causes other dependent components to become unusable or inaccessible. In particular, when the trigger event occurs, the dependent components fail with probability $p_d \leq 1$; the separate failure of a dependent component, on the other hand, has no effect on the trigger event. FDEP has also a non-dependent output, that simply reflects the status of the trigger event and is called dummy output (i. e. not used in the analysis).

PDEP Gate

We have generalized the FDEP by defining a new gate, called *Probabilistic Dependency* (PDEP) gate (Portinale et al., 2010). In the PDEP, the probability of failure of dependent components, given that the trigger has failed, is $p_d \leq 1$.

PAND Gate

Finally, the PAND gate reaches a failure state if and only if all of its input components have failed in a preassigned order (from left to right in the graphical notation). While the SEQ gate allows the events to occur only in a preassigned order and states that a different failure sequence can never take place, the PAND does not force such a strong assumption: it simply detects the failure order and fails just in one case (in Figure 2 (c)) a failure occurs iff *A* fails before *B*, but *B* may fail before *A* without producing a failure in *G*).

DFT Analysis

The quantitative analysis of DFT typically requires to expand the model in its state space, and to solve the corresponding *Continuous Time Markov Chain* (CTMC) (Dugan et al., 1992). Through a process known as modularization (Dutuit & Rauzy, 1996; Gulati & Dugan, 2003), it is possible to identify the independent sub-trees with dynamic gates, and to use a different Markov model (much smaller than the model corresponding to the entire DFT) for each one of them. In Codetta, 2005, the modules are first translated into a Petri net by a suitable graph transformation technique, and then the corresponding CTMC is automatically generated from the Petri net. Nevertheless, there still exists the problem of state explosion.

In order to alleviate this limitation, as stated above, we propose a conversion of the DFT into a DBN. With respect to CTMC, the use of a DBN allows one to take advantage of the factorization in the temporal probability model. As a matter of fact, the conditional independence assumptions implicit in a DBN enable to confine the statistical dependence to a subset of the random variables representing component failures, providing a more compact representation of the probabilistic model. The system designer or analyst is faced with a more manageable and tractable representation where the complexity of specifying and using a global-state model (like a standard CTMC) is avoided; this is particularly important when the dynamic module of the considered DFT is significantly large.

Dynamic Bayesian Networks

Bayesian Networks (BN) (Koller & Friedman, 2009) have become a widely used formalism for representing uncertain knowledge in probabilistic systems. BN are defined by a DAG in which discrete random variables are assigned to each node, together with the conditional dependence on the parent nodes. In particular, each node has associated a *Conditional Probability Table* (CPT) specifying the probability of each value of the node, conditioned by every instantiation of parent nodes. Root nodes are nodes with no parents, and marginal prior probabilities are assigned to them. In this way, it is possible to include local conditional dependencies, by directly specifying the causes that influence a given effect. This allows computing the probability distribution of any variable given the observation of the values of any subset of the other variables.

Dynamic Bayesian Networks (DBN) (Murphy, 2002) extend standard BN formalism by providing an explicit discrete temporal dimension. DBN represent a probability distribution over the possible histories of a time-invariant process; the advantage with respect to a classical probabilistic temporal model like Markov Chains is that a DBN is a stochastic transition model factored over a

number of random variables, over which a set of conditional dependency assumptions is defined.

Time invariance ensures that the dependency model of the variables is the same at any point in time. While a DBN can in general represent semi-Markovian stochastic processes of order k-1, providing the modeling for k time slices, the term DBN is usually adopted when $k=2$ (i.e. only 2 time slices are considered in order to model the system temporal evolution; for this reason such models are also called 2-TBN or 2-*time-slice Temporal Bayesian Network*).

Given a set of time-dependent state variables $X_1...X_n$ and given a BN N defined on such variables, a DBN is essentially a replication of N over two time slices t and $t+\Delta$ (Δ being the so called discretization step), with the addition of a set of arcs representing the transition model. Letting X_i^t denote the copy of the variable X_i at time slice t, the transition model is defined through a distribution $Pr[X_i^{t+\Delta} \mid X_i^t, Y^t, Y^{t+\Delta}]$ where Y^t is any set of variables at slice t other than X_i (possibly the empty set), while $Y^{t+\Delta}$ is any set of variables at slice $t+\Delta$. other than X_i. Arcs interconnecting nodes at different slices are called inter-slice edges, while arcs interconnecting nodes at the same slice are called intra-slice edges. For each internal node, the conditional probabilities are stored in the *Conditional Probability Table* (CPT) in the form $Pr[X_i^{t+\Delta} \mid X_i^t, Y^t, Y^{t+\Delta}]$.

The conversion of the dynamic gates of Figure 2 into a DBN is considered in length in (Portinale, et al. 2007; Portinale et al., 2010), where it is shown that $Y^{t+\Delta}$ is non empty only in the case of the PDEP gate conversion. Of course a DBN defined as above (i.e. a 2-TBN) represents a discrete Markovian model. The two slices of a DBN are often called the anterior and the ulterior layer. Finally, it is useful to define the set of canonical variables as *{Y: $Y^t \in \cup_k parents[X_k^{t+\Delta}]$}*; they are the variables having a direct edge from the anterior layer to another variable in the ulterior layer. A DBN is in canonical form if only the canonical variables are represented at slice t (i.e. the anterior layer contains only variables having influence on the same variable or on another variable at the ulterior layer).

Given a DBN in canonical form, inter-slice edges connecting a variable in the anterior layer to the same variable in the ulterior layer are called temporal arcs; in other words, a temporal arc connects the variable X^t to the variable $X^{t+\Delta}$. The role of temporal arcs is to connect the nodes representing the copies of the same variable at different slices. It follows that no variable in the ulterior layer may have more than one entering temporal arc.

In previous works (Portinale et al., 2007; Portinale et al., 2010), we have shown that a DFT characterized as above, can be translated into a DBN in canonical form and the software tool *Radyban* has been developed to automate this process, as well as to edit and working with the resulting DBN for possibly augmenting the modeling features.

Algorithms for DBN Analysis

Concerning the analysis of a DBN, different kinds of inference algorithms are available. In particular, let X^t be a set of variables at time t, and $y_{a:b}$ any stream of observations from time point a to time point b (i.e. a set of instantiated variables Y_i^t with $a \leq t \leq b$). The following tasks can be performed over a DBN:

- **Filtering or Monitoring:** Computing $Pr(X^t \mid y_{0:t})$, i.e. tracking the probability of the system state taking into account the stream of received observations.
- **Prediction:** Computing $Pr(X^{t+h} \mid y_{0:t})$ for some horizon $h > 0$, i.e. predicting a future state taking into consideration the observation up to now (filtering is a special case of prediction with $h = 0$).
- **Smoothing:** Computing $Pr(X^{t-l} \mid y_{0:t})$ for some $l < t$, i.e. estimating what happened l

steps in the past given all the evidence (observations) up to now.

In particular, the difference between a filtering and a smoothing inference relies on the fact that in the former case, while computing the probability at time t ($0 \leq t \leq T$), only the evidence gathered up to time t is considered; on the contrary, in the case of smoothing the whole evidence stream is always considered in the posterior probability computation. It should also be clear that the specific task of prediction can be obtained by asking for a time horizon T greater than the last time point considered for an observation.

The classical computation of the unreliability of the top event of a DFT is a special case of filtering, with an empty stream of observations (i.e. it is a filtering assuming $y_{0:0}$). Smoothing may be, for instance, exploited in order to reconstruct the history of the system components for a kind of temporal diagnosis (e.g. given that the system has been observed failed at time t, to compute the probability of failure of basic components prior to t).

Different algorithms, either exact (i.e. computing the exact probability value that is required by the task) or approximate, can be exploited in order to implement the above tasks and some of them are available in *Radyban* (see Portinale et al., 2007 for more details).

Junction Tree

A way to efficiently compute conditioned probabilities on a (D)BN, consists of generating and analyzing the *Junction Tree* (JT) according to the procedures detailed in Huang & Darwiche, 1996. A JT is an undirected unrooted tree where each node (also called a cluster) corresponds to a set of nodes in the original (D)BN. The *Boyen-Koller* (BK) algorithm (Boyen & Koller, 1998) is a parametric JT-based inference strategy: the algorithm depends on some input parameters (set of nodes) called "*bk-clusters*"; according to the bk-clusters provided, it can produce approximate inference results with different degrees of accuracy. In particular, if the input is a unique bk-cluster containing all the so-called "*interface nodes*" of the DBN, the BK algorithm performs exact inference (see Boyen & Koller, 1998 for the details). The main reason for implementing approximate inference is that, in case of network models which are particularly hard to solve with exact inference, a reasonable approximation can trade-off time/space complexity and quality of the results[1].

Conversion of DFT into DBN

In this section, we present the conversion of each dynamic gate (WSP, PDEP, PAND) in the corresponding DBN. The rules to convert Boolean gates (AND, OR, K out of N) can be found in (Bobbio et al., 2001).

WSP Gate

In a DFT, different configurations of warm spares can be designed. Of particular interest are those in which the same pool of spares is shared across a set of WSP. In this case, each principal component is allowed to request the items in the pool in a precise order - if more than one is still dormant. As an example, let us consider a situation where two components A and B can be substituted by two spares $S1$ and $S2$. In particular, $S1$ is B's spare, and will substitute A only if B is working and $S2$ is failed. If B fails, it will request the activation of $S1$, and only if it is unavailable, it will activate $S2$. $S2$ is A's spare: analogous considerations hold. Every gate fails iff its principal component and all the available (i.e. working and dormant) spares in the pool fail. The DBN corresponding to this situation is shown in Figure 3.

It can be observed that each component node at time $t+\Delta$ depends on its copy at time t (we consider persistence of faults). Moreover, each spare depends on the two principal components, and on the other spare. Each spare is modeled as

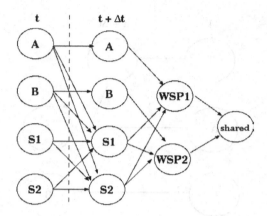

Figure 3. DBN for the WSP gate

a stochastic variable assuming four values, namely: dormant, operative on A, operative on B and failed. If both principal components are working, each spare maintains a failure rate equal to $\alpha\lambda$ at time $t+\Delta$. On the other hand, if B is down, $S1$ switches to a failure rate equal to λ (since the spare is now in the active mode); the same happens if B is working, but A and $S2$ are both failed. $S2$ works dually on its principal component A. Each WSP gate (in the example, the one having A as its principal component, and the one having B as its principal component) is modeled as a deterministic AND node among its three inputs: the principal components and the two spares in the pool. The overall set of WSP sharing the pool can be modeled as a $k{:}n$ Boolean gate (2:4 in the example), where n is the number of principal components and of available spares in the pool, and k is equal to the number of WSP gates sharing the spares.

PDEP Gate

Since the trigger event of a PDEP gate determines with a given probability, an immediate failure of its dependent components, a subsystem including a PDEP can be completely characterized resorting to intra-slice (i.e. static) conditional dependencies. Nevertheless, exploiting a dynamic network allows

Figure 4. DBN for the PDEP gate

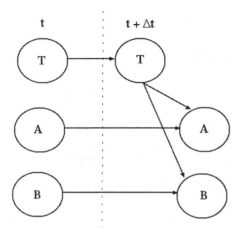

Figure 5. DBN for the PAND gate

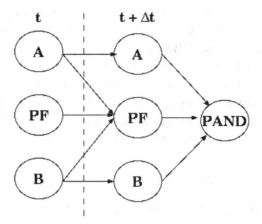

us to resort to a common framework for dynamic gates representation. Figure 4 shows the DBN for a PDEP gate in a configuration in which the trigger event T has two dependent components A and B. As usual, each component at time $t+\Delta$ depends on the component itself at time t. Moreover, the dependent components will fail (with probability p_d) if the trigger has failed in the same time slice.

PAND Gate

PAND gates model situations where a control component may prevent the system to crash (with ruinous consequences) because of the failure of a standard component. In such cases, a failure of the control component before the failure of the standard one prevents the recovery action of the control component, leading to a (sub)system failure. Consider the gate of Figure 2 (c): we can model the failure sequence by introducing a new stochastic variable PF, that explicitly keeps track of the order in which A and B fail.

PF at time $t+\Delta$ depends on all the variables at time t. In particular, if it was already failed at time t, it will remain failed at time $t+\Delta$. It will also fail iff $A(t)=1$ and $B(t)=0$, i.e. A fails before B. The PAND gate is modeled as a logic AND among its three inputs A, B and PF at time $t+\Delta$.

Figure 5 shows the resulting DBN. An hypothesis on how to deal with contemporary faults of A and B has to be made; for example, we have made the choice that a contemporary fault sets $PF(t + \Delta)$ to 1, and therefore leads to a fault of the whole gate.

A CASE STUDY

An example case study we have used to test ARPHA, concerns the power supply subsystem of a Mars rover, with a particular attention to the following aspects.

Solar Arrays

We assume the presence of three solar arrays (SA), namely SA1, SA2, SA3. In particular, SA1 is composed by two redundant strings, while SA2 and SA3 are composed by three strings. Each SA can generate power if both the following conditions hold: 1) at least one string is not failed; 2) the combination of sun aspect angle (SAA), optical depth (OD), and local time (day or night) is suitable. In particular, OD is affected by the presence or absence of shadow or storm. The total amount of generated power is proportional to the number of SAs which are actually working.

Load

The amount of load depends on the action performed by the rover. Actions may concern the plan or the recovery. Example of actions are: Wait, Drill, GNC (navigation), Pancam (use of panoramic camera).

Battery

We assume the battery to be composed by three redundant strings. The charge of the battery may be steady, decreasing or increasing according to the current levels of load and generation by SAs. The charge of the battery may be compromised by the damage of the battery occurring in two situations: all the strings are failed, or the temperature of the battery is low.

Scenarios

We are interested in four failure or anomaly scenarios. Each scenario can be recovered by specific policies:

S1: Low (anomaly) or very low (failure) power generation while SAA is not optimal.

Recovery policies:

- **P1:** Suspension of the plan in order in order to reduce the load.
- **P2:** Change of inclination of SA2 and SA3 in order to try to improve SAA and consequently the power generation (the tilting system cannot act on SA1).
  - **S2:** Low (anomaly) or very low (failure) power generation while OD is not optimal.

Recovery policies:

- **P3:** Movement of the rover into another position in order to try to avoid a shadowed area and improve OD and the power generation as a consequence.
- **P4:** Modification of the inclination of SA2 and SA3, retraction of the drill, and suspension of the plan.
  - **S3:** Low (anomaly) or very low (failure) battery level while drilling.

Recovery policies:

- **P4:** As above.
- **P5:** Retraction of the drill, suspension of the plan.
  - **S4:** Low (anomaly) or very low (failure) battery level while the battery is damaged.

Recovery policies:

- **P4:** As above.

MODELLING AND OPERATIONAL FRAMEWORK

Off-Board Process

The off-board process starts with a fault analysis phase concerning some basic knowledge about the system faults and failures, together with some knowledge about environmental/contextual conditions and their effects and impacts on the system behavior (possibly either nominal or faulty). This phase is aimed at constructing (by standard and well-known dependability analysis procedures) a first dependability model that we assume to be a DFT. The choice of this formalism is due to several reasons: reliability engineers are familiar with DFT, dependencies can be represented, conversion rules are available to obtain the equivalent DBN.

The DFT produced by the fault analysis phase can be automatically compiled into a DBN. The added value given by the use of DBN consists of the possibility to easily compute probability measures conditioned by the observation of specific events or conditions. This possibility is essential in the onboard process, in order to perform diagnosis, prognosis and recovery conditioned by the observation of sensor data and plan data.

The DBN obtained from the DFT represents the same stochastic process: the DBN initially contains only binary variables, dependencies due to dynamic gates, and deterministic relations due to Boolean gates.

Some properties in the DFT have to be relaxed or extended in order to represent particular aspects of the system behaviour that the DFT formalism cannot express. In order to improve the accuracy of the model, the DBN model is enriched with knowledge about more specific system capabilities and failures, with particular attention to the identification of multi-state components and stochastic dependencies not captured at the DFT language level. Multi-state components require variables whose number of possible values is equal to the number of possible states. So, existing variables may be increased in terms of size (number of possible values), or new variables may be introduced with a size greater than two. The introduction of new or more complex dependencies may require the addition of new variables and new arcs connecting variables, with the consequent update of the CPTs. Boolean relations established by Boolean gate can be modified in order to be non-deterministic, by introducing some noise in the relation (Noisy-OR, Noisy-AND); this can be done by changing the entries of the CPTs of the variables corresponding to Boolean gates.

The aim is to generate a DBN representing all the needed knowledge about failure impacts. In particular, during the enrichment of the DBN, both knowledge about plan actions or recovery actions can be incorporated into the DBN. In particular, we model the effects of action on the state of components or services. Actions will be modelled by introducing new variables, and their effect will be represented by adding new influence arcs between such variables and those already present in the model.

The design that has been done with the DFT model is preserved at DBN level, for those parts of the DFT which actually capture the system behaviour. If specific aspects are not represented by the DFT, then some parts of the DBN will be modified or added.

In ARPHA, we decided to implement the DBN analysis by resorting to JT inference algorithms. So, another role of the off-board process is the generation of the JT from the DBN. This is performed according to the procedures presented in Huang & Darwiche, 1996.

The DFT definition, its compilation into DBN, and the enrichment of the DBN are supported by the *Radyban* tool (Portinale et al., 2007), previously realized and exploiting *Draw-Net* (Codetta et al. 2006) as graphical interface in order to edit both the DFT and the DBN. An ad-hoc JT generator has been implemented inside VERI-FIM, and the resulting JT can be visualized still by means of *Draw-Net*. The XML interchange format of *Draw-Net* has been exploited to define the formalisms DFT, DBN, JT, and generate the respective models.

The off-board process is completed by the definition of the *utility function* which will be necessary in the on-board process: the *expected utility* (EU) of recovery policies is computed according to the utility function and the probability distribution of the variables involved in such function. We provide the utility function on a [0, 1] scale and is necessary to compare the recovery policies in case of failure or anomaly detection due to power supply problems.

DFT Model of the Case Study

The DFT model of the case study (Figure 7) represents the combinations of events or states leading to the top event (*TE*) corresponding to the anomaly or failure of the whole system. *TE* is the output of an OR gate and occurs if the event *S1*, *S2*, *S3*, or *S4* happens. The event *S1* represents the scenario S1 and is the output of an AND gate. *S1* occurs if both the events *PowGen* and *AngleSA2* occur. They represent an anomaly/failure about the power generation (for instance, a low level of generated power) and a not optimal SAA for SA2 (we assume that SAA of SA2 is similar to SAA of SA1 and SA3). *PowGen* occurs if all the events *PowGenSA1*, *PowGenSA2* and *PowGenSA3* happen. Each of them represents the fact that a SA is not producing energy. For example, *PowGenSA1* concerns SA1 and happens if *StringsSA1* occurs (all the strings of SA1 are failed) or *SA1perf* occurs (the combination of local time (day or night), OD and SAA of SA1 does not allow the generation of energy). OD is not optimal in case of storm or shadow.

The event *S2* occurs if both *PowGen* and *OpticalDepth* happen. *S3* occurs if both *BattCharge* and *Drill* occur; they represent an anomaly/failure about the level of charge of the battery, and the drill actions in execution, respectively. *BattCharge* in turns occurs if both the events *Balance* and *BattFail* happen.

Balance represents the fact that the use of the battery is necessary: *Balance* happens if both *PowGen* and *Load* occur. The second event represents the presence of a load (consume of energy). The event *BattFail* models the damage of the battery because of the failure of all its strings (event *BattStrings*) or a low temperature (event *Temp*). Finally, *S4* occurs if both the events *BattCharge* and *BattFail* happen.

The model contains two FDEP gates. The first one represents the influence of *ActionId* on other events, such as *Load*, *Drill* (in case of drilling actions), *DrillRetract* (drill in or out), *AngleSA1*, *AngleSA2*, *AngleSA3* (in case of tilting actions), *Shadow* (in case of travelling actions), and *MechShock* (possibility of mechanical shock damaging the battery strings, in case of drilling or travelling

Figure 6. ARPHA off-board process and on-board process

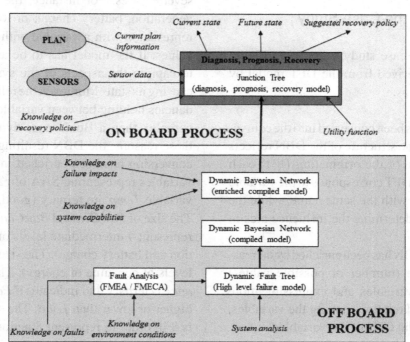

Figure 7. DFT model of the case study

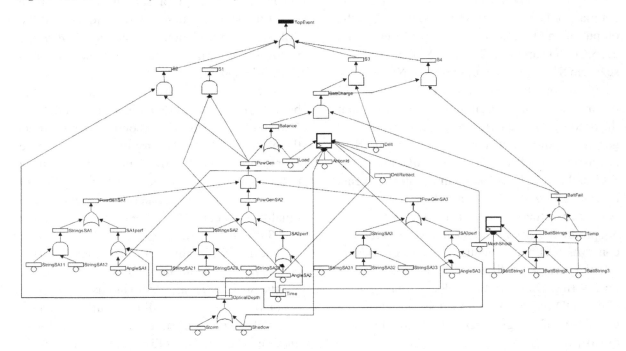

actions). *MechShock* influences in turns the events *BattString1, BattString2, BattString3* by means of the second FDEP gate.

DBN Model of the Case Study

The DBN of the case study reported in Figure 8 (a) has been derived from the DFT model by following two steps:

1. The DFT has been converted into the equivalent DBN: the structure of the DBN reflects the structure of the originating DFT: each event in the DFT corresponds to the variable in the DBN with the same name, while the DFT gates determine the influence arcs in the DBN.
2. Then, the DBN has been enriched by increasing the size (number of possible values) of several variables and expressing more complicated relations among the variables, by editing the CPT of the variables.

The DFT contains Boolean (binary) events (variables) representing the state of components or subsystems. This lacks of modeling power in several cases. For instance, the level of power generation, battery charge, or load needs to be represented with a variable with more than two values, if the model has to be accurate enough to capture the aspects of the system behaviour causing its state. Moreover, the relations or dependencies holding between variables may be more complex than a Boolean or dynamic gate. For these reasons, the DBN resulting from the DFT conversion has been enriched in this sense: the variables representing SAA of each SA, and the variable *Temp* are ternary (good, discrete, bad). The size of *PowGen* and *BattCharge* is 4 (we can represent 4 intermediate levels of power generation and battery charge). The size of *Load* is 5 (5 levels of consume of energy). The variable *Balance* is ternary and indicates if *PowGen* is equal, higher or lower than *Load*. The size of *ActionId* is 8 in order to represent 8 actions of interest in

Figure 8. a) DBN model of the case study. b) utility function

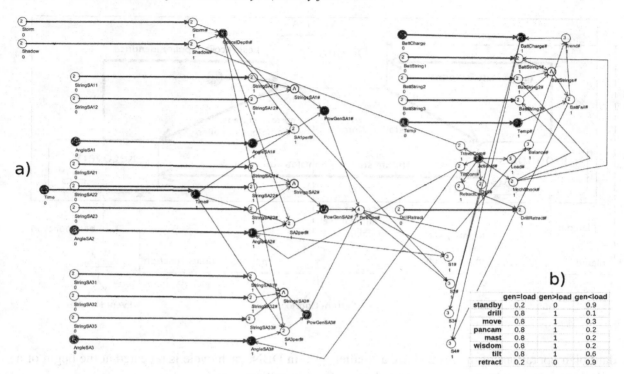

	gen=load	gen>load	gen<load
standby	0.2	0	0.9
drill	0.8	1	0.1
move	0.8	1	0.3
pancam	0.8	1	0.2
mast	0.8	1	0.2
wisdom	0.8	1	0.2
tilt	0.8	1	0.6
retract	0.2	0	0.9

the model (6 plan actions and 2 recovery actions). The variables *S1*, *S2*, *S3*, *S4* are ternary in order to represent the states Normal, Anomalous and Failed in each scenario (the Normal state indicates that the scenario is not happening).

In the DBN we added some support variables in order to reduce the number of entries in the CPT of the non binary variables by applying the so-called "divorcing" technique (Portinale et al., 2007). The support variables are: *TravelCom*, *Drill-Com* and *RetractCom* depending on *ActionId*, and *Trend* depending on *Balance* and *BattFail*. In the DBN, if a variable has a temporal evolution, it has two instances, one for each time slice (*t, t+Δ*); the two instances are connected by a "temporal" arc appearing as a thick line in Figure 8 (a). For instance, *StringSA11* and *StringSA11#* are connected by a temporal arc, in order to express that the state of the first string of SA1 at *t+Δ* depends on its state at *t*. Still in Figure 8 (a), the observable variables are put in evidence (black nodes); the values com-

ing from the sensors will become observations for such variables during the analysis of the model. The plan actions and the recovery actions will become observations for the variable *ActionId*.

The JT is derived from the DBN model in Figure 8 (a). The utility function in Figure 8 (b) is exploited for Recovery and provides utility values for the combinations of the possible actions and the balance between power generation and load. Notice that there are actions (standby and retract of the drill) that, when used in recovery policies, are meant to avoid the rover halting in an unsafe condition (for example with the drill locked on the ground, with the danger of icing during the night); such actions have a large utility for cases corresponding to low power supply situations (meaning that they are useful for recovering situations where the generated power is less than the load), while they have a small utility in case the power supply is sufficient to cover the required load. Remaining actions (which are also usual stan-

Figure 9. The UML-like diagram of the functionalities of ARPHA

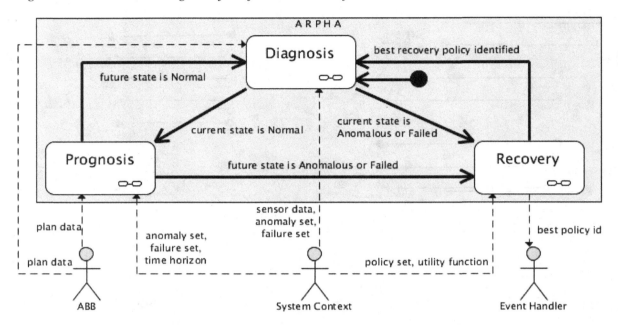

dard plan operations of the rover) have a smaller utility in correspondence to cases related to low power supply situations, since in such cases one should avoid power consuming actions.

On-Board Process

The on-board process is performed by the ARPHA prototype and operates on a JT as actual operational model, receiving observations from both sensors and plan actions (Figure 6). It is intended to perform Diagnosis (current state detection), Prognosis (future state detection) and Recovery (evaluation of the best recovery policy). Figure 9 shows the external components (actors) that interact with ARPHA: *System Context* (memory area that contains data received from sensors, and the configuration of the system), *Autonomy Building Block* or ABB (dedicated to plan execution and plan generation), *Event Handler* (the manager of events, receiving from ARPHA the id of the policy to be performed to recover the system).

ARPHA cyclically performs the following functionalities (Figure 9). Since time is discrete in DBN, each cycle is repeated at the begin of a new time step.

Diagnosis

Diagnosis begins with the retrieval of data necessary for on-board reasoning. In particular, sensor and plan data are retrieved from System Context and ABB respectively. Both kinds of data are converted in form of observations concerning specific variables of the on-board model. Observations are loaded into the on-board model; then, the model inference (analysis) is performed at the current time and returns the probability distribution of the variables in the model. The inspection of the probabilities of specific variables representing the system state, can provide the diagnosis at the current mission time: the possible system states are Normal (no anomalies or failures are detected), Anomalous (an anomaly[2] is detected) or Failed (a failure is detected). If the current state detected is Normal, then Prognosis is performed, else Recovery is performed (as depicted in Figure 9).

Prognosis

Prognosis is performed only if the current state is Normal, and consists of the future state detection. The on-board model is analyzed in the future according to a specific time horizon and taking into account observations given by future plan actions. Future state is detected according to the probability distribution obtained for the variable representing the system state. The future state can be Normal, Anomalous, or Failed. In case of Normal state, the ARPHA on-board process restarts at the next time step, with the Diagnosis phase, otherwise Recovery is performed (Figure 9).

Recovery

Recovery can be distinguished in Reactive Recovery (performed if the current system state is Failed) or Preventive Recovery (performed in case of Anomalous current state, Anomalous future state, or Failed future state). In both cases, Recovery is performed in this way: given the detected anomaly or failure, the recovery policies facing that anomaly or failure are retrieved from System Context. In particular, each recovery policy is composed by a set of recovery actions, possibly to be executed at different times. Each policy is evaluated in this way:

1. The policy is converted into a set of observations for the on-board model variables representing actions.
2. Such observations are loaded in the on-board model which is analyzed in the future.
3. According to the probability distribution returned by the analysis, and a specific utility function, the *expected utility* (EU) of the policy is computed. In other words, EU quantifies the future effects of the recovery policy on the system. The policy providing the best EU is selected and notified to the Event Handler for the execution. Then, the

ARPHA on-board process restarts at the next time step, with Diagnosis (Figure 9).

ARPHA's Architecture

ARPHA is composed by several modules. In particular, JT Handler implements the BK inference algorithm with the goal of providing the posterior probabilities over the variables of interest to the other components that need them (e.g. State Detector and Policy Evaluator). The details about the internal architecture of ARPHA are provided in (Portinale & Codetta, 2011b). In order to perform an empirical evaluation of the approach, ARPHA has been deployed in an evaluation platform composed by a workstation linked to a PC via Ethernet cable. A rover simulator (called ROSEX) has been installed on the workstation. On the PC we installed the TSIM environment, emulating the on-board computing hardware/OS environment (LEON3/RTEMS), and the ARPHA executable. ARPHA will run in parallel to other processes of the on-board software.

Executing ARPHA on the Case Study.

We provide an example of ARPHA execution during a simulated mission; for the sake of brevity, we describe only the initial steps of the mission. Sensors data and plan data that simulator provides are the following: OD, power generated by each SA, SAA of SA1, SA2, SA3, charge of the battery, temperature of battery, mission elapsed time, action under execution, plan under execution.

Figure 10 (a) shows a graphical representation of the plan where the x-axys represents the mission time step, while the y-axis represents the possible plan actions (it does not include recovery actions). In Figure 10 (b) we show the OD profile generated by rover simulator. Figure 10 (c) shows the power generation profile related to the OD profile in Figure 10 (b).

At the begin of each cycle of the on-board process (Figure 9), the current sensor data and

Figure 10. Scenario S2: a) plan. b) Optical Depth (OD). c) Power generation by SA1, SA2, SA3

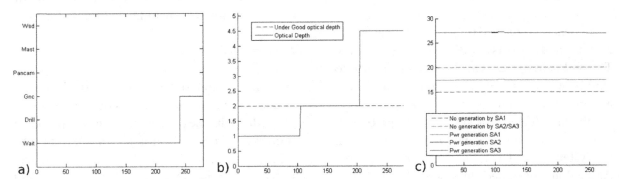

plan data are retrieved and converted into current or future observations for specific variables in the on-board model. Such observations are expressed as the probability distribution of the possible variable values. For example, the "*wait*" action in the plan at time step 3, is converted in the probability distribution 1, 0, 0, 0, 0, 0, 0, 0 concerning the variable *ActionId* in the same step. The first value of the distribution indicates that the first possible value of the variable (0) has been observed with probability 1. This is due to the fact that ActionId represents in the model the current plan action (or recovery action). In particular, the value 0 corresponds to the "*wait*" action.

An example about sensor data is the sensor *pwrsa1* providing the value 17.22273 at time step 3. This value becomes the probability distribution 1, 0 for the values of the variable *PowGenSA1*. In other words, *PowGenSA1* is observed equal to 0 with probability 1 at the same mission step, in order to represent that SA1 is generating power in that step (the value 1 represents instead the absence of power generation).

Diagnosis

At time steps 0, 1, 2, ARPHA detects Normal state as the result of both diagnosis and prognosis. Figure 11 shows the output of ARPHA at time step 3 (corresponding to 218 sec. of the

mission time): lines 01-04 contain the values of the sensors (generated by the rover simulator) and the plan action under execution (SVF action); lines 06-16 concern the diagnosis. In particular, at lines 07-08, the plan action (SVF action=1="*wait*") performed in the current time step, is converted into the observation *ActionId*=0; at lines 09-12, the sensor values are mapped into observations of the corresponding variable values: *pwrsa1*=17.22273 becomes *PowGenSA1*=0 (power generation by SA1 is high), *pwrsa2*=26.67850 becomes *PowGenSA2*=0 (power generation by SA2 is high), *pwrsa1*=6.67641 becomes *PowGenSA3*=0 (power generation by SA3 is high), *saa1*=0.51575 becomes *AngleSA1*=0 (SAA1 is optimal), *saa2*=0.515750 becomes *AngleSA2*=0 (SAA2 is optimal), *saa3*=0.515750 becomes *AngleSA3*=0 (SAA3 is optimal), *opticaldepth*=4.50000 becomes *OpticalDepth*=1 (OD is not optimal), etc. Given such observations, ARPHA performs the inference of the model at the current time step (line 13), querying the variables *S1#*, *S2#*, *S3#*, *S4#* representing the occurrence of the scenarios (lines 14-15). The probability that *S1#* = 1 (anomaly) or *S1#* = 2 (failure) is lower than a predefined threshold, so S1 is not detected. The same condition holds for scenarios S2, S3, S4, so the result of diagnosis is Normal state (line 16).

Figure 11. ARPHA output at time step (or mission step) 3

```
00   *** MISSION STEP: 3 (MISSION TIME: 218 sec.) ***
01   *************** ROSEX VALUES ***************
02   opticaldepht = 4.50000  pwrsa1 = 17.22273  pwrsa2 = 26.67850  pwrsa3 = 26.67641
03   saa1 = 0.51575          saa2 = 0.51575     saa3 = 0.51575     batterycharge = 90.28925
04   batttemp = 273.00000    time = 10.05112    SVF_action = 1     SVF_plan = 1
05   *********************************************
06   ## Diagnosis ##
07   Propagate PLAN STREAM
08   3:ActionId#:1 0 0 0 0 0 0 0
09   Propagate SENSORS STREAM
10   3:OpticalDepth#:0 1  3:PowGenSA1#:1 0  3:PowGenSA2#:1 0  3:PowGenSA3#:1 0
11   3:AngleSA1#:1 0 0  3:AngleSA2#:1 0 0  3:AngleSA3#:1 0 0  3:BattCharge#:0 0 0 1
12   3:Temp#:0 1 0      3:Time#:1 0
13   Current inference (STEP 3)
14   Pr{S1#=2}=0.00<0.59  Pr{S2#=2}=0.00<0.59  Pr{S3#=2}=0.00<0.59  Pr{S4#=2}=0.00<0.59
15   Pr{S1#=1}=0.00<0.59  Pr{S2#=1}=0.00<0.59  Pr{S3#=1}=0.00<0.59  Pr{S4#=1}=0.00<0.59
16   SYSTEM STATE: "Normal"
17   ## Prognosis ##
18   Propagate PLAN STREAM
19   4:ActionId#:1 0 0 0 0 0 0 0  5:ActionId#:1 0 0 0 0 0 0 0
20   6:ActionId#:1 0 0 0 0 0 0 0  7:ActionId#:0 0 1 0 0 0 0 0
21   Future inference (STEP 7)
22   Pr{S1#=2}=0.384715<0.59  Pr{S2#=2}=0.606048>=0.59        Pr{S3#=2}=0.019669<0.59
23   Pr{S4#=2}=0.052145<0.59  Pr{S1#=1} excluded because under recovery or minor criticality
24   Pr{S2#=2} excluded because under recovery or minor criticality  Pr{S3#=1}=0.099446<0.59
25   Pr{S4#=1}=0.298603<0.59
26   FUTURE SYSTEM STATE: "Failed" (S2#=2)
27   ## Preventive Recovery ##
28   Policy to convert: P3
29   Propagate POLICY STREAM
30   4:ActionId#:0 0 1 0 0 0 0 0  5:ActionId#:0 0 1 0 0 0 0 0
31   Future inference (STEP 13)
32   Utility Function = 0.0890
33   Policy to convert: P4
34   Propagate POLICY STREAM
35   4:ActionId#:0 0 0 0 0 0 1 0  5:ActionId#:0 0 0 0 0 0 1 0  6:ActionId#:0 0 0 0 0 0 0 1
36   7:ActionId#:0 0 0 0 0 0 0 1
37   8:ActionId#:1 0 0 0 0 0 0 0  9:ActionId#:1 0 0 0 0 0 0 0  10:ActionId#:1 0 0 0 0 0 0 0
38   11:ActionId#:1 0 0 0 0 0 0 0
39   12:ActionId#:1 0 0 0 0 0 0 0  13:ActionId#:1 0 0 0 0 0 0 0
40   Future inference (STEP 13)
41   Utility Function= 0.8764
42   Best policy for Preventive Recovery is P4
```

Prognosis

Since Diagnosis has returned Normal state, Prognosis is activated (lines 17-26). The future actions in the plan become observations for the variable ActionId (lines 18-20); then, the model inference is executed (line 21), still querying the variables $S1\#$, $S2\#$, $S3\#$, $S4\#$ (lines 22-25), but analyzing the model in the future (next four time steps). At line 22, $Pr(S2\# = 2)$ is greater than a given threshold, so ARPHA detects S2 and in particular, the Failed state (line 26).

Recovery

Preventive recovery is activated (lines 27-42) due to Prognosis result, with the aim of evaluating the policies P3 and P4, suitable to deal with S2. At lines 28-30, the actions inside P3 become observations in the next time steps, for the variable *ActionId*. In particular, we observe the "*move*" action in the future time steps 4 and 5 (line 30). Given such observations, the model is inferenced for 10 time steps in the future (line 31) and EU is computed (line 32). The same procedure is applied to P4 (lines 33-41). The actions inside P4 become evidences for *ActionId* (lines 34-39): the "*tilt*" action (SA inclination) is observed at time steps 4 and 5, "*retract drill*" is observed at time steps 6 and 7, "*wait*" is observed at time steps from 8 to 13[3]. According to such observations, the model is analyzed in the future, still for the next 10 time steps (line 40) and EU is computed (line 41). P4 provides a better EU, so P4 is suggested by ARPHA for execution (line 42)[4].

FUTURE RESEARCH AND DIRECTIONS

The DFT formalism is rather simple, so the design of the DFT model does not require a modeller with particular skills. The DBN enrichment instead, actually requires a modeller with a specific experience in Bayesian modelling. In particular, the editing of CPTs needs a particular attention in order to consider any possible case and avoid cases not compatible with observations. In order to limit this problem, inside VERIFIM, DFT formalism has been extended to EDFT (Portinale & Codetta, 2011a). If an automatic translator from EDFT to DBN was developed, the effort to enrich the DBN would be less relevant because several features may be directly modelled in EDFT form, and translated into DBN in automatic way. In order to design an accurate stochastic model, knowledge about probability parameters, such as component failure rates, has to be provided. Such values may not be immediately available. Another not negligible aspect is the link between computing time and model accuracy. The complexity of the DBN model depends on the number of entries in the CPTs of variables. This number depends on the number of possible values and the number of parents of the variables. It is necessary to perform a trade-off between the model accuracy and the computing time, taking into account that on-board hardware has limited computing power.

CONCLUSION

ARPHA aims at keeping as much standard as possible the fault analysis phase, by allowing reliability engineers to build their fault models using an intuitive and familiar modelling language such as DFT. By the enrichment of the DBN obtained from the DFT, we are able to address issues that are very important in the context of innovative on-board FDIR: multi-state components with different fault modes, stochastic dependencies among system components, system-environment interactions. A case study has been presented in order to show the steps of the modelling phase and the innovative capabilities of ARPHA: diagnosis under partial observability of the system and the environment, possibility to perform the prognosis, dealing with recovery policies composed by several actions performed at different times, evaluation of the future effects of recovery policies. Actually, ARPHA is a reasoning based FDIR system: diagnosis, prognosis and recovery decisions derive from the analysis (inference) of the on-board model, while traditional FDIR is simply based on sensor monitoring for diagnosis, and look-up tables for recovery actions, without any prognosis capability.

ACKNOWLEDGMENT

This work has been funded by European Space Agency (ESA/ESTEC) under the VERIFIM study (grant n. TEC-SWE/09259/YY).

REFERENCES

Bobbio, A., Franceschinis, G., Gaeta, R., & Portinale, L. (2003). Parametric fault tree for the dependability analysis of redundant systems and its high-level Petri net semantics. *IEEE Transactions on Software Engineering*, 29(3), 270–287. doi:10.1109/TSE.2003.1183940.

Bobbio, A., Portinale, L., Minichino, M., & Ciancamerla, E. (2001). Improving the analysis of dependable systems by mapping fault trees into Bayesian networks. *Reliability Engineering & System Safety, 71*(3), 249–260. doi:10.1016/S0951-8320(00)00077-6.

Boyen, X., & Koller, D. (1998). Tractable inference for complex stochastic processes. In *Proceedings of the Conference on Uncertainty in Artificial Intelligence* (pp. 33–42). AUAI

Codetta-Raiteri, D. (2005). *Extended fault trees analysis supported by stochastic Petri nets*. (Ph.D. Thesis). University of Turin, Turin, Italy.

Codetta-Raiteri, D., Franceschinis, G., & Gribaudo, M. (2006). Defining formalisms and models in the draw-net modelling system. In *Proceedings of the International Workshop on Modelling of Objects, Components and Agents* (pp. 123-144). IEEE.

Codetta-Raiteri, D., Franceschinis, G., Iacono, M., & Vittorini, V. (2004). Repairable fault tree for the automatic evaluation of repair policies. In *Proceedings of the International Conference on Dependable Systems and Networks* (pp. 659-668). Florence, Italy: IEEE.

Dugan, J., Bavuso, S., & Boyd, M. (1992). Dynamic fault-tree models for fault-tolerant computer systems. *IEEE Transactions on Reliability, 41*, 363–377. doi:10.1109/24.159800.

Dutuit, Y., & Rauzy, A. (1996). A linear-time algorithm to find modules of fault trees. *IEEE Transactions on Reliability, 45*, 422–425. doi:10.1109/24.537011.

Glover, W., Cross, J., Lucas, A., Stecki, C., & Stecki, J. (2010). The use of PHM for autonomous unmanned systems. In *Proceedings of the Conference of PHM Society*. PHM.

Gulati, R., & Dugan, J. B. (2003). A modular approach for analyzing static and dynamic fault-trees. In *Proceedings of the Annual Reliability and Maintainability Symposium* (pp. 57-63). IEEE.

Huang, C., & Darwiche, A. (1996). Inference in belief networks: A procedural guide. *International Journal of Approximate Reasoning, 15*, 225–263. doi:10.1016/S0888-613X(96)00069-2.

Koller, D., & Friedman, N. (2009). *Probabilistic graphical models: Principles and techniques*. Cambridge, MA: MIT Press.

Manian, R., Coppit, D. W., Sullivan, K. J., & Dugan, J. B. (1999). Bridging the gap between systems and dynamic fault tree models. In *Proceedings of the Annual Reliability and Maintainability Symposium* (pp. 105-111). IEEE.

Murphy, K. (2002). *Dynamic Bayesian networks: Representation, inference and learning*. (Ph.D. Thesis). UC Berkeley, Berkeley, CA.

Portinale, L., Bobbio, A., Codetta-Raiteri, D., & Montani, S. (2007). Compiling dynamic fault trees into dynamic Bayesian nets for reliability analysis: The Radyban tool. In *Proceedings of CEUR Workshop Proceedings*. CEUR.

Portinale, L., & Codetta-Raiteri, D. (2011a). Using dynamic decision networks and extended fault trees for autonomous FDIR. In *Proceedings of the International Conference on Tools with Artificial Intelligence* (pp. 480-484). IEEE.

Portinale, L., & Codetta-Raiteri, D. (2011b). ARPHA: An FDIR architecture for autonomous spacecrafts based on dynamic probabilistic graphical models. In *Proceedings of ESA Workshop on AI in Space*. ESA.

Portinale, L., Codetta-Raiteri, D., & Montani, S. (2010). Supporting reliability engineers in exploiting the power of dynamic Bayesian networks. *International Journal of Approximate Reasoning, 51*(2), 179–195. doi:10.1016/j.ijar.2009.05.009.

Robinson, P., Shirley, M., Fletcher, D., Alena, R., Duncavage, D., & Lee, C. (2003). Applying modelbased reasoning to the FDIR of the command and data handling subsystem of the ISS. In *Proceedings of the International Symposium on Artificial Intelligence, Robotics and Automation in Space*. IEEE.

Schneeweiss, W. G. (1999). *The fault tree method*. LiLoLe Verlag.

Schwabacher, M., Feather, M., & Markosian, L. (2008). Verification and validation of advanced fault detection, isolation and recovery for a NASA space system. In *Proceedings of the International Symposium on Software Reliability Engineering*. IEEE.

KEY TERMS AND DEFINITIONS

2-TBN: 2-time-slice Temporal Bayesian Network.

ABB: Autonomy Building Block.

ARPHA: Anomaly Resolution and Prognostic Health management for Autonomy.

BN: Bayesian Network.

CPT: Conditional Probability Table.

CTMC: Continuous Time Markov Chain.

DBN: Dynamic Bayesian Network.

DFT: Dynamic Fault Tree.

EU: Expected Utility.

JT: Junction Tree.

FDEP: Functional Dependency gate.

FDIR: Failure Detection, Identification and Recovery.

FMEA: Failure Mode Effect Analysis.

FT: Fault Tree.

FTA: Fault Tree Analysis.

OD: Optical depth.

PAND: Priority and gate.

PDEP: Probabilistic Dependency gate.

SA: Solar Array.

SAA: Sun Aspect Angle.

SEQ: Sequence Enforcing Gate.

TE: Top Event.

VERIFIM: Verification of Failure Impact by Model-checking.

WSP: Warm Spare gate.

ENDNOTES

[1] The assumption is also that, since the networks used by ARPHA have a reasonable number of observed variables (i.e. each relevant system component is a sensored component and sensors have a high accuracy), then the approximation error is bounded by conditioning on the next set of observations during a temporal inference.

[2] An anomaly is a malfunctioning possibly leading to a failure in the near future.

[3] The number of actions inside a policy is not constant. Therefore the duration of a policy depends on the number of actions and the duration of each action. For instance, P3 and P4 generate observations for 2 and 10 time steps in the future, respectively, because of their internal actions.

[4] This is justified, since the movement in another position (P3) does not guarantee to improve power generation, while the tilting action in P4 is more effective.

Chapter 12
A Model–Driven Methodology to Evaluate Performability of Metro Systems

Roberto Nardone
Università di Napoli "Federico II", Italy

Stefano Marrone
Seconda Università di Napoli, Italy

ABSTRACT

Metro systems are required to continuously achieve acceptable levels of reliability, availability, maintainability, and performance (performability) in order to comply with the target values reported in operation and maintenance contracts. These requirements are regulated by several international standards that control the lifecycle defining both processes, documentation flows, and enabling techniques, aiming at controlling disturbances on service performed by the system. This chapter focuses on a complete model-driven methodology with the aim to support the performability evaluation of a metro system during design and in-service phases, as well as requirements assessment. In detail, the methodology allows the automatic generation of those formal models required for performability analysis, specialized according to the specific track layout and the defined operational strategies. The proposed methodology is perfectly coherent with the European Standard CENELEC EN 50126 and it allows the generation of all the technical reports needed in the related documentation.

INTRODUCTION

Metro systems are rapid transit train systems, operating in an urban area with a high capacity and frequency, totally independent from other traffic. These systems are demand-oriented systems, since the reasons why they are built are strongly related to people transportation. The achievement of good Quality of Service levels, offered to passengers, is, for the most part, linked to the attainment of acceptable levels of Reliability, Availability, Maintainability and Performance (Performability). More and more often target values are defined in contracts for the designer companies, and their attainment is strictly connected with economic bonus (when exceeded) and penalties (when not reached). Lastly the achievement of good Quality of Service levels increases the system competitive-

DOI: 10.4018/978-1-4666-4659-9.ch012

ness in the people transportation domain, which is really important for system operators.

A Metro system can be classified as a complex system, due to its large-sized distributed architecture and to the components heterogeneity, both hardware and software, as well as their continuous and discrete temporal evolution. This complexity makes the design, construction and maintenance very difficult, in particular with the aim of controlling both the Quality of Service and the Performability: it is necessary a continuous assessment during all the lifecycle, including also operation phase.

Quality of Service (QoS) offered to customers hence represents the main requirement a Metro System shall satisfy, and it needs to be considered by operators (Kotler, 1991). The QoS is a measure of the "customers' satisfaction", it estimates different issues such as cost of tickets, waiting time at stations, total on-board travel time, cleanness, safety level, travel time variability and so on. According to classical literature in the field of transportation engineering (Cascetta, 2009), customer satisfaction is maximized when the so called "users' generalized cost" is minimized, where the independent variables are bounded among a certain set of discrete alternatives. Specifically for a single passenger, the generalized cost (C_i), choosing an alternative i, can be expressed as a linear combination of the K attributes ($X_{K,i}$) concerning that alternative, weighted by their respective homogenization coefficients $\beta_{K,i}$, which mostly represent specific costs of the attribute: C_i = SUM ($\beta_{K,i} * X_{K,i}$). As previously mentioned, for a single customer attributes $X_{K,i}$ can represent both quantitative variables as well as qualitative variables correctly discretized.

The perceived QoS is strongly dependent on Performability levels delivered by the system. The Performability indexes estimate "the ability to maintain performance, also degraded, in presence of failures", properly combining system performance with its dependability. For a Metro System, as well as other service-providing systems, Performability indexes are expressed through mathematical formulas referred to the offered service, measuring both the correct and the degraded service carried out by the system; these indexes are defined in tender documents and may vary for the specific project. They are often described by the ratio between performed (actual) and target (designed) service; as an example, a common Performability index is given by "Punctuality (P)", which can be defined as $P = (t_s - t_l)/t_l$, where t_s is the number of scheduled trips within a certain time period and t_l is the number of lost and delayed trips (i.e. the number of not-realized trips, or those which arrive over a certain delay threshold at the measurement station) calculated over the same time interval. Performability indexes are commonly known, wrongly, as "RAM indexes" due to the strict relationships with Reliability, Availability, Maintainability attributes.

The European Standard CENELEC EN 50126 (CENELEC, 1999) defines a complete process for the management of Reliability, Availability, Maintainability and Safety, denoted by the acronym RAMS, of Railway and Metro Systems. This norm suggests a common "V" lifecycle (the RAMS lifecycle), decomposed in fourteen phases; for each one of them objectives, inputs, requirements, deliverables and verification techniques are defined. The RAMS lifecycle is depicted in Figure 1, where, neglecting the minor, main phases are indicated. All these phases can be grouped together into the following macro-phases: definition, design, installation and operation. If, on one hand, this norm is well focused on the process, on the other hand it does not impose any approaches for the Performability evaluation, leaving a wide margin to adopt an appropriate methodology depending on the adopted formulas that, as said previously, are specifically defined for each project.

To date, the Performability evaluation of a complex system during development stages can be carried out through analytical approaches or relying on the model usage. The adoption of the first, especially in the industry, has the enormous

Figure 1. RAMS lifecycle

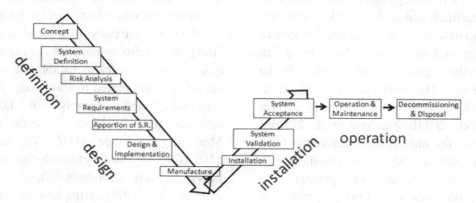

advantage of making unnecessary the presence of skilled personnel in the use of formal languages but it is based on difficult-to-prove assumptions (e.g. failure independence) and excessive simplifications on the failure consequences (e.g. penalizing worst case). The disadvantages of the first, however, are the advantages of the latter: the use of formal models, although highly recommended if not mandatory, makes it feasible to contemplate internal dynamics, even though complex. Obviously, the better is the accuracy of the models with respect to the real system, the higher is the difficulty of their implementation and solution. To better clarify the differences between the two approaches, an example would be the following assumption: after a failure stopping a vehicle, the entire system is assumed as down when analytical approaches are implemented; with formal modelling, some complex dynamics can be modelled as, for example, the degraded "shuttle service", where a set of trains travel along a portion of the entire line.

The Performability evaluation techniques, not only for railway or Metro systems, based on the usage of formal models have been conducted in many works but they always are performed at sub-system level (to evaluate the Performability of a single sub-system, i.e. a vehicle); on the other hand a lot of service models have been presented in the classical literature in transporta-

tion domain, commonly at three detail levels that are macroscopic, mesoscopic, and microscopic. As an example, in (Hagalisletto et al., 2007), a model-based approach for large-scale railways, based on a compositional approach, has been exploited; all the basic models are developed using Petri Nets formalism but they are not able to represent failures and to evaluate dependability attributes. To the best of our knowledge, there are not noteworthy experiments combining service models at system level with dependability models at sub-system level.

In general, to cope with the Metro system Performability evaluation and to increase the models utilization in industry, it is necessary to develop not only a complete model-based approach, but also a model-driven process able to make it easy the usage of formal models. In this paper a complete model-driven methodology is presented; the aim of the paper is not to address specific problems encountered during development of the methodology, but to give a complete overview of the methodology itself, showing the followed steps and the developed elements. The entire methodology is implementable into cost-effective processes in order to reduce the effort of RAM analysis, to support definition of operational strategies during design stages, and to support re-schedule activities, after the occurrence of a failure during the service. Furthermore the proposed methodology can be combined with standard practices that drive development and verification, so its adoption in industrial processes does not need expensive extra-efforts, but it can support also the required technical reports in the standard formats. This work constitutes an extension of previous papers (Nardone et al., 2011a; Nardone et al., 2011b; Nardone et al., 2011c); in these works the models architecture has been discussed in detail, and results obtained with a simulative approach have been presented. In detail, in (Nardone et al., 2011a) a comparative analysis between two different "own built" railway simulators (a microscopic and a mesoscopic) has been presented with the aim of focusing on the necessity of a dynamic integration. In (Nardone et al., 2011b) the overall architecture which contains all the models has been depicted; this architecture enables the integration of the dynamic-scale railway model with the dependability and with the passengers demand models. Lastly, (Nardone et al., 2011c) focuses on the necessity to evaluate together the QoS and the Performability to assess the effects of architectural and operational choices, which not improve always both of them. All these works does not cope with model-driven processes and methodologies, but they are focused on the benefits of a model-based approach, providing some technical details about the models.

This paper does not aim at providing extended methodologies but rather than wants to show the complexity of the application of existing model-driven and multiformalism methodologies to a real case study taken from complex rail and metro systems.

MODEL DRIVEN METHODOLOGY

In this Section we propose a three stages approach (Figure 2), able to combine the use of an appropriate Domain Specific Modelling Language (DSML), compositionality and automatic genera-

tion to evaluate Metro Systems Performability: the stages are hence described from top to down.

The first stage consists in the high-level modelling of a Metro system, annotating also its requirements. In order to establish a usable and completely automated methodology, it is necessary that all models comply with a DSML, specific designed for Metro Systems: the Metro Modelling Language (*MML*). The semantic of *MML* is obtained directly from the specific domain, the syntax has been formally defined. As explained in the following, *MML* is implemented using UML profile mechanism (Fuentes-Fernández et al., 2004), where Metro domain concepts have been identified and then mapped on UML as stereotypes, tags and constraints. *MML* is structured in packages, according to the concerns separation paradigm. *MML* is the basic point of the approach and it represent the interface between the automated model-driven methodology and system modellers, who need to interact with a language which provide concepts familiar to them.

At the second stage several formal models for quantitative analysis are generated on the basis of high-level one: the generated models are expressed in different formal languages depending on aspects that they take into account. In detail, these models are developed using Stochastic Activity Networks (SANs) for the behavioural aspects, Fault Trees for the dependability aspects and C++ code for the operational strategies. At this stage, furthermore, technical reports, necessary to document RAM process, are also generated, according to the standard format defined in (CENELEC, 1999); the generated reports concern with RAM analysis at sub-system and at system levels and, in particular, they deal with Product Breakdown Structures (PBSs), Failure Mode Effects Analyses (FMEA) and Fault Trees analysis (FTs).

At the third stage single-formalism models are tied together in order to create a composed multi-formal System Model (*SM*) of the entire Metro system under analysis. The relationships among high-level model sub-parts are translated

Figure 2. Conceptual schema of the methodology

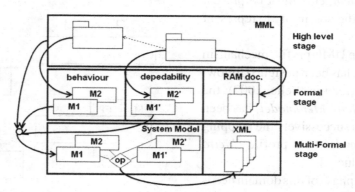

into compositionality operators that define the model composition and information passing rules. At this stage the *SM* is finally translated in specific *xml* files, written into the concrete syntax of the Möbius analysis tool.

The passing from a stage to another is possible by means of model-to-model (M2M) and model-to-text (M2T) transformations. These transformations are defined between the source and the target metamodel, and are applied to a model conforms to the source language in order to produce a model conforms to the target one. The final transformation, able to generate XML files, understood by Möbius, from *SM* uses a particular M2T transformation.

The described methodology produces a System Model that is perfectly coherent with the CEN-ELEC EN 50126 norm and it is usable during the critical phases of the lifecycle; the generated RAM information are usable during deliverables editing and allow to have a continuous update of technical documentation. In detail the *MML* is useful to describe the system since earlier stages of the lifecycle: it is possible to annotate from requirements to the complete final design of the specific Metro System. In fact:

- During the definition phase of a new system *MML* is useful to establish target values reachable with the current technology relying on past experiences.

- During the design stage it is possible to describe in a unique language all the architectural choices that have an impact on Performability levels reached by the system (as the application of more dependable component, different service operational strategies, different configuration of the maintenance staff, and so on.)

- During service, lastly, thanks to the computational efficiency of the *SM*, it is possible to use the same approach for the run-time evaluation of the best strategy to perform after the occurrence of a specific failure in the specific degraded situation.

In the following major details about the *MML*, the *SM* and the transformations are given.

METRO MODELING LANGUAGE (MML)

The starting point of a model-driven methodology is a defined language: the automatic generation at first of atomic formal models, and subsequently of the entire System Model is possible just if a complete DSML for Metro systems has been defined. This language is the only language that the system modelers need to know; it must be complete, graphical, practical and easy to use. In this language all domain concepts as *track*, *vehicle, signalling system*, etc., must be present as well as it must give the possibility to represent operational strategies.

To design *MML*, the UML profile mechanism has been chosen. *MML* has been designed following the approach described in (Selic, 2007): the domain metamodel (*Metro Metamodel*) has been previously defined and successively the mapping of the domain metamodel to a profile (*Metro Profile*) has been conducted.

The metamodeling phase of this domain needs simultaneously to take care of services provided by the different subsystems with their dependability aspects: as an example, one of the services provided by the vehicles is the *movement*; this service is performed at 100% of the maximum speed if no failures affect the vehicle, but the speed ratio decreases up to reach the 0% (vehicle stoppage) if a severe combination of failures happened. Hence, for each basic service provided by the subsystems, all the degraded modes that they can offer must be specified.

Dependability aspects are also present, over multiple application domains, in existing aspect-oriented languages as in MARTE-DAM (Bernardi et al., 2011). So the overall *Metro Metamodel* is obtained by an extension of MARTE and MARTE-DAM (Figure 3).

The *Metro Metamodel* is composed of the following packages: the *System* package describes the structural features of metro domain. It is composed of several sub packages: each of one devoted to a specific technology (*Track, Rolling Stocks, Signaling*, etc.) where each of these packages can be considered as a vertical DSML itself. The *Operation* package deals with the modeling of the service: it includes the concepts of a mission to be accomplished by a certain set of vehicles, having the others as hot spares; for the specific mission it must be defined the dwell times at stations and the crossing times of the sections. The role of joint point between vertical and horizontal languages is addressed by a specific package (*MetroNFP*), that synthesizes the huge

Figure 3. Package structure of metro metamodel

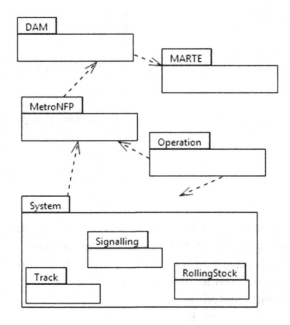

amount of concepts of MARTE and MARTE-DAM, increasing the usability of such languages since metamodeling phases. In concrete, a *MetroComponent* concept is introduced: this concept inherits DAM *DaComponent*. A *MetroComponent* can operate with different performance and dependability levels so the concept *OperatingMode* has been added to annotate these states.

The *Metro Profile* is structured in similar packages of *Metro Metamodel*, the concepts coming from the metamodel are stereotypes that extend UML metaclasses, adding, where necessary, additional properties. A UML model is perfectly coherent with the Metro Domain Language just if all UML modeling elements have been stereotyped with the stereotypes of *Metro Profile*; otherwise, if there is at least one element without the application of a *Metro Profile* stereotype, the model is not consistent and cannot be considered as an high-level source model for the following transformation steps.

For the sake of clarity it is important to show an extract of the track representation that have been adopted inside the *Track* package. The Figure 4 shows the UML profile that has been developed for the track representation: according to industrial track representation, a track is composed of generic *TrackElement*s. The abstract concept of *TrackElement* is the generalization of the *Segment*, *Crossing* and *Point* stereotypes where the first corresponds to the common track with two connections while the others are in turn specialized.

The *Crossing* element represents the crossing between two tracks that can be made of two crossing segments (*CrossingSegment*) or of two parallel segments where there is no sufficient space to consider them separated. The *Point* is the general concept of railway interchange and specializes in three types: the *SinglePoint* that is the simplest way to change direction with one entrance and two exits or vice versa, the *SingleSlipPoint* allows the mixing of a crossing segment with a slip point and, lastly, the *DoubleSlipPoint* connects two entrances with two exits, allowing all possible directions interchanges.

SYSTEM FORMAL MODEL (SM)

The Performability evaluation of a Metro System, as sustained before, needs to assess the failures impact on the system under analysis and their consequences on the service performed. For this reason the goal is to generate automatically a multi-formal qualitative *SM* from a high-level one expressed in *MML*. In addition, the goals that we intend to analyze with the *SM* are three: (a) evaluate the impact of disturbances on service, estimating the variation induced on the Performability; (b) estimate the efficiency having different configurations of track layout allowing to choose the one that has the greater impact on cost reduction; (c) identify the optimal configuration of the plants and of operation and maintenance staff.

To this aim, formal models of two different nature must cooperate: on one hand there are the behavioural models of the service and, on the other hand, dependability models of system components.

Figure 4. UML profile for track topology representation

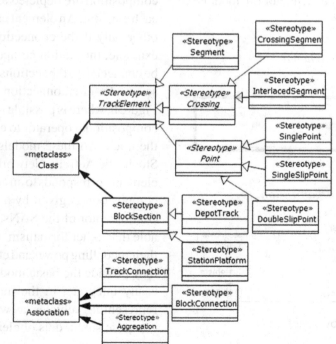

In Figure 5 the overall models organization has shown: it is decomposed into two main blocks that are *State of critical components* and *Behaviour*. In the first block, models able to reproduce the state of each component are present, these models represent the evolution between different service modes (nominal, degraded and not-working) according to the redundancies, failure rates and repair times; the overall state, given by the set of all the components states, is an input of the latter block where models represent the performed service, taking into account the infrastructure configuration (track layout) and the operational strategies, both during nominal service and after failure occurrences.

The final System Model organization is depicted in Figure 6. It is composed of a four modules which reflect, at the same time, three different views of the Metro System, each one obtainable isolating one component from the others. These three views are: (1) *Management vs. System* - classical operational unit and control unit decomposition adopted in computers science, (2) *State vs. Behaviour* - distinguishing between dependability models and behavioural models,

Figure 5. Formal models schema

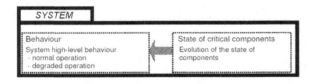

Figure 6. System model organization

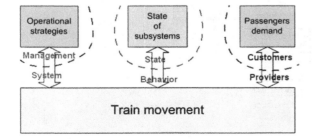

(3) *Customers vs. Providers* - splitting supply system from demand according to transportation literature. The four models of the *SM* are described in the following:

- **Train Movement Module:** This is the principal module of the *SM* including all the behavioural models of the service, relying on the modelling of the track topology. In this module a compositional approach is implemented, the basic elements are standard components, each one models a specific track portion (e.g. station, depots, terminals for turn back, sections between stations, sections with pocket track, etc.). For each basic element specific input data are defined; these data regard infrastructure characteristics (track length and gradient, speed limits, etc.) and service (travel times, dwell times, etc.).

These elementary blocks are tied together from precise composition rules that identify possible connections: in the Figure 7 the rules for the composition are depicted as outgoing links from each element. An element can be connected to the other only if the connection rule enables it, for example, the station component of Figure 7 can be connected to the sections and / or terminals and so on. An interconnection example is shown in Figure 8, where is possible to find a more complex compositional operator to connect the depot with the track. All these models are developed using Stochastic Activity Networks (SANs); each basic element corresponds to an atomic model while the composition is given by a specific rule into the *Join* operator of the SANs. SANs are more suitable than other formalism to our aims because of their modelling power and efficiency. Specifically, they provide the basic modelling mechanisms to easily integrate, in the models, data structures representing vehicles, as well as to replicate and compose submodels of elementary blocks.

Figure 7. Compositional approach

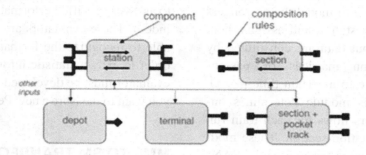

Figure 8. Example of interconnection

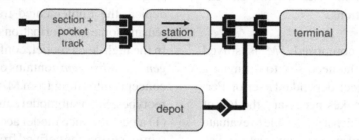

- **Operational Strategies Module:** This module implements operational strategies controlled by control centre managing vehicles routes and accesses into block sections. It considers, as input data, both operational timetable (scheduled train arrival and departure times at/from each station), and different operational strategies which are addressed to manage ordinary train movements (e.g. train movements towards the depot at the end of the daily service time) as well as degraded conditions to restore normal service after failures of system components (e.g. train movements towards the nearest pocket track after a failure occurrence on itself). More precisely this module authorizes train movements from stations and block sections, according to timetable and obviously respecting signalling semaphores, which safely regulate train movements on the track. In case of degraded mode of operation instead, this module activates the specific operation

strategies to recover ordinary conditions after a certain failure event. This module is implemented as small SANs to manage timetable and clocks, and C++ code to evaluate the movement authorizations inside the input and output gates elements of the SANs.

- **State of Sub-Systems Module:** This module simulates operating states of system components, considering the transition from ordinary to degraded functioning for each sub-system, in accordance to failure rates which constitute in fact input data of such module. In particular different degraded operating modes are considered for each component, and transitions from normal working to degraded conditions are modeled. This module is realized by Fault Tree models where top event are failure events that enable the state passing of a hierarchically higher SAN, which in turn communicates with SAN models of other modules.

- **Passenger Demand Module:** Such module is responsible to model the passengers demand at each station and assigns them to vehicles. Input data are constituted by origin/destination matrices of passenger trips relative to a certain time period. Specifically this module determines onboard passengers flows for each train run and each interstation section. These models are implemented through trivial SANs where an action models the stochastic distribution of arriving and leaving passengers flows at stations.

The multiformal composed *SM* is solved through simulations; the necessity to estimate a not-defined (and project dependant) set of Performability indexes makes necessary the log of simulation events on which it is possible to evaluate an enormous variety of interest parameters. The Performability evaluation mechanism is shown in Figure 9: the *SM* reproduces system service taking into account stochastic disturbances due to failures; the outputs are log files which contain the list of all arrival and departure instants of time for each train at each station; a set of *evaluators* is able to analyse these log file with the aim to evaluate interest parameters. Each *evaluator* is able to assess a specific Performability index (or QoS index). These evaluators are simple text parsers able to recognize the format of the log files in order to extract statistic information; just a new evaluator must be developed in the project when you want to measure a new Performability index.

MML TO SM TRANSFORMATION

Regarding model transformations, Figure 10 depicts the implemented transformation chain, reusing some transformations present in literature. In the high-level model, conforms to the MML, a *generic subsystem* contains elements tagged with concepts inheriting from MARTE and DAM stereotypes. Such submodel can be transformed into (1) a performance model according to *dam2gspn* (similar to the one defined from AADL in (Rugina et al., 2007)) and *gspn2san* transformations and into (2) an availability model according to the *dam2rft*, *rft2gspn* and *gspn2san* transformation subchain. System structure can bring to a Möbius model according to a *system2mobius* transformation; such model can be used to integrate the SAN models previously defined. Several *model-to-text* transformations end the chain, transforming the Möbius model into the concrete syntax understood by Möbius analysis tool.

As said before, it is possible to generate automatically also RAM technical report. In the high level model, in fact, RAM aspects have been modeled in order to create dependability models of the subsystems, for this reason it is possible to apply some *model-to-text* transformation able to generate technical information (Figure 11). The information generated are XML and/or CSV files, that include reports needed by the RAM analyses; the output format is the one described in the standard (CENELEC, 1999).

Figure 9. Performability analysis

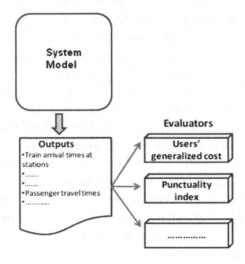

Figure 10. MML to system model transformation chain

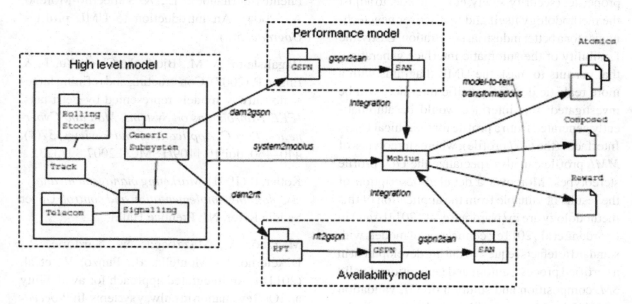

Figure 11. MML to RAM documentation transformations

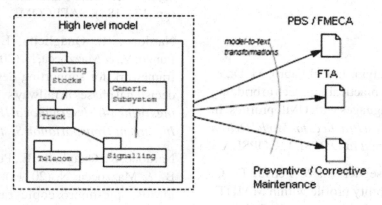

CONCLUSION

This paper presents a novel approach in formal modeling of Metro Systems in order to evaluate Performability. The model-driven methodology exploits the benefits of a Domain Specific Modeling Language (*MML*) creation and usage, multiformalism, submodels composition and automatic model generation. The methodology is perfectly coherent with the most common European standard for RAMS in railway systems, and furthermore the same high-level model allows to generate technical reports, ready to be inserted into the RAM documentation, in the format pointed out by the same norm. An important benefit is the application of model-driven engineering making the methodology more attractive to the industrial settings, offering to the domain modeler a language with concepts very familiar to them.

Future research efforts will investigate the application of the same methodology on other complex systems (as computer networks or sensor networks) where Performability evaluations are needed and to focus on other non functional properties (security, safety, etc...) in order to adjust the methodology itself and to discover new techniques for a better industrial penetration. Lastly, the feasibility of the automatic interface generation, that permits to mask the UML diagrams with a more realistic domain specific interface, will be investigated; this interface would be automatically generated from a profile for Graphical Users Interfaces (the *GUI* profile), where stereotypes of *MML* profile can also specialize the *GUI* profile stereotypes. Moreover a detailed description of the results obtainable from the application of this methodology are in (Nardone et al., 2011b) and in (Nardone et al., 2011c); connection of models with standard artefacts requested during development in a certified process, automated generation of valid *SM*, composition and solution of *SM*, validation of *MML* here are just addressed but they will be the object of extensions of this work.

REFERENCES

Abouzahra, A., Bezivin, J., Del Fabro, M. D., & Jouault, F. (2005). A practical approach to bridging domain specific languages with UML profiles. In *Proceedings of the Best Practices for Model Driven Software Development at OOPSLA*. OOPSLA.

Bernardi, S., Merseguer, J., & Petriu, D. C. (2011). A dependability profile within MARTE. *Software & Systems Modeling, 10*(3), 313–336. doi:10.1007/s10270-009-0128-1.

Bondavalli, A., Dal Cin, M., Latella, D., Majzik, I., Pataricza, A., & Savoia, G. (2001). Dependability analysis in the early phases of UML-based system design. *Comput. Syst. Sci. Eng., 16*(5), 265–275.

Cascetta, E. (2009). *Transportation system analyses, models and applications*. Berlin: Springer. doi:10.1007/978-0-387-75857-2.

CENELEC. (1999). *Railway applications - Specification and demonstration of reliability, availability, maintainability and safety (RAMS), EN 50126*. Author..

Fuentes-Fernández, L., & Vallecillo-Moreno, A. (2004). An introduction to UML profiles. *Upgrade, 5*(2).

Hagalisletto, A. M., Bjork, J., Chieh Yu, I., & Enger, P. (2007). Constructing and refining large-scale railway models represented by Petri nets. *IEEE Transactions on Systems, Man and Cybernetics. Part C, Applications and Reviews, 37*(4), 440–460. doi:10.1109/TSMCC.2007.897323.

Kotler, P. (1991). *Marketing management, analysis, planning, implementation and control*. Upper Saddle River, NJ: Prentice Hall..

Mazzeo, A., Mazzocca, N., Nardone, R., D'Acierno, L., Montella, B., Punzo, V., et al. (2011b). An integrated approach for availability and QoS evaluation in railway systems. In *Proceedings of the International Conference on Computer Safety, Reliability, and Security (SAFECOMP)* (pp. 171-184). SAFECOMP.

Nardone, R., Quaglietta, E., D'Acierno, L., Punzo, V., & Mazzocca, N. (2011c). A simulation framework for supporting design and real-time decisional phases in railway systems. In *Proceedings of the 14th International IEEE Conference on Intelligent Transportation Systems (ITSC)*. IEEE.

Nardone, R., Quaglietta, E., Punzo, V., Montella, B., & Mazzocca, N. (2011a). Towards a hybrid mesoscopic-microscopic railway simulation model. In *Proceedings of the 2nd International Conference on Models and Technologies for ITS*. ITS.

Rugina, A. E., Kanoun, K., & Kaâniche, M. (2007). A system dependability modeling framework using AADL and GSPNs. [LNCS]. *Proceedings of Architecting Dependable Systems IV, 4615*, 14–38. doi:10.1007/978-3-540-74035-3_2.

Selic, B. (2007). A systematic approach to domain-specific language design using UML. In *Proceedings of Object and Component-Oriented Real-Time Distributed Computing*. IEEE. doi:10.1109/ISORC.2007.10.

Compilation of References

Abouzahra, A., Bezivin, J., Del Fabro, M. D., & Jouault, F. (2005). A practical approach to bridging domain specific languages with UML profiles. In *Proceedings of the Best Practices for Model Driven Software Development at OOPSLA*. OOPSLA.

Ajmone, M., Balbo, G., Conte, G., Donatelli, S., & Franceschinis, G. (1995). *Modeling with generalized stochastic petri nets*. Hoboken, NJ: Wiley.

Avritzer, A., & Weyuker, E. J. (1997). Monitoring smoothly degrading systems for increased dependability. *Empirical Software Engineering*, 2, 59–77. doi:10.1023/A:1009794200077.

Bachmann, J., Riedl, M., Schuster, J., & Siegle, M. (2009). An efficient symbolic elimination algorithm for the stochastic process algebra tool CASPA. In *Proceedings of the 35th Int. Conf. on Current Trends in Theory and Practice of Computer Science* (SOFSEM'09) (LNCS), (vol. 5404, pp. 485–496). Berlin: Springer.

Balsamo, S., & Marin, A. (2008). From BCMP queueing networks to generalized stochastic petri nets: An algorithm and an equivalence definition. In *Proceedings of the European Simulation and Modeling Conference*, (pp. 447–455). Academic Press.

Balsamo, S., & Marzolla, M. (2005). Performance evaluation of UML software architectures with multiclass queueing network models. In *Proceedings of the Fifth International Workshop of Software and Performance*, (pp. 37–42). Academic Press.

Balsamo, S., Di Marco, A., Inverardi, P., & Simeoni, M. (2004). Model-based performance prediction in software development: A survey. *IEEE Transactions on Software Engineering*, 30(5), 295–310. doi:10.1109/TSE.2004.9.

Barbero, M., Jouault, F., Gray, J., & Bezivin, J. (2007). A practical approach to model extension. In *Proceedings of the 3rd European Conference on Model Driven Architecture-Foundations and Applications, ECMDA-FA'07* (pp. 32-42). Berlin: Springer-Verlag.

Barbierato, E., Bobbio, A., Gribaudo, M., & Iacono, M. (2012). Multiformalism to support software rejuvenation modeling. In *Proceedings of ISSRE Workshops* (pp. 271-276). IEEE.

Barbierato, E., Dei Rossi, G., Gribaudo, M., Iacono, M., Marin, A. (2012). Exploiting product form solution techniques in multiformalism modeling. *Electr. Notes Theor. Comput. Sci.*

Barbierato, E., Gribaudo, M., & Iacono, M. (2011). Exploiting multiformalism models for testing and performance evaluation in SIMTHESys. In *Proceedings of the Fifth International Conference on Performance Evaluation Methodologies and Tools* (Valuetools), (pp. 121-130). Valuetools.

Barbierato, E., Iacono, M., & Marrone, S. (2012). PerfBPEL: A graph-based approach for the performance analysis of BPEL SOA applications. In *Proceedings of VALUETOOLS* (pp. 64-73). IEEE.

Barbierato, E., Dei Rossi, G., Gribaudo, M., Iacono, M., & Marin, M. (2013). Exploiting product forms solution techniques in multiformalism modeling. *Electronic Notes in Theoretical Computer Science*, 296(16), 61–77. doi:10.1016/j.entcs.2013.07.005.

Barbierato, E., Gribaudo, M., & Iacono, M. (2013). *Performance evaluation of NoSQL big-data applications using multi-formalism models*. Fut. Gen. Comp. Sys.

Barbierato, E., Gribaudo, M., Iacono, M., & Marrone, S. (2011). Performability modeling of exceptions-aware systems in multiformalism tools. In K. Al-Begain, S. Balsamo, D. Fiems, & A. Marin (Eds.), *ASMTA* (pp. 257–272). Berlin: Springer. doi:10.1007/978-3-642-21713-5_19.

Baudry, B., Fleurey, F., France, R., & Reddy, R. (2005). *Exploring the relationship between model composition and model transformation.* Paper presented at the 7th International Workshop on Aspect-Oriented Modeling. Montego, Jamaica.

Bause, F. (1993). Queueing petri nets - A formalism for the combined qualitative and quantitative analysis of systems. In *Proceedings of 5th International Workshop on Petri nets and Performance Models.* IEEE Computer Society.

Bause, F. (1994). QPN-tool for qualitative and quantitative analysis of queueing Petri nets. In *Proceedings of the 7th International Conference on Computer Performance Evaluation: Modelling Techniques and Tools.* Vienna, Austria: Springer-Verlag.

Bause, F., Buchholz, P., & Kemper, P. (1998). A toolbox for functional and quantitative analysis of DEDS. In R. Puigjaner, N. N. Savino, & B. Serra (Eds.), *Computer Performance Evaluation (Tools)* (pp. 356–359). Berlin: Springer. doi:10.1007/3-540-68061-6_32.

Bechta-Dugan, J., Bavuso, S. J., & Boyd, M. A. (1992). Dynamic fault-tree models for fault-tolerant computer systems. *IEEE Transactions on Reliability, 41,* 363–377. doi:10.1109/24.159800.

Bernardi, S., & Campos, J. (2009). Computation of performance bounds for real-time systems using time Petri nets. *IEEE Transactions on Industrial Informatics, 5*(2), 168–180. doi:10.1109/TII.2009.2017201.

Bernardi, S., Flammini, F., Marrone, S., Mazzocca, M., Nardone, R., Merseguer, J., & Vittorini, V. (2013). Enabling the usage of UML in the verification of railway systems: The DAM-rail approach. *Reliability Engineering & System Safety.* doi:10.1016/j.ress.2013.06.032.

Bernardi, S., Flammini, F., Marrone, S., Merseguer, J., Papa, C., & Vittorini, V. (2011a). Model-driven availability evaluation of railway control systems. *Lecture Notes in Computer Science, 6894,* 15–28. doi:10.1007/978-3-642-24270-0_2.

Bernardi, S., Merseguer, J., & Petriu, D. C. (2011b). A dependability profile within MARTE. *Software & Systems Modeling, 10*(3), 313–336. doi:10.1007/s10270-009-0128-1.

Bernardi, S., Merseguer, J., & Petriu, D. C. (2012b). Dependability modeling and analysis of software systems specified with UML. *ACM Computing Surveys, 45*(1), 2. doi:10.1145/2379776.2379778.

Bernardo, M., Cortellessa, V., & Flamminj, M. (2011). TwoEagles: A model transformation tool from architectural descriptions to queueing networks. In *Proceedings of Computer Performance Engineering, European Performance Engineering Workshop* (EPEW), (pp. 265-279). EPEW.

Berthomieu, B., & Vernadat, F. (2006). Time petri nets analysis with TINA. In *Proceedings of Third International Conference on the Quantitative Evaluation of Systems (QEST 2006),* (pp. 123-124). Riverside, CA: IEEE Computer Society.

Berthomieu, B., & Diaz, M. (1991). Modeling and verification of time dependent systems using time Petri nets. *IEEE Transactions on Software Engineering, 17*(3), 259–273. doi:10.1109/32.75415.

Bertoli, M., Casale, G., & Serazzi, G. (2006). Java modeling tools: An open source suite for queueing network modeling and workload analysis. In *Proceedings of Quantitative Evaluation of Systems.* QEST.

Best, E., & Devillers, R. et al. (2001). *Petri net algebra.* Berlin: Springer Publishing Company, Incorporated. doi:10.1007/978-3-662-04457-5.

Blanc, J. P. C. (2011). *Queueing models - Analytical and numerical methods.* Retrieved from http://lyrawww.uvt.nl/~blanc/qm-blanc.pdf

Bobbio, A., Garg, S., Gribaudo, M., Horvath, A., Sereno, M., & Telek, M. (2008). Compositional fluid stochastic petri net model for operational software system performance. In *Proceedings of IEEE 1st Intl Workshop Software Aging and Rejuvenation* (WoSAR) (pp. 1–6). IEEE.

Bobbio, A., Franceschinis, G., Gaeta, R., & Portinale, L. (2003). Parametric fault tree for the dependability analysis of redundant systems and its high-level Petri net semantics. *IEEE Transactions on Software Engineering*, *29*(3), 270–287. doi:10.1109/TSE.2003.1183940.

Bobbio, A., Portinale, L., Minichino, M., & Ciancamerla, E. (2001). Improving the analysis of dependable systems by mapping fault trees into Bayesian networks. *Reliability Engineering & System Safety*, *71*(3), 249–260. doi:10.1016/S0951-8320(00)00077-6.

Bohnenkamp, H. C., Hermanns, H., Katoen, J.-P., & Klaren, R. (2003). The modest modeling tool and its implementation. In P. Kemper, & W. H. Sanders (Eds.), *Computer Performance Evaluation / TOOLS* (pp. 116–133). Berlin: Springer. doi:10.1007/978-3-540-45232-4_8.

Bondavalli, A., Dal Cin, M., Latella, D., Majzik, I., Pataricza, A., & Savoia, G. (2001). Dependability analysis in the early phases of UML-based system design. *Comput. Syst. Sci. Eng.*, *16*(5), 265–275.

Bonet, P., Lladó, C. M., Puigjaner, R., & Knottenbelt, W. J. (2007). PIPE v2.5: A petri net tool for performance modelling. In *Proceedings of 23rd Latin American Conference on Informatics* (CLEI 2007). CLEI.

Booch, G. (1994). *Object-oriented analysis and design with applications* (2nd ed.). New York: Benjamin-Cummings Publishing Co., Inc.

Bortolussi, L., & Hillston, J. (2012a, September). Fluid approximation of CTMC with deterministic delays. In Proceedings of 2012 Ninth International Conference on Quantitative Evaluation of Systems (pp. 53–62). London: IEEE.

Bortolussi, L., & Hillston, J. (2012b, March). Fluid model checking. Retrieved from http://arxiv.org/abs/1203.0920

Bortolussi, L., & Policriti, A. (2008). Modeling biological systems in stochastic concurrent constraint programming. *Constraints*, *13*(1-2), 66–90. doi:10.1007/s10601-007-9034-8.

Boulanger, F. (2008). Simulation of multi-formalism models with ModHel'X. In *Proceedings of the 2008 International Conference on Software Testing, Verification, and Validation*. IEEE Computer Society.

Boyen, X., & Koller, D. (1998). Tractable inference for complex stochastic processes. In *Proceedings of the Conference on Uncertainty in Artificial Intelligence* (pp. 33–42). IEEE.

Bryant, R. E. (1986). Graph-based algorithms for Boolean function manipulation. *IEEE Transactions on Computers*, *C-35*(8), 677–691. doi:10.1109/TC.1986.1676819.

Bucci, G., Sassoli, L., et al. (2004). ORIS: A tool for state-space analysis of real-time preemptive systems. In *Proceedings of the The Quantitative Evaluation of Systems, First International Conference*. IEEE Computer Society.

Buchholz, P. (1991). *Die strukturierte analyse Markovscher modelle*. (PhD thesis). Universität Dortmund, Dortmund, Germany.

Campos, J., & Silva, M. (1992). Structural techniques and performance bounds of stochastic Petri net models. *Lecture Notes in Computer Science*, *609*, 352–391. doi:10.1007/3-540-55610-9_178.

Carley, K. M. (1999). On the evolution of social and organizational networks. *Research in the Sociology of Organizations*, *16*, 3–30.

Carley, K. M., & Columbus, D. (2012). *Basic lessons in ORA and AutoMap 2012*. Pittsburgh, PA: Carnegie Mellon University, School of Computer Science, Institute for Software Research.

Carnevali, L., Ridi, L., & Vicario, E. (2011). Sirio: A framework for simulation and symbolic state space analysis of non-markovian models. In *Proceedings of the 30th International Conference on Computer Safety, Reliability, and Security*, (pp. 409–422). Springer-Verlag.

Carvalho, R., Santos, L., Matsumoto, S., Ladeira, M., & Costa, P. (2008). UnBBayes - MEBN: Comments on implementing a probabilistic ontology tool. In *Proceedings of IADIS, Applied Computing 2008 Conference*. Algarve, Portugal: IADIS.

Cascetta, E. (2009). *Transportation system analyses, models and applications*. Berlin: Springer. doi:10.1007/978-0-387-75857-2.

Castiglione, A., Gribaudo, M., Iacono, M., & Palmieri, F. (2013). Exploiting mean field analysis to model performances of big data architectures. *Future Generation Computer Systems*. doi:10.1016/j.future.2013.07.016.

CENELEC. (1999). *Railway applications - Specification and demonstration of reliability, availability, maintainability and safety (RAMS), EN 50126.* Author.

Chaintreau, A., Boudec, J.-Y. L., & Ristanovic, N. (2009). The age of gossip: Spatial mean field regime. In Proceedings of Joint International Conference on Measurement and Modeling of Computer Systems. IEEE.

CHESS. (n.d.). *Composition with guarantees for high-integrity embedded software components assembly.* Retrieved from http://www.chess-project.org

Chiola, G., Franceschinis, G., Gaeta, R., & Ribaudo, M. (1995). GreatSPN 1.7: Graphical editor and analyzer for timed and stochastic Petri nets. *Performance Evaluation, 24*(1-2), 47–68. doi:10.1016/0166-5316(95)00008-L.

Ciardo, G., & Miner, A. (1996). SMART: Simulation and Markovian analyzer for reliability and timing. In Proceedings of IEEE International Computer Performance and Dependability 20 Symposium. IEEE.

Ciardo, G., & Miner, A. S. (2004). SMART: The stochastic model checking analyzer for reliability and timing. In *Proceedings of QEST* (pp. 338-339). IEEE Computer Society.

Ciardo, G., & Tilgner, M. (1996). *On the use of Kronecker operators for the solution of generalized stochastic Petri nets* (Technical Report 96-35). Institute for Computer Applications in Science and Engineering.

Ciardo, G., Blakemore, A., Chimento, P. F. J., Muppala, J. K., & Trivedi, K. S. (1993). Automated generation and analysis of Markov reward models using stochastic reward nets. *IMA Volumes in Mathematics and its Applications, 48,* 145–191.

Ciardo, G., Jones, R. L., Miner, A. S., & Siminiceanu, R. (2001). SMART - Stochastic model analyzer for reliability and timing. In *Proceedings of Tools of Aachen 2001 Int. Multiconference on Measurement, Modelling and Evaluation of Computer Communication Systems* (pp. 29-34). Tools of Aachen.

Ciardo, G., Jones, R. L., Miner, A. S., & Siminiceanu, R. I. (2006). Logic and stochastic modeling with SMART. *Performance Evaluation, 63*(6), 578–608. doi:10.1016/j.peva.2005.06.001.

Ciardo, G., Miner, A. S., & Wan, M. (2009). Advanced features in SMART: The stochastic model checking analyzer for reliability and timing. *SIGMETRICS Performance Evaluation Review, 36,* 58–63. doi:10.1145/1530873.1530885.

Ciocchetta, F., Duguid, A., Gilmore, S., Guerriero, M. L., & Hillston, J. (2009, September). The Bio-PEPA tool suite. In Proceedings of 2009 Sixth International Conference on the Quantitative Evaluation of Systems, (pp. 309–310). IEEE.

Ciocchetta, F., Degasperi, A., Heath, J. K., & Hillston, J. (2010). Modelling and analysis of the NF-kB pathway in Bio-PEPA. *Transactions on Computational Systems Biology, 12,* 229–262. doi:10.1007/978-3-642-11712-1_7.

Ciocchetta, F., & Hillston, J. (2009). Bio-PEPA: A framework for the modelling and analysis of biological systems. *Theoretical Computer Science, 410*(33-34), 3065–3084. doi:10.1016/j.tcs.2009.02.037.

Ciocchetta, F., & Hillston, J. (2010). Bio-PEPA for epidemiological models. *Electronic Notes in Theoretical Computer Science, 261,* 43–69. doi:10.1016/j.entcs.2010.01.005.

Clark, A. (2008). State-aware performance analysis with eXtended stochastic probes. In *Proceedings of the 5th European Performance Engineering Workshop on Computer Performance Engineering.* Palma de Mallorca, Spain: Springer-Verlag.

Clark, G., Courtney, T., Daly, D., Deavours, D., Derisavi, S., & Doyle, J. M. … Webster, P. (2001). The Mobius modeling tool. In *Proceedings of the 9th International Workshop on Petri Nets and Performance Models,* (pp. 241-250). Aachen, Germany: IEEE.

Codetta Raiteri, D., Franceschinis, G., Iacono, M., & Vittorini, V. (2004). Repairable fault tree for automatic evaluation of repair policies. In *Proceedings of the Performance and Dependability Symposium.* Washington, DC: IEEE Computer Society.

Codetta-Raiteri, D. (2005). *Extended fault trees analysis supported by stochastic Petri nets.* (Ph.D. Thesis). University of Turin, Turin, Italy.

Codetta-Raiteri, D., & Portinale, L. (2010). Generalized continuous time Bayesian networks and their GSPN semantics. In *Proceedings of European Workshop on Probabilistic Graphical Models* (pp. 105-112). IEEE.

Codetta-Raiteri, D., Franceschinis, G., & Gribaudo, M. (2006). Defining formalisms and models in the draw-net modelling system. In *Proceedings of International Workshop on Modelling of Objects, Components and Agents* (pp. 123–144). IEEE.

Codetta-Raiteri, D., Franceschinis, G., Iacono, M., & Vittorini, V. (2004). Repairable fault tree for the automatic evaluation of repair policies. In *Proceedings of the International Conference on Dependable Systems and Networks* (pp. 659-668). Florence, Italy: IEEE.

Colom, J., Teruel, E., & Silva, M. (1998). Logical properties of P/T systems and their analysis. In Proceedings of Performance Models for Discrete Event Systems with Synchronization: Formalisms and Analysis Techniques, MATCH Human Capital and Mobility CHRX-CT-94-0452. CHRX-CT.

Cortellessa, V., Di Gregorio, S., & Di Marc, A. (2008). Using ATL for transformations in software performance engineering: A step ahead of java-based transformations? In *Proceedings. of the 7th Int. Workshop on Software and Performance*, (pp. 127–132). ACM.

Cotroneo, D., Natella, R., Pietrantuono, R., & Russo, S. (2011). Software aging and rejuvenation: Where we are and where we are going. In *Proceedings of IEEE 3rd Int Workshop Software Aging and Rejuvenation* (WoSAR). IEEE.

Courtney, T., Gaonkar, S., Keefe, K., Rozier, E., & Sanders, W. H. (2009). Möbius 2.3: An extensible tool for dependability, security, and performance evaluation of large and complex system models. In *Proceedings of DSN* (pp. 353-358). IEEE.

Cuadrado, J. S., & Molina, J. C. (2010). A model-based approach to families of embedded domain specific languages. *IEEE Transactions on Software Engineering, 35*(6).

D'Ambrogio, A., Iazeolla, G., & Mirandola, R. (2002). A method for the prediction of software reliability. In *Proceedings of the 6th IASTED Software Engineering and Applications Conference (SEA2002)*. IASTED.

Darling, R. W. R., & Norris, J. R. (2007). Differential equation approximations for Markov chains. *Probability Surveys, 5*, 37–79.

Davis, J. (2003). GME: The generic modeling environment. In *Proceedings of Conference on Object-Oriented Programming, Systems, Languages, and Applications (OOPSLA 2003)*. Anaheim, CA: OOPSLA.

de Lara, J. (2002). AToM3: A tool for multi-formalism and meta-modelling. In *Proceedings of the 5th International Conference on Fundamental Approaches to Software Engineering*. Berlin: Springer-Verlag.

Deavours, D. D., Clark, G., Courtney, T., Daly, D., Derisavi, S., & Doyle, J. M. et al. (2002). The Möbius framework and its implementation. *IEEE Transactions on Software Engineering, 28*, 956–969. doi:10.1109/TSE.2002.1041052.

Derisavi, S., Kemper, P., Sanders, W. H., & Courtney, T. (2002). The Möbius state-level abstract functional interface. In T. Field, P. G. Harrison, J. T. Bradley, & U. Harder (Eds.), *Computer Performance Evaluation / TOOLS* (pp. 31–50). Berlin: Springer. doi:10.1007/3-540-46029-2_2.

Didonet Del Fabro, M., & Valduriez, P. (2007). Semi-automatic model integration using matching transformations and weaving models. In *Proceedings of 22nd ACM Symposium on Applied Computing - Model Transformation Track (SAC 2007)* (pp. 963-970). ACM.

Distefano, S., & Puliafito, A. (2009). Dependability evaluation with dynamic reliability block diagrams and dynamic fault trees. *IEEE Transactions on Dependable and Secure Computing, 6*(1), 4–17. doi:10.1109/TDSC.2007.70242.

Dutuit, Y., & Rauzy, A. (1996). A linear-time algorithm to find modules of fault trees. *IEEE Transactions on Reliability, 45*, 422–425. doi:10.1109/24.537011.

Ehrig, H., & Hoffmann, K. et al. (2006). Transformations of petri nets. *Electronic Notes in Theoretical Computer Science, 148*(1), 151–172. doi:10.1016/j.entcs.2005.12.016.

El-Hay, T., Friedman, N., & Kupferman, R. (2008). Gibbs sampling in factorized continuous time Markov processes. In *Proceedings of Conference on Uncertainty in Artificial Intelligence*. IEEE.

Engblom, S. (2006). Computing the moments of high dimensional solutions of the master equation. *Applied Mathematics and Computation*, *180*(2), 498–515. doi:10.1016/j.amc.2005.12.032.

Fan, Y., & Shelton, C. (2008). Sampling for approximate inference in continuous time Bayesian networks. In *Proceedings of International Symposium on AI and Mathematics*. IEEE.

Ferré, X., & Vegas, S. (1999). An evaluation of domain analysis methods. In *Proceedings of the* 4th CASE/IFIP8 *International Workshop in Evaluation of Modeling Methods in Systems Analysis and Design*. CASE/IFIP.

Fishwick, P. A. (2004). Toward an Integrative multimodeling interface: A human-computer interface approach to interrelating model structures. *Simulation. Fuseki.* (2011). Retrieved from http://jena.apache.org/documentation/serving_data

Fleurey, F., Baudry, B., France, R., & Ghosh, S. (2007). A generic approach for automatic model composition. In *Proceedings of AOM at MoDELS*. MoDELS.

Florin, G., & Natkin, S. (1985). Les reseaux de Petri stochastiques. *Technique et Science Informatiques, 4*(1).

Fox, B. L., & Glynn, P. W. (1988). Computing Poisson probabilities. *Communications of the ACM, 31*(4), 440–445. doi:10.1145/42404.42409.

Franceschinis, G., Gribaudo, M., Iacono, M., & Vittorini, V. (2002). Towards an object based multi-formalism multi-solution modeling approach. In *Proceedings of Second International Workshop on Modelling of Objects, Components, and Agents* (MOCA'02). Aarhus, Denmark: MOCA.

Franceschinis, G., Gribaudo, M., Iacono, M., Marrone, S., Mazzocca, N., & Vittorini, V. (2004). Compositional modeling of complex systems: Contact center scenarios in OsMoSys. In J. Cortadella & W. Reisig (Eds.), *Proceedings of ICATPN* (pp. 177-196). Berlin: Springer.

Franceschinis, G., Gribaudo, M., Iacono, M., Marrone, S., Moscato, F., & Vittorini, V. (2009). Interfaces and binding in component based development of formal models. In G. Stea, J. Mairesse, & J. Mendes (Eds.), *Proceedings of VALUETOOLS* (p. 44). ACM.

Franceschinis, G., Gribaudo, M., Iacono, M., Vittorini, V., & Bertoncello, C. (2002). DrawNet++: A flexible framework for building dependability models. In *Proceedings of DSN* (p. 540). IEEE Computer Society.

Fritzsche, M., Picht, M., Gilani, W., Spence, I., Brown, J., & Kilpatrick, P. (2009). Extending BPM environments of your choice with performance related decision support. In *Proceedings of the 7th Int. Conference on Business Process Management* (BPM '09), (pp. 97-112). Berlin: Springer-Verlag.

Fritzsche, M., & Johannes, J. (2008). Putting performance engineering into model-driven engineering: Model-driven performance engineering. In H. Giese (Ed.), *Reports and Revised Selected Papers* (pp. 164–175). New York: Springer. doi:10.1007/978-3-540-69073-3_18.

Fuentes-Fernández, L., & Vallecillo-Moreno, A. (2004). An introduction to UML profiles. *Upgrade, 5*(2).

Garg, S., Puliafito, A., Telek, M., & Trivedi, K. (1995). Analysis of software rejuvenation using Markov regenerative stochastic Petri nets. In *Proceedings of the 6-th International Symposium on Software Reliability Engineering*. Toulouse, France: IEEE.

Garlan, D., Carley, K. M., Schmerl, B., Bigrigg, M., &Celiku, O. (2009). Using service-oriented architectures for socio-cultural analysis. *Int'l J. of Software Engineering and Knowledge Engineering*.

Gholizadeh, H. M. (2010). A meta-model based approach for definition of a multi-formalism modeling framework. *International Journal of Computer Theory and Engineering, 2*, 87–95.

Gillespie, D. T. (1977). Exact stochastic simulation of coupled chemical reactions. *Journal of Physical Chemistry, 81*(25), 2340–2361. doi:10.1021/j100540a008.

Gillespie, D. T., & Petzold, L. R. (2003). Improved leap-size selection for accelerated stochastic simulation. *The Journal of Chemical Physics, 119*(16), 8229. doi:10.1063/1.1613254.

Glover, W., Cross, J., Lucas, A., Stecki, C., & Stecki, J. (2010). The use of PHM for autonomous unmanned systems. In *Proceedings of the Conference of PHM Society*. PHM.

Gopalratnam, K., Kautz, H., & Weld, D. S. (2005). Extending continuous time bayesian networks. In *Proceedings of AAAI Conference on Artificial Intelligence* (pp. 981–986). AAAI.

Gordon, W., & Newell, G. (1967). Closed queueing systems with exponential servers. *Operations Research, 64*(2), 254–265. doi:10.1287/opre.15.2.254.

Götz, N. (1994). *Stochastische prozessalgebren – Integration von funktionalem entwurf und leistungsbewertung verteilter systeme.* (PhD thesis). Universität Erlangen-Nürnberg, Erlangen, Germany.

GreatSPN. (n.d.). *Graphical editor and analyzer for timed and stochastic Petri nets version 2.0.* Retrieved from www.di.unito.it/~greatspn

Gribaudo, M., & Sereno, M. (1997). GSPN semantics for queueing networks with blocking. In *Proceedings of the 6th International Workshop on Petri Nets and Performance Models.* Washington, DC: IEEE Computer Society.

Gribaudo, M., Cerotti, D., & Bobbio, A. (2008). Analysis of on-off policies in sensor networks using interacting markovian agents. In Proceedings of 6th IEEE International Conference on Pervasive Computing and Communications PerCom (2008), (pp. 300–305). IEEE.

Gribaudo, M., Codetta Raiteri, D., & Franceschinis, G. (2006). *The DrawNET modelling system: A framework for the design and the solution of single-formalism and multi-formalism models.* Technical Report TR-INF-2006-01-UNIPMN.

Gribaudo, M., Codetta-Raiteri, D., & Franceschinis, G. (2005). DrawNET, a customizable multi-formalism, multi-solution tool for the quantitative evaluation of systems. In *Proceedings of QEST 2005.* QEST.

Gribaudo, M., Codetta-Raiteri, D., & Franceschinis, G. (2005). Draw-net, a customizable multi-formalism, multi-solution tool for the quantitative evaluation of systems. In Proceedings of Second International Conference on the Quantitative Evaluation of Systems (QEST'05) (pp. 257–258). Torino, Italy: IEEE.

Gribaudo, M., Iacono, M., Mazzocca, N., & Vittorini, V. (2003). The OsMoSys/DrawNET XE! languages system: A novel infrastructure for multi-formalism object-oriented modelling. In *Proceedings of ESS 2003: 15th European Simulation Symposium And Exhibition.* ESS.

Gribaudo, M., Raiteri-Codetta, D., et al. (2005). DrawNET, a customizable multi-formalism, multi-solution tool for the quantitative evaluation of systems. In *Proceedings of QEST 2005.* QEST.

Guenther, M. C., & Bradley, J. T. (2011). Higher moment analysis of a spatial stochastic process algebra. In Proceedings of 8th European Performance Engineering Workshop - EPEW 2011. EPEW.

Guenther, M. C., & Bradley, J. T. (2013). Journey data based arrival forecasting for bicycle hire schemes. In Proceedings of Twentieth International Conference on Analytical & Stochastic Modelling Techniques & Applications ASMTA. ASMTA.

Guenther, M. C., Stefanek, A., & Bradley, J. T. (2012). Moment closures for performance models with highly non-linear rates. In Proceedings of 9th European Performance Engineering Workshop (EPEW). Munich, Germany: EPEW.

Gulati, R., & Dugan, J. B. (2003). A modular approach for analyzing static and dynamic fault-trees. In *Proceedings of the Annual Reliability and Maintainability Symposium* (pp. 57-63). IEEE.

Hagalisletto, A. M., Bjork, J., Chieh Yu, I., & Enger, P. (2007). Constructing and refining large-scale railway models represented by Petri nets. *IEEE Transactions on Systems, Man and Cybernetics. Part C, Applications and Reviews, 37*(4), 440–460. doi:10.1109/TSMCC.2007.897323.

Haider, S., & Levis, A. H. (2005). Dynamic influence nets: An extension of timed influence nets for modeling dynamic uncertain situations. In *Proceedings of 10th International Command and Control Research and Technology Symposium.* Washington, DC: IEEE.

Haider, S., & Levis, A. H. (2007). Effective course-of-action determination to achieve desired effects. *IEEE Trans. on Systems, Man, and Cybernetics, Part A: Systems and Humans, 37*(6), 1140–1150. doi:10.1109/TSMCA.2007.904771.

Hamadi, R. (2003). A Petri net-based model for web service composition. In *Proceedings of the 14th Australasian Database Conference* (vol. 17). Adelaide, Australia: Australian Computer Society, Inc.

Harrison, P. G., Lladó, C. M., & Puigjaner, R. (2009). A unified approach to modelling the performance of concurrent systems. *Simulation Modelling Practice and Theory*, *17*(9), 1445–1456. doi:10.1016/j.simpat.2009.06.003.

Harwarth, S. (2006). *Computation of transient state probabilities and implementing Moebius' state-level abstract functional interface for the data structure ZDD*. (Master Thesis). University of the Federal Armed Forces, Munich, Germany.

Hayden, R. (2012). Mean field for performance models with deterministically-timed transitions. In Proceedings of 9th International Conference on Quantitative Evaluation of Systems (QEST 2012). London: IEEE.

Hayden, R. A. (2011). *Mean-field approximations for performance models with generally-timed transitions*. ACM SIGMETRICS Performance Evaluation Review. doi:10.1145/2160803.2160877.

Hayden, R. A. (2012b). Mean-field models for interacting battery-powered devices. In *Proceedings of Imperial College Energy and Performance Colloqium*. London: Imperial College.

Hayden, R. A., & Bradley, J. T. (2010). A fluid analysis framework for a Markovian process algebra. *Theoretical Computer Science*, *411*(22-24), 2260–2297. doi:10.1016/j.tcs.2010.02.001.

Hayden, R. A., Bradley, J. T., & Clark, A. (2013). Performance specification and evaluation with unified stochastic probes and fluid analysis. *IEEE Transactions on Software Engineering*, *39*(1), 97–118. doi:10.1109/TSE.2012.1.

Hayden, R. A., Stefanek, A., & Bradley, J. T. (2012). Fluid computation of passage-time distributions in large Markov models. *Theoretical Computer Science*, *413*(1), 106–141. doi:10.1016/j.tcs.2011.07.017.

Hemingway, G., Neema, H., Nine, H., Sztipanovits, J., & Karsai, G. (2011). Rapid synthesis of high-level architecture-based heterogeneous simulation: A model-based integration approach. *Simulation*. PMID:22919114.

Hermanns, H., Herzog, U., Klehmet, U., Mertsiotakis, V., & Siegle, M. (1998). Compositional performance modelling with the TIPPtool. In *Proceedings of 10th International Conference on Modelling Techniques and Tools for Computer Performance Evaluation* (TOOLS'98) (LNCS), (vol. 1469, pp. 51–62). Berlin: Springer Verlag.

Hermanns, H., Herzog, U., Mertsiotakis, V., & Rettelbach, M. (1997). Exploiting stochastic process algebra achievements for generalized stochastic Petri nets. In *Proceedings of the 6th International Workshop on Petri Nets and Performance Models*. Washington, DC: IEEE Computer Society.

Hermanns, H., Herzog, U., & Mertsiotakis, V. (1998). Stochastic process algebras – Between LOTOS and Markov chains. *Computer Networks and ISDN Systems*, *30*(9-10), 901–924. doi:10.1016/S0169-7552(97)00133-5.

Hillah, L., Kindler, E., Kordon, F., Petrucci, L., & Trèves, N. (2009). A primer on the Petri net markup language and ISO/IEC 15909-2. *Petri Net Newsletter*, *76*, 9–28.

Hillston, J. (1994). *A compositional approach to performance modelling*. (PhD thesis). University of Edinburgh, Edinburgh, UK.

Hillston, J. (2005). Fluid flow approximation of PEPA models. In Proceedings of Second International Conference on the Quantitative Evaluation of Systems (QEST'05) (pp. 33–42). IEEE.

Hoare, C. (1985). *Communicating sequential processes*. Upper Saddle River, NJ: Prentice-Hall, Inc.

Höfferer, P. (2007). Achieving business process model interoperability using metamodels and ontologies. In *Proceedings of 15th European Conference on Information Systems*. IEEE.

Holanda, H., Merseguer, J., Cordeiro, G., & Serra, A. (2010). Performance evaluation of web services orchestrated with WS-BPEL4People. *International Journal of Computer Networks & Communications*, *2*(11), 18.

Huang, Y., Kintala, C., Kolettis, N., & Fulton, N. D. (1995). Software rejuvenation: analysis, module and applications. In *Proceedings of Fault Tolerant Computing Symp* (FTCS-25) (pp. 381–390). FTCS.

Huang, C., & Darwiche, A. (1996). Inference in belief networks: A procedural guide. *International Journal of Approximate Reasoning, 15*, 225–263. doi:10.1016/S0888-613X(96)00069-2.

Huszerl, G., Majzik, I., Pataricza, A., Kosmidis, K., & Dal Cin, M. (2002). Quantitative analysis of UML statechart models of dependable systems. *The Computer Journal, 45*(3), 260–277. doi:10.1093/comjnl/45.3.260.

Iacono, M., & Gribaudo, M. (2010). Element based semantics in multi formalism performance models. In *Proceedings of MASCOTS* (pp. 413-416). IEEE.

Iacono, M., Barbierato, E., & Gribaudo, M. (2012). The SIMTHESys multiformalism modeling framework. *Computers & Mathematics with Applications (Oxford, England), 64*, 3828–3839. doi:10.1016/j.camwa.2012.03.009.

International Electrotechnical Commission. (2004). *ISO/IEC 15909-1: Systems and software engineering – High-level Petri nets - Part 1: Concepts, definitions and graphical notation.* Author.

International Electrotechnical Commission. (2011). *ISO/IEC 15909-2: Systems and software engineering - High-level Petri nets - Part 2: Transfer format.* Author.

Isserlis, L. (1918). On a formula for the product-moment coefficient of any order of a normal frequency distribution in any number of variables. *Biometrika, 12*(1/2), 134–139. doi:10.2307/2331932.

Jansen, D. (2003). *Extensions of statecharts: With probability, time, and stochastic timing.* (PhD thesis). University of Twente, Enschede, The Netherlands.

Jena. (2011). Retrieved from http://jena.apache.org/about_jena/about.html

Kansal, S., Abusharekh, A., & Levis, A. H. (2007). Computationally derived models of adversary organizations. In *Proceedings of the IEEE Symp. On Computational Intelligence for Security and Defense Applications.* Honolulu, HI: IEEE.

Kappel, G., Kapsammer, E., Kargl, H., Kramler, G., Reiter, T., & Retschitzegger, W. …Wimmer, M. (2006). Lifting metamodels to ontologies: A step to the semantic integration of modeling languages. In Model Driven Engineering Languages and Systems (pp. 528-542). Berlin: Springer.

Kleppe, A. (2008). *Software language engineering: Creating domain-specific languages using metamodels.* Reading, MA: Addison-Wesley Professional.

Kleppe, A., Warmer, S., & Bast, W. (2003). *MDA explained: The model driven architecture: Practice and promise.* Boston, MA: Addison-Wesley Longman Publishing Co.

Kohut, M., Stefanek, A., Hayden, R., & Bradley, J. T. (2012). Specification and efficient computation of passage-time distributions in GPA. In Proceedings of Ninth International Conference on Quantitative Evaluation of Systems (QEST'12). London: IEEE.

Koller, D., & Friedman, N. (2009). *Probabilistic graphical models: Principles and techniques.* Cambridge, MA: MIT Press.

Kotis, K., & Lanzenberger, M. (2008). Ontology matching: Current status, dilemmas and future challenges. In *Proceedings of International Conference on Complex, Intelligent and Software Intensive Systems.* IEEE.

Kotler, P. (1991). *Marketing management, analysis, planning, implementation and control.* Upper Saddle River, NJ: Prentice Hall.

Koutrasa, V., Platisa, A., & Gravvanisb, G. (2007). On the optimization of free resources using non-homogeneous Markov chain software rejuvenation model. *Reliability Engineering & System Safety, 92*, 1724–1732. doi:10.1016/j.ress.2006.09.017.

Kuntz, M., Siegle, M., & Werner, E. (2004). Symbolic performance and dependability evaluation with the tool CASPA.[LNCS]. *Proceedings of EPEW, 3236*, 293–307.

Kwiatkowska, M., Gethin, N., et al. (2011). PRISM 4.0: Verification of probabilistic real-time systems. In *Proceedings of the 23rd International Conference on Computer Aided Verification.* Snowbird, UT: Springer-Verlag.

Kwiatkowska, M., Norman, G., & Parke, D. (2011). PRISM 4.0: Verification of probabilistic real-time systems. In Proceedings of the 23rd International Conference on Computer Aided Verification (CAV) (LNCS), (Vol. 6806, pp. 585–591). Berlin: Springer.

Kwiatkowska, M., Mehmood, R., Norman, G., & Parker, D. (2002). A symbolic out-of-core solution method for Markov models. *Electronic Notes in Theoretical Computer Science*, *68*(4), 589–604. doi:10.1016/S1571-0661(05)80394-9.

Lagarde, F., Espinoza, H., Terrier, F., & Gérard, S. (2007). Improving UML profile design practices by leveraging conceptual domain models. In *Proceedings of 22nd Int.l Conf. on Automated Software Engineering* (pp. 445-448). ACM.

Lampka, K. (2007). *A symbolic approach to the state graph based analysis of high-level Markov reward models*. (PhD thesis). Universität Erlangen-Nürnberg, Erlangen, Germany.

Lampka, K. (2008). A new algorithm for partitioned symbolic reachability analysis. In *Proceedings of ENTCS 223, Workshop on Reachability Problems*. ENTCS.

Lampka, K., & Siegle, M. (2006). Activity-local state graph generation for high-level stochastic models. In *Proceedings of 13th GI/ITG Conf. on Measuring, Modelling and Evaluation of Computer and Communication Systems* (MMB'06), (pp. 245–264). GI/ITG.

Lampka, K., & Siegle, M. (2006). Analysis of Markov reward models using zero-supressed multi-terminal decision diagramms. In *Proceedings of VALUETOOLS 2006*. VALUETOOLS.

Lampka, K., Harwarth, S., & Siegle, M. (2007). Can matrix-layout-independent numerical solvers be efficient? In *Proceedings of the International Workshop on Tools for solving Structured Markov Chains*, (vol. 2, pp. 1–9). Nantes, France: ACM.

Lampka, K., Siegle, M., Ossowski, J., & Baier, C. (2010). Partially-shared zero-suppressed multi-terminal BDDs: Concept, algorithms and applications. *Formal Methods in System Design*, *36*, 198–222. doi:10.1007/s10703-010-0095-8.

Langseth, H., & Portinale, L. (2007). Bayesian networks in reliability. *Reliability Engineering & System Safety*, *92*, 92–108. doi:10.1016/j.ress.2005.11.037.

Laprie, J. C. (1992). *Dependability: Basic concepts and terminology*. New York: Springer-Verlag.

Lazowska, E. D., Zahorjan, J., Graham, G., & Sevcik, K. (1984). *Quantative system performance: Computer system analysis using queueing network models*. Upper Saddle River, NJ: Prentice Hall.

Ledeczi, A., Maroti, M., Bakay, A., Karsai, G., Garrett, J., & Thomasson, C., Volgyesi, P. (2001). *The generic modeling environment*. Paper presented at the Workshop on Intelligent Signal Processing. Budapest, Hungary.

Ledeczi, A., Nordstrom, G., Karsai, G., Volgyesi, P., & Maroti, M. (2001). On metamodel composition. In *Proceedings of the 2001 IEEE International Conference on Control Applications*. IEEE.

Lee, C. Y. (1959). Representation of switching circuits by binary-decision programs. *The Bell System Technical Journal*, *38*, 985–999. doi:10.1002/j.1538-7305.1959.tb01585.x.

Levis, A. H., Zaidi, A. K., & Rafi, M. F. (2012). *Multi-modeling and meta-modeling of human organizations*. Paper presented at the 4th International Conference on Applied Human Factors and Ergonomics. San Francisco, CA.

Llodrà, J., Lladó, C. M., Puigjaner, R., & Smith, C. U. (2011). FORGE: Friendly output to results generator engine. In *Proceedings of the Second Joint WOSP/SIPEW International Conference on Performance Engineering* (ICPE '11). ACM.

Loewe, L., Guerriero, M., Watterson, S., Moodie, S., Ghazal, P., & Hillston, J. (2011). Translation from the quantified implicit process flow abstraction in SBGN-PD diagrams to bio-PEPA illustrated on the cholesterol pathway. *Transactions on Computational Systems Biology*, *13*, 13–38. doi:10.1007/978-3-642-19748-2_2.

Lohmann, N., Verbeek, H., Ouyang, C., & Stahl, C. (2009). Comparing and evaluating Petri net semantics for BPEL. *International Journal of Business Process Integration and Management*, *4*(1), 60–73. doi:10.1504/IJBPIM.2009.026986.

Manian, R., Coppit, D. W., Sullivan, K. J., & Dugan, J. B. (1999). Bridging the gap between systems and dynamic fault tree models. In *Proceedings of the Annual Reliability and Maintainability Symposium* (pp. 105-111). IEEE.

Maria, A. (1997). Introduction to modeling and simulation. In *Proceedings of the 29th Winter Simulation Conference*. IEEE.

Marrone, S., Mazzocca, N., Nardone, R., & Vittorini, V. (2012). *Combining heterogeneity, compositionality and automatic generation in formal modeling*. Paper presented at the International Workshop on Research and Use of Multiformalism Modeling Methods. London, UK.

Marrone, S., Mazzocca, N., Nardone, R., Presta, R., Romano, S. P., & Vittorini, V. (2012). A SAN-based modeling approach to performance evaluation of an IMS-compliant conferencing framework. *T. Petri Nets and Other Models of Concurrency*, *6*, 308–333. doi:10.1007/978-3-642-35179-2_13.

Marrone, S., Papa, C., & Vittorini, V. (2010). Multiformalism and transformation inheritance for dependability analysis of critical systems. In *Proceedings of 8th Integrated Formal Methods, IFM'10* (pp. 215–228). Berlin: Springer-Verlag. doi:10.1007/978-3-642-16265-7_16.

Massink, M., Latella, D., Bracciali, A., Hillston, J., & Faedo, I. A. (2011). Modelling non-linear crowd dynamics in bio-PEPA. In D. Giannakopoulou, & F. Orejas (Eds.), *Fundamental approaches to software engineering* (Vol. 6603, pp. 96–110). Berlin: Springer Berlin Heidelberg. doi:10.1007/978-3-642-19811-3_8.

Mazzeo, A., Mazzocca, N., Nardone, R., D'Acierno, L., Montella, B., Punzo, V., et al. (2011b). An integrated approach for availability and QoS evaluation in railway systems. In *Proceedings of the International Conference on Computer Safety, Reliability, and Security (SAFECOMP)* (pp. 171-184). SAFECOMP.

Mehmood, R. (2004). *Disk-based techniques for efficient solution of large Markov chains*. (PhD thesis). University of Birmingham, Birmingham, UK.

Meier, S., Kounev, P., & Koziolek, H. (2011). Automated transformation of component-based software architecture models to queueing petri nets. In *Proceedings of 19th IEEE/ACM International Symposium on Modeling, Analysis and Simulation of Computer and Telecommunication Systems (MASCOTS)*. IEEE/ACM.

Mernik, M., Heering, J., & Sloane, A. M. (2005). When and how to develop domain-specific languages. *ACM Computing Surveys*, *37*, 316–344. doi:10.1145/1118890.1118892.

Michalski, R., & Tecuci, G. (Eds.). (1994). *Machine learning: A multistrategy approach*. San Mateo, CA: Morgan Kaufmann.

Milner, R. (1989). *Communication and concurrency*. Upper Saddle River, NJ: Prentice-Hall, Inc.

Minato, S. (1993). Zero-suppressed BDDs for set manipulation in combinatorial problems. In *Proceedings of the 30th Design Automation Conference* (DAC), (pp. 272–277). Dallas, TX: ACM / IEEE.

Miner, A. S. (2007). Decision diagrams for the exact solution of Markov models. *Applied Mathematics and Mechanics*, *7*(1).

Moebius. (n.d.). *Page*. Retrieved from www.mobius.uiuc.edu

Montecchi, L., Lollini, P., & Bondavalli, A. (2011). Towards a MDE transformation workflow for dependability analysis. In *Proceedings of ICECCS* (pp. 157-166). ICECCS.

Moscato, F., Flammini, F., Lorenzo, G. D., Vittorini, V., Marrone, S., & Iacono, M. (2007). The software architecture of the OsMoSys multisolution framework. In P. W. Glynn (Ed.), *VALUETOOLS* (p. 51). ACM. doi:10.4108/valuetools.2007.1913.

Munsing, E., & Lamb, C. (2011). *Joint interagency task force - South: The best known, least understood interagency success*. Washington, DC: National Defense University Press.

Muppala, J. K., & Ciardo, G. et al. (1994). *Stochastic reward nets for reliability prediction*. Communications in Reliability, Maintainability and Serviceability.

Murphy, K. (2002). *Dynamic Bayesian networks: Representation, inference and learning*. (Ph.D. Thesis). UC Berkeley, Berkeley, CA.

Nardone, R., Quaglietta, E., D'Acierno, L., Punzo, V., & Mazzocca, N. (2011c). A simulation framework for supporting design and real-time decisional phases in railway systems. In *Proceedings of the 14th International IEEE Conference on Intelligent Transportation Systems (ITSC)*. IEEE.

Nardone, R., Quaglietta, E., Punzo, V., Montella, B., & Mazzocca, N. (2011a). Towards a hybrid mesoscopic-microscopic railway simulation model. In *Proceedings of the 2nd International Conference on Models and Technologies for ITS*. ITS.

Nicol, D. M., Sanders, W. H., & Trivedi, K. S. (2004). Model-based evaluation: From dependability to security. [IEEE.]. *IEEE Transactions on Dependable and Secure Computing*, *1*, 48–65. doi:10.1109/TDSC.2004.11.

Niles, I., & Pease, A. (2001). Towards a standard upper ontology. In *Proceedings of International Conference on Formal Ontology in Information Systems*. IEEE.

Nodelman, U., Shelton, C. R., & Koller, D. (2005). Expectation propagation for continuous time Bayesian networks. In *Proceedings of Conference on Uncertainty in Artificial Intelligence* (pp. 431–440). IEEE.

Novak, J. D., & Cañas, A. J. (2006). *The theory underlying concept maps and how to construct and use them*. Pensacola, FL: IHMC.

O'Cinneide, C. A. (1990). Characterization of phase-type distributions. *Communications in Statistics: Stochastic Models*, *6*(1), 1–57. doi:10.1080/15326349908807134.

OASIS. (2007). *Business process execution language*. Retrieved from https://www.oasis-open.org/committees/wsbpel/

Obal, W. D. (1999). State-space support for path-based reward variables. *Performance Evaluation*, *35*(3-4), 233–251. doi:10.1016/S0166-5316(99)00010-3.

Object Management Group. (2011). *MOF core specification*. Retrieved from http://www.omg.org/technology/documents/modeling_spec_catalog.htm#MOF

OMG. (2002). *UML profile for MARTE: Modeling and analysis of real-time embedded systems, version 1.1, formal/11-06-02*. OMG.

OMG. (2011). *Business process model and notation (BPMN)*. Retrieved from http://www.omg.org/spec/BPMN/

OMG. (2011). *Unified modeling language: Infrastructure and superstructure, version 2.4, formal/11-08-05, May 2011*. OMG.

OMG. (2012). *Object constraint language, version 2.3, formal/12-01-01, January 2012*. OMG.

Opper, M., & Saad, D. (2001). *Advanced mean field methods: Theory and practice*. Cambridge, MA: The MIT Press.

Pachowicz, P., Wagenhals, L. W., Pham, J., & Levis, A. H. (2007). Building and analyzing timed influence net models with internet-enabled pythia. In *Proceedings of SPIE, Defense and Security Symposium*. Orlando, FL: SPIE.

Pacini, E., Bernardi, S., & Gribaudo, M. (2009). ITPN-PerfBound: A performance bound tool for interval time Petri nets.[LNCS]. *Proceedings of TACAS*, *5505*, 50–53.

Pai, G. J., & Dugan, J. B. (2002). Automatic synthesis of dynamic fault trees from UML system models. In *Proceedings of the 13th International Symposium on Software Reliability Engineering* (pp. 243-254). Washington, DC: IEEE.

Parker, D. (2002). *Implementation of symbolic model checking for probabilistic systems*. (PhD thesis). University of Birmingham, Birmingham, UK.

Petriu, D., & Shen, H. (2002). Applying the UML performance profile: Graph grammar-based derivation of LQN models from UML specifications. In *Proceedings of the 12th International Conference on Computer Performance Evaluation, Modeling Techniques and Tools*, (pp. 183-204). Academic Press.

Plateau, B. (1985). On the stochastic structure of parallelism and synchronization models for distributed algorithms. [New York: ACM Press.]. *Proceedings of SIGMETRICS*, *85*, 147–154. doi:10.1145/317786.317819.

Portinale, L., & Codetta-Raiteri, D. (2011a). Using dynamic decision networks and extended fault trees for autonomous FDIR. In *Proceedings of the International Conference on Tools with Artificial Intelligence* (pp. 480-484). IEEE.

Portinale, L., & Codetta-Raiteri, D. (2011b). ARPHA: An FDIR architecture for autonomous spacecrafts based on dynamic probabilistic graphical models. In *Proceedings of ESA Workshop on AI in Space*. ESA.

Portinale, L., Bobbio, A., Codetta-Raiteri, D., & Montani, S. (2007). Compiling dynamic fault trees into dynamic Bayesian nets for reliability analysis: The RADYBAN tool. In *Proceedings of CEUR Workshop*. CEUR.

Portinale, L., Codetta-Raiteri, D., & Montani, S. (2010). Supporting reliability engineers in exploiting the power of dynamic bayesian networks. *International Journal of Approximate Reasoning, 51*(2), 179–195. doi:10.1016/j.ijar.2009.05.009.

Potier, D., & Veran, M. (1985). QNAP2: A portable environment for queueing systems modelling. In *Proceedings of the First International Conference on Modeling Techniques and Tools for Performance Analysis*, (pp. 25-63). IEEE.

Prieto-Diaz, R. (1990). Domain analysis: An introduction. *Software Engineering Notes, 15*(2), 47. doi:10.1145/382296.382703.

PRISM. (n.d.). *Web page*. Retrieved from www.prismmodelchecker.org

Reisig, W. (2009). Simple composition of nets.[LNCS]. *Proceedings of Applications and Theory of Petri Nets, 5606*, 23–42. doi:10.1007/978-3-642-02424-5_4.

Robinson, P., Shirley, M., Fletcher, D., Alena, R., Duncavage, D., & Lee, C. (2003). Applying modelbased reasoning to the FDIR of the command and data handling subsystem of the ISS. In *Proceedings of the International Symposium on Artificial Intelligence, Robotics and Automation in Space*. IEEE.

Rodriguez, R. J., Julvez, J., & Merseguer, J. (2012) PeabraiN: A PIPE extension for performance estimation and resource optimisation. In J. Brandt & K. Heljanko (Eds.), *Proceedings of the 12th International Conference on Application of Concurrency to System Designs* (pp. 142-147). Hamburg, Germany: IEEE Computer Society.

Rugina, A. E., Kanoun, K., & Kaâniche, M. (2007). A system dependability modeling framework using AADL and GSPNs.[LNCS]. *Proceedings of Architecting Dependable Systems IV, 4615*, 14–38. doi:10.1007/978-3-540-74035-3_2.

Saeki, M., & Kaiya, H. (2006). On relationships among models, meta models and ontologies. In *Proceedings of the 6th OOPSLA Workshop on Domain-Specific Modeling*. Jyväskylä, Finland: University of Jyväskylä.

Sahner, R. A., Trivedi, K. S., & Puliafito, A. (1996). *Performance and reliability analysis of computer systems: An example-based approach using the SHARPE software package*. Boston: Kluwer Academic Publisher. doi:10.1007/978-1-4615-2367-3.

Sahner, R., Trivedi, K., & Puliafito, A. (1997). Performance and reliability analysis of computer systems. *IEEE Transactions on Reliability, 46*(3), 441. doi:10.1109/TR.1997.664017.

Sanders, W. H. (1988). *Construction and solution of performability models based on stochastic activity networks*. (PhD thesis). University of Michigan, Ann Arbor, MI.

Sanders, W. H. (1999). Integrated frameworks for multi-level and multiformalism modeling. In *Proceedings of the 8th International Workshop on Petri Nets and Performance Models*. Washington, DC: IEEE.

Sanders, W. H., Courtney, T., Deavours, D., Daly, D., Derisavi, S., & Lam, V. (2007). Multi-formalism and multi-solution-method modeling frameworks: The Möbius approach. In *Proceedings of Symp. on Performance Evaluation–Stories and Perspectives*, (pp. 241–256). IEEE.

Sanders, W. (2002). *Stochastic activity networks: Formal definitions and concepts*. New York: Springer-Verlag.

Sanders, W. H. (1999). *Integrated frameworks for multi-level and multi-formalism modeling*. Washington, DC: IEEE Computer Society. doi:10.1109/PNPM.1999.796527.

Sanders, W. H., & Meyer, J. F. (1991). A unified approach for specifying measures of performance, dependability, and performability. *Dependable Computing and Fault-Tolerant Systems: Dependable Computing for Critical Applications, 4*, 215–237. doi:10.1007/978-3-7091-9123-1_10.

Sanders, W., Courtney, T., Deavours, D., Daly, D., Derisavi, S., & Lam, V. (2003). *Multiformalism and multi-solution method modeling frameworks: The Mobius approach*. Academic Press.

Saria, S., Nodelman, U., & Koller, D. (2007). Reasoning at the right time granularity. In *Proceedings of Conference on Uncertainty in Artificial Intelligence* (pp. 421–430). IEEE.

SATURN. (n.d.). SysML based modeling, architecture exploration, simulation and synthesis for complex embedded systems. Retrieved from http://www.saturn-fp7.eu/

Schneeweiss, W. G. (1999). *The fault tree method*. LiLoLe Verlag.

Schuster, J., & Siegle, M. (2008). A symbolic multilevel method with sparse submatrix representation for memory-speed-tradeoff. In *Proceedings of 14th GI/ITG Conference on Measurement, Modeling and Evaluation of Computer and Communication Systems*, (pp. 191-205). VDE-Verlag.

Schwabacher, M., Feather, M., & Markosian, L. (2008). Verification and validation of advanced fault detection, isolation and recovery for a NASA space system. In *Proceedings of the International Symposium on Software Reliability Engineering*. IEEE.

Selic, B. (2007). A systematic approach to domain-specific language design using UML. In *Proceedings of 10th IEEE Int.l Symposium on Object and Component-Oriented Real-Time Distributed Computing (ISORC'07)*. IEEE.

SISC. (2000). *IEEE standard for modeling and simulation high level architecture (HLA) - framework and rules*. Washington, DC: IEEE.

SMART. (n.d.). *Web page*. Retrieved from www.cs.ucr.edu/~ciardo/SMART

Smith, C. U., & Lladó, C. M. (2004). Performance model interchange format (PMIF 2.0), XML definition and implementation. In *Proceedings of the First International Conference on the Quantitative Evaluation of Systems* (pp. 38-47). IEEE Computer Society Press.

Smith, C. U., Cortellessa, V., Di Marco, A., Lladó, C. M., & Williams, L. G. (2005). From UML models to software performance results: An SPE process based on XML interchange formats. In *Proceedings of the Fifth International Workshop of Software and Performance* (pp. 87–98). Palma de Mallorca, Spain: ACM.

Smith, C. U., Lladó, C. M., Puigjaner, R., & Williams, L. G. (2007). Interchange formats for performance models: Experimentation and output. In *Proceedings of the Fourth International Conference on the Quantitative Evaluation of Systems* (pp. 91-100). IEEE Computer Society Press.

Smith, C. U., Lladó, C. M., & Puigjaner, R. (2010). Performance model interchange format (PMIF 2): A comprehensive approach to queueing network model interoperability. *Performance Evaluation, 67*(7), 548–568. doi:10.1016/j.peva.2010.01.006.

Smith, C. U., Lladó, C. M., & Puigjaner, R. (2011). Model interchange format specifications for experiments, output, and results. *The Computer Journal, 54*(5), 674–690. doi:10.1093/comjnl/bxq065.

Smith, C. U., & Williams, L. G. (1999). A performance model interchange format. *Journal of Systems and Software, 49*(1), 63–80. doi:10.1016/S0164-1212(99)00067-9.

Smith, C. U., & Williams, L. G. (2002). *Performance solutions: A practical guide to creating responsive, scalable software*. Boston, MA: Addison-Wesley.

Somenzi, F. (1998). *CUDD: Colorado university decision diagram package, release 2.3.0: User's manual and programmer's manual*. Boulder, CO: Colorado University.

Starke, P. H. (n.d.). *Integrated net analyzer version 2.1*. Retrieved from http://www2.informatik.hu-berlin.de/lehrstuehle/automaten/ina/

Stefanek, A., Guenther, M. C., & Bradley, J. T. (2011). Normal and inhomogeneous moment closures for stochastic process algebras. In Proceedings of 10th Workshop on Process Algebra and Stochastically Timed Activities (PASTA'11). PASTA.

Stefanek, A., Hayden, R. A., & Bradley, J. T. (2010). A new tool for the performance analysis of massively parallel computer systems. In Proceedings of Eighth Workshop on Quantitative Aspects of Programming Languages QAPL. QAPL.

Stefanek, A., Hayden, R. A., & Bradley, J. T. (2011). Fluid analysis of energy consumption using rewards in massively parallel Markov models. In Proceedings of ICPE'11 - Second Joint WOSP/SIPEW International Conference on Performance Engineering. ACM Press.

Stefanek, A., Hayden, R. A., & Bradley, J. T. (2013). Mean-field analysis of large scale Markov fluid models with fluid dependent and time-inhomogeneous rates. Technical report.

Stefanek, A., Hayden, R. A., Gonagle, M. M., & Bradley, J. T. (2012). Mean-field analysis of Markov models with reward feedback. In Proceedings of ASMTA (pp. 193–211). ASMTA.

Steinberg, D., Budinsky, F., Paternostro, M., & Merks, E. (2009). *EMF: Eclipse modeling framework 2.0* (2nd ed.). Reading, MA: Addison-Wesley Professional.

Stewart, W. J. (1994). *An introduction to the solution of Markov chains.* Princeton, NJ: Princeton University Press.

Szabo, C. (2007). On syntactic composability and model reuse. In *Proceedings of the First Asia International Conference on Modelling & Simulation.* IEEE Computer Society.

Tadano, K., Xiang, J., Kawato, M., & Maeno, Y. (2011). Automatic synthesis of SRN models from system operation templates for availability analysis. In *Proceedings of the 30th International Conference on Computer Safety, Reliability, and Security, SAFECOMP'11* (pp. 296-309). Berlin: Springer-Verlag.

Taivalsaari, A. (1996). On the notion of inheritance. *ACM Computing Surveys, 28,* 438–479. doi:10.1145/243439.243441.

Total, R., & Development. (2007). *Grif.* Retrieved from http://grif-workshop.com/3

Trivedi, K. S. (2002). SHARPE 2002: Symbolic hierarchical automated reliability and performance evaluator. In *Proceedings of the 2002 International Conference on Dependable Systems and Networks, DSN '02.* Washington, DC: IEEE Computer Society.

Trivedi, K. S., Vaidyanathan, K., & Goseva-Popstojanova, K. (2000). Modeling and analysis of software aging and rejuvenation. In *Proceedings of the 33rd Annual Simulation Symposium,* (p. 270). IEEE Computer Society.

Trivedi, K. S., & Sahner, R. (2009). SHARPE at the age of twenty two. *ACM SIGMETRICS Performance Evaluation Review, 36*(4), 52–57. doi:10.1145/1530873.1530884.

Uschold, M., & Gruninger, M. (1996). Ontologies: Principles, methods and applications. *The Knowledge Engineering Review, 11,* 93–136. doi:10.1017/S0269888900007797.

van der Aalst, W., & ter Hofstede, A. (2012). Workflow patterns put into context. *Software & Systems Modeling, 11,* 319–323. doi:10.1007/s10270-012-0233-4.

Vittorini, V., Iacono, M., Mazzocca, N., & Franceschinis, G. (2004). The OsMoSys approach to multi-formalism modeling of systems. *Software & Systems Modeling, 3,* 68–81. doi:10.1007/s10270-003-0039-5.

W3C. (2008). *SPARQL query language for RDF.* Retrieved from http://www.w3.org/TR/rdf-sparql-query/

Wagelaar, D., Van Der Straeten, R., & Deridder, D. (2009). Module superimposition: A composition technique for rule-based model transformation languages. In *Software and Systems Modeling.* Berlin: Springer. doi:10.1007/s10270-009-0134-3.

Wagenhals, L. W., & Levis, A. H. (2007). Course of action analysis in a cultural landscape using influence nets. In *Proceedings of the IEEE Symp. On Computational Intelligence for Security and Defense Applications.* Honolulu, HI: IEEE.

Walter, M., Munchen, T. U., et al. (2009). Lares: A novel approach for describing system reconfigurability in dependability models of fault-tolerant systems. In *Proceedings of European Safety and Reliability Conference* (ESREL 2009). New York: Taylor and Francis Ltd.

Whitney, P. D., & Walsh, S. J. (2010). Calibrating Bayesian network representations of social-behavioral models. [LNCS]. *Proceedings of Advances in Social Computing, 6007,* 338–345. doi:10.1007/978-3-642-12079-4_42.

Whittle, P. (1957). On the use of the normal approximation in the treatment of stochasticprocesses. *Journal of the Royal Statistical Society. Series B. Methodological, 19*(2), 268–281.

Zimmermann, D. (2005). *Implementierung von Verfahren zur lösung dünn besetzter linearer gleichungssysteme auf basis von zero-suppressed multi-terminalen binären entscheidungs-diagrammen.* (Master Thesis). Universität der Bundeswehr München, Munich, Germany.

Zimmermann, A., & Knoke, M. (2007). *TIMENET 4.0: A software tool for the performability evaluation with stochastic and colored Petri nets: User manual.* Berlin: Technische Universitat Berlin - Real-Time Systems and Robotic Group..

About the Contributors

Marco Gribaudo is a senior researcher at the Politecnico di Milano, Italy. He works in the performance evaluation group. His current research interests are multi-formalism modeling, queueing networks, mean-field analysis, and spatial models. The main applications to which the previous methodologies are applied comes from cloud computing, multi-core architectures, and wireless sensor networks.

Mauro Iacono is a tenured Assistant Professor and Senior Researcher in Computing Systems at Dipartimento di Scienze Politiche, Seconda Università degli Studi di Napoli, Caserta, Italy. He received a Laurea in Ingegneria Informatica (MSc) degree cum laude (Hon) in 1999 by Università degli Studi di Napoli "Federico II," Napoli, Italy, and a Dottorato in Ingegneria Elettronica (PhD) degree by Seconda Università degli Studi di Napoli, Aversa, Italy. He has published over 35 peer-reviewed scientific papers on international journals and conferences and has served as scientific editor, conference scientific committee chairman, and member and reviewer for several journals, and is a member of IEEE and other scientific societies. His research activity is mainly centered on the field of performance modeling of complex computer-based systems, with a special attention to formultiformalism modeling techniques. More information is available at http://www.mauroiacono.com.

* * *

Enrico Barbierato has worked in the IT industry (Finance, Telecom, and Energy and Utilities) since 1993. He earned a BSc (Hon) in Computer Science at University of Turin (Italy) and an MSc in Advanced Studies in Artificial Intelligence, Katholieke Universiteit of Leuven, Belgium. Currently, he is completing his PhD at University of Turin. His interests focus on performance evaluation of multiformalism models. Most of his work relates to SIMTHESys, a framework for the development of modeling languages and the solution of multiformalism models. SIMTHESysER is the complementary tool to the SIMTHESys framework, which includes numerous modelling formalisms from queueing to Business Process Execution Language (BPEL).

Simona Bernardi is professor at the Centro Universitario de la Defensa, in the General Militar Academy of Zaragoza (Spain). From 2005 to 2010, she held a researcher position at the University of Torino. Her research interests include software performance, dependability and security engineering, UML and object-oriented software development methodologies, formal methods for the modelling, and analysis of software systems. She received the MS degree in mathematics and the PhD degree in computer science, in 1997 and 2003, respectively, both from the University of Torino (Italy). She has been visiting researcher at the Department of Computer Science and System Engineering of the University of Zaragoza, Spain, and at the Department of System and Computer Engineering of the Carleton University, Canada. She has been serving as a referee for international journals and as a program committee member for several international conferences and workshops.

Andrea Bobbio graduated from Politecnico di Torino in 1969. His research work was then focused on the modeling and analysis of the performance and reliability of stochastic systems. He addressed his interests in the study of aggregation techniques in large and stiff Markov chains, and in the analysis of non-Markovian systems through stochastic Petri Nets. Recently, he contributed to the development of a new formalism, called Fluid Petri Nets, and to the study of heterogeneous modeling techniques for dependable systems, ranging from combinatorial techniques to Bayesian belief networks to state-space based techniques. Currently, he is full professor at the University of Piemonte Orientale, Italy. He has spent various research periods in well-recognized foreign universities (Duke University, Technical University of Budapest, Indian Institute of Technology, Ecole Normale Superieure de Cachan). He has been principal investigator and leader of research groups in various research projects with public and private institutions.

Pere Bonet received the Computer Engineering degree in 2006 and a Master's degree in Computer Science in 2012, both from the Universitat de les Illes Balears (Palma de Mallorca, Spain). His final university project consisted on the development of a new version of PIPE2, a Petri Net tool, for which he obtained a qualification with Honors. He works at the Performance Engineering Group (Universitat de les Illes Balears) where he currently participates in a research project funded by the Ministerio de Educacion y Ciencia of Spain called "A General Performance Interoperability Framework." More specifically, his research interests are in the area of model transformations and he also follows with the development of PIPE2.

Jeremy T. Bradley is a Reader in Scalable Performance Analysis in the Department of Computing at Imperial College London. He obtained his Ph.D. in Computer Science at the University of Bristol in 2000. After research posts at Bristol and Durham, he was appointed Lecturer at Imperial College London in 2003. His research has produced parallel algorithms for transient and response-time analysis of large semi-Markov processes. Latterly, he has focussed on fluid analysis of performance and energy models, as derived from stochastic Petri nets and stochastic process algebras augmented with rewards.

Daniele Codetta-Raiteri received the Ph.D. in Computer Science from the University of Turin, Italy, in 2006. Currently, he is an assistant professor at University of Piemonte Orientale, Italy. His research focuses on probabilistic models for Reliability evaluation, with a particular experience in Fault Trees, Petri Nets, Bayesian Networks, multi-formalism models. He published his works in relevant journals such as *Reliability Engineering and System Safety, International Journal of Approximate Reasoning, International Journal of Modelling and Simulation, Engineering Applications of Artificial Intelligence,* etc. He has been a reviewer for relevant journals such as *Simulation Modelling Practice and Theory, Reliability Engineering and System Safety, IEEE Transactions on Reliability, Transactions on Petri Nets and Other Models of Concurrency, International Journal of Electrical Power and Energy Systems, Journal of Risk and Reliability, IEEE Transactions on Dependable and Secure Computing, Process Safety and Environmental Protection, IEEE Transactions on Systems, Man and Cybernetics,* etc.

Marcel Christoph Guenther is a doctoral student at Imperial College London. He is a member of the AESOP performance analysis group and his main research interests lie in the development and application of modelling and performance evaluation techniques to complex spatial population processes.

Andrea Guiotto works at Thales Alenia Space as Technical Support Specialist, Software Specialist, UML architect, Study Manager in the aerospace sector. He participated in the following projects: SMART-FDIR, OMC-ARE, VeriFIM, MPLM.

Richard A. Hayden obtained his Ph.D. in performance modelling from the Department of Computing at Imperial College London in 2011. He was awarded the Best Computational Science Student of the Year at the 2007 Science, Engineering and Technology Student of the Year Awards, a national award sponsored by Microsoft Research. He is now a Research Associate at Imperial College and his research interests lie in tackling the state-space explosion problem for massive performance models using fluid analysis and related techniques.

Ahmed Abu Jbara is a candidate for Ph.D. in Information Technology at George Mason University. His education includes B.S. in Computer Engineering from Islamic University of Gaza, Palestine (2002), and M.S. in E-Commerce / Computer Science from George Mason University (2006). From 2006 to 2008, he worked as Head of Information Technology Department and then Vice Dean for Academic Affairs at the University College of Applied Sciences in Palestine. He has been affiliated with the System Architectures Laboratory at George Mason University since 2006, first as a Software Engineer, and then as Research Assistant. His research interests include System Architectures, Service Oriented Architectures, Multi-Modeling, and Meta-Modeling.

Kai Lampka obtained his Master and PhD degree in computer science from the Frederic-Alexander University Erlangen-Nuremberg (Germany) in 2001 and 2007, respectively. One of his publications related to his PhD thesis has been awarded with the "Best-Paper-Award" at the Int. Conf. on "Measurement, Modeling, and Evaluation of Computing Systems 2006." From 2007 – 2011, Kai Lampka was a post graduated research fellow in the Computer Engineering Group at ETH Zurich. There, he turned from stochastic verification to the modeling, analysis, and the design of algorithms for Embedded Systems with (hard) real-time constraints. In 2009, Kai was awarded with the ACM SIGBED "Best-Paper-Award" (EmSoft 2009). Since 2012, he is an assistant Professor in Embedded Systems in the Department of Information Technology at Uppsala University, Sweden.

Alexander H. Levis is University Professor of Electrical, Computer, and Systems Engineering and heads the System Architectures Laboratory in the Volgenau School of Engineering, George Mason University, Fairfax, VA. From 2001 to 2004, he served as the Chief Scientist of the U.S. Air Force at the Pentagon. He was educated at Ripon College where he received the AB degree (1963) in Mathematics and Physics and then at MIT where he received the BS (1963), MS (1965), ME (1967), and Sc.D. (1968) degrees in Mechanical Engineering with control systems as his area of specialization. For the last fifteen years, his areas of research have been architecture design and evaluation, resilient architectures for command and control, and adversary multi-modeling for behavioral analysis. Dr. Levis is a Life Fellow of the

Institute of Electrical and Electronic Engineers (IEEE) and past president of the IEEE Control Systems Society, a Fellow of the American Association for the Advancement of Science (AAAS), a Fellow of the International Council on Systems Engineering (INCOSE), and an Associate Fellow of the American Institute of Aeronautics and Astronautics (AIAA).

Catalina M. Lladó is a lecturer at the Departament de Ciències Matemàtiques i Informàtica of the Universitat de les Illes Balears (Palma de Mallorca, Spain). She received the Computer Engineering degree in 1998 from the Universitat de les Illes Balears and the Ph.D. in Computer Science from the Imperial College of London (UK) in 2002. She frequently works on conferences and program committees (for example, MASCOTS, EPEW, Valuetools, Sigmetrics) and serves as reviewer of international journals, as for instance Performance Evaluation. She is now leading a research project funded by the Ministerio de Educacion y Ciencia of Spain called "A General Performance Interoperability Framework." In a broader view, her research interests are on performance modeling of computer and communications systems, and performance engineering.

Stefano Marrone got the degree in Computer Engineering at the Università degli Studi di Napoli "Federico II" in 2002 and the Ph.D. in Electronic Engineering at Seconda Università di Napoli in 2006. From 2002 to 2008, he had worked in Ansaldo STS on the verification and validation of critical computer-based railway signalling controllers. In September 2008, he became assistant professor at Dipartimento di Matematica e Fisica of the Seconda Università di Napoli. His research interests include the development of methodologies and techniques for performance and dependability evaluation of complex critical computer-based systems: such evaluations are mainly conducted by means of multiformalism-based approaches and Model Driven Engineering.

Nicola Mazzocca is currently a full professor of High-Performance and Reliable Computing and head of the "Dipartimento di Ingegneria Elettrica e Tecnologie dell'Informazione" of the University of Naples Federico II, Italy. He owns an MSc Degree in Electronic Engineering and a Ph.D. in Computer Engineering, both from the University of Naples Federico II. He authored over 200 papers in international journals, books, and international conferences in the field of computer architecture, reliable and secure systems, distributed systems, and performance evaluation in high-performance systems. His research activities include methodologies and tools for design/analysis of distributed systems; techniques for modelling and analysis of distributed heterogeneous systems and communication networks; secure and real-time systems; distributed control applications; models and tools for configuration and performance evaluation of distributed, heterogeneous systems, and communication networks; dedicated parallel architectures.

José Merseguer is currently the Director of the Master in Computer Science and Systems Engineering at the University of Zaragoza, Spain. He teaches software engineering courses at graduate and undergraduate levels. Dr. Merseguer has developed postdoctoral research at Carleton University, Ottawa, Canada, and at Iowa State University, USA. His main research interests include performance and dependability analysis of software systems, UML semantics, and service-oriented software engineering. Dr. Merseguer received BS and MS degrees in computer science and software engineering from the Technical University of Valencia, and a PhD degree in computer science from the University of Zaragoza. Dr. Merseguer has been serving as a referee for international journals and as a program committee member for several international conferences and workshops. Among them the International Conference on Performance Engineering (ICPE), he is now serving as Program Co-chair for ICPE'14. He is a member of the Aragón Institute for Engineering Research (I3A).

Roberto Nardone received his Ph.D. in 2013 at the Federico II University of Naples, Italy. He collaborates with Ansaldo STS, a worldwide company operating in the field of railways and urban rail transport systems. He is currently a post-doc researcher. His main works are in the area of quantitative evaluation of non-functional properties in critical systems, in particular the focus is on the dependability, performability, and vulnerability assessment using formal models. His research interests are both in the Model-Based and Model-Driven techniques supporting the lifecycle of critical systems, from the requirement specification to the verification and validation phase, increasing their automation and reducing their costs.

Luigi Portinale earned a PhD in Computer Science on 1994, from University of Torino, Italy. He is currently a Full Professor of Computer Science at the University or Piemonte Orientale, Italy. He is currently Head of the Computer Science Institute of the Department of Sciences and Technological Innovation. His reasearch interests focus on knowledge representation and reasoning in Artificial Intelligence systems, with particular attention devoted to Case-Based Reasoning (CBR) methodologies and Probabilistic-Based Uncertain Reasoning (Bayesian Belief Networks). The first research stream concerns: CBR foundations, the intergration of CBR and Model-Based Reasoning (multi-modal reasoning), the use of CBR in medical informatics, studies concerning the relationships between distance-based and fuzzy-based approaches to case retrieval. The "reasoning under uncertainty" stream concerns: the use of probabilistic formalisms based on Bayesian Networks for the monitoring and diagnosis of systems, the relationships among classical reliability and dependability methodologies and AI-based techniques grounded on Bayesian Networks.

Markus Siegle studied computer science with electrical engineering as a minor subject at the University of Stuttgart (Germany). After finishing his degree, he spent one year as a Fulbright scholar at North Carolina State University (USA) where he earned a Masters degree. He obtained both the doctoral degree and the habilitation degree from the University of Erlangen (Germany) where he was a member of the chair for Computer Networks and Communication Systems under the supervision of Ulrich Herzog. Since 2003, Markus Siegle has held the professorship for Design of Computer and Communication Systems at Bundeswehr University Munich (Germany). The focus of his research is on the model-based analysis of performance and dependability properties of IT systems. His group works on stochastic models specified by formal methods, where the development of tools for modelling, analysis, and optimisation is a key concern.

Connie U. Smith is CTO of the Performance Engineering Services Division of L&S Computer Technology, Inc. She received a BA in mathematics from the University of Colorado and MA and Ph.D. degrees in computer science from the University of Texas at Austin. She is the author of Performance Engineering of Software Systems, co-authored the book *Performance Solutions: A Practical Guide to Creating Responsive, Scalable Software*, and numerous scientific papers. She is the principal developer of the performance engineering tool, SPE•ED™. Her research interests include software performance modeling and evaluation, tool interoperability, and software engineering. Dr. Smith received the Computer Measurement Group's AA Michelson Award for technical excellence and professional contributions for her SPE work. She frequently serves on conference and program committees, and currently serves on the steering committee of the Workshop on Software and Performance.

Anton Stefanek is a doctoral student in the Department of Computing at Imperial College London, where he works on the Analysis of Massively Parallel Systems project. His research focuses on the development of efficient modelling techniques for analysing performance and energy efficiency of large scale computer systems. He is the main developer of the GPA tool.

Valeria Vittorini graduated in Mathematics at University of Napoli "Federico II" in 1991, and she received her Ph.D in Computer Science and Systems from the University of Napoli "Federico II" in 1995. She joined the "Dipartimento di Ingegneria Elettrica e Tecnologie dell'Informazione" where she was a Researcher from 1999. She is an Associate Professor since October 2005. She has been the Advisor or Co-Advisor of several PhD Theses. She is Associate Editor of the *International Journal of Critical Computer-Based Systems* (IJCCBS). She is currently involved in the organization of the 30th International Conference on Computer Safety, Reliability, and Security (SAFECOMP2011). Her current research interests include complex and critical systems, performance, and dependability evaluation of distributed systems, formal modeling, service orientation. She has published over several journal and conference papers in these and related areas.

Yuri Yushtein works as a Software Engineer at ESA-ESTEC. He is or has been Technical Officer of the R&D projects on Formal Techniques in Software Engineering, System-Software Co-Engineering, System-Software Dependability and Safety, Failure and Anomaly Management Software Support to operational projects: ExoMars, Solar Orbiter, Lunar Lander. Previously, he has been Senior Software Engineer at National Aerospace Laboratory NLR, where his activities regarded Aircraft On-Board Software Development, Avionics Architectures Analysis Tools, Real-Time Simulation Environments, and Software Engineer at Triple P Telematics B.V., where he focused on Private Mobile Communication Systems, Communication Switches Software, Digital Signal Processing.

Index

T

Timed Influence Net 74-76, 80

V

VERIFIM 240, 248, 256, 258
WSP 241-242, 245, 258

X

XML 35, 37, 40, 42-43, 51, 54, 99, 105, 107, 109,
    111-113, 198, 200, 202-203, 236, 248, 263, 268